ARGUMENTATION AND CRITICAL DECISION MAKING

LONGMAN SERIES IN RHETORIC AND SOCIETY

Bruce Gronbeck, Editor
University of Iowa

Malcolm O. Sillars
Messages, Meanings, and Culture:
Approaches to Communication Criticism

Richard D. Rieke and Malcolm O. Sillars
Argumentation and Critical Decision Making, Fourth Edition

Joseph P. Folger, Marshall Scott Poole, and Randall K. Stutman
Working Through Conflict: Strategies for
Relationships, Groups, and Organizations, Third Edition

ARGUMENTATION AND CRITICAL DECISION MAKING

Fourth Edition

Richard D. Rieke
University of Utah

Malcolm O. Sillars
University of Utah

 LONGMAN

An imprint of Addison Wesley Longman, Inc.

New York • Reading, Massachusetts • Menlo Park, California • Harlow, England
Don Mills, Ontario • Sydney • Mexico City • Madrid • Amsterdam

Senior Editor: Deirdre Cavanaugh
Editorial Assistant: Kwon Chong
Project Coordination and Text Design: Ruttle, Shaw & Wetherill, Inc.
Cover Designer: Kay Petronio
Cover Photograph: PhotoDisk, Inc.
Electronic Production Manager: Christine Pearson
Manufacturing Manager: Helene G. Landers
Electronic Page Makeup: Ruttle, Shaw & Wetherill, Inc.
Printer and Binder: R. R. Donnelley & Sons Company
Cover Printer: The Lehigh Press, Inc.

Library of Congress Cataloging-in-Publication Data

Rieke, Richard D.
    Argumentation and critical decision making / Richard D. Rieke,
Malcolm O. Sillars. — 4th ed.
        p.   cm. — (Rhetoric and society series)
    Includes bibliographical references and index.
    ISBN 0-673-98079-0
    1. Debates and debating. I. Sillars, Malcolm O. (Malcolm
Osgood), 1928–   . II. Title. III. Series.
PN4181.R47   1997
808.53—dc20   95-53272
                                                   CIP

ISBN 0-673-98079-0

12345678910—DOC—99989796

Brief Contents

Detailed Contents

Preface

Writing in London, England, more than one hundred years ago, George Jacob Holyoake said, "To be able to take a subject well in hand, as a stagecoach driver does his horses, to hold the reins of argument firmly, to direct and drive well home the burden of meaning, is a power useful to every man [and woman]. . . ."[1] That sentiment is equally true today. Whether it is understood as argumentation, informal logic, critical thinking, composition, rhetoric, or forensics, the ability to participate effectively in reasoned discourse leading to critical decision making is required in virtually every aspect of life in a democracy. Competency in reasoned discourse, written or oral, is increasingly expected of those who are involved in government, business, citizen action, or any of the professions.

Argumentation and Critical Decision Making is designed to contribute to meeting those demands. Using this book to learn reasoned discourse does not require prior background in any discipline. It is aimed at helping people develop argumentation skills within the world of their daily, practical affairs. It is equally applicable to written or oral discourse, and it provides for multiple perspectives such as composition, critical thinking, debate, or informal logic.

In this, the fourth edition, there are significant changes. The importance of narrative to argumentation and the relevance of culture to critical decision making are given greater emphasis. There is more emphasis on interpersonal argument and greater use of resources from many disciplines. In response to the continuing development of intellectual thought on the concept of spheres of argument, there is increased discussion throughout the book on this subject.

The process of critical assessment of arguments is strengthened in several places. Chapter 2 emphasizes human involvement in argument appraisal, chapter 3 adds material on the role of values in analysis, and chapters 12 and 13 draw more heavily upon informal logic to clarify argument assessment. The discussion of the language of argumentation in chapter 15 is completely revised to develop the importance of meaning-in-use as part of critical analysis.

These changes have been made with the intention of keeping the book tied to the basic principles that have driven it for more than twenty years. This edition, like the earlier ones, is indebted to the work of Chaim Perelman, Stephen Toulmin, and C. L. Hamblin. These and other contemporary argumentation theorists are included without rejection of the rich thought of Classical writers such as Plato and Aristotle. Chapter 1 draws upon over 2,500 years of thought about arguments and critical decision making. The focus of the discussion is still human-centered. The audience, whether readers or lis-

---

[1]George Jacob Holyoake, *Public Speaking and Debate*. London: T. Fisher Unwin Ltd., 1895.

teners, immediate or over time, is vital to understanding argumentation. And, the orientation and examples are drawn from actual situations representative of the kinds of challenges readers will encounter throughout life. The relevance of argumentation to a broad spectrum of human activity is still a fundamental principle.

Pedagogy and Instructional Support

As in previous editions, we provide a variety of elements designed to make this book more teachable and accessible to students. These elements include the following:

- —Each chapter begins with a list of key terms.
- —Important concepts are printed in italics the first time they occur in the text.
- —Each chapter concludes with a summary.
- —Suggested student projects are provided at the end of chapters.
- —Research citations and additional readings are provided throughout.
- —An *Instructor's Manual* with pedagogical suggestions, overviews, possible syllabi, and suggested test items is available from the publisher.

Acknowledgments

This edition was influenced by all those whom we acknowledged for assisting us in the first three editions and many other students and colleagues over the twenty years of the book's use. The following persons have provided distinctly helpful contributions to this edition: Dennis C. Alexander, Ronald Sathoff, and Mary Louise Willbrand of the University of Utah; Kathleen Farrell, University of Iowa; Raymie McKerrow, Ohio University; David Zarefsky, Northwestern University; and Jon Bruschke, Baylor University. The students in Kathleen Farrell's argumentation classes at the University of Iowa pointed out where difficult concepts needed to be clarified. We were ably assisted at Longman by Kwon Chong, Deirdre Cavanaugh, and Christine Pearson. Finally, we thank Charlane Sillars for extraordinary editorial and manuscript preparation work.

Richard D. Rieke
Malcolm O. Sillars

1
The Domain of Argumentation

Key Terms

adherence
decision maker
claim
evidence
credibility
uncertainty
internal dialogue
reflective thinking
argument

support
values
criticism
critical thinking
dialectic
critical
decision
rhetoric

A rgumentation is at once a familiar and mysterious concept. It is familiar in the sense that the word is one you know, it probably appears in your conversation occasionally, and, research suggests, you have been making up reasons since you were about four years old. In fact, you still use a lot of the reasons that came to mind when you were just a child (Willbrand and Rieke).

Argumentation is mysterious because people so rarely take time to reflect on what they mean and do under the heading of argument or argumentation. If we were to ask a group of people what argumentation means, we would get many different answers, and most of them would be fairly superficial.

The difficult part about studying argumentation is keeping your mind open to new ways of thinking about a familiar process. In this book, we will not suggest that your ideas about argumentation are wrong. In fact, we will not spend time labeling anything right or wrong.

Instead, in this chapter and the next, we will offer our perspective on argumentation for your consideration. Subsequent chapters will present information about engaging in argumentation that we expect will provide you with some valuable insights.

In this chapter, we will begin by introducing you to the key elements of argumentation. Then, we will explain how argumentation is inherent in critical decision making.

ELEMENTS OF ARGUMENTATION

Argumentation is the communicative process of advancing, supporting, criticizing, and modifying claims so that appropriate decision makers may grant or deny adherence. Let us briefly discuss the important terms in this working definition.

Adherence

The objective of argumentation, as Chaim Perelman and L. Olbrechts-Tyteca have noted, is to gain *adherence*, which is the informed support of others (1). By informed, we mean people commit themselves to your claim consciously aware of the reasons for doing so. By support, we mean that people stand ready to act on your claims, not just grant lip service.

We have said that argumentation is a communication process, and that means it involves engaging people's minds through interaction. As we will see in the next chapter, different people make different demands on arguments before committing themselves to them. The responsibility for decision making is shared, including the responsibility for bad decisions.

Appropriate Decision Makers

The appropriate *decision makers* are those necessary to the ultimate implementation of the decision. You may win adherence of fellow students to the proposition that the midterm exam should count less than the final paper in grading your class, but if the professor says no, what have you accomplished?

The conservative advocacy organization Empower America argued through an ad campaign against some of the rock and gangsta-rap music produced by such organizations as HBO. If Empower America wants music they find offensive either eliminated or subject to a rating system, who are the appropriate decision makers?

They made their argument to the top officers of Time Warner, the world's largest media company and, at that time, the corporate parent of HBO. If those officers committed themselves to the argument, changes would occur. If Empower America successfully argued to the U.S. Supreme Court that such music lyrics fall within the category of obscene speech, changes would occur. These are some of the appropriate decision makers on this issue, but not all of them.

The appropriate decision makers need not be powerful persons. All citizens have a part in implementing decisions. By participating in such groups as Empower America or those who take the opposite position, by actively participating in the political process and by voting, you can become an appropriate decision maker on the issue of censoring music lyrics. It is important for you as an arguer to recognize who the appropriate decision makers are.

Because argumentation functions as a social-interactive process and because people's critical decisions are the products of argumentation, we speak of argumentation as audience-centered.

The word *audience* is used in its broadest sense to include all argumentative situations including interpersonal interaction between two people.

Claims

A *claim* is a statement that you want others to accept and act upon (to grant their adherence). It may be linked to a series of other claims that constitute a case.

In chapter 3 we explain the different kinds of claims and how they are analyzed to determine the best way to argue them. In chapter 4 we examine how they are combined into cases.

Support

Whatever communication (including both words and objects) is necessary and available to secure adherence, what it takes to get others to accept and act on your claim, falls within the concept of *support*. Sometimes, nothing more than your statement of the claim is required:

> JERI: This university should not torture animals in the name of research.
>
> MARY LOU: You're right!

We often put support alongside a claim without waiting to find out if others will demand it.

> JERI: This university should not torture animals in the name of research, because [support] wanton cruelty to living creatures is never acceptable.

It is also common to give reasons where the claim is understood but not spoken. In your conversation, you might just say, "Animals have rights against unnecessary suffering." In more complex situations, where disagreement is expressed or anticipated, support of more explicit kinds is used. We will discuss the following:

Evidence   We can strengthen a claim and increase its potential for adherence if we add to it examples, statistics, or testimony, the three broad categories of *evidence*. This is discussed in chapter 7.

Values   Claims are supported when they are identified with social *values*—generalized conceptions of what are desirable ends or ways of behaving—of the decision makers. Values are discussed in chapter 9.

Credibility   Claims are more acceptable when the person making the claim is regarded as credible, as believable, and worthy of adherence. *Credibility* is discussed in chapter 10.

Argument

An *argument,* in our usage, is a single unit of argumentation comprising a claim and its support. Both claim and support may be explicitly stated or one or both may be implied but understood by the persons participating in the argumentation process. To qualify as an argument, the support must potentially provide justification to relevant decision makers to grant adherence to the claim.

A caution is necessary here. In English usage argument can also refer to the open expression of disagreement, as in "My roommate and I had a terrible argument last night." An angry exchange will involve arguments, but the term *argument* includes much more than angry exchanges. Argument includes the argument a lawyer prepares for a trial, the argument supporting a scientific principle, or the argument of a friend that you should join her in studying for the test.

Daniel O'Keefe explains the two meanings of argument. What he calls argument$_1$ "is a kind of utterance or a sort of communicative act" (121). This speaks of an argument as a product as we have just defined it. What O'Keefe calls argument$_2$ is a communicative process, what we have defined as argumentation. Argumentation (argument$_2$) refers to the ongoing process of advancing, rejecting, modifying, and accepting claims, while argument (argument$_1$) refers to a single claim with its support. Our interest is in arguments functioning within argumentation in whatever context, ranging from informal interpersonal communication to such complex situations as law, politics, religion, or science.

Criticism

Argumentation involves *criticism* of claims with the open potential for modifying them. Dogmatic defense of positions is not argumentation, it is fanaticism. Criticism involves refutation, which is discussed in chapters 12–14. Stephen Toulmin says that the test of an argument is its ability to "stand up to criticism" (9).

A colleague reported this exchange with his wife, which exemplifies a type of argument criticism you may recognize.

> JEFF: Honey, I won't be able to go to Palm Springs next week. I know I promised to go with the family, but that company seminar changed its meeting time to next Wednesday.
>
> JOAN: We've had that on our schedule for months. Why didn't you just tell them you had a prior commitment?
>
> JEFF: This is really an important chance to make a move in the company. If I tell them I can't come because I have to go on vacation with my family, they'll think I'm not serious about my career.
>
> JOAN: Well, if you tell me that your promises to us are less important than what the boss thinks of you, what are we supposed to think of you, and doesn't that count?

So far, Jeff has offered two supporting statements to justify the claim of not going to Palm Springs: (1) the seminar changed its meeting time; (2) the seminar is important to his advancement in the company.

Joan has presented two critical arguments in response: (1) Jeff had a commitment that should take priority over a changing seminar time; (2) Jeff's standing in his family should be at least as important as his standing in the company.

The outcome of this exchange was that the family left for Palm Springs on Monday, as scheduled, and Jeff joined them Wednesday night after the seminar. Through critical interaction, Jeff and Joan managed to modify their initial positions and come to a decision that served their common interests. We cannot help feeling, however, that Jeff will be well-advised to pay more attention to his family calendar. In future argumentation, Joan will be able to recall this instance with good critical effect.

This example of argumentation comes from what we call an interpersonal sphere. Critical decision making there is based heavily on cooperation and compromise of personal preferences. In other spheres such as those falling within such activities as law, science, politics, or business, you will discover critical decision making based less on personal preferences and more on historically and institutionally established criteria, as we will explain in chapter 2.

ELEMENTS OF CRITICAL DECISION MAKING

A critical decision is one that survives the test of a relevant set of criteria. Choice is made on the basis of clearly articulated arguments that have been held open to refutation or disagreement. It stands up to criticism, and it remains open to further criticism as long as possible. When the arguments change, when new arguments occur, when the criteria for decision change, the decision changes accordingly.

Critical decisions are the opposite of those we make unconsciously, impulsively, dogmatically. Many people say they make their voting decisions based on the qualifications of the candidates and without regard to party. But curiously, year after year, millions of people vote precisely the way their parents did, and for the same party they have supported before.

How many of us have gotten into the voting booth only to discover there are races for such things as county clerk, recorder, treasurer, or medical examiner about which we know little or nothing? Knowing nothing about the candidates and little if anything about the nature of the office, we go ahead and vote for someone, possibly because we like the candidate's name or party affiliation. Those are uncritical decisions.

However, critical decision making does not demand certain knowledge or unanimous agreement. Within the domain of argumentation, questions have no sure answers to which all reasonable people must agree. When we say decisions must stand up to criticism, we mean that before action is taken, people must engage in a critical process and act, when the time comes, on the results of that process. While there is no single way this must be done, we will explain the process by focusing on some of the more important elements: toleration of *uncertainty*, *internal dialogue*, *dialectic*, *rhetoric*, and the willingness to act even though no certain answers or unanimous agreement has been produced.

Toleration of Uncertainty

To call decision making critical is to say that the claims of argumentation are inherently open to ongoing criticism. Decisions must be made and actions taken on them without knowing for certain that they are correct. In religion, politics, science, ethics, business, law, government, education, and many more pivotal areas of your life, you must decide and act without being able to wait until you are certain.

In ancient Greece, Socrates was sure that an absolute truth was out there waiting to be discovered, but he also recognized how very difficult it is to find. His solution was simply to continue searching, indefinitely if necessary, until absolute truth was found. Philosophers may have the luxury of an endless search for truth, but you rarely do.

Those human tasks that must be accomplished through reason within a context of *uncertainty* lie within the domain of argumentation. To engage in argumentation is to tolerate uncertainty.

Uncertainty Is Pervasive   As you proceed in the study of argumentation, you will probably be surprised to find uncertainty so pervasive. Throughout modern times, many scholars (followers of Socrates) have refused to teach argumentation because it operates in arenas of uncertainty, and they were interested only in the absolute. As one-by-one those issues once thought to be susceptible to certain answers have proven to be, at best, uncertain, the study of argumentation has become increasingly important.

In the past, doctors used leeches or surgery to draw blood from their patients because the best medical knowledge at the time indicated that this would help people recover from some illnesses. To most people today, bleeding sounds horribly ignorant, outdated, and dangerous. But today, doctors are using leeches to draw blood from patients to control swelling in some situations. It still sounds repulsive, but is it the right thing to do or not? Medicine cannot wait until some treatment is proved absolutely correct before using it to try to save lives.

As in all other argumentation situations, medical researchers develop the best arguments possible, subject them to the best criticism possible, and then go ahead even though they are not absolutely certain it is the right thing to do.

Language Is Inherently Ambiguous   One of the things that allowed people in the past to think they could find certainty was their belief that language could be precise as to meaning, and that meaning was derived from a tight link between language and the regularity of the universe. Aristotle's idea of fallacies (argument practices that are persuasive but illogical), which is still influential today, rests largely on such assumptions about language (Hamblin 50–63). Aristotle believed in language precision. He noted how many times argumentation is frustrated by ambiguity, frequently by people who intentionally hope to mislead, and so he labeled those instances as fallacies or sophistical refutations. His system loses much of its meaning today, when we believe language cannot be made as precise as Aristotle wanted it to be.

As we will make clear in chapters 13 and 15, language is inherently ambiguous. The idea of certain language practices always being fallacious does not square with contemporary thought. Language is a human product generated through social interaction and the assignment of meanings. You make interpretations of language that are based on your understanding, and you make guesses about how others will interpret your language. But in virtually all the decision making you will be a part of, there is never certainty as to what interpretations will dominate in any situation.

Take, for example, the concept of equal opportunity. In the debate over affirmative action, which we discuss in chapter 4, we note that everybody supports equal opportunity. But for some, equal opportunity means creating an even playing field by giving added weight to those whose opportunities have been degraded by past discrimination. To others, equal opportunity means letting each individual be judged by the same criteria without discrimination in any direction. There is no single, correct meaning for equal opportunity.

The Attraction of Certainty Is Powerful   History documents a search for truth and certainty. Whether it is a genetic characteristic of humans or something learned, people deplore doubt. It is an uncomfortable state of mind from which people seek to free themselves (Peirce 7–18). We like to think of science and mathematics as bedrock, certain reality. "We demand truths that are absolute, leaders who are blameless and doctors who are omniscient" (Salzer B5). We expect arguments that are true and valid for everyone.

Perelman and Olbrechts-Tyteca note that Rene Descartes, the influential 17th century philosopher and mathematician, declared that anything that was not certain was false. "It was this philosopher who made the self-evident the mark of reason, and considered rational only those demonstrations which, starting from clear and distinct ideas, extended, by means of apodictic [incontestable] proofs, the self-evidence of the axioms to the derived theorems" (1). Descartes believed his certainty was divine because God does not play tricks on us. His ideas struck a chord with Europeans who had suffered long and terrible wars and were desperate for something secure to hold to (Kagan, et al. 467–78).

The attraction of certainty seems stronger than ever today. Many of the most important debates are predicated on the presumption of self-evident and absolute rights. There is a religious fervor behind many claims, and those who disagree are characterized as evil. Issues of abortion, genetic engineering, in vitro fertilization, welfare, nuclear power, environmental protection, euthanasia, prayer in the schools, the size of government, and many more are frequently approached in such absolute terms. Ross Perot said the U.S. should withhold diplomatic recognition from Vietnam until every single MIA (missing in action) is accounted for. Because all MIAs have never been accounted for in any wars (in part because some people don't want to be accounted for), this essentially means absolutely no recognition of Vietnam.

From the perspective of argumentation, none of these issues can be resolved absolutely and certainly. Argumentation scholars say that it would be more productive to address all such issues as opportunities for critical decision making. But that requires learning to tolerate uncertainty.

Tolerance of Uncertainty Must Be Genuine Argumentation comes into play when you must choose, and choice inherently involves uncertainty. It may be uncertainty about future consequences of what you do today, future preferences, or how you will feel about today's actions tomorrow (Simonson 158). *Argumentation and Critical Decision Making* describes a process by which you seek the best possible choices within a context of uncertainty and ambiguity. Most of the decision making people do occurs in this context. From trying to understand how your own mind works to characterizing the universe, from deciding what to do on Saturday night to what to do with your life, you engage in argumentation and critical decision making. The better you use the process, the better you are at making decisions. But unless you are genuinely willing to open your mind to alternate ideas, you cannot make critical decisions.

Critical Thinking—The Internal Dialogue

A second element of critical decision making is critical thinking. While argumentation is a social process (audience-centered), it involves engaging individuals in making up their minds on how to act through communication with other people. As we will see in chapter 2, making up your mind means working with who you are and how you think.

Sometimes, your mind can lead you astray. People fear heights, crowds, closed spaces, snakes, and the like, even though society calls the fears groundless. Even though most of us think they are fantasizing, people truly believe they have been taken into a spaceship by extra terrestrials. You don't have to be insane to hold sincere beliefs that others call nonsense.

But following the lead of society or the majority opinion of others can also lead you astray. Peer pressure often justifies self-abuse even when the mind screams in alarm. Some young people sincerely believe gang membership is good for them as their only source of social support, even as they become more and more alienated from the rest of society. Plenty of people are dead because they could not resist a dare.

The term *critical thinking* calls attention to the fact that who you are, how your mind works, and what roles you play in society are inextricably linked. Self-awareness or reflection upon your own thinking and open-mindedness in relation to others' become essential features of critical thinking (Millman 48–49). Such phrases as "sensitive to context," "reflective," "thinking appropriate to a particular mode or domain of thinking," and "to assess the force of reasons in the context in which reasons play a role" are other ways to characterize critical thinking.

Critical thinking is the *personal* phase of critical decision making. It is the first step in the conscious reconciliation between your inner thoughts and your social experience. If the individuals engaging in argumentation are not willing and able to think critically, they will be unable to participate effectively in critical decision making.

When we say that critical thinking is the personal phase of critical decision making, we are not suggesting that it is all that different from the social act of argumentation. Indeed, research suggests that critical thinking is really a mini-debate you carry on with yourself. What is often mistaken for private thought is more likely an "internalized conversation" (Mead 173), an "internal dialogue" (Mukarovsky), or an "imagined interaction" (Gotcher and Honeycutt 1–3). All of these concepts refer essentially to the same thing, which we will call an internal dialogue.

The idea is this: you are able to carry on a conversation in your mind that involves both a "self" that represents you and "others" who stand for those people, real or imagined, with whom you wish to try out an argument. In a sense, all of our communication behaviors are pretested in social simulations (internal dialogue) prior to being shared in actual social situations (Wenburg and Wilmot 21). It may be misleading, in fact, to distinguish between imagined and actual interactions. During any conversation, you may find yourself doing some of the dialogue mentally while some of it may be spoken aloud, and, at any moment, you may not be able to say with confidence which is which. Some societies make no such distinction (Regal 61–66).

In critical thinking, you become keenly aware of your internal dialogues. You identify and put aside the tendency to think only of how to justify your thoughts while denigrating the thinking of others. Instead, you must apply critical tests, reflect on what you are doing, and try to open your mind to the potential weaknesses in your position while truly looking for other and better ways of thinking. It is critical thinking that makes you able to become a working partner in the next element of critical decision making: *dialectic*.

Dialectic—The External Dialogue

Dialectic is an ancient process that is very much on the minds of contemporary scholars. As an element of critical decision making, *dialectic* is the social dialogue in which people seek to come to understanding by opening themselves to the thinking of others with an interest in learning and changing.

Aristotle defines dialectic as a counterpart of rhetoric—a companion in the critical decision making process, a philosophical disputation. He believed that people are inherently rational: "The function of man is an activity of the soul which follows or implies a rational principle" (*Nicomachean Ethics* 1098a).

In dialectic, individuals engage in conversation, one person advances a claim tentatively, seeks to point out the logic behind it, and then responds to the probing questions of the others. "Dialectic proceeds by question and answer, not, as rhetoric does, by continuous exposition" (Kennedy in Aristotle. *On Rhetoric*: 26). The focus in dialectic is on providing logical bases for claims without all the persuasive elements found in rhetoric. The claims in dialectic are more general than those ultimately appearing in rhetorical argument. Through dialectic, you explore the values relevant to the decision making, the criteria by which tentative decisions are to be judged, and do all the other work identified in chapter 3 prior to the point at which a specific proposition is selected for argumentation: identify the question, survey the range of objectives and values, canvass alternative decisions, weigh the costs and risks, search for new information, criticize the alternatives, and note biases that block alternatives.

Some contemporary scholars suggest that failure to understand and engage in dialectic is at the heart of some of our most painful difficulties. They suggest that the dogmatic, rights-based diatribes that too often replace argumentation demonstrate the absence of dialectic in our society. We need to be aware, say Floyd W. Matson and Ashley Montagu,

> . . . that the end of human communication is not to *command* but to *commune*; and that knowledge of the highest order (whether of oneself, or of the other) is to be sought and found not through detachment but through connection, not by objectivity but by intersubjectivity, not in a state of estranged aloofness but in something resembling an act of love (6).

Hamblin suggests that the difficulty in identifying fallacies in argumentation reflects an unhealthy drive for certainty. "What is, above all, necessary," says Hamblin, "is to de-throne deduction from its supposed pre-eminent position as a provider of certainty" (250). He would replace it with dialectic through which people can determine the specific demands of the question and thereby identify what are truly misuses of logic.

Richard H. Gaskins says that argumentation runs into trouble when debates boil down to an inability to prove any position beyond question, resulting in decisions being made not on solid, critical grounds, but by default (1–11). He proposes more effective use of dialectic through which values, presumptions, and criteria can be worked out in advance (240–72).

Derek Edwards and Jonathan Potter argue that psychological research into such human cognitive behavior as perception, memory, language and mental representation, knowledge, and reasoning must proceed from the fact that these processes are socially and culturally embedded (14). They are to be understood through an examination not of the individual mind (which is all but impossible to examine) but in naturally occurring conversation, an informal dialectic. "The phenomena of thought and reasoning, of mind and memory, are best understood as culturally formed, socially shaped and defined, constituted in talk and text. . . . " Cognitive processes, they say, " . . . are ideas generated within cultures, conceptions of sense, action and motive that people invent to mediate their dealings with each other and to engage in social forms of life" (18).

Rhetoric

The fourth element in critical decision making is *rhetoric*. Aristotle defined *rhetoric* as the "ability [of a person, group, society, or culture] in each [particular] case to see [perceive] the available means of persuasion" (*On Rhetoric* 36). To perceive the available means of persuasion is to understand an issue from all points of view and ways of thinking. It is not necessary to use all of the available means, just take them into account (13).

While the meaning of rhetoric has varied dramatically in the almost 2,500 years since Aristotle, we will discuss its contemporary relevance to argumentation and critical decision making. There are three key rhetorical elements we need to explain here: audience, probability, and proof.

Audience   Rhetoric is concerned with people, how they think, act, and communicate. When we say our perspective of argumentation is audience-centered, we are saying it is a rhetorical perspective. In dialectic, the focus is on the soundness of reasoning and availability of support for claims. In rhetoric, the focus is the bases on which people will grant or deny adherence to claims. As we will see in the discussion of proof, people resort to a wide variety of bases in making up their minds.

In his discussion of rhetoric, Aristotle observed rhetoric occurring throughout society: deciding on public policy, resolving legal disputes, and developing and strengthening the values that underlie most arguments. He noticed that different people respond differently to arguments, so he talked about how rhetoric can be adapted to the young, middle-aged, and elderly; to the wealthy and the powerful; to those in all stations of society.

Aristotle divided knowledge into two groups: scientific demonstration, which he believed was not audience-centered, and rhetoric, which dealt with those issues not susceptible to certain demonstration and thus turning on human judgment. Today, scholars are much less likely to accept this division. Scientists of all kinds are more inclined to see their work as audience-centered, and we now read of rhetorical analyses of almost all aspects of human endeavor. Thomas Kuhn speaks of scientific revolutions in discussing his contention that science rests on paradigms or groups of people with common models, perspectives, problems, and procedures. When paradigms come into conflict, they work it out, says Kuhn, by using what is essentially political rhetoric.

Probability   As we have said in the discussion of uncertainty, argumentation deals with those tasks that require decision under uncertainty. Aristotle identified probable reasoning as belonging to rhetoric. We need to talk about two different meanings for the word *probability*.

In statistics and other forms of mathematical analyses of frequencies or chance, objective calculations can be made of the probability with which a certain phenomenon will occur or the probability that the phenomenon that did occur was the result of pure chance. For example, serious gamblers can say with high confidence the frequency with which certain combinations of numbers will appear on dice or roulette. Weather forecasters can calculate the frequency with which certain weather patterns will occur. Experimenters can say that their results could have been explained by chance alone, say, once in a thousand times.

Rhetorical probability is a more general concept that embraces mathematical probability as well as what might be called human or subjective probability. Early research into decision making revealed that people do not necessarily stick to mathematical probability even when it is explained to them and guaranteed to produce greater profits (Edwards and Tversky 71–89). They coined the term "subjective probability" to describe the experience in which, for example, people were told to bet on a single outcome because it was certain to produce a victory where all other options would not. In spite of this information, people varied their bets because they *felt* like doing so. Feelings, intuitions, values, and emotions are part of rhetorical probability.

Rhetorical probability works two ways: the extent to which one person is willing to advance a claim and be held responsible for it, and the extent to which people are willing to accept and act upon a claim. In critical decision making, both of these probability judgments apply.

We have said that argumentation deals with the uncertain, but there is no law that says you cannot say you are certain about a claim. People do it all the time. We use such words as "absolutely," "certainly," "unquestionably," or "without a doubt" to describe our claims. If your claim really cannot be advanced with objective certainty, how can you say it is so? Because you are not describing the mathematical probability of your claim or some other measure of reality, you are describing the extent to which you are willing to be associated with the claim and be held responsible for the outcome.

You may say that certainly the safest bet on the typical game of craps is the "come" or "pass." But if you were asked to guarantee a $1 million bet, you might withdraw your claim of certainty.

Consider, for example, the decision to drop atomic bombs on two Japanese cities during World War II. There were scientific probabilities about whether the bombs would work and whether they would cause extensive destruction. There were tactical probabilities about whether the Japanese would surrender once the bombs were dropped, or if they were about to surrender anyhow. The alternative, dropping the bombs on a deserted area while Japanese leaders looked on, was rejected as unlikely (improbable) to cause surrender. There was the military probability of how many lives would be lost on both sides if an invasion of the Japanese home islands occurred. There was the moral probability whether history would judge the dropping of the bombs to be justified.

The debate over this decision continues. There is no consensus on most of these questions. President Harry S. Truman, however, could not wait a half century to make the decision. He had little time and knew he would live forever with the consequences of the decision. He committed himself to those consequences, and that is rhetorical probability. Had the United States lost the war, he might have been tried as a war criminal.

Proof   Mathematical calculations and experimental demonstrations constitute proof for some scientific probability claims. Rhetorical proof, which includes such scientific proof, is more complex.

Aristotle included three forms of proof in his discussion of rhetoric. *Logos* represented the use of logic and reasoning as support for claims. In Aristotle's system, examples served as the rhetorical equivalent to induction, and the enthymeme (a rhetorical syllogism) served as rhetorical deduction. In a symbolic format, induction and deduction are forms of logic that work on problems outside the domain of argumentation. A pure induction requires itemization of 100% of the elements under consideration. A rhetorical induction or example requires sufficient instances to satisfy the audience. A symbolic deduction or syllogism is proved simply by demonstrating that it satisfies the rules of internal validity. A rhetorical deduction or enthymeme depends upon its link to established beliefs, values, and ways of thinking already held by the audience.

Pathos included the feelings, emotions, intuitions, sympathies, and prejudices that people bring to decisions. It suggests the fact that people accept or reject claims, make or refuse to make decisions on the basis of the values that are connected to the arguments.

Ethos identified the extent to which people are inclined to go along with an argument because of who expresses it. In contemporary research, ethos is seen as part of credibility.

In the chapters that follow, we will discuss the various forms of support that are available to prove your claims. The important point to remember here is that rhetorical proof is addressed to people (audience-centered) and the quality of proof is measured by the extent to which the appropriate decision makers find it sufficient for their needs.

Acting Within Uncertainty

The final element in critical decision making is the willingness and ability to act even when you are uncertain. Philosophers are adept at thorough criticism and dialectic. They are able to express themselves with rhetorical effectiveness. But often they take the position of Socrates and refuse to act until they have achieved certainty. The result is that they are not usually identified as action-oriented people.

In many college curricula, critical thinking is taught alone, without being subsumed under critical decision making. That approach to critical thinking is similar to the philosophers mentioned above. You may have well-developed critical skills, but unless you have learned how to act on them, they are of little value in a practical sense.

We come then, in this final element of critical decision making, back to where we began—the tolerance of uncertainty. It is not sufficient to tolerate uncertainty if you allow yourself to be frozen by doubt and end up like Hamlet. Critical decision making includes ultimately the willingness to make and act upon your decisions knowing that you may later regret it, or knowing like President Truman, that history might condemn you a half-century later.

CONCLUSION

We have introduced you to the domain of argumentation by identifying the elements of argumentation and critical decision making. In argumentation a key term is adherence, which characterizes the audience-centered focus of argumentation on the appropriate decision makers, who have also been defined. Claims, the points or propositions you offer for others' consideration, the support or materials provided to help others understand and subscribe to your claims, and the nature of argument as the intersection of a claim and its support have been discussed. Criticism, the give and take of making your claims and noting the weaknesses in alternate claims, has been explained as a key feature of argumentation.

The essential elements of critical decision making have also been identified. To participate in critical decision making, you must understand that you will necessarily be working with uncertain knowledge, and you must keep your mind open to alternatives and resist the temptation to rush to belief. Critical thinking is a concept that describes reflective, open-minded attention to your own thinking and the search for alternatives and complete information. Dialectic and rhetoric have been defined as counterparts in the development of critical decisions. Dialectic is the question-answer process through which you and others inquire, seek to understand the values and criteria appropriate to your decision, and entertain various points of view. Rhetoric, on the other hand, is the process of persuasion through which claims are presented to decision makers (audience) with the appropriate proof to help them understand and grant adherence.

Finally, we have said that to be a part of critical decision making you must be willing not only to tolerate uncertainty but to take action in its presence. In summary, we have said that argumentation provides the mechanism that mediates the tension between individual judgment (your mind) and social judgment (your culture) to bring the most powerful and relevant criteria to bear on any decision. The product is social (audience-centered) critical decision making.

PROJECTS

1.1 Read the editorials in one issue of a newspaper and answer these questions for each:
   a. What adherence is sought from the reader?
   b. Who are the appropriate decision makers? Why?
   c. What claims does the editorial make?
   d. What support is provided for the claims?
   e. What criticism can you make of the arguments?

1.2 Share your criticism of the editorials with other members of the class. Notice how you and the other students are similar and different in your answers. What does that tell you about your class as an audience?

1.3 Discuss the AIDS epidemic and see if the class can come to a common decision on the appropriate response to the problem. Does this social interaction (dialectic?) help you make a better personal decision? Does it make you uncertain or even uncomfortable? Does it help you to make an argument for a particular claim?

1.4 List three times in your life you believe you have made uncritical decisions that you later regretted. Describe why you think they were uncritical, and how you might have avoided them.

REFERENCES

Aristotle. *Aristotle on Rhetoric: A Theory of Civic Discourse*. Trans. George A. Kennedy. New York: Oxford UP, 1991.

Aristotle. *Nicomachean Ethics. Works of Aristotle*. Ed. by Richard McKeon. New York: Random House, 1949, 935–1112.

Benderson, Albert. "Critical Thinking: Critical Issues." *Focus* 24. Educational Testing Service, 1990.

Brookfield, Stephen D. *Developing Critical Thinkers*. San Francisco: Jossey-Bass, 1987.

Edwards, Derek, and Jonathan Potter. *Discursive Psychology*. Newbury Park: Sage, 1992.

Edwards, Ward, and Amos Tversky, Eds. *Decision Making*. Baltimore: Penguin. 1967.

Gaskins, Richard H. *Burdens of Proof in Modern Discourse*. New Haven: Yale UP, 1992.

Gotcher, J. Michael, and James M. Honeycutt. "An Analysis of Imagined Interactions of Forensic Participants." *The National Forensic Journal* 7 (1989): 1–20.

Halpern, Diane F. *Thought and Knowledge*. Hillsdale, NJ: Erlbaum, 1989.

Hamblin, C. L. *Fallacies*. London: Methuen, 1970.

Honeycutt, James M., Kenneth S. Zagacki, and Renee Edwards. "Intrapersonal Communication, Social Cognition, and Imagined Interactions." *Readings in Interpersonal Communication*. Eds. Charles Roberts and Kittie Watson. Birmingham: Gorsuch Scarisbruck, 1989.

———. "Imagined Interaction and Interpersonal Communication." *Communication Reports* 3 (1990): 1–8.

Kagan, Donald, Steven Ozment, and Frank M. Turner. *The Western Heritage*. New York: Macmillan, 1983.

Kuhn, Thomas. *The Structure of Scientific Revolutions*. Chicago: U of Chicago P, 1970.

Manktelow, K. I., and D. E. Over. *Inference and Understanding*. London: Routledge, 1990.

Matson, Floyd W., and Ashley Montagu, Eds. *The Human Dialogue*. New York: Macmillan, 1967.

Mead, G. H. *Mind, Self, and Society*. Chicago: U of Chicago P. 1934.

Millman, Arthur B. "Critical Thinking Attitudes: A Framework for the Issues." *Informal Logic* 10 (1988): 45–50.

Mukarovsky, Jan. *Structure, Sign and Function*. Trans. Peter Steiner and John Burbank. New Haven: Yale UP, 1976.

O'Keefe, Daniel J. "Two Concepts of Argument." *Journal of the American Forensic Association* 13 (1977): 121–28.

Peirce, Charles S. "The Fixation of Belief." *Philosophical Writings of Peirce*. Ed. Justus Buckler. New York: Dover, 1955. 7–18.

Perelman, Chaim. *The New Rhetoric and the Humanities*. Dordrecht, Holland: Reidel, 1979.

Perelman, Chaim, and L. Olbrechts-Tyteca. *The New Rhetoric: A Treatise on Argumentation*. Notre Dame: U of Notre Dame P, 1969.

Plato. *Phaedrus*. Trans. William C. Helmbold and W. G. Rabinowitz. New York: Liberal Arts, 1956.

Regal, Phillip J. *The Anatomy of Judgement*. Minneapolis: U of Minnesota P, 1990.

Salzer, Beeb. "Quotable," *The Chronicle of Higher Education* 21 July 1995: B5.

Simonson, Itamar. "Choice Based on Reasons: The Case of Attraction and Compromise Effects." *Journal of Consumer Research* 16 (1989): 158–59.

Toulmin, Stephen E. *The Uses of Argument*. Cambridge: Cambridge UP, 1958.

Walker, Gregg B., and Malcolm O. Sillars. "Where is Argument? Perelman's Theory of Values." *Perspectives on Argumentation: Essays in Honor of Wayne Brockriede*. Eds. Robert Trapp and Janice Schuetz. Prospect Heights, IL: Waveland, 1990, 134–50.

Wenburg, John R., and William Wilmot. *The Personal Communication Process*. New York: Wiley, 1973.

Willbrand, Mary Louise, and Richard D. Rieke. "Strategies of Reasoning in Spontaneous Discourse." *Communication Yearbook* 14. Ed. James A. Anderson. Newbury Park, CA: Sage, 1991.

2

Critical Appraisal of Argumentation

Key Terms

criteria

critical decision

commonsense

reasonableness

world views

starting points

interpretation strategies

facts

probabilities

commonplaces

spheres

ultimate purpose

patterns

interaction

informal logic

good reasons

science

good story

When you interview for a job, you and the interviewer are engaged in the critical appraisal of argumentation. The position announcement should set the broad *criteria* that will be used to judge your application, and the interview will flesh them out. Here's an announcement that appeared in the *Los Angeles Times*:

> Friendly Publishing Co. in Costa Mesa has immediate opening in Marketing Dept. Assist w/direct mail promotions & brochure production. Good writer, good w/numbers & xlnt organizational skills a must. College degree & 1 yr exp. required. Call Mary . . . (G–7).

During your interview with Mary, she could well ask, "Why should we hire you?" This is an invitation for you to present arguments on your behalf, complementing those in your application. What will be the strongest arguments you can make? At this stage, your best bet is to follow the criteria set out in the job announcement and argue the following: (1) I am a good writer; (2) I am good with numbers; (3) I have excellent organizational skills; (4) I have a college degree; (5) I have one year of experience.

If you can convince Mary of each of these points, and if they truly represent the criteria she is using to make this decision, it would be reasonable for her to hire you. It would be a *critical decision*. Of course, she could interview five people, all of whom meet these broad criteria. It would be reasonable to hire any one of them. So a critical decision does not mean resolution of uncertainty. It does not necessarily mean finding the one correct decision. It means selecting and applying a set of criteria designed to generate the best possible decision.

What will probably happen is this: during the interview, Mary will refine the criteria as you develop your arguments. She will try to make value judgments about the quality of your credentials compared to other applicants, and, before making a hiring decision, she will probably discuss the applicant pool with her colleagues to add their particular criteria.

Before a job offer is made, still other criteria may be applied, partly in response to arguments you made. For example, you may argue that you are a friendly person who would fit easily into a friendly publishing company. While this was not specifically listed as a criterion for hiring, the fact that they chose to call themselves a friendly publishing company says it has some importance to them. You might get the job over someone who has more experience but who seemed to be less friendly. It would still be a critical decision, because Mary and her colleagues would be consciously applying tests of your arguments and those of other candidates to produce the best hire.

In chapter 1, we defined a critical decision as one that can survive the test of a relevant set of criteria, one that can stand up to *criticism*. We also said that argumentation and critical decision making involve choice in a context of uncertainty.

In this chapter, we will talk about how people apply criteria to arguments, and how they can use such criticism to increase the quality of their decisions even in the face of uncertainty. First, we will discuss at some length the forces that can work against reasonable decision making, and go on to explain how reasonable arguments resist these forces. Then, we will introduce you to some of the established mechanisms people have developed over the years to improve the reasonableness of their argumentation.

ARGUMENTATION AND BEING REASONABLE

Critical appraisal of argumentation applies to you in two interacting ways: (1) When you *present* an argument, the better you understand the way it will be evaluated the stronger you can make it; (2) When you *evaluate* an argument, the better you understand the relevant criteria (tests for argument evaluation), the better (more critical) will be your decisions. These two points interact in the sense that presenters and evaluators of argumentation do their jobs best when they consciously operate within a common set of criteria (a sphere).

Characteristics of Unreasonable Arguments

What is an unreasonable argument? It is one that cannot stand up to critical appraisal, one that cannot survive criticism. If Mary decided she would not consider anyone under 30 or of Asian American extraction, she would certainly not tell anyone because she would be breaking the law. She knows those criteria are improper, cannot withstand the light of day, and thus would yield an unreasonable decision. Whenever the argumentation is evaluated according to tests that cannot be publicly announced, or cannot withstand the light of public scrutiny, chances are an unreasonable decision is at hand.

Your Reality May Not Be Reasonable   Your mind functions as the central processing unit with which you evaluate arguments and make decisions. What is sensible or reasonable to you is shaped by the genetic forces that act on you at any point in time (Konner). While people like to think of themselves as superior to other animals, some comparisons are possible. If you want to buy a dog, you can read books that tell you in advance how different dogs will behave. They can do that because generations of selective breeding can produce desired behaviors. It is not just chance that one puppy will come to you immediately, lick your hand, and try to cuddle, while another will retreat, whine, and even snap at your hand. Individual puppies behave in response to criteria selected by those who breed them. Humans as well as other animals come to each situation with some criteria of choice bred into them (Konner 59–105).

Your brain, while it is marvelous to behold in action, is not without potential problems. It creates its own reality by selecting from among the innumerable stimuli around you, those that make it possible for you to function. Take perspective, for instance. As you look off into the distance, your eyes could see big objects and little objects, but the brain works its own reality to help you see the objects as near or far away. Or consider selective perception. You are surrounded, virtually inundated, with stimuli day and night. But your brain sifts through these stimuli, essentially eliminating most of them, so you can focus on the few important ones. Of course, *important* is sometimes a function of hidden factors: when you are hungry, your brain takes notice of food related stimuli that it ignores at other times; when you have just bought a new car, your brain either eliminates positive messages about types of cars you rejected, or it interprets them in ways that diminish them.

Since your brain creates its own reality, no matter how helpful that may be, it could be seen as Philip Regal sees it, as an "illusion organ" (69). That means that sometimes your reality could get you in trouble. Pilots use an artificial horizon to tell them when they are flying level, because their brain may tell them they are on the level even when they are almost upside down.

Even though Regal calls the brain an illusion organ, he does believe it to be at least partly synchronized with the realities of others. People do a pretty good job of sharing realities, whether it is surviving in a threatening world, developing wonderful technologies, creating magnificent art, or conquering disease (Jones 48–50).

Through social influences (shaped by our genetic history), we develop *world views*, or complex schemata, that define our beliefs, attitudes, values, stereotypes, prejudices, norms, folkways, language, and culture. World views enable us to make it through life more comfortably. Having a common language is obviously important. So is sharing common narratives, scripts, or stories of how to go about our daily life: how to dress, eat, play, worship, form relationships, educate children, and care for the elderly. People behave according to the dictates of what they call commonsense, which means they are following the lead of their world view. At any particular moment, however, people are probably unaware of how their world view shapes their idea of commonsense.

Artificial intelligence specialists trying to program computers to exercise something like human reasoning are hard-put to reduce commonsense to computer logic. Ernest Davis is working on that problem. He says,

> Commonsense knowledge and commonsense reasoning are involved in most types of intelligent activities, such as using natural language, planning, learning, high level vision, and expert-level reasoning (1).

Commonsense, operating below a level of awareness, can produce unreasonable behavior. Researcher Linda Jackson, writing in *Social Psychology Quarterly*, reports that good-looking men are viewed as more intelligent and competent in their work than their not so handsome but quite capable co-workers. Beautiful women, however, do not necessarily benefit from a similar social judgment. If your interviewer Mary is like the people in this study, she may decide to hire the most attractive male applicant thinking that he is the most competent. He may, indeed, be the most intelligent and competent, but Mary's basis for choosing fails the critical test. She is operating on social influence that cannot hold up under close scrutiny. Like Dracula, her reasons die in sunlight.

Solomon Asch reports experiments in which he aked people to judge the length of one line compared to a series of other lines. He adjusted the task until people judging alone made almost no errors. He then selected four experimenters who were instructed to announce an incorrect answer, and put them with a series of naive subjects who did not know the experimenters were being intentionally incorrect. One by one, the experimenters would announce an incorrect choice, and then the naive subject was asked to respond. Imagine the social pressure this placed on the naive subjects. They had just heard four apparently honest people give answers that seemed obviously wrong. In the research, about a third of the naive subjects chose to give the same incorrect answer rather than disagree with the others.

Some of these later said they actually saw the incorrect response as correct, while others said they just went along with the group, being unwilling to oppose the majority or deciding the majority must be right. In this instance, social influence moved people to doubt their personal judgment, which almost certainly would have produced a correct response.

So, both your mind's reality and social judgment (they are virtually inseparable) can produce commonsense that is unreasonable. Yet, both forces constitute your most valuable source of reasoned behavior. How can you test commonsense to increase the frequency of reasonable behavior? That is the function of argumentation.

When you engage in the evaluation of arguments, some of the criteria influencing your judgment will be the product of your genetic and experiential background. Because you are mostly unconscious of these criteria, they may drive you toward unreasonable decisions. These will not necessarily be bad decisions, they will just be based on criteria you may not understand or that you are unwilling to open to public scrutiny.

When you exercise judgment, some of the criteria you bring to bear on the question will be the product of your brain's version of reality, which may or may not help you decide wisely. You could be acting on the basis of bias, ignorance, or selective perception. If you look into a mirror and your brain's reality is that you are a fat person needing to lose weight, this may improve your health or drive you into a fatal anorexia nervosa. Argumentation provides the means of testing the reasonableness of your reality (world view, common-sense).

A number of people in the United States believe that the federal government is engaging in a conspiracy with the United Nations to establish a New World Order. They may be right, but their arguments are not reasonable. They rely on assertions and support unavailable for public scrutiny, and they have no interest in listening to refutations of their positions. They are sometimes called paranoid, and their beliefs may, indeed, be partly influenced by genetic and experiential peculiarities.

Michael Kelly, writing in *The New Yorker*, quotes one conspiracist named Bob Fletcher this way:

> Oh, they been planning this for years, for years. They built a bomb during the Gulf War that they are planning to use in a big way. . . . It's called a fuel-air bomb, and the way it works is you drop the thing and it explodes, sends out this spray of vapor . . . and then, just a second or two after that, while the stuff is still in the air, a second bomb explodes: boom! And the thing is, if you have breathed in during those one or two seconds, well when the second bomb explodes, it not only ignites the vapor in the air, it ignites the vapor in *you*, see, so you explode inside *and* out. Boom! Vaporized! You just freaking disappear! And that's what happened during the Gulf War, my intelligence sources told me, to two hundred thousand Iraqi soldiers. You remember those videos they showed every day? You saw all those Iraqi vehicles on the road? You never saw a damned body. Why? "Cause they freaking vaporized them is why" (60).

Can you identify the unreasonable elements in this line of argument?

Characteristics of Reasonable Arguments

So, what makes one argument better, more sound, stronger, more reasonable than another argument? Why should appropriate decision makers be more influenced by one argument than another? From the examples we have just given, you should see that arguments derive their power or force either from the criteria already in the minds of the decision makers, or from criteria that emerge in the decision makers' minds during the course of the interaction.

When your arguments—claims and support—square directly with the criteria in the minds of the decision makers, the arguments will draw power from those criteria and thus be more influential. In contrast to past philosophical thought, arguments are not necessarily more powerful by virtue of their internal logical validity or by passing some scientific test of truth. As we will explain in this chapter, concepts of logical validity and scientific truth, *when they are part of the criteria decision makers apply*, will play a role in the appraisal of your arguments. But you cannot count on this always happening.

If arguments are tested by criteria in the minds of decision makers, how does argumentation differ from persuasion in general? What makes argumentation different from what we see on TV, read on billboards, hear from some fast-talking sales person or a conspiracist? The answer is, first, that argumentation *is* a relatively distinct dimension of persuasion that includes many of the strategies found in ordinary advertising or political campaigning (Willbrand and Rieke, "Reason Giving" 57).

Second, argumentation is a *distinct* dimension of persuasion in that it tends to be used in those situations in which people want to make wise decisions, and the strategies used in argumentation tend to be different from other forms of persuasion. Arguments employ more of the forms of criteria that we discuss later in this chapter than do common persuasive messages, and argumentation occurs within spheres that demand such criteria, as we will discuss. Argumentation appeals to the reasonableness of the decision makers by consciously focusing on criteria that are carefully selected, subjected to criticism, publicly accessible, and open to continual reexamination.

Argumentation serves as the process through which people seek to enhance the positive contributions of their personal reality while holding in abeyance its unreasonable tendencies. Argumentation is the process through which people take advantage of the positive influences in their society and culture while holding in abeyance the perilous social pressures that produce unreasonable behavior. By employing messages predicated upon carefully chosen and socially scrutinized criteria, argumentation becomes that form of persuasion dedicated to making the best possible decisions. This almost always means taking advantage of types of criteria and social processes that have proved helpful over the years in yielding reasonable decisions.

In the next section, we discuss some of those types of criteria that contribute to reasonableness. We explain the concept of spheres through which people acting together can demand reasonable arguments, and we will close by describing several common patterns of criteria. As you read this section, keep in mind that all these systems for argumentation depend upon the willingness and ability of the relevant decision makers to use them effectively.

THE BASES OF REASON IN ARGUMENTATION

Argumentation is the product of centuries of evolution in social practices aimed at resolving or creating uncertainty. We try to resolve uncertainty by making wise decisions that cannot be held absolutely, and we create uncertainty by raising doubts about ideas that may no longer deserve support (Goodnight 215). During this evolution, people have developed a number of systematic practices designed to improve the quality of argumentation and the decisions it produces. In this section, we describe some of these processes. We identify some powerful concepts that provide the necessary common bonding for reasoned interaction to take place and that form a fundamental test of the strength of an argument.

Starting Points for Argumentation

Argumentation works by connecting what people already accept (know; their personal reality) with claims they are being asked to accept. If they grant adherence to those claims, then the newly accepted claims can be used as the connectors to still other claims, leading finally to a decision. The energy or power that drives argumentation is found in people: that which they believe provides the foundation for that which they are asked to believe. In any argumentative interaction, then, some starting points must be identified—those powerful concepts that will start the connecting process: language interpretation strategies, facts, presumptions, probabilities, and commonplaces.

A general focus for appraisal of arguments is to examine the nature and quality of the powerful concepts invoked. If they are mistaken—either not shared by all the relevant decision makers or controversial—then the arguments that flow from them become suspect.

Language Interpretation Strategies   The most fundamental starting point, as we explain in chapter 15, is language and shared interpretation strategies. English is widely spoken in India because of the many years of British rule, and English is spoken in the United States, but such sharing of a common language does not guarantee sufficient commonality for argumentation. The interactants will need to negotiate some common strategies for interpreting their common language before critical argumentation can occur. The United States and the United Kingdom have been described as two nations separated by a common language.

You do not have to look at such extremes to discover the importance of common interpretative strategies as a starting point of argumentation. Even within the close group of your friends or even family, there is never absolute commonality in the interpretation of language. It is necessary to make guesses about others' interpretation strategies, and then try to understand where you must revise to improve communication.

The first step in evaluating arguments is to open up interpretation strategies for examination. Disagreements may dissolve as strategies are made to coincide but so might agreements. Before evaluating an argument, you must satisfy yourself that you understand what is being communicated.

Facts   In the discussion of analysis in chapter 3, we observe that facts can become issues, questions around which controversy occurs. However, as starting points of argumentation, *facts* are empirical knowledge derived from observation or experience over which there is no controversy.[1] The morning sun

---

[1] We do not mean to say that these so-called facts are beyond controversy. At one time, people held as fact that the world was flat. We use *fact* here to mean a powerful concept that is widely accepted without controversy, *at the time of the argument*, to the extent it can be invoked as the starting connection for further argumentation. Today, we might be able to invoke the "fact" that the universe is constantly expanding as a starting point for the argument, only to have people a hundred years from now laugh at the idea the same way we laugh at the idea that the world is flat.

appears in the east. Caviar costs more than chopped liver. Mothers who abuse alcohol or drugs during pregnancy endanger the health of their babies. These are facts that could very well be the starting points of arguments, because the decision makers regard them as facts beyond question.

There are profound differences in what is accepted as fact as you move from one sphere to another. What is a fact for conspiracist Bob Fletcher is not even close to fact for the FBI. Millions of people acknowledge the "fact" that Jesus is the Messiah, and millions reject the idea totally. Even among scientists, there is significant disagreement about what to count as fact. A physics professor who studies UFOs was seriously challenged by colleagues who doubted there was any factual basis for such research.

In appraising arguments, one place to look is at the facts used as starting points, because people may accept facts that, upon reflection, they should not. First time backpackers in the mountains whose knowledge of high country is based more on beer commercials than on serious study sometimes look at cold streams cascading over smooth rocks and conclude it must be safe to drink from them:

> CURLY: It's a fact that bacteria can't live in rapidly moving water that's almost freezing.
> MOE: Yeah, I've heard that, too.
> CURLY: So, it's okay to drink it.

Unfortunately, many mountain streams contain *Giardia* bacteria that thrive in cold rushing water and cause severe intestinal distress. Curly's argument would not have led to trouble if Moe had challenged the factual starting point.

Presumptions   Another powerful concept that serves as a starting point for arguments is presumption. A *presumption* occurs when one arguer occupies the argumentative ground or position "until some sufficient reason is adduced against it" (Whately 112). Like facts, presumptions may reflect considerable experience and observation, but they usually involve a broader generalization or a point taken hypothetically for the sake of argument.

Many presumptions have been formally stated in legal decisions. Children are presumed to have less ability to look out for themselves than adults, so society demands more care for them. Some mentally handicapped persons are presumed to be unable to understand the difference between right and wrong, so courts send them to hospitals rather than prisons. Property lines that have been marked by fences and have remained uncontested for many years are presumed to be correct and may be accepted even when a survey shows otherwise. People are presumed to behave rationally, so the law punishes those who, for example, drive under the influence of drugs or alcohol.

U.S. criminal law presumes people to be innocent until proved guilty. As this presumption suggests, all presumptions are subject to challenge and may be overturned. In fact, people may start with a presumption they really do not believe, just to get the argumentation going. If they didn't have a presumption to work from (say, the presumption of innocence), they would not know who has to start the argument and who wins in the absence of clear superiority of one argument over another. The U.S. criminal law presumes innocence just so it is the state that has to open with a claim of guilt, not the individual citizen who has to prove innocence. And if the state fails to win the argument, we choose to let the citizen go free rather than risk convicting the innocent. We expand the concepts of presumption, burden of proof, and prima facie cases in chapter 4 during the discussion of case building.

Part of the critical appraisal of argumentation is examination of presumptions. Because presumption is more or less arbitrary, it is possible for one position in the discussion to claim presumption and use it as a tool to force others to defend their positions. This may put an unreasonable burden on one point of view and lead to an unreasonable decision (Gaskins).

Probabilities   As starting points of argument, *probabilities* consist of commonly held beliefs about what is likely to happen, what is ordinary and to be expected. Such beliefs can be used as premises for arguments. After extensive observations, we hold powerful concepts of such probabilities as the times of the tides, the movements of the planets, the changing of the seasons, or the behavior of matter under various conditions. We reason from biological probabilities such as what plants will survive in certain climates, how animals will respond to loss of habitat, and how diseases disseminate. We hold concepts of how people will probably act under certain circumstances: they will look to such basic needs as food, clothing, and shelter before considering such abstract needs as self-fulfillment; they will seek pleasure and avoid pain; they will organize themselves into societies.

Like presumptions, probabilities vary from one sphere to another. Many hold the probability that human beings will seek to avoid death, but other spheres hold that death under prescribed circumstances is preferable.

Where presumptions may be points that are taken for the sake of argument without solid proof of their validity, probabilities get arguments started because they are likely to be accepted as well established by proof but still falling short of the confidence given to facts. Their susceptibility to challenge makes it necessary to present claims resting on probabilities with some statements of *qualification*.

Stephen Toulmin says that when people qualify claims, they "authorize . . . hearers to put more or less faith in the assertions . . . treat them as correspondingly more or less trustworthy" (*The Uses of Argument* 91). Since argument functions within uncertainty, there is always some degree of qualification on claims. Sometimes you use words: likely, almost certainly, probably, maybe. Sometimes you use numbers: 90 percent chance, $p < .05$, three to one odds. No matter how you express these probabilities, they communicate the force with which an argument is advanced, the degree of faith you authorize others to place on your claims.

Appraising arguments, then, necessarily involves an examination of the probabilities on which they rest and the qualifications with which they are presented. A point of criticism is to ask the basis of the probability statement.

In deciding what, and how much, higher education you need, you may turn to statistics that indicate probabilities about what kinds of majors will be most in demand when you graduate and what value advanced degrees may produce. In 1995, the major most likely to produce a job at good pay was computer science in engineering. But you must decide now on your major, based on such a probability, knowing that in two or three years conditions may change. If enormous numbers of people act on that probability and major in computer science, in a few years the field may be over-supplied leaving no job for you. By adopting a new major and agreeing to devote several years of your life to school, you express a high confidence in the probability of that major producing what you expect; you hold few qualifications.

The probability of one team winning a championship is a function of past behavior and current performance. The loss of a key player changes the odds. But the foundation of probability is the extent to which you and others agree to commit yourselves. In horse racing, the odds of a horse winning change depending on how people bet. The horses do not vary in their ability, the people vary in their degree of commitment. The critic must always examine the basis of the probability assessment, and remember how probabilities change.

Commonplaces   In argumentative practice, various ways of putting arguments together become standardized, common, widely recognized, and accepted. These *commonplaces* are lines of argument or places from which arguments can be built. Aristotle speaks of rationales such as opposites: what goes up must come down. He called them, depending upon which translation you use, *topoi*, topics, lines of argument, or commonplaces (Roberts 1396). Perelman and Olbrechts-Tyteca call them *loci* (83). We will call them commonplaces.

In appraising arguments, the commonplaces on which they are developed must be examined. We have mentioned the commonplace of opposites as an example. If one argues from this commonplace, the critic must test the assumption of opposition. Up and down do not work the same in the weightlessness of space, which Aristotle never heard of.

Another commonplace in use since the time of Aristotle is based on the meaning of words. Contracts, treaties, and other documents anticipate arguments on word meaning, and the critic must do more than look in the dictionary. Chapter 15 elaborates on the role of language in argument. Language varies with interpretive strategies.

An argument based on genealogy was also common in Aristotle's time, but it is less likely to survive critical scrutiny today. To argue, for example, that people are suitable for high office because of the high status of their parents is not well received in a democracy. Neither are the arguments by some researchers who claim African Americans are less intelligent than people with different genes.

However, genealogy still functions as a commonplace in certain argumentative contexts. Some religions pay particular attention to genealogy in defining membership. The selection of a British monarch or a Japanese emperor rests on that commonplace. And, in a looser way, many people point with pride to their distinguished ancestors, however far-fetched; we pay attention to how the children of movie, sports, and music celebrities succeed or fail; we follow closely the ins and outs of distinguished or notorious families such as the Kennedys or Rockefellers.

We will mention, as examples, two other commonplaces. *A fortiori* (more or less) argues that if you can perform the more difficult task, you can surely perform the easier one. Or, conversely, if you can't do an easy task, you won't be able to do a more difficult one. The argument "If we can put a man on the moon, we should be able to solve the hunger problem" rests on the commonplace of *a fortiori*. So does this: if you cannot pass the introductory course, you surely will flunk the advanced one.

Considerations of *time* work as commonplaces. Professionals charge fees based on the time spent for a client or patient. Most wages are calculated on time. Forty hours is deemed enough work for a week, and any more deserves better pay. Students argue for a better grade on the basis of how much time was spent on an assignment. We presume that a person can't be in two places at the same time, so the accused may argue an alibi based on the time to go from point A to point B.

It is impossible to list all commonplaces because they vary from time to time and from sphere to sphere. The potency of the commonplaces of induction and deduction has been the subject of much debate during this century. The commonplace of cause and effect is interpreted in quite different ways by different spheres.

Language interpretation strategies, facts, presumptions, probabilities, and commonplaces are powerful concepts that work as socially generated starting points for argument. When you make an argument, you will want to think carefully about where you can start it with reasonable assurance that there is common ground between you and your decision makers. In your critical appraisal of the argumentation of others, you must scrutinize the starting points to see whether they were well selected.

SPHERES

We have spoken frequently of appropriate decision makers as the object of your argumentation. Now we will locate decision makers within decision making groups, forums, organizations, societies, professions, disciplines, generations, or other such arrangements, which we will refer to as *spheres*. We will provide a general definition of spheres first, and then discuss some of the ways spheres work in argumentation and critical decision making.

Definition of Spheres

Spheres are collections of people in the process of interacting upon and making critical decisions. They are real sociological entities (Willard 28). You cannot make a critical decision completely alone. No matter how private you believe your thoughts to be, your internal dialogue involves a myriad of "voices" from your life's experiences.

Spheres function in the present tense: they are in the process of making critical decisions. While they quite often have a history of the same or similar people doing similar activities, that history functions for the purposes of critical decision making only as it is construed in the present. Derek Edwards and Jonathan Potter argue that perception, memory, language, knowledge, and reasoning are neither fixed in our brains nor guaranteed in documents and protocols. They are to be found in our interactions in the present. What we recall as facts, they say, are really what we put in our present rhetorical accounts and accept as facts (44–57).

Spheres operate as task oriented small groups. Although millions of people may ultimately play a part in a single decision, in practical terms, the process occurs in multiple, overlapping small groups.

When people interact about some common problem or goal with the ability to exert influence over one another, they constitute a group. Gerald Wilson and Michael Hanna say that while two people could meet this definition, it is easier to think of three or more, because then people can form coalitions to influence the others. They also say that a decision making group is one in which the members are aware of each others' roles (6).

B. Aubrey Fisher and Donald G. Ellis focus on communicative behaviors in groups—what is said, what is said in reply, what is said in reply to the reply, and so on. From this perspective, a group exists when the communicative behaviors become "interstructured and repetitive in the form of predictable patterns" (18).

While they are, as spheres, operating in the present, their interactions observed over time demonstrate patterns that are related to one another and used time after time. In critical decision making, these patterns of interaction include the starting points of argument, the way argumentation is conducted, and the criteria used to evaluate arguments and form critical decisions. Because they are thus predictable, the patterns guide your guesses about how your arguments will be understood and criticized. Because they are predictable, patterns of argumentation come to be associated with some groups and serve to increase the likelihood that critical decisions will result. *Groups are called spheres when their interstructured, repetitive, and therefore predictable patterns of communicative behavior are used in the production and evaluation of argumentation.*

Spheres, then, consist of people functioning as a group who share a cluster of criteria for the production and appraisal of argumentation. People in spheres share language interpretation strategies, facts, presumptions, probabilities, and commonplaces. But remember, that sharing is in the present, subject to ongoing change, and is never certain to yield a critical decision.

Location of Spheres

Spheres may consist of only a few people or may constitute groups within complex organizations involving many people. Spheres may be transitory or enduring. At any time, you may be a member of many spheres. Your *internal dialogue*, because it includes many voices, can work as a sphere. Basic *social groups* such as families, friends, or people with common interests, can function as spheres. Standing or temporary *task oriented small groups* such as committees or task forces, function as spheres.

Groups working within the rubric of a religion, profession, academic discipline, vocation, civic or charitable organization, business, or governmental unit, may function as spheres. Sometimes the defining characteristic of a sphere is ethnic association, social movements, or a political entity such as a state or nation. All spheres function within a culture and during a certain time or generation, both of which supply some of the argumentation patterns of a sphere.

Spheres and Level of Activity

G. Thomas Goodnight identifies three levels of activity of spheres: personal, technical, and public. By level of activity, Goodnight means the "grounds on which arguments are built and the authorities to which arguers appeal" (216).

In *personal spheres*, the level of activity is more spontaneous, negotiated interpersonally or in your internal dialogues. The interstructured and repetitive patterns of argumentation tend to be less easily discerned and predicted, so the chances of a critical decision are lower than at other levels of activity.

Technical spheres are those in which formal argumentative patterns are enforced. The highly specialized criteria are appropriate to the nature of the decisions made by such professional groups as lawyers, managers, scholars, engineers, physicians, and technicians. Those with advanced education, possessing a special kind of knowledge, are most likely to be found in technical spheres. Toulmin (*The Uses of Argument*) uses the term *field* to describe special criteria for the appraisal of arguments within a particular technical sphere. Charles Arthur Willard notes that a technical sphere may restrict access to its patterns of argumentation by requiring decision participants to, " . . . master specialized codes, procedures, knowledge, and language to limit what can count as reasonable argument. . . ." (50). This may insulate it from interacting with other spheres without substantial translation.

Public spheres usually involve those people who seek participation in public debate and are recognized by the relevant decision makers. They may be elected politicians or publicly recognized spokespersons. While politicians may use highly formalized arguments, their decision making must be comprehensible to the public. The chief problem with the public sphere is complexity. Public decision makers face complex organizations representing different values, interests, and influence.

Goodnight's idea of the personal, technical, and public spheres is useful in understanding that some issues require only the most informal and commonsense demands for support of arguments, while other issues demand highly specialized argumentation. The public sphere is neither as casual as the personal nor as specialized as the technical. Yet, as Goodnight says, "it provides forums with customs, traditions, and requirements for arguers" because the consequences of public disputes go beyond either the personal or technical spheres.

Ultimate Purpose

Each sphere involves an ultimate purpose that provides a relatively enduring set of tests of arguments. Toulmin speaks of this concept as "doing what there is there to be done" (*Human Understanding*, 485). What critical tests arguments and decisions must satisfy are themselves rooted in " . . . what we [people in the sphere] want now, constructed from our sense of purpose and what we are here for" (Willihnganz, et al. 202). This generalized sense of purpose resists change to the extent that it is unlikely that one person or one argumentative interchange will have much effect on it.

In the history of American business, for example, there has been sharp debate over its ultimate purpose, and this has slowly modified the way in which business arguments are appraised. A hundred years ago, the single ultimate purpose of business was to make money. Arguments about raising wages, improving working conditions, accepting unions, protecting the environment, or contributing to the community rarely survived the test of the profit criterion.

Today, these arguments stand a better chance of passing the test because of the slow evolution of the ultimate purpose of business. Concern for the well-being of the work force is now often justified as a contributor to profit. Many businesses now see being a good neighbor as part of their ultimate purpose. And the public sphere, through laws, has required businesses to revise their ultimate purpose to include concern for safety, consumers, individual rights, and control of their hazardous by-products.

Adjusting Arguments to Spheres

We have said that when you argue, you must make guesses about how your communication will be understood and criticized by the appropriate decision makers. And, we have just said that appropriate decision makers invariably function within a sphere or spheres that have predictable patterns of argumentation and criticism. So, the way to make the best possible guesses about the way your argumentation will be treated is to base them on the predictable patterns being employed by the people with whom you are interacting. We will suggest four levels of adjustment to spheres.

First Level: Formal Pattern Analysis   In preparing to participate in a critical decision making process, the first question to be asked is this: "What are the interstructured, repetitive, predictable patterns of argumentation and decision making?" Professional and graduate schools operate in large part to explain and inculcate in students the communicative patterns characteristic of their category of spheres. Law professors talk about how students must learn to "think like a lawyer." English departments insist that graduate students learn to argue like a literary scholar. Business schools stress quantitative, statistical, and accounting patterns. So, at a highly general level, you can study the historic behavior of the sphere into which you will go to discover how to develop your arguments and how to criticize others.

Second Level: Patterns-in-Use Analysis   The formal or historical patterns of argumentation that have come to be associated with certain activities such as science, law, religion, or commerce are what Toulmin characterized as fields. Considered at this highly generalized level, there is only a gradual evolution in what is to be done and how decisions are made. Knowledge of the characteristics of the field is helpful in framing your argumentation, but you really do not actually argue to fields, you argue to people.

So, the second level of argument adjustment is to examine the argumentative patterns-in-use by the people who will actually function as decision makers. At any moment within a field there will be significant variations.

Within law, the difference between civil and criminal proceedings cannot be ignored. Nor can the specific patterns-in-use within a particular judge's court be overlooked.

One business setting may continue with traditional authoritarian, line of command procedures while another may have turned completely to total quality management. Within academic fields there are profound differences in patterns-in-use. In sociology, some scholars may be involved in interpretive studies while others focus on demographics. In literature, some may be committed to formal literary criticism while others may have turned to post-modern thinking. In communication, some scholars who began their careers as dedicated experimental, behavioral scientists now find themselves working with semiotics or cultural studies.

Within any field at any time there will be spheres that are testing the limits of their ultimate purpose and acceptable methodologies. Arbitration is a test of the limits of jurisprudence, and attorneys who are successful trial lawyers still must adjust both to the specific characteristics of arbitration and to the particular practices within each arbitration setting. Teamwork in business is testing the limits of management. A highly successful manager in one firm may move to another and find it necessary to adjust to profound changes in decision making processes.

So, the second step in adjusting your argumentation to the sphere is to survey the work of contemporary decision makers. Your job is to test your sense of the sphere derived in the first step against the patterns currently in place. You must find the interstructured, repetitive, and predictable patterns of communication currently in place and adjust to them.

Lawyers who insist that judges and juries adjust to their standards; scientists who think they know the scientific method and that everyone should acknowledge it; people in business who expect the boss to play by their rules are naive at best and usually do not last long. Some people start this practice while still in college. Students who lecture the professor on how papers should be evaluated and debaters who shout at judges telling them how to decide are starting out on the road to disaster.

Third Level: Interaction Analysis   If you have conscientiously conducted the first two levels of adjustment, you should be in good shape, but not necessarily. As you participate in the argumentation, advancing your arguments and criticizing others, it is vital that you pay attention to the communication patterns being used during the ongoing argumentative interaction. Remember, spheres operate in the present. The appropriate decision makers with whom you are immediately working will have idiosyncratic language interpretation strategies and may well work from a particular sense of what is a fact, probability, presumption, or common-place. You must be prepared to listen carefully, make conscious observations about the argumentative process, and make immediate adjustments.

An attorney was presenting a case to a sheriff's merit commission consisting of people appointed by the governor. Before he began, he was told that none of the commissioners was a lawyer and that he should keep that in mind as he made his argument. He replied, "OK, I'm going to make this very simple." The Chair of the Commission, who held an earned Ph.D., replied, "I said we are not lawyers. I did not say we are simple." That lawyer's attempt at interaction adjustment was a disaster.

Interaction analysis means just that. Listen carefully, ask for clarification, avoid making hasty generalizations, and always remain open to adjustment.

Fourth Level: Critique   Finally, following your participation in an argumentation experience, after the decisions have been made, it is useful to critique your work. Look back on what happened, try to make sound judgments about what you did well and where your work was either irrelevant to the decision or even detrimental to your point of view. Try to locate where your adjustments did not work, and remember that for your next experience.

Many young managers are invited to make presentations to the key people in the company. They are understandably nervous, and quite often their arguments are given little attention. What many do not realize, however, is that one of the reasons for giving them the chance to present is so they can begin to get a sense of how decision making in this corporation works. The smart ones go to their boss and other people who were in the room and ask, "How did I do? What can I do better?" This may lead to training opportunities that will improve both their presentation skills and their ability to respond appropriately to particular situations. Those who fail to critique their work usually end up with little involvement in decision making.

This introduction to the concept of spheres should help you understand that critical decision making is a function of the behavior of people working in groups. Whether the argumentation really can stand up to criticism or not depends on the willingness and sense of ultimate purpose of the people working together at the time in relation to the ongoing standards of the sphere.

In the next section, we will identify some common patterns of criteria that have been developed over centuries of work toward critical decision making. Of course, each sphere will demonstrate its particular patterns, but these common patterns can be used as a guide.

COMMON PATTERNS OF CRITERIA

People appraise arguments on the basis of what they think makes sense, but if you were to discuss this with a few of your friends, you would probably find many different definitions of *sensible*. Among the common notions of what it means to be sensible are four that we will describe in detail:

1. Being sensible means being logical. Like Mr. Spock on "Star Trek," the premises are related to one another according to a clear pattern of inference.
2. Being sensible means having good reasons. We look at the ways claims are justified through reasoned discourse.
3. Being sensible means being scientific. If claims are derived from systematic observation of the world through our senses of sight, sound, taste, touch, and smell, they make sense: "Seeing is believing."
4. Being sensible means telling a good story. We listen to "what happened" and decide if it makes sense on the basis of how coherent and realistic the story is.

We will take some time to develop these four ways of making sense because, first, they appear in some form or another in the communication patterns of many spheres, and, second, you can use them to become more sensitive to the ways you appraise argumentation. It is more important that you understand the underlying rationale of making sense in each of these patterns than it is to try to memorize details.

Logic

Aristotle set out a pattern of formal relations by which arguments could be tested for validity. That is to say, if you begin with true premises, this logic can dictate the ways in which they can be combined to yield true conclusions. The pattern is called syllogism (deduction) and is taught, with the modifications that have been made over the years, as formal logic.

Typical examples of the validity patterns in syllogisms are the categorical, hypothetical, and disjunctive. We will give simple examples of each.

Categorical: If all A is B,
And if all C is A,
Then all C is B
Hypothetical: If A, then B
So if A exists
Then B exists
Disjunctive: Either A or B
So if A exists
Then B does not exist

Modern formal logic texts (Gensler) illustrate the various valid forms of these syllogisms and show how validity can be tested symbolically in a method closely resembling mathematics. Because of different basic assumptions and requirements, this logic deals with such tasks as computer programming that fall outside the domain of argumentation.

During the last half of the twentieth century, there was much philosophical discussion of the viability of formal logic in argumentation (Toulmin, *The Uses of Argument*; Perelman and Olbrechts-Tyteca). At the same time, work in artificial intelligence presented computer programmers with the need for a goal-directed, knowledge-based logic suited to describing how people actually go about the business of practical reasoning (Walton).

The result has been what is called *informal logic* (Johnson and Blair). In many ways, its contribution is directed toward the discussion of fallacies, as we explain in chapter 13. In its more conservative form, informal logic employs the patterns of deductive logic to criticize arguments within the realm of argumentation. Thus, the concept of validity is retained, but the force of conclusions does not reach the certainty of formal logic. Perelman and Olbrechts-Tyteca speak of *quasi-logic*, meaning the use of syllogistic forms in presenting arguments to benefit from the widespread respect given to logic by many decision makers.

Douglas Walton offers a goal-directed pattern of informal logic appropriate for both artificial intelligence and practical reasoning. Walton sees informal logic, unlike formal logic, as working with reasoning in a problem-solving context, involving some value-laden mandate (must, should), premised on known requirements and consequences, projecting into the future, assessing costs and benefits, calling for a shift or adjustment in the collective commitments of the relevant decision makers (83).

The argumentation scheme Walton offers is this:

A is the goal.
B is necessary to bring about A.
Therefore, B is necessary.

This is used, says Walton, to convince someone to take whatever action is entailed in B. Critical appraisal of such argumentation, according to Walton, follows these questions:

1. Are there alternatives to B?
2. Is B an acceptable (or the best) alternative?
3. Is it possible to bring about B?
4. Does B have bad side effects? (85)

Is it logical, for example, for you to complete a college degree if your goal is to make lots of money? Is a college degree necessary, sufficient, acceptable, or even the best way to establish a career that produces lots of money? Will you, in fact, be wasting time and money in college when you would be better served by starting your own business now?

Frans H. van Eemeren and Rob Grootendorst have proposed a set of rules by which critical decision making can be guided. They speak of dialectical constituents of argument as the logical or reasonable foundation. They list ten rules for critical discussion:

1. Participants must not try to silence each other to prevent the exchange of arguments and criticism.
2. If you make a claim, you must be willing to provide support if it is requested.
3. When you criticize someone's argument, you should be sure you are talking about what they really said.

4. You should defend your claims with arguments relevant to them.

5. You should not claim that others have presumed something they have not, and you should be willing to admit your own presumptions.

6. You should not try to start argumentation with a starting point others do not accept, and you should not deny a genuine starting point.

7. You should not say your claim has been established unless you have provided proper argumentative support.

8. You should stick to arguments that are logically valid or can be made valid.

9. If you fail to establish your claim, admit it; if others establish their claims, admit it.

10. Avoid unnecessary ambiguity, and try to interpret other's arguments as clearly as possible (1993).

Good Reasons

In the rhetorical tradition, also attributable to Aristotle (Roberts), the focus is on reasoned discourse. What reasons are offered in support or justification of a claim? Are they good reasons, or good enough to warrant adherence to the claim?

When children or adults are asked to generate reasons in support of a claim, they typically call upon their own authority ("I believe it"); *power authority* ("The textbook says it's so"); *moral obligation* ("It's the right thing to believe"); *social pressure* ("Everyone believes it"); or *listener benefit* ("If you want to pass this test, you will be well advised to believe it"), among other kinds of reasons (Willbrand and Rieke 420). Reasons generated in this way are learned from early childhood on and reflect the enculturation each person has experienced (Toulmin, "Commentary"). Coming up with good reasons is learned in response to challenges:

"Why did you do that?"
"Because."
"Because why?"
"Just because."
"That's not good enough!"[2]
"The teacher said I could." (power authority)
"Okay."

Some of the ways we test reasons to see if they are good enough are these:

1. The reasons should speak with one voice. This test advises you to look for contradictions. When the religious leader who preaches faithfulness in marriage is found in a motel room with someone other than a spouse, the sermon loses its punch. In reasons, the old cliché, "Don't do as I do; do as I say," does not overcome contradiction.

---

[2]Children quickly learn that "because, just because" is not a good reason. Four-year-olds use it frequently, but by the time they reach eight years of age, it is almost never used alone.

2. The reasons should be consistent. Here, the critic looks to see if all parts of the argumentation play by the same rules. If a politician argues for big reductions in defense spending but opposes the closure of a military base in the home district, the argument is weakened by lack of consistency. The pro-life advocate who supports capital punishment communicates inconsistency.

3. The argument should locate starting points within the appropriate audience. Arguments should neither patronize the audience by telling them what they already know nor presume starting points that do not exist.

4. The reasons should be expressed in language that communicates to the appropriate decision makers. Critics should check to see if everyone involved in the argumentation is on the same wavelength.

5. The reasons should be complete. A critic searches for points necessary to the claim that are not addressed, exceptions or variations to the materials included.

6. The reasons must be reasonably related to the point they support. As we explain in our discussions of evidence in chapter 7, there are specific tests to which reasons must be put.

Science

There are many versions of the "scientific method," depending upon the particular sphere involved. However, we can identify the use of science as a means of evaluating arguments in a more general way. Simply put, scientific logic rests on carefully performed observations, successful predictions, and the ability of others to obtain the same results. Ronald Pine provides these essential elements (42):

1. Observations are conducted: your empirical faculties are engaged in relation to a problem or phenomenon (sight, sound, taste, touch, smell).

2. Creative thought about the observations is done.

3. A hypothesis is generated in which you state the product of your creative thought in the form of a prediction.

4. Specific tests or experiments based on the hypothesis are conducted. The effort is to see if these now focused observations still make sense in relation to the hypothesis.

5. A claim is advanced in support of the hypothesis using the exposition of the first four steps and is presented with enough detail that others can repeat your work and get the same result.

Richard Parker advanced these steps as tests of scientific logic:

1. The argument must be internally consistent.

2. Its premises must be acceptable to the decision makers for whom it is intended.

3. It must survive refutation.

4. It must survive confutation or the critical examination of all arguments for and against it (7–16).

When your car refuses to start on a cold morning, you may use scientific argumentation to decide what to do. First, you look carefully at the engine, the gas gauge, the battery. If the battery seems weak, you may try a jump start. When that doesn't work, you may need to engage in some creative thought. There is plenty of gas, nothing apparent is wrong in the engine compartment. There is plenty of cranking power. Maybe (prediction) there is water in the gas. You put a gasoline additive in the tank based on your prediction, crank the engine, and it starts.

A Good Story

Recent scholarly attention (Fisher) has turned to narrative logic or storytelling as a test of argumentation:

> From the stone-age Tasaday people of the Philippine rain forest to the suburban-ites in Scarsdale, narrative is the only art that exists in all human cultures. It is by narrative that we experience our lives. . . . imaginative narrative, which in its re-fined and printed form we call fiction, was decisive in the creation of our species, and is still essential in the development of each human individual and necessary to the maintenance of his health and pursuit of his purposes (Morton 2).

Reginald Twigg provides this brief description of the elements contained in a narrative presentation of an argument:

1. Link experiences of reality to ideas.
2. Create and trace the actions of characters (heroes, lovers, tyrants, weak-lings, and villains) as they unfold in time and space.
3. Locate, impose, or reject social or moral hierarchy.
4. Provide lessons or "morals" in the form of ideas.
5. Provide understanding of how people, ideas, actions, motives, and values compare and contrast (26–27).

According to W. Lance Bennett and Martha S. Feldman, we organize our understanding around stories from early childhood. What counts as real and what makes sense is learned as central actions and the way those actions are characterized in relation to the people and motivations that make them up. Roger C. Schank and Robert P. Abelson claim that people have scripts that, in the absence of any more immediate or reliable input, are default positions they can use. You probably have scripts on how argumentation is to be carried out in different situations: with parents, lover, teacher, cop.

Scripts are used in building arguments. For instance, people may support a claim by considering all the scenarios, or other ways the events could have happened, that would lead to a different conclusion. Showing that none of these scenarios is reasonable supports the claim by the method of residues, or the elimination of all alternatives save one (Johnson-Laird 45). During the O. J. Simpson trial, the defense advanced a scenario that they claimed would ex-plain away all the forensic evidence that connected Simpson with the mur-ders. They claimed the Los Angeles police conspired to plant evidence just to convict Simpson because he is an African American. By showing instances of racism by the Los Angeles police and instances of apparent sloppiness in evidence handling, they sought to give Simpson a plausible alternative story that would constitute reasonable doubt in the jurors' minds.

In the political arena, "plausible deniability" is a term frequently used. If a political campaign turns to mud-slinging, it is often done by people outside the actual candidate's advisory group so that the candidate has a plausible basis for saying, "I had nothing to do with it."

CONCLUSION

When you appraise argumentation, when you try to decide what arguments are acceptable, what ones are not, and what decision makes the most sense, you will necessarily make your judgments under the influence and within the limits of your genetic make-up, the environments in which you have lived, your world views, and the social interactions you have experienced. Sometimes these factors will help you act wisely, and sometimes they will get you in trouble.

Over many centuries, people have developed systematic argumentation practices that can increase the likelihood that you will make sensible decisions. When properly used, these will help you make critical decisions. Powerful concepts such as language interpretation strategies, facts, presumptions, probabilities, and commonplaces can serve as starting points for argumentation. They establish a foundation on which everyone can argue and provide some ready rationales on which to build claims.

When people functioning in groups develop communicative behaviors that are interstructured and repetitive and thus occur in predictable patterns for the purposes of producing and evaluating argumentation, they constitute spheres. In spheres, people share both common ground and an ultimate purpose that set relatively enduring standards by which argumentation is judged.

In spheres, there are established patterns of criteria that help people evaluate arguments. Such common patterns as logic, good reasons, science, and storytelling may be employed singly, together, or in some modified form. Having a basic understanding of these common patterns will help you understand how to argue from sphere to sphere.

PROJECTS

2.1 Write a description of a job interview you have had. Did you understand the criteria to be used in making a hiring decision? Did you make arguments in response to the criteria? Did the job decision rest on the criteria? In all, do you think the decision was critical or uncritical, and why?

2.2 Think of three instances in which your commonsense helped you act wisely and three instances in which it got you in trouble.

2.3 Think of at least one example of each of the following: language interpretation strategies, facts, presumptions, probabilities, commonplaces.

2.4 Think of courses you have taken in science, social science, humanities, or art. Think of the teachers in these subjects as operating in different spheres. Look at textbooks you have used. Identify as many ways as you can that show different ways of making arguments in different subjects. What methods are similar?

REFERENCES

Asch, Solomon E. "Effects of Group Pressure Upon the Modification and Distortion of Judgments." *Groups, Leadership and Men*. Ed. Harold Guetzkow. Pittsburgh: Carnegie, 1951. 171–90.

Bennett, W. Lance, and Martha S. Feldman. *Reconstructing Reality in the Courtroom*. New Brunswick, NJ: Rutgers UP, 1981.

Davis, Ernest. *Representations of Commonsense*. San Mateo, CA: Morgan Kaufmann, 1990.

Edwards, Derek, and Jonathan Potter. *Discursive Psychology*. Newbury Park, CA: Sage, 1992.

Fisher, B. Aubrey, and Donald G. Ellis. *Small Group Decision Making*. New York: McGraw, 1990.

Fisher, Walter R. *Human Communication as Narration: Toward a Philosophy of Reason, Value, and Action*. Columbia: U of South Carolina P, 1987.

Gaskins, Richard H. *Burdens of Proof in Modern Discourse*. New Haven: Yale UP, 1992.

Gensler, Harry J. *Logic*. Englewood Cliffs, NJ: Prentice, 1989.

Goodnight, G. Thomas. "The Personal, Technical, and Public Spheres of Argument: A Speculative Inquiry into the Art of Public Deliberation." *Journal of the American Forensic Association* 18 (1982): 214–27.

Jackson, Linda, John E. Hunter, and Carole N. Hodge. "Physical Attractiveness and Intellectual Competence: A Meta-Analytic Review." *Social Psychology Quarterly* 58 (1995): 108–22.

Johnson, Ralph H., and J. Anthony Blair. "The Recent Development of Informal Logic." *Informal Logic*. Eds. J. Anthony Blair and Ralph Johnson. Inverness, CA: Edge, 1980. ix-xvi.

Johnson-Laird, Philip N. "Reasoning Without Logic." *Reasoning and Discourse Processes*. Eds. Terry Myers, Keith Brown, and Brendan McGonigle. London: Academic P, 1986. 13–49.

Jones, Roger S. *Physics as Metaphor*. Minneapolis: U of Minnesota P, 1982.

Kelly, Michael. "The Road to Paranoia." *New Yorker* 19 June 1995: 60–75.

Konner, Melvin. *The Tangled Wing: Biological Constraints on the Human Spirit*. New York: Holt, 1982.

Morton, Kathryn. "The Story-Telling Animal." *New York Times Book Review* 28 Dec. 1984: 1–2.

Parker, Richard. "Toward Field-Invariant Criteria for Assessing Arguments." Western Speech Communication Association Convention. Denver, 1982.

Perelman, Chaim, and L. Olbrechts-Tyteca. *The New Rhetoric: A Treatise on Argumentation*. Notre Dame: U of Notre Dame P, 1969.

Pine, Ronald. *Science and the Human Prospect*. Belmont, CA: Wadsworth, 1989.

Regal, Philip J. *The Anatomy of Judgment*. Minneapolis: U of Minnesota P, 1990.

Roberts, W. Rhys. "Rhetorica." *The Works of Aristotle*. Ed. W. D. Ross. Oxford: Clarendon, 1945. 1354–1462.

Schank, Roger C., and Robert P. Abelson. *Scripts, Goals and Understanding*. Hillsdale, NJ: Erlbaum, 1977.

Toulmin, Stephen E. *The Uses of Argument*. Cambridge: Cambridge UP, 1964.

———. *Human Understanding*. Princeton: Princeton UP, 1972.

———. "Commentary on Willbrand and Rieke." *Communication Yearbook* 14. Ed. James A. Anderson. Newbury Park, CA: Sage, 1991. 445–50.

Twigg, Reginald J. "History Versus Her Story: Toward A Theory of Appellate Narrative." Thesis. U of Utah, 1990.

van Eemeren, Frans H., and Rob Grootendorst. *Argumentation, Communication, and Fallacies: A Pragma-Dialectical Perspective*. Hillsdale, NJ: Erlbaum, 1993.

Walton, Douglas N. *Practical Reasoning*. Savage, MD: Rowman & Littlefield, 1990.

Whately, Richard. *Elements of Rhetoric*. Ed. Douglas Ehninger. Carbondale: Southern Illinois UP, 1963.

Willard, Charles A. "Argument Fields." *Advances in Argumentation Theory and Research*. Eds. J. Robert Cox and Charles A. Willard. Carbondale: South Illinois U P, 1982.22–77.

Willbrand, Mary Louise, and Richard D. Rieke, "Reason Giving in Children's Supplicatory Compliance Gaining." *Communication Monographs* 53 (1986): 47–60.

———. "Strategies of Reasoning in Spontaneous Discourse." *Communication Yearbook* 14. Ed. James A. Anderson. Newbury Park, CA: Sage, 1991. 414–40.

Willihnganz, Shirley, Joy Hart Seibert, and Charles Arthur Willard. "Paper Training the New Leviathan: Dissensus, Rationality and Paradox in Modern Organizations." *Argument and the Postmodern Challenge*. Ed. Raymie E. McKerrow. Annandale, VA: Speech Communication Association, 1993.

Wilson, Gerald L., and Michael S. Hanna. *Groups in Context*. New York: McGraw-Hill, 1990.

3

Analysis in Argumentation

Key Terms

claim	uncontroversial matter
factual claim	alternatives
value claim	argumentative case
policy claim	analysis of a proposition
issue	stock issues
proposition	comparative advantage
criteria	critical analysis

In the first two chapters, we have described the domain of argumentation and the methods of critical appraisal. Now it is time to look more closely at the way argumentation is practiced. We will clarify the most important terms of argumentation, see how critical appraisal is applied to a general problem, and then describe how you can apply critical appraisal to an argumentative proposition.

Clearly, not all communication is argumentative. Much of your communication will consist of other modes of speech in which you ask questions, inform others, request information, or greet others. While there is a potential for argumentation in every communication situation, it does not always develop. Argumentation comes into play when you and the others with whom you are communicating become interested in justifying claims. Remember, we have defined argumentation as the advancing, supporting, criticizing, and modifying of claims so that appropriate decision makers may grant or deny adherence. Adherence is not involved in many interactions such as this one where Alice is only giving information:

ANGIE: "Where are you going?"
ALICE: "I'm going to the store."
ANGIE: "See you later."

Even when adherence is sought, argumentation may not emerge if adherence is granted uncritically:

EMPLOYEE: "I believe I deserve a few extra days of vacation."
EMPLOYER: "You do, but we can't afford to have you gone right now."
EMPLOYEE: "OK, I'll be back next Monday."

When adherence is sought and will not necessarily be granted uncritically, argumentation may emerge:

STUDENT: "I want to turn the paper in tomorrow."
PROFESSOR: "It is due today."
STUDENT: "But my computer is down."
PROFESSOR: "You will have to find another computer."

Now the student will either begin to practice argumentation, find some way to print out the paper, or take a hit on the grade. Consider this interaction:

KEVIN: "I think I'll go to the gymnastics meet Saturday night."
DANIEL: "You have a history exam and you need the weekend to study."
KEVIN: "That's true but the gymnastics meet will give me a break from the books."
DANIEL: "It seems to me that you can't afford any time away from the books considering your grade on the last history exam."
KEVIN: "All work and no play makes Jack a dull boy."
DANIEL: "All play and no work puts Jack on probation."

The more complex the situation, the more elaborate and involved the argumentation process becomes. People advance claims with the intention that they be shared by others, but not uncritically. That is, when a claim is advanced and argumentation occurs, others recognize that the process includes the right to know why the arguer holds the claim and what support that person has to go on.

All argumentation, whether it is interpersonal like the example above, political and social, or specialized like that of lawyers, scientists, or economists, requires *analysis*: *the examination of an argumentative situation for its claims and opposing claims to discover the issues and what arguments and support (evidence, values, and credibility) are most important.*

Analysis of argument is necessary no matter at what point you enter the argumentation process. It may be your intention to seek the adherence of someone else to a claim or refute another's claim. You may also want to evaluate someone else's argumentation.

Analysis should be undertaken systematically and in advance of presenting arguments to decision makers. Analysis is not just a matter of acquiring knowledge. It is a process whereby all the constituents of the argumentative situation are examined in such a way that what needs to be argued and what it will take to gain adherence is known. With careful analysis, you can develop more effective arguments supported by evidence, values, and credibility. And even more, analysis involves learning about the others with whom you will argue. What arguments might they make that could damage your position with the appropriate decision makers?

Understanding the process of analysis, the subject of this chapter, requires that you first understand some terms we will be using throughout this book. Then we will look at how you go about discovering claims. Finally, we will discuss the analysis of different kinds of claims.

TERMS IN ARGUMENTATION

To understand systematic analysis in argumentation, certain terms need to be more clearly understood. In chapter 1 we briefly defined the term *claim*. We will now look at claims more carefully and introduce two new terms: *issue* and *proposition*.

Claim

As we noted in chapter 1, a *claim is a single statement advanced for the adherence of others*. "Gangsta-Rap is violent and degrades women," is a claim. Claims are used to justify other claims. So, "Gangsta-Rap is violent and degrades women" could be used to justify the claim, "Record companies should not produce Gangsta-Rap music." When a claim is used to justify another claim it is called a *subclaim*.

There are three kinds of claims: *fact*, *value*, and *policy*. Later in this chapter we will see how they interrelate and are used to support one another. For now let us see what they are.

Factual Claim   A *factual* claim *affirms that certain conditions exist in the material world and could be observed*. Decision makers are asked to adhere to a factual claim because it is confirmed by objective data from reliable sources. The following are examples of factual claims:

> Washington State University is in Pullman, Washington.
> Twenty-four species of animals run faster than humans.
> New Mexico became a state in 1912.
> Next year there will be reduced benefits for Medicare recipients.

These are all factual claims. Each makes a claim that decision makers might verify by reference to some kind of data. The first two are claims of *present fact* and the third is a claim of *past fact*. The fourth claim about Medicare is worth special note as it is a claim of *future fact* (Cronkhite). A visit tells you that Washington State University is in Pullman, a count confirms there are twenty-four species of animals faster than humans, and a historical record shows that New Mexico became a state in 1912. But, a future fact cannot be confirmed by looking at objective data from reliable sources. Decision makers will require more extensive reasoning to give it adherence. However, it is still a factual claim because at some point you, or someone, will be able to check it by objective data or observation. If, for instance, Congress has changed the Medicare law this year to provide fewer benefits, you can reason that benefits will be lower next year, and next year you can check it, if you wish.

Nonetheless, whether of past, present, or future, factual claims all have similar characteristics. All make assertions about what a situation was, is, or will be. All can be identified by some variety of the verb "to be." Note the examples above: "Washington State University *is* . . . ," "Twenty-four species of animals *are* . . . ," "New Mexico *became* . . . ," "Next year there *will be*. . . ." And, all are analyzed in the same way.

Value Claim   *A claim that asserts the quality of a person, place, thing, or idea* is called a *value claim*:

> Natural gas is our best energy source.
> Drugs and alcohol are a threat to public morality.
> "It's [Pepsi] the right one, Baby."

All of these statements make claims about the value of something; they make a value judgment that cannot be checked against data. "Drugs and alcohol are a threat to public morality" is clearly a value claim. "Public morality" is a condition that can be defined only by the participants in argumentation. It has no generally accepted means of verification. Natural gas, on the other hand, might be shown to have less pollutants, cost less per BTU than other energy sources, and have other characteristics that seem to make this claim as verifiable as a factual claim. But *best* means more than verifiable characteristics. Some people find gas *better* than electricity for cooking. How is that to be verified? So, value claims may vary from personal choice to definition in the strictest verifiable terms. "It's the right one, Baby," is a claim almost without content. It cannot be verified because no one knows what "right" is. There can be no question that you are being asked to attach your definition of "right" ("refreshing," "tasty," "pleasant") to Pepsi and adhere to it as a value claim.

The value claim is frequently confused with the factual claim because it has the same form. It is built around some version of the verb "to be." Note the examples above: "Drugs and alcohol *are* . . . ," "Natural gas *is* . . . ," "*It's* the right one. . . . " Furthermore, as we will show later in this chapter, the value claim is analyzed the same way as is the factual claim. But, the value claim can always be distinguished from the factual claim because it has in it a value term ("public morality/immorality," "best/worst," "right/wrong," "just/unjust," "beautiful/ugly") that contains a judgment that cannot be objectively verified and depends on the decision makers' concepts of what is good and bad.

Policy Claim   *A claim that tells someone or some agency how to behave* is called a *policy claim*. Any statement of a rule, law, or regulation is a policy claim and is a proposed change in the way people or agencies currently behave:

> No left turn.
> Don't walk on the grass.
> The balanced budget amendment to the constitution should be passed.
> Marijuana use ought to be legalized.
> The United States must control illegal immigration.

Because policy claims have to do with behavior, it will help you to identify them by checking to see if they state or imply the word *should*. The first two claims do not specifically state "You should not turn left" or "You should not walk on the grass," but they are commands based on policy decisions. The last two policy claims use terms *ought* and *must* that mean the same as *should*.

Note the differences in these three related claims:

Left turns are against the law at Fifth and Elm streets (factual claim).
Left turns at Fifth and Elm are dangerous (value claim).
You should not turn left at Fifth and Elm Streets (policy claim).

All three claims deal with the same subject matter but they are quite different. They require different kinds of analysis and argumentation, primarily because asking for a change of behavior is more than asserting a fact or value.

Notice that a claim is a single statement, but it is possible that you could have a sentence with more than one claim in it. Consider this sentence: "The average composite American College Testing Program score for American high school students is 20.8, a significant drop from twenty years earlier." There is a factual claim about the scores and a value claim about their significance. You may need to separate these two for your analysis.

Issue

The term *issue*, as frequently used in our society, can be confused with the term *claim*. A politician will argue "my opponent has missed the issue; we need a balanced budget amendment." But, an issue is more than an important claim. An *issue* is *the clash of two opposing claims stated as a question.*

To make analysis more pointed, you should always state issues in a hypothetical form allowing only two responses: yes or no. In this way, the statement of the issue points the response either toward one claim or a continued search.

For example, you might ask, "Are current tuition rates too low?" One person says yes, another says no: there is an issue. Issues are best stated with such words as *should, will, does, can,* or *is* because such words clearly imply a "yes" or "no" answer. If the decision makers decide the answer is no, it does not mean the discussion of tuition is over; it merely means those interested in change must revise their analysis and open another issue. For example, they might move to the question, "Will higher tuition rates improve our education?"[1]

By the same token, issues *never* begin with such words as *who, what, where, when, why,* or *how.* These and similar words lead to an open-ended question such as, "What is the impact of livestock grazing on federal lands?" The response to such a question is wide-open and does not focus the analysis, nor does it identify the burden of proof.

Many political leaders in western states oppose wilderness designation for federal lands because that will restrict the economic development of those lands for livestock grazing, mining, and logging. Environmental groups favor a greater designation of wilderness to preserve more land in the natural state. They claim: "More federal land should be designated as wilderness." Others argue against such designation. Here, then, is a policy issue: "Should more

---

[1]In some logic systems this point is made by substituting for yes or no, yes or not yes. All you have decided to do was not to say yes to the question this particular issue poses, not to reject anything else on this subject.

public land be designated as wilderness?" No, opponents say, because designated wilderness land hurts the local economy. While supporters claim that it does not. Here is a value issue: "Does wilderness designation of federal land hurt the local economy?" But, say the supporters, "Wilderness attracts tourists who strengthen the local economy." Opponents say, "Tourism adds less to the economy than does mining, grazing, and lumbering." This clash of claims results in an issue of fact: "Does tourism add more to the economy than mining, grazing, and lumbering?"

Not all claims result in issues but any claim (policy, fact, or value) may become an issue. If you say to a friend, "We should go to the basketball game tonight," you have a claim. But, if she says, "sure, let's go," you have no issue. As you will see as we look further at analysis, issues are important because they identify the points where controversy exists and, therefore, where, if the issues are significant, you must concentrate your argument. Consequently, it is important to maintain a clear distinction between an issue and a claim.

Proposition

A *proposition* is *a claim that expresses the judgment that decision makers are asked to accept or reject.* Generally speaking, like other claims a proposition may be of fact, value, or policy.[2] But, while other claims may serve as subclaims to one another and to propositions, a proposition cannot be a subclaim because it represents the point where you want the decision makers to be when your argumentation is finished.

Claims accumulate to form other claims. These claims support propositions. You may change your proposition when new information is added or when your proposition is rejected. Argumentation is a continuing process of changing issues, claims, and propositions. But, at the point you choose to build a case (see chapter 4) you select a judgment for decision makers to accept or reject. The claim that states that judgment is the proposition.

The following is a brief outline of a controversy to illustrate the relationship between a proposition and its supporting claims.

Proposition of Policy: The Associated Students of this University should provide low-cost day care for the children of students.

---

[2]Among students of argumentation there have been attempts to define a wider variety of propositions than the three most traditional ones we have identified here. However, these mostly show that fact, value, and policy come in a variety of forms. As long as you recognize that all fact, value, or policy claims will not look exactly alike you can be a successful arguer using these three.

There are definitional propositions (Ehninger and Brockriede 218–229) in which people argue how to define a term (e.g: "What is a democracy?"). We treat these as factual claims. Definition is discussed in chapter 15. Some people treat some value claims that imply a policy claim ("War is immoral") as a "quasi-policy claim." Some differentiate "comparative value claims" from value claims ("Rape victims are more important than a free press") and treat some value claims ("Television is an important literary genre") as what they call "value-object claims" (Zarefsky). "Historical/scientific claims" (Zarefsky) and "historical inference claims" (Church and Wilbanks 37) are sometimes used to identify a particular kind of claim of fact ("The Battle of the Little Big Horn was a military victory, not a massacre").

I. Almost 20 percent of the students have children (factual claim).

II. Acceptable day care is expensive (value claim).

III. Many students have to restrict their educations because they do not have affordable day care available (value claim).

IV. The Associated Students should spend money on things that students need rather than unnecessary social events and expensive popular lectures (policy claim).

V. A day care program would cost less than 5 percent of the annual Associated Students budget (factual claim).

PURPOSE OF ANALYSIS IN ARGUMENTATION

Argumentation can be a lengthy and involved process with hundreds of arguments and issues developing around a single claim of fact, value, or policy. Consider, for instance:

There is a God.
Democracy is a superior form of government.
Individual freedom should be guaranteed to all persons.

On such claims there are potentially an infinite number of related arguments because by one chain of reasoning or another all potential arguments can be related. Certainly, that is the assumption of the theologian who looks at the factual claim, "There is a God." But, even the theologian will select from all the potential claims those that will build the best case for the proposition, "There is a God." The propositions that you argue will be based on a limited number of claims. To find the proposition you wish to argue and the claims that support it requires analysis.

Analysis has two somewhat distinctive parts. One part deals with developing claims from questions, when you have only a vague realization that some problem requires resolution—what Charles Sanders Peirce called a "feeling of doubt." The second part is used after the proposition has been identified and it is necessary to find the crucial issues. You will see that these two overlap and interact, that a single analysis may move back and forth from one to the other, but we will treat them separately because they are rather different approaches. We will first look at how to develop the proposition you wish to argue.

CRITICAL ANALYSIS TO FIND A PROPOSITION

When you realize that there is some kind of a problem, when you have a feeling of doubt, you frequently aren't sure what to do about it. Critical decision making can be used to help you to discover the proposition you will argue. If you only express your feeling of doubt you may gain the adherence of some others who are equally frustrated, but to solve the problem you need a clearer statement of the proposition. Statements like the following have to be refined into propositions to which decision makers can respond:

Something is wrong with the library fine system.
How serious is sexual harassment on this campus?
Why can't the city coordinate traffic lights?
When will America recognize the needs of people with disabilities?

Argumentation takes place in a broader societal context of decision making. There are stages that individuals, groups, and even whole societies go through to deal with problems. The stages in critical analysis are intended to determine a proposition.

These stages of critical analysis involve the dialectical process of posing questions and searching for answers and the rhetorical process of finding claims and support for them so that others may grant adherence to your claims (Rieke 42–43). There are eight stages to the selection of a proposition.

An arguable proposition may appear at any stage and you need not go through each stage. Your analysis should help you to decide at what point to enter the process. If no one recognizes that a problem exists you must develop claims about the problem. But, if everyone agrees that there is a problem, you may skip that stage. Suppose everyone agrees "the library fine system is unfair." If everyone is agreed on the unfairness, you can slight the analysis of the problem and search for a proposition in the solution.

Identify the Question

The feeling of doubt that you have needs to be refined into a clearly stated question that represents the problem. In order to do this you must entertain genuine doubt (Dewey; Peirce). Ask yourself "what are the potential meanings to my concern?" Entertain the possibility of alternatives. From these, identify and face squarely the question that represents that feeling of doubt (Browne and Keeley; Ruggiero 92; Millman 45). Let us use your generalized concern over library fines as an example. Here are some examples of the thoughts you might have about the library that could set the basis for you to ask the question "What is actually the problem with library fines?"

I forgot the due date last quarter and it cost me $16.
Fines are stupid. People ought to be trusted.
Many students complain that the statement of the fine system is confused and confusing.
Fines cost more to enforce than they bring in.

Can you phrase a question from one of these, or some other statement, that will define the problem and provide a basis for further critical analysis?

Survey Implicated Objectives and Values

From your experience, research, and thought identify those objectives and values that seem to be related to the question that concerns you. You need to ask: what problems seem to need addressing? What might an ideal system look like? What values do you wish to see embodied in such a program?

Knowing what is sought in the decision making and the values to be served sets up the criteria upon which arguments will be tested (Janis and Mann 11). This includes your values and those of others involved as decision makers or critics. On the library question, you might consider what the objectives of a library should be; what values, such as knowledge and service, should govern the situation. The library values having books available when people want them. People value finding the books they want when they want them. No one likes to pay fines, but we often need books beyond the due date or we carelessly forget to return them. Notice how values tend to come into conflict.

Canvass Alternative Decisions

Sometimes people look for alternative decisions only long enough to find the first one that fits, sometimes they look only for the alternatives that seem most attractive, sometimes they use a small list of handy criteria and eliminate alternatives until one is left, and sometimes people just muddle through, choosing by hit or miss (Janis and Mann 21–41; Ruggiero 92). To be critical means to examine the widest range of alternative propositions, including some that you are tempted to dismiss at once. You might consider ending all library fines, adapting them more to specific situations, or basing fines on ability to pay. Or, you might decide the library should have more copies of important books, put all material on-line and eliminate hard copies, or find some other punishment for delinquent patrons.

Weigh the Costs and Risks

Being critical means looking at the negative as well as the positive arguments on all alternative decisions (Janis and Mann 11). Cost means more than money; it means values and goods sacrificed by rejecting one alternative for another. Risk includes the degree of uncertainty involved and the strength of the worst-case scenario. So, what are the costs and risks of the possible solutions to the library fine problem? It is expensive to buy multiple copies or go on-line. Other punishments might be more onerous than fines.

Search for New Information

Using words like *facts* or *data* often masks the complexity of information seeking. Information means overcoming ambiguity in language, developing a measure of the quality of evidence, searching for errors in discovery or measurement of data, and thinking about significant information that is missing (Browne and Keeley).

Criticize the Alternatives

Each alternative claim must be tested against the objectives and values sought in the decision and the relevant information (Ruggiero 92; Millman 46–47). This includes reexamination of the positive and negative consequences of each alternative proposition, even when this puts originally attractive alternatives at risk (Janis and Mann 11; Browne and Keeley).

Note Your Biases that Block Alternatives

The brain has been called a variably synchronized illusion organ (Regal 48–69), which means that people can create their own reality and feel confident about it while others perceive them as wrong. One extreme case is of three people in one city who were certain they were Christ, even when confronted by others making the same claim (Rokeach).

You are not likely to have that problem, but everyone has blind spots. So, you must notice what biases and prejudices are driving you toward or away from some alternatives (Browne and Keeley). This is where your awareness of the thinking of others is most useful. It is not reasonable to hold to positions simply because *you* feel strongly about them. Remember the library fine example? Perhaps you are bothered by the library fine system because you had to pay. Perhaps others will see this as your problem, not the library's. This does not mean that you must change your position just because others disagree with it. It does mean that a careful examination of others' views will help you to check your biases.

Select a Proposition

Using the results of the earlier stages, you are ready to select the proposition you find most reasonable. Perhaps you will discover that many people believe the statement of the library fine policy is confusing, so you decide the policy should be rewritten. Or, finding that, unlike other libraries, yours has no grace period, you might then decide that the library fine system should provide for a seven-day grace period for all except reserve books. Perhaps you will discover that there is no arguable problem and, therefore, you have no proposition.

These seven stages of critical decision making are used to find a proposition from a feeling of doubt when you believe there is a problem but do not know what to do about it. Perhaps you went through such stages when you wondered what to do when you were graduated from high school. You may be going through them right now as you try to decide what your major should be. You may be familiar with this process from your job. It is a system widely advocated by management experts.

Traditionally, after you have selected a proposition you will be expected to consider three other steps: (1) Make plans to implement the proposition, (2) Prepare contingency plans, and (3) Build a case for your decision. These will be covered in chapter 4 (Case Building). Critical analysis, as we will consider it in this chapter, involves finding a proposition and analyzing it for issues.

The result of the analysis discussed here is a proposition. Frequently, the stages of critical decision making do not enter in because the proposition has already been identified. That is true of most public propositions. Even so, you would be wise to go through the stages to give yourself a better understanding of the proposition and make yourself a more valuable participant in the discussion.

The state should legalize assisted suicide.
Affirmative action programs are unnecessary.
The People's Republic of China violates human rights.

These and many other propositions you might wish to argue came to your attention through the news and the arguments of others. Whether you found your proposition by critical appraisal or had it presented to you through public debate, the process of identifying your supporting claims begins. That requires the second part of critical analysis.

CRITICAL ANALYSIS OF A PROPOSITION

Any proposition is analyzed by identifying the various claims (fact, value, and policy) that are available to support or oppose it. Take note of what others are saying and what you can think of about the proposition, then state the claims that are both expressed and implied. Search out the crucial issues. These issues are generated by looking to the clash of arguments, as in a debate. Not all argumentative situations are debates, but each is potentially a debate. If you wish to advance arguments, you must be prepared to answer objections to them. You need to meet even unstated objections that are likely to be known by decision makers. Therefore, it is best to treat every argumentative situation as a potential debate.

In chapter 1, we spoke of the internal dialogue through which you engage in a mini-debate in your own mind. That debate should involve imagining how others would react to your proposition. You should pursue both sides of the proposition with equal vigor. Critical decision making requires that you find the issues and you will only find issues if you study both sides of a proposition.

Determining the Issues

A simple method for determining the issues is to make a list of arguments for and against the proposition and then match them up. For instance, in 1994 California voters had an opportunity to vote on ballot Proposition 187 which prohibits "state and local government agencies from providing publicly funded education, health care, welfare benefits, or social services to any person they do not verify as either a U.S. citizen or a person legally admitted to the United States." (51).

In the *California Ballot Pamphlet* for November 8, 1994, there are statements for and against Proposition 187 and rebuttals of each statement. Here are the main arguments (not necessarily in the order they were made). The numbers identify the main claims made. The unnumbered statements are claims made in opposition to the numbered claims. This matching up of claims and counterclaims can help you set the issues.

For	*Against*
1. California must "stop the flow of illegal aliens." If we don't it will lead to "economic and social bankruptcy."	"Something must be done to stop the flow of illegal immigrants coming across the border."
2. "Illegal aliens are costing taxpayers in excess of $5 billion per year." "How could getting rid of present costs end up costing more?"	"Because Proposition 187 is in conflict with federal laws, California could lose billions in federal funding." a. "Education, health care, and legal analysts all come to the same conclusion." b. U.S. Secretary of Education says California would lose more than $3 billion. c. National Health Law Program says it would cost the state $7 billion in Medicaid and Medicare funds.
"Nonsense."	3. Proposition 187 conflicts with state and federal laws and U.S. Constitutional protections, according to California Senate Office of Research.
"Welfare, medical, and educational benefits are the magnets that draw these illegal aliens across our borders."	4. It does not stop illegal immigration. a. Doesn't "beef up enforcement" b. Doesn't "crack down on employers who hire illegal immigrants."
5. Illegal aliens "buy and sell forged documents without penalty."	
6. Taxpayer subsidized education for illegal aliens leads to overcrowded classrooms.	"Proposition 187 would turn our schools into immigration offices." a. "It will be a paperwork nightmare" to verify the citizenship of . . . more than 10 billion people." b. It will divert money from classrooms already suffering from budget cuts.

7. "Citizens and legal resid-
   dents go wanting," and
   illegal aliens get
   "royal treatment."
   a. Senior citizens are
      denied full services to
      subsidize illegal aliens.
   b. In July the state
      removed dental care and
      increased the cost of
      prescription drugs for
      Medicaid recipients and
      "voted to continue free
      prenatal care for
      illegal aliens."

8. "Increased crime and graffiti
   because 400,000 kids have been
   kicked out on the street."
9. "Creates a police state
   mentality."
10. "Undocumented workers handle
    our food supply in fields and
    restaurants. Denying them
    basic health care would only
    spread communicable diseases."

The Save Our State Coalition
(sponsoring Proposition
187) is made up of Democrats,
Republicans, and
Independents of all races
and all colors. "We are
Americans."

11. Proposition 187 says that
    "suspected" illegal immigrants
    must be checked but does not
    define "suspected." Will it be
    by their speech? Their last
    name? Shade of skin?
    (Proposition 187 is racist).
    The California Teachers
    Association and the California
    Medical Association do not
    profit from the current situation
    but their members are the
    people who will have to enforce
    this unfair legislation.[3]

12. Greedy special interests
    oppose Proposition 187 for their
    own profit.
    a. The California Teachers
       Association
    b. The California Medical
       Association
    c. "Tax-paid bureaucrats . . .
       give sanctuary to those
       illegals in our country."

(54–55)

---

[3]Claim number 12 was made in rebuttal. This response was summarized from other sources.

These arguments, matched up for and against, are organized to determine issues—the places where opposing claims clash. First, look at the opposing claims that do not suggest an issue because they agree with one another.

1. California must stop the flow of illegal immigrants.

This is called *uncontroversial matter*. Both sides agree to this claim. It is not an issue. Does that mean that it is not important to your analysis? No! It may be quite important in supporting other issues. For instance, the supporters of Proposition 187 could argue that their opponents say that illegal immigration must be stopped but have no plan like Proposition 187 to stop it.

There are five other claims that are not opposed and that, therefore, do not constitute issues:

5. Illegal aliens buy and sell forged documents without a penalty.
7. "Citizens and legal residents go wanting" and illegal aliens get "royal treatment."
8. There will be increased crime and graffiti because 400,000 kids will have been kicked out on the street.
9. Proposition 187 creates a police-state mentality.
10. Undocumented workers handle our food supply in fields and restaurants. Denying them health care would only spread communicable diseases.

These constitute a rather large number of claims that one side or the other did not choose to make an issue. Perhaps this is caused by the fact that some are really not questioned. For instance, number 5 is not quite true: there were state and federal penalties for selling forged documents, but the section in Proposition 187 raising the penalties to a felony were not objected to because that was not the part of Proposition 187 to which opponents objected. They objected to the core of the proposition: the denial of services.

Three of the other four numbers, 7, 8, and 10, could be contested and, at one time or another, in the political campaign, they were issues. As we find them in this ballot pamphlet, however, they are not issues, though they still serve as arguments for the side that made them. Decision makers would consider them in their deliberations in relation to other arguments. For instance, those in favor of Proposition 187 could argue that if the illegal immigrants were kept out of school and denied health care, they would leave the country and thus the problems in numbers 8 and 10 are not so great. These claims could be refuted by the proponents' claim in issue 4 as we will shortly see. Claim 9, about creating a police state mentality, was probably ignored by supporters of Proposition 187, because they are sure that it is too abstract an argument to have much impact on voter decision making. These claims are not issues but they can be used as factual and value claims that support a position on the issues.

With these claims put to one side, here are six issues suggested by placing claims in opposition:

2. Will Proposition 187 save taxpayers money?
3. Does Proposition 187 conflict with state and federal law?
4. Will Proposition 187 stop illegal immigration?
6. Will Proposition 187 damage our educational system?

11. Is Proposition 187 a racist proposal?
12. Are greedy interests behind the opposition to Proposition 187?

There were many more arguments raised, but these six from the ballot arguments are a reasonable summary of the issues. They reflect the fundamental questions to be addressed in order to make a critical voting decision.

Rank-Order the Issues

The first stage in this process of locating the issues more specifically is to rank-order them based on their importance to the decision makers. Permit us to illustrate how you might examine these issues based on what we know from following the 1994 campaign on Proposition 187 in California.

Both sides agreed that illegal immigration should be stopped. The major issues about Proposition 187 were whether it would save or cost taxpayers money (issue 2); the possible damage to the educational system (issue 6); whether it conflicts with state and federal law (issue 3); and the possibility it was a racist proposal (issue 11). For opponents, cost meant costs from increased regulation and paperwork, from loss of federal funds, and human costs from denial of public services. For supporters of Proposition 187 cost meant the cost of services for illegal immigrants. Its opponents implied that Proposition 187 was racist while supporters implied that it was not.

Proposition 187 passed by a two-to-one margin, primarily, it is thought, because of the frustration people felt about illegal immigration and the need to do *something* about it. In November 1995 a U.S. District Judge ruled that most of Proposition 187 was unconstitutional. The Judge let stand only the provision for increased penalties for buying and selling forged documents (claim 5). As of November 1995 the case was expected to go all the way to the U.S. Supreme Court. It is interesting that the Judge let stand only an uncontroversial provision. Furthermore, the irony of this proposition is that it won because of uncontroversial matter (issue 1) and is challenged in the legal sphere because what appears to have been a lesser issue in the election (issue 3) violates state and federal laws.

For the judges, legality is the only issue. However, rank-ordering issues for 51 percent of the most populated state in the United States is a difficult task. Polling experts and political consultants are paid a lot of money to do that and they aren't always successful. When you argue, hopefully, your decision makers will be more restricted and better known to you. However, using Proposition 187 as our example, we can probably estimate that for the electorate, stopping illegal immigration was most important, saving money next, damage to the educational system after that, and finally, racism. Assuming this is the order of importance, you will want your case to emphasize the issues in the same order. If you believe that the racism issue is the most important one, you would need to realize that it will take a lot more argumentation to raise it in the consciousness of decision makers.

The arguments over Proposition 187 are complex and sometimes implied, but there are six issues here that are probably at the center of the controversy, and are the questions on which the decision makers will decide. In chapter 4 we will discuss Case Building. We will show you several ways of organizing your case. Two of these case formats are useful in analysis as you try to understand the issues regardless of what case you build: stock issue and comparative advantage analysis.

Stock Issue Analysis

Many people use *stock issue analysis* as a means of understanding the issues in a policy claim. They are called *stock* because they serve as a generic guide to policy analysis. It is frequently used to organize a case (see chapter 4). Users of stock issue analysis say that to gain adherence to a policy claim you have to get a positive response from decision makers on three questions:

1. Is there a need for a change from the status quo?
2. Is the proposed change practical?
3. Is the proposed change desirable? (Will its advantages outweigh its disadvantages?)[4]

Here are the Proposition 187 issues and one major item of uncontroversial matter, organized by stock issues.

Need for a change
1. California must stop the flow of illegal immigrants.
Practicality
3. Does Proposition 187 conflict with state and federal laws?
Desirability
2. Will Proposition 187 save taxpayers money?
4. Will Proposition 187 stop illegal immigration?
6. Will Proposition 187 damage our educational system?
11. Is Proposition 187 a racist proposal?
12. Are greedy interests behind the opposition to Proposition 187?

There are a few interesting points about these issues:

1. They represent issues of fact, value, and policy. Issues 2, 3, 4, and 6 are all factual issues. Once people have common meanings (see chapter 15) for judgment phrases as "conflict with state and federal laws" or "save," the claims in these issues have the potential of objective verification. They will be difficult to verify, however, for they all deal with future fact and that, as we noted earlier, requires some more complex reasoning. Issues 11 and 12 are value issues. They call for value judgments (*racist* and *greedy*) that cannot be verified by anything except the decision maker's values.

2. Uncontroversial matter number 1 is a policy claim that both sides agree to: "California must stop the flow of illegal immigrants." When it is agreed to by all parties, it controls the argumentation and blocks any attempt

---

[4]The stock issues of policy as we have identified them here are the most traditional. Others have used some variation of (1) Ill (need), (2) Blame, (3) Cure (the proposed change), (4) Cost/Benefit (Warnick and Inch 240–43; Ziegelmueller, Kay, and Daues 38–46; Lee and Lee 163–64). See Robert O. Weiss 76–77 for an examples of a writer who uses stock issues as we do.

by the opponents of Proposition 187 to say or imply that illegal immigration is beneficial. For instance, consider number 10, "Undocumented workers handle our food supply in fields and restaurants. Denying them health care would only spread communicable disease." A legitimate argument is possible here that illegal immigrants are necessary to the economy because they do the work that others will not do. But, such an argument is not possible in this case because it is inconsistent with a claim that illegal immigration should be stopped. Inconsistency (see chapter 4) is a potent basis of refutation.

3. Issue 11 requires some additional comment. Some things are not said directly even when they are strongly held, and this is one. Consequently, the opposition argument about how officials could know who is suspected of being illegal points to speech styles or accents, "ethnic" last names, and shade of skin to imply that Proposition 187 is a racist proposal. As a way of saying that it is not racist, supporters counter by saying that they come from all races and colors. Sometimes when you look for issues you have to look for what is implied by the arguments.

4. Issue 12 about "greedy interests" is a case of a direct attack on the credibility of the opponents. Some writers on argumentation regard this as a fallacy, the *ad hominem* fallacy (against the person) and not legitimate in judging a policy claim, but such credibility questions can be influential on decision makers. The same is true of the implied credibility question in number 11. If the proposal is racist, then perhaps its sponsors are, many will reason.

5. It is worth noting from the stock issue analysis that there is no disagreement over need; number 1 is not an issue. Both sides believe that illegal immigration needs to be controlled. The issues all deal with the desirability and workability of Proposition 187 as a means to meet that need and limit its costs. It is not unusual for everyone to recognize a problem but disagree on the solution. It can also be the case that even though they agree on the problem they disagree on its severity. Such a situation is possible here.

Comparative Advantage

When a need is agreed to and only questions of workability and desirability remain, analysis usually proceeds on a comparative advantage basis. Comparative advantage means that you analyze the advantages and disadvantages of the proposal against the status quo or some other alternative. Suppose your analysis revealed that Proposition 187 had these advantages and disadvantages:

Advantages	*Disadvantages*
It will save money.	It conflicts with state
It will stop (or slow)	and federal law.
illegal immigration.	It will damage the education system.
	It is a racist proposal.

Your judgment on how to build a case for or against will be based on the values that warrant the arguments. The advantages make the case for Proposition 187 on economic grounds while the arguments against are rooted in legal and social values. You can then build your case to show from evidence and argument how one set of values is more advantageous (should have higher priority) in this situation than the other. The argument then becomes, for instance, that the proposition is more advantageous than the *status quo* because it will stop illegal immigration and save money. At the same time, one arguing for the proposition would say that the disadvantages are nonexistent or minor when compared to these major advantages. Thus, in comparative advantage analysis, you search for the basis on which you can argue that your values are more advantageous than any possible alternative.

ANALYSIS OF CLAIMS

When the policy claim is reduced to a workable series of issues of fact and value, you must further refine your analysis by focusing on each claim that argues for one position or another in each issue. The objective here is to develop a plan for assessing the strength with which the claims resolve the issue.

Identify the Most Significant Claims

The significance of a claim is judged by the extent to which it directly provides a potential answer to the issue. Sometimes this is easily found because the claims are straightforward in their relation to the issue. In practical argumentation, however, people often make numerous claims that have only an indirect relation to specific issues. In analysis, you must match claims to issues and identify those most significant in answering the question posed in the issue. In doing this work, you will frequently uncover new issues generated by the ambiguity in the language of the arguments. This will require making what is implied by the language of the claim as specific as possible.

For instance, there is a hidden issue in issue 4. Opponents say Proposition 187 does not crack down on employers who hire illegal immigrants and supporters say medical and educational benefits are what draws illegal immigrants across the border. Behind this issue is another issue: Do people come to the United States illegally because of services?

Clarify What Each Claim Asserts

At this point you have a rank-ordered series of issues, you know their significance to the stock issues, and you have recognized the comparative advantages of each. Next, you need to analyze each of them to locate the specific nature of the issue. For instance, on the issue "Are greedy interests behind the opposition to Proposition 187?" what level and kind of support will an arguer need to prove to decision makers that the motive for the California Medical Association's opposition is greed? Making the issue more specific will tell you where to concentrate evidence, values, and credibility.

Unfortunately, there are no stock issues of fact or value because values change with decision makers and spheres. However, there are some guidelines for such analysis.[5] Those guidelines involve establishing criteria for evaluating each claim and then finding what more specific issues may be lodged in potential disagreements over those criteria, the relationship of the claim to the criteria, and the relationship of the support to the criteria.

Each claim has a subject term and a judgment term. For instance, opponents of Proposition 187 claim: "Proposition 187 will cost taxpayers money." There is little difficulty in understanding the subject term. The subject of this sentence is *Proposition 187*. However, the judgment term, *will cost taxpayers money* presents a problem in definition. What criteria define *costs the taxpayer money*?

When opponents of Proposition 187 made this claim they supported it with the following statement:

> Proposition 187 could end up costing taxpayers $10 billion. Education, health care, and legal analysts all come to the same conclusion. Because Proposition 187 is poorly drafted it directly conflicts with several important federal laws. As a result, California could lose billions in federal funding. Even the U.S. Secretary of Education has concluded Proposition 187 could cause California schools to lose more than $3 billion. Health care experts have further determined Proposition 187 could cost California $7 billion in lost federal funding for Medicaid for seniors and other legal residents [italics removed] (55).

It is clear that $10 billion satisfies the opponent's criteria ($10 billion or less) by which to judge that Proposition 187 will cost the taxpayers money. Let us use this claim as a basis for the next problem in the analysis of issues of fact and value: what is the specific point of clash on this issue?

Locate the Points of Disagreement

To evaluate a claim you must locate the points of disagreement over it. As you do this work, you will be setting up the basis on which to evaluate the strength of the claim. We will suggest four locations for disagreement:

Location I: By what criteria should the claim be judged?
Location II: What are the most important criteria?
Location III: To what extent does the claim satisfy the criteria?
Location IV: What is the strength of support for the claim?

By What Criteria Should the Claim Be Judged?   Those who favor Proposition 187 could argue that $10 billion is not too much to pay to restrict illegal immigration. Or they could argue that since their plan saves $5 billion, the actual cost is

---

[5]Some writers have called something similar to what we are suggesting here the four stock issues of propositions of value. For instance:
1. What are the definitions of the key terms?
2. What are the criteria for the values?
3. Do the facts correspond to the definitions?
4. What are the applications of the values? (Freeley 55: Warnick and Inch 218–22).

not great ($5 billion, not $10 billion). The issue would, therefore, be over the criteria for the judgment term. What amount of money is too much cost?

What Are the Most Important Criteria?   Supporters of Proposition 187 could question some of the criteria. For instance, the $10 billion estimate is of lost federal payments to the state. The issue might be over the relative importance of savings by denial of services and lost federal revenue. Suppose the supporters said that federal subsidies always come with harmful controls, and, therefore, the state would be better off with the savings from Proposition 187 and avoiding the federal payments. Thus, the most important issue would be over the relative importance of the criteria of specific dollar amounts and state autonomy.

To What Extent Does the Claim Satisfy the Criteria?   Even if it is agreed that $10 billion is an excessive loss, supporters of Proposition 187 could argue that it won't cost anything because it doesn't violate federal law. So the issue would not be over the criteria, but over whether Proposition 187 would meet them. If Proposition 187 won't cost too much then the cost issue is defeated.

What Is the Strength of Support for the Claim?   Every argument must ultimately rest on some kind of support (evidence, values, or credibility). The issue then becomes one of testing the support. Opponents cited the testimony of the National Health Law Program, the U.S. Secretary of Education, and the California Senate Office of Research while supporters cited no outside authorities; they did have figures about savings and perhaps there are authorities to support their positions. Furthermore, they might have argued, "these experts were not independent and, therefore, their evidence cannot be accepted" (credibility and values). They might have made them part of the "tax paid bureaucrats" they attacked in issue 12.

Particularly on factual claims, the support necessary will usually emphasize evidence (examples, statistics, testimony). An arguer needs to find the strongest possible evidence for a position. Though values and credibility can be strong bases to support arguments, they are most effective when linked to evidence. Remember the response of the supporters of Proposition 187 to the claim (in issue 3) that it conflicted with state and federal laws, even the U.S. Constitution? Their response was one word "Nonsense." Its support is strictly the credibility of the arguer. It is weak because it does not counter the evidence provided by the opponents.

All propositions depend for their adherence on the acceptance by the decision makers of one or more claims of fact or value. You must discover what claims are most crucial to this adherence. You do this by looking on the analysis as a debate in the minds of the decision makers and observing the major locations where issues might be found. Frequently, actually discussing claims with others, listening to the questions they raise, and reading arguments on both sides is the best way to locate issues.

From a process of putting aside those claims that are not issues and identifying those that are, a small group of issues will be identified as requiring support. Claims in these issues may be classified by stock issues and comparative advantage. The individual claims of fact and value can be further examined for issues to decide where to concentrate an argumentative case. From this analysis you can determine your strategy for organizing and supporting your case. That subject will be covered in chapter 4, Case Building.

CONCLUSION

People determine where argumentation begins. They discover problems and determine how these problems will be resolved. They frequently do this in a hit-or-miss fashion from limited knowledge and analysis. The adherence of others can be more easily developed if the analysis of problems takes place systematically rather than haphazardly.

To understand how to engage in such analysis, some terms need to be understood. A claim is the single statement that is advanced for the adherence of others. It may stand by itself or it may involve one or more subclaims that support it. There are three kinds of claims: fact, value, and policy. They are different in that one claims that certain observable conditions exist, the second claims the quality of something, and the third proposes a change in the way people or agencies behave. An issue reflects the clash of two opposing claims. A proposition is the claim that expresses the judgment that decision makers are asked to accept or reject. Because any statement may be linked to any other statement and thus generate an infinite number of claims, the number of arguments must be reduced to some workable basis. This is achieved in two parts: first, the critical process of finding a proposition when only a general problem (a "feeling of doubt") is recognized; and, second, the process of finding the crucial issues in the argumentation after the proposition has been identified.

Propositions are discovered through a process of analysis involving eight potential steps: identify the question, survey implicated objectives and values, canvass alternate decisions, weigh the costs and risks, search for new information, criticize the alternatives, note your biases that block alternatives, and, then, select a proposition.

Once a proposition has been determined, it can be more specifically analyzed. A policy proposition is analyzed by looking for the clash of arguments as in a debate, rank-ordering the issues, applying stock issue analysis, and examining comparative advantages. Thus, by looking at both sides of the proposition, the arguer can discover the issues of fact or value that are likely to be most crucial. Each value and factual claim is analyzed by finding criteria for the judgment term in the claim with which to measure the subject term. Issues about fact and value claims will be found in one of four locations:

1. Over the formation of appropriate criteria.
2. Over the relative importance of various criteria.
3. Over whether or not the claims meets the criteria.
4. Over the strength of support for the criteria.

When the proposition is identified, the issues discovered, and their specific natures identified, the arguer can then determine what must be argued and how best to build a case for it.

PROJECTS

3.1 With a small group of your classmates, discuss a general problem area such as America's energy needs, crime prevention, Mideast peace, world hunger, the future of higher education. How many policy claims can you generate? What kinds of claims did you leave out because they seem to conflict with your understanding of the facts and values? What did you learn about narrowing to a claim?

3.2 Many newspapers, including *USA Today*, have a regular feature of printing two opposing editorials on current topics. *Congressional Quarterly* also features such exchanges. Find one of these exchanges and find the issues in the controversy.

3.3 Find the issues in the following controversy.

In 1994, in the same election in which Californians voted on Proposition 187, another measure appeared on their ballot. It provided for the amendment of the state constitution to establish a "health services system to provide medical, prescription drugs, long term, mental health, dental, emergency, and other benefits, available to California residents, replacing existing health insurance, premiums, programs." The following are the arguments for and against Proposition 186.

Argument in Favor of Proposition 186

Does your health insurance pay for long term care at home or in a nursing home?

Can you keep your insurance forever, even if you lose or change your job?

Does your insurance allow you to see any doctor you choose?

Is your doctor free to prescribe the treatment you need, without outside interference?

Will you still be insured, even if you have cancer or another "pre-existing condition?"

Does your insurance pay for prescription drugs, preventive care, chiropractors, nursing care, and mental health?

Will Medicare take care of all your health needs during retirement?

Are you free from fear of losing your life savings due to a major illness?

If you answered "no" to any of these questions, you don't have the health insurance you need and deserve.

Right now a huge amount of our health care money—money paid by California consumers, businesses and taxpayers—is wasted by insurance companies.

Insurance companies spend up to 30 cents of every dollar we pay them for health care on something else: paperwork, advertising, profits, big buildings and big salaries for their executives.

Proposition 186 ends the insurance company rip-off and puts the money back where it belongs: buying more and better health services.

186 covers long term care and prescription drugs. All medically necessary health care—as determined by you and your doctor—is covered.

186 guarantees your choice of doctors.

If you lose or change jobs, or start your own business, or retire, your health insurance goes with you and you can keep the same doctor.

With Proposition 186, your coverage can never be taken away, as long as you are a legal California resident. You cannot be denied coverage for "pre-existing conditions."

Proposition 186 helps California's economy.

Businesses now providing employee health benefits pay more than ten percent of their payroll costs for health insurance. 186 significantly reduces these employer costs and provides employees with better coverage.

Proposition 186 also lowers the cost of doing business—and living—in California because it eliminates the need to purchase duplicate medical coverage in our automobile, worker's compensation, homeowners', and business liability insurance.

Proposition 186 helps our schools.

Proposition 186 saves our schools more than $600 million by reducing what they pay for health care for teachers and other school employees. That's $600 million to improve our schools.

Proposition 186 is a consumer movement for the health insurance we need.

Over a million Californians signed petitions to put 186 on the ballot. Thousands more are giving $1, $5, and $10 in this crusade to end our health care worries forever.

Insurance companies are spending millions of dollars to oppose 186. Every time you see one of their ads, remember:

They are spending your money to deny you the health care you and your loved ones deserve.

We can do it. Stop the insurance rip-off. Vote yes on Proposition 186.

Argument Against Proposition 186

Proposition 186: Bad Medicine
for Californians

"This initiative is exactly the wrong medicine for California's recovering economy. It's a budget buster and a job killer."

Governor Pete Wilson

"We all want to achieve universal health coverage for Californians, but this measure is not the right way to go."

Treasurer Kathleen Brown

Californians from every walk of life and every corner of the state, including Governor Wilson, Treasurer Brown, Democrats, Republicans, Independents, nurses, senior citizens, consumers, taxpayers, businesses, and physicians, oppose Proposition 186. We need health care reform, but this measure creates more problems than it solves and jeopardizes health care quality. Proposition 186 deserves your no vote.

A Government-Run Experiment with
Our Health Care

Under this proposal, most Californians would lose private health coverage and instead, be forced to get coverage through a massive new government-run bureaucracy—a completely untested and experimental system in the United States.

$40 Billion in New Taxes

According to the Legislative Analyst, Proposition 186 will cost $40 billion in new taxes, including huge increases in income taxes and payroll taxes. That's the biggest tax increase in California history and there are no limits on how high taxes could be raised!

Nothing in this proposal prohibits the politicians from raising taxes again and again to pay for this huge new health care experiment.

Massive Income Tax Increases
for Californians

A study by the California Taxpayers' Association has determined that under Proposition 186, a married couple filing jointly with an income of $32,000 (two children, standard deductions) would pay 229% more in California income tax!

Hurts Small Businesses. 300,000 Lost Jobs?

Spectrum Economics, a respected California economic consulting firm, concludes that over 300,000 jobs could be lost over the next four years because of the huge new costs of the payroll tax. Small businesses would be hit hardest and many could be forced to go out of business, layoff employees, or leave California.

We can't afford to send more California jobs to Arizona, Nevada, and Utah.

Huge Funding Deficit on Top of New Taxes?

Spectrum Economics found that even with the $48 billion in new taxes, this government-run system, when fully implemented, could face shortfalls of some $48 billion.

A $48 billion shortfall could double the new income and payroll taxes imposed by the measure.

Bureaucrats and "Health Czar" Make
Health Care Decisions

An elected "Health Czar," with billions to spend on state and regional bureaucracies to regulate health care, makes crucial health care decisions, can stop new facilities and purchases of equipment and will impose statewide limits on health care spending.

With a potential deficit of $48 billion, the "Czar" can ration and eliminate services and institute co-payments with little legislative oversight. Rationing, limited choices and long lines are not the health care reforms Californians want, especially when this vague measure may allow many non-Californians, who don't pay the taxes, to get coverage.

Join us in voting NO on Proposition 186, the Health "Insecurity" Act (48–49).

REFERENCES

Aristotle. *The Basic Works of Aristotle*. Ed. Richard McKeon. New York: Random House, 1941.

Browne, M. Neil, and Stuart M. Keeley. *Asking the Right Questions: A Guide to Critical Thinking*. Englewood Cliffs, NJ: Prentice, 1990.

California Ballot Pamphlet: General Election. California Secretary of State Office, 8 Nov. 1994.

Church, Russell T., and Charles Wilbanks. *Values and Policies in Controversy: An Introduction to Argumentation and Debate*. Scottsdale, AZ: Gorsuch Scarisbrick, 1986.

Cronkhite, Gary. "Propositions of Past and Future Fact and Value: A Proposed Classification." *Journal of the American Forensic Association* 3 (1966): 11–17.

Dewey, John. *How We Think*. Boston: Heath, 1910.

Ehninger, Douglas, and Wayne Brockriede. *Decision By Debate*. New York: Dodd Mead, 1967.

Fisher, Roger, and William Ury. *Getting to Yes*. Boston: Houghton, 1981.

Freeley, Austin J. *Argumentation and Debate: Critical Thinking for Reasoned Decision Making*. Belmont, CA: Wadsworth, 1990.

Janis, Irving L., and Leon Mann. *Decision Making*. New York: Free Press, 1977.

Lee, Ronald, and Karen King Lee. *Arguing Persuasively*. White Plains, NY: Longman, 1989.

Millman, Arthur B. "Critical Thinking Attitudes: A Framework for the Issues." *Informal Logic* 10 (1988): 45–50.

Minnich, Elizabeth K. *Transforming Knowledge*. Philadelphia: Temple UP, 1990.

Northrop, F. S. E. *Logic of the Sciences and the Humanities*. New York: Macmillan, 1947.

Peirce, Charles S. "The Fixation of Belief." *Philosophical Writings of Peirce*. Ed. Justus Buckler. New York: Dover, 1955: 7–16.

Regal, Philip J. *The Anatomy of Judgment*. Minneapolis: U of Minnesota P, 1990.

Rieke, Richard D. "The Judicial Dialogue." *Argumentation* 5 (1991): 39–55.

Rokeach, Milton. *Three Christs of Ypsilanti: A Psychological Study*. New York: Knopf, 1964.

Ruggiero, Vincent R. *The Art of Thinking*. New York: Harper, 1964.

Warnick, Barbara, and Edward S. Inch. *Critical Thinking and Communication*. New York: Macmillan, 1994.

Weiss, Robert O. *Public Argument*. Lanham, MD: UP of America, 1995.

Zarefsky, David. "Criteria for Evaluating Non-policy Argument." *Perspectives on Non-policy Argument*. Ed. Don Brownlee. Long Beach, CA: Cross-Examination Debate Association, 1980. 9–16.

Ziegelmueller, George W., Jack Kay, and Charles A. Dause. *Argumentation: Inquiry and Advocacy*. Englewood Cliffs, NJ: Prentice Hall, 1990.

4

Case Building

Key Terms

presumption

burden of proof

prima facie case

burden of rejoinder

brief

contexts

counterargument

convincing vision

clarity

significance

relevance

inherency

consistency

chain of reasoning

problem-solution

criteria

In our discussion of the steps in critical decision making in chapter 3, we closed with the mandate to build an argumentative case for the proposition you want adopted by the decision makers. We recalled Aristotle's belief that you should be as prepared to defend yourself in decision making as you are to protect yourself physically. We also explained analysis, which forms the backbone of case building. In this chapter, we tell you how to build a case.

Sometimes we hear people condemn the argumentative effort involved in presenting a well-prepared case with the claim that the truth needs no defense. Looking back over thousands of years of history and noting the frequency with which poor decisions have been made, we can only conclude that people who believe truth needs no defense are dangerously naive.

A lawyer approached the annual meeting of her firm's salary committee with the belief that she was outperforming many of the male attorneys but was not being rewarded accordingly. She was aware of an "Old Boys" network that operated during the firm's daily basketball games and discussions that followed in the locker room among the male partners, so she decided to prepare a case for herself.

When she went to the salary committee meeting, she had charts demonstrating her performance in each of the firm's criteria for rewards: billable hours, new clients brought to the firm, revenue generated, pro bono work, successful overall performance, and so on. Her charts demonstrated a growth curve in each criterion and compared it with the firm's standards to reveal that she was, indeed, one of the top producers.

The response was disappointing. The senior and managing partners said it was unseemly to make such a "case" out of the annual salary review. One was expected to be more sedate and cool about the whole thing and let the true qualities of one's performance emerge quietly.

Does that mean that preparing a case was a mistake? No. If she had waited for her true qualities to emerge on their own, they might never have been recognized. It does say, however, that cases must be adapted to the sphere in which they will be presented. In this law firm, cases for salary and other professional rewards were expected to emerge subtly through interpersonal interaction throughout the year. The annual salary meeting was designed as an opportunity to present a relaxed and confident summary of a case already made.

If the women in the firm do not choose to play basketball at noon, or if they do not feel truly welcome to do so, they must find other opportunities for interaction with senior partners or those on the salary committee through which to make their case according to the cultural rules of the firm. And, in spite of the resistance to formal presentations to the salary committee, it still makes sense for those in less powerful positions to prepare a formal case, because they have to confront the power establishment with the reasonableness of their positions.

So when we talk about making an argumentative case, we are referring to preparing a plan, a strategy, a comprehensive series of arguments that combine to support a decision persuasively. In a sense, a case is a complete story that helps others see that your proposed decision is the right and sensible thing to do. The context in which a case is communicated and the manner of communication will vary according to the argumentative or decision rules of the particular sphere in which the decision will be made.

In this chapter, we discuss the preliminary steps toward building cases, the process of briefing arguments, developing a vision of the case, and communicating the case to specific decision makers. We aim our discussion toward more formal situations, in the belief that if you can handle the complex cases you can surely adjust downward toward less formality (an argument using the commonplace *a fortiori* as we explain in chapter 2).

PRELIMINARY STEPS IN CASE BUILDING

As academic debaters, business executives, lawyers, legislators, or scientists will tell you, good cases are the result of both thorough preparation and knowing how to build them. No matter how clever you are at argumentation, you will have a tough time defending a position against others who have done more and better research, assuming they are also accomplished in argumentation. The preliminary steps in case building are vital and must not be overlooked.

Follow Critical Decision Making

In chapter 3, we set out a series of steps in critical decision making. This process constitutes the bulk of the preliminary work to be done in the preparation of a case. Even though you begin wanting to defend a certain point of view or specific decision, you are wise to set that aside momentarily and analyze the situation with as open a mind as possible. Looking seriously at all alternatives with as much knowledge and as little prejudice as possible will strengthen your position in one or more of the following ways: (1) you will have available the strongest possible statement of your case; (2) you will have a realistic knowledge of the strengths and weaknesses of other alternatives (we often assume weaknesses that do not exist); (3) you will be able to modify your position to avoid weaknesses and maximize strengths; (4) you will be able to abandon your position entirely if you find it not worthy of your support.

Identify the Nature of the Proposition

Having worked your way through the steps in critical decision making, you should be ready to advance the point of view or outcome of your research. You will be required to establish adherence to a series of specific claims that, when combined, will add up to support for your more encompassing claim, which we call a proposition (legislators call it a resolution or bill; lawyers call it a cause of action, claim, or motion; scholars call it a thesis, hypothesis, or theory; and people in business call it a presentation, pitch, or sales message). Propositions are explained in chapter 3.

Let's look at a case prepared by the Bose Corporation in support of this proposition: You should buy their small radio. Suppose you are in the market for a new radio, and you have already worked your way through the initial steps in critical decision making. The criteria that you have decided upon to guide your decision are these: (1) The radio must be able to fit comfortably in your small apartment; (2) The sound must be superior; (3) There must be integration with other elements in your entertainment system, the TV, VCR, CD; (4) the price must be within your means.

You have looked at several products that meet some but not all your criteria, and now you are testing the claims made in a Bose advertisement. To what extent does the case stand up to your criticism?

I. The Bose "radio gives sound that is richer, more natural, more lifelike than you've ever heard from a radio."
   A. The radio employs the patented acoustic waveguide speaker technology.
      1. "Just as a flute strengthens a breath of air to fill an entire concert hall, the waveguide produces room-filling sound from a small enclosure."
      2. *Popular Science* honored this radio with a "Best of What's New" award.
      3. *Business Week* named the radio a "Best Product of 1994."
   B. You can test sound quality yourself.
      1. You can use the radio for fourteen days and return it if not completely satisfied.
II. The Bose radio is small.
   A. It will fit almost anywhere: bedroom, living room, kitchen.

1. This can be seen in the picture.
2. You can try it out in your apartment.

III. The Bose includes the most current technology.
    A. It integrates with other sound system elements: CD, cassette player, TV, or VCR.
    B. It has an array of easy-to-use features.
        1. Operates from across the room with a credit card-sized remote control.
        2. You can pre-set six AM and six FM stations and shift with the touch of a button.

IV. The $349 Bose is affordable.
    A. You can pay in six easy payments.
    B. Bose will pay the $15 shipping charge ("Why you Should").

Go back and review the list of criteria. Look at the Bose arguments and test them one-by-one against the criteria. Now answer to what extent you believe the Bose is the radio for you. Would you need to see the cases for other products before deciding? Is the meaning of "affordable" a sticking point?

Assess Presumptions and Burden of Proof

In chapter 2 we introduced you to presumptions, which, alongside shared interpretative strategies, facts, probabilities, and commonplaces, are starting points of argument. Now we extend the concept of presumption to include decision makers' state of mind regarding your proposition and introduce the concept of burden of proof to describe the challenge to overcoming presumption.

Presumption   In 1828, Richard Whately defined a presumption in favor of any proposition as the "preoccupation of the ground, which implies that it must stand good till some sufficient reason is adduced against it; in short, that the burden of proof lies on the side [that] would dispute it" (Whately 112). This says nothing about the truth or quality of that position. Presumption identifies the state of mind or prejudice people hold regarding some proposition.

Because propositions emerge from the basic concepts of fact, value, and policy, you can usually expect to find decision makers presuming that what they now regard as fact, value, and policy will continue to be so regarded unless and until someone undertakes the burden of proving otherwise. Frequently, this means that there is a presumption in favor of the status quo (Latin for the way things are now), but not always.

The only presumption that matters, however, is what is actually in the minds of those who will ultimately make the decision. To find presumption, then, you must go to the decision makers and listen carefully. They will not always tell you the truth. Because we extol open-mindedness, people are often reluctant to confess their prejudices. Everyone has prejudices or established world views, as we describe in chapter 2 in the discussion of argumentation and critical appraisal. You must build your case on your best analysis of your decision makers' genuine presumptions.

In the debate over affirmative action, which we will discuss later, the presumption is hard to figure. Because affirmative action policies have been in place for many years, you might assume they benefit from the usual presumption in favor of the status quo. But, since the U.S. Supreme Court has, in a series of decisions, ruled against affirmative action plans, you might see the burden of proof on those who defend affirmative action. And, of course, political trends and associations will influence people's thinking.

If presumption favors your proposition, your case need only be aimed at maintaining and reinforcing it. You may need no case at all if no one is arguing for another proposition. The best case often consists of few words. If you were already familiar with the Bose radio, if you had seen and heard it before, and if you were already inclined to buy one, the Bose case might consist of nothing more than their 800 number and ordering instructions. If, on the other hand, you presumed that no small radio is worth $349, if you really never considered that the sound from a small radio could be good enough to justify that kind of money, then the Bose company will need to make the strongest case possible. That may explain why their ad appears in *The New Yorker,* which also includes ads for Rolex watches and luxury cars.

Burden of Proof   Burden of proof identifies the responsibility to initiate argument and set out a case sufficient in argumentative strength and breadth to bring the decision makers to doubt their presumptions and then see themselves, at least potentially, able to adhere to your proposition. From a communicative perspective, fulfilling a burden of proof means moving decision makers to the point that if no further argument were to occur, they will grant adherence to your proposition. In that way, you will have shifted the initiative to your opponents, who now have the burden of rejoinder. If they do not reply to your case, their position will erode.

Prima Facie Case   What we have just described, a case that provides sufficient argument to justify adherence to its proposition if no counterargument occurs, is called a *prima facie case*. This is a Latin term still used in law that says, in essence, the case is sufficient on its face or at first glance to justify adherence. The Bose company could publish a thousand ads for their little radio, and if you still felt that the price was far out of line, they will have failed to undermine your presumption. They would lack a prima facie case.

A prima facie case does nothing more than shift the burden of carrying the argument forward from you to those who previously were protected by presumption. They now have the *burden of rejoinder*: they must supply counterargument to stay in contention. You should not expect that just because you have made a prima facie case you will win the adherence of the decision makers. It just means you are now a vital part of the decision process. Remember, also, that all these technical terms become meaningful only in what goes on in the decision makers' minds. In some abstract sense, you may have every reason to believe you have set out a prima facie case, when the decision makers remain unmoved.

We were discussing the abortion question with a colleague one day, when he finally announced the discussion was over. When we asked why, he said "I cannot refute your arguments, but I will not change my mind. So there is no point in talking further." We felt we had done all that was needed to make a prima facie case, but our case was to no avail if it did not bring the colleague's presumptions into doubt. A common saying is, "If you don't want to change, don't listen." Our colleague chose to listen no longer.

The preliminary steps in case building, then, include following the critical decision making process, identifying the nature of the proposition, assessing the presumptions and burden of proof, and deciding what will be needed for a prima facie case. Now you can proceed to prepare a brief of available arguments.

BRIEFING ARGUMENTS

There are two significant responsibilities in case building: (1) clear, well-supported, and defensible arguments; (2) a convincing vision of the rightness of your cause. Neither is sufficient alone.

Old-fashioned law professors used to tell their students that knowing the law and doing their homework was all that was needed. Advocacy was both unnecessary and rather shady. On the other hand, some trial lawyers used to say a convincing vision (a "theory of the case") and powerful advocacy was all that was needed. The law isn't the law until some judge is moved to say so, they proclaimed.

Scientists often say that science speaks for itself, and it is unnecessary and even improper to become a scientific advocate. Technicians, however, may reply that science is just "blue sky" until someone translates it into practical terms.

It is a mistake to act as if reason and advocacy are at odds. When a lawyer enters court knowing the law thoroughly and able to communicate a compelling vision of justice as well, the other one-dimensional opponents are swept aside. Scientists who combine powerful research with eloquent presentation of their work become the giants of their time. Charles Darwin is an example of one who combined solid science with rhetorically powerful advocacy (Campbell). In this section, we describe how to brief the arguments, and in the next we talk about developing a convincing vision of your case.

The concept of a *brief* comes from the act of reducing mountains of information to manageable proportions. A brief sets out in argumentative outline form the essential elements of the proposition, including likely counterarguments. An argumentative outline form differs from other types of outlines in the sense that it identifies the lines of argument and support for the claims stated. It does not represent subdivisions of major concepts, and thus you might have only one subitem identifying support under a stated claim. The brief also demonstrates the various reasoning strategies that might be used to strengthen the case.

The Elements of the Brief

A fully developed brief should contain the following elements.

Identification of the Decision Contexts   Within a single decision making sphere, there are frequently many contexts in which argumentation functions. Dennis Jaehne has found many different and complex contexts for argumentation just within the bureaucratic system of the U.S. Forest Service. An environmental group that wants, for example, to stop helicopter shooting of coyotes must carry its case from local Forest Service personnel all the way through several administrative levels ending in Washington, DC.

Before any idea becomes law, it will probably need to be argued among interested citizens, special interest groups, legislative research personnel, legislative committees, in formal floor debate, and among executive bureaucrats who must translate law into administrative policies. Each context is likely to bring up different arguments and issues, and all should be accounted for in the brief.

Statement of the Proposition   Sometimes you may be assigned a proposition by someone else and sometimes it will be your job to state the proposition. In either case, as you move through time and contexts, it may be necessary to modify the proposition, however slightly.

Statement of Uncontroversial Matter   Definitions of terms, shared criteria, admitted facts, and shared claims should be stated explicitly. These are the starting points of argument discussed in chapter 2.

Recall also our discussion of the California initiative against providing social services to illegal immigrants. All the parties to the debate agreed, among other things, that illegal immigration should be limited. Such points of agreement must be made clear so that they can be used to support other arguments and ultimately contribute to a joint critical decision. Unless you know these uncontroversial starting points, you will have problems finding issues.

Statement of Potential Issues   The propositional analysis we discussed in chapter 3, provides you with a series of issues that seem to be the most important. You will use these to build this part of the brief. However, these are only the *potential issues*, those most likely to become central to the decision. Furthermore, as you examine these issues in the light of the significance of various contexts, issues will probably change.

In business, for example, you may start with a presentation to your manager for whom staying within the budget is a major issue. Having obtained your manager's support, you next go to the assistant vice president, for whom meeting schedules is prime. If you are successful at that level, you may present to the regional vice president, for whom distribution and quarterly return on investment count most. And if that is successful, your presentation to the CEO may need to focus on issues of company vision and market share, with cost, schedule, distribution, and even quarterly return being of less importance.

Statement of Arguments and Counterarguments   For each issue, you need to state the claims you intend to support with argument and the possible opposing claims or refutations that might detract from them. At this point in your preparation, you are trying to cast the widest net for all claims that tend to support your proposition. For each context, you will select those arguments that are most relevant to the decision makers at hand.

An Example of a Brief

The best examples of briefs will be found in the hands of people engaged in real argumentation, those in law, business, scholarship, government, politics, and so on. If possible, interview such a person or secure an internship to work on a proposition. This will give you the best example of what we have been talking about. Short of that, we will present a highly compressed example that does not go as far in detail as to state explicitly the forms of support. We have chosen to look at the debate over affirmative action policies in higher education.

Decision Contexts   In the summer of 1995, Governor Pete Wilson of California asked officials at public colleges and universities to "end the unfairness of granting seats in our finest schools on the basis of skin color or ethnicity" (Lively). He issued an executive order to curb affirmative action programs that give preferential treatment to women and members of minority groups in admissions, hiring, and contracts.

This set up a series of immediate decision contexts:

1. The University of California Board of Regents
2. The Board of Trustees of the California State Colleges and Universities
3. The Board of Trustees of the California Community Colleges

Each of these contexts presented slightly different argumentative challenges. Governor Wilson had appointed at least half of the members of the boards of California State and Community Colleges systems, so he could anticipate a presumption in his favor. While this was not the case for the Regents of the University of California, there seemed to be members inclined to support his position.

There were larger contexts at play as well. They ultimately involved virtually all U.S. citizens.

1. Because Wilson was seeking the nomination of the Republican Party for President of the United States, he first wanted the adherence of party members.
2. Because officials in higher education all over the country were facing similar arguments, Wilson's action spurred their debate on the question.
3. Because the courts have been actively involved in affirmative action for more than forty years, judges could not fail to watch the debate.
4. Because Congress has the power to decide on laws and appropriations relevant to affirmative action, legislators formed a decision context.

5. To the extent that opposition to affirmative action constituted a reason to vote for or against a candidate for president, the entire electorate formed a decision context.

State the Proposition   The specific proposition under consideration changes from context to context. In California, the proposition was that all parts of the higher education system should eliminate policies giving preferences to women and minorities in admission and hiring decisions. In other states, the propositions dealt with various alternatives to the established affirmative action practices.

Courts only consider specific cases involving specific legal issues. So their propositions are likely to be stated as in a case that became influential in the debate, Adanan and Constructors v. Pena. Here the Court supported the proposition that federal affirmative action programs involving the use of race as a basis for preferential treatment are lawful only if they can withstand federal courts' "strict scrutiny." This term means that the courts give the highest possible presumption against any preferential treatment based on race or gender, and those who would advocate affirmative action bear the highest possible burden of proof.

In the political arena, the question of affirmative action became attached to the proposition that Pete Wilson or another candidate with the same position should be elected to the presidency. Or, whether Congress should enact laws to weaken or eliminate affirmative action programs and whether candidates advocating that action should be elected.

Uncontroversial Matter   The concept behind affirmative action programs rests on key values that do not come into contention. As you will see when we turn to potential issues, the debate centers on how the values are carried into practical application. Here are some of the points that remain uncontroversial.

1. No practice in higher education should be in violation of federal and state law or court orders.
2. Society should be "colorblind."
3. Affirmative action should continue only as long as it is needed to overcome past or present discrimination.
4. All people should be treated fairly.
5. In college admissions, there should not be quotas set on the basis of race, gender, or ethnicity.
6. Increasing the number of people who are the first generation in their family to attend college is a good thing.
7. Affirmative action should rest only on a compelling national interest to remove barriers to higher education and increase the diversity of graduates.
8. Affirmative action should be narrowly focused to meet a specific, actual need.

Potential Issues   Potential issues can be found by examining carefully the arguments used by people already involved in the question of affirmative action. You will see that some of the issues stated below are broad in scope while others are narrow, and some of the narrow ones are really implied in the broad ones. We will list them all, because as the debate goes on, there will be shifts in issues that need to be anticipated. When we present examples of arguments, you will see that some subordinate issues identify potential arguments in support of the broader issues.

1. Is affirmative action in higher education inherently unfair?
2. Does affirmative action in higher education lower the bar on qualifications for admission?
3. Does affirmative action limit educational resources and opportunities for white males?
4. Are race- and gender-specific scholarships and fellowships illegal?
5. Has affirmative action achieved its goal of redressing the effects of past discrimination?
6. Will policies aimed at helping only the disadvantaged fulfill any continuing affirmative action needs?
7. Is affirmative action in higher education necessary to achieve a colorblind society?
8. Does higher education require a diverse student body?
9. Are diverse student bodies a significant source of increased social and professional diversity?
10. Does affirmative action on campuses open employment to women and minorities as faculty and staff that were previously closed?
11. Will the United States face critical shortages of talent in crucial jobs in science, education, and professions if college graduates do not come from all sectors of society?

Potential Arguments and Counterarguments   What we present below is a highly shortened version of what arguments and counterarguments should look like. The important point to note is that we have tried to put arguments that develop opposing claims on the same issue opposite each other.

Arguments Supporting the Ban	Arguments Opposing the Ban
I. Affirmative action in higher education is unfair. A. Admission should be based on merit alone. 1. Merit is a basic American value. B. Giving minorities preference lowers the bar on qualifications. 1. Scholarships are denied qualified candidates.	I. Affirmative action promotes fairness. A. Merit works only if discrimination is abolished. 1. Fairness demands an even field. B. Unqualified students are not admitted. 1. Money to afford college is given to qualified applicants.

2. Qualified students are passed over for those less qualified.

3. Graduating less qualified students lowers professional hiring standards.

C. Minority preference reduces opportunities for whites and males.
1. Support given minorities is support not given others.
2. Lost education yields lost occupations.

II. There is no longer a need for affirmative action.
A. Minorities today have not specifically been discriminated against.
1. The law has removed discrimination in education: Brown v. Board.
2. The Civil Rights Act has had over 30 years to correct discrimination.
B. To discriminate on the basis of race, even for purposes of helping, is to demean minority people.
1. Race is alien to U.S. Constitution.

2. Successful minorities lose individual credit for their work.
C. Special help to the disadvantaged will do all that needs to be done.

2. Quotas are not defended, let all who are qualified be admitted.

3. Students must meet the same graduation standards.

C. Minorities have suffered lost opportunity for years.
1. Some preference is needed to level the playing field.

2. Help to minorities does not deny access to others.

II. Affirmative action is still needed.

A. Discrimination is still practiced.

1. The schools are segregated by neighborhood and income.
2. There is discrimination despite the law.
B. It is more demeaning to deny a person access to education because of race, ethinicity, or gender.
1. Equality of opportunity is central to the Constitution.
2. There are plenty of people who receive credit.
C. There is not enough data to support this claim.

1. Minorities who are
   disadvantaged are the
   ones deserving
   special help.
2. Disadvantaged people
   represent all races
   and genders.

III. Affirmative action in
   higher education is
   illegal.
   A. Courts say a race-based
   scholarship is not legal
   at U of Maryland.
   B. Other decisions have
   denied affirmative
   action laws.

   1. Adanan and
      Constructors v. Pena
   2. City of Richmond v.
      J. A. Croson Company

IV. Higher education will be
   diverse enough without
   affirmative action.
   A. All qualified students
   will be admitted.

   B. Diversity is not needed
   in higher education.

III. The courts have not
   definitively decided
   this.
   A. U.S. Supreme Court did
   not consider this
   case.
   B. These cases did not
   address higher
   education affirmative
   action plans.

IV. Higher education must
   have diversity through
   affirmative action.
   A. No affirmative action
   means a drop in
   minority students.
   B. Education must reflect
   the larger society,
   which is diverse.
   C. The United States will see a
   shortfall of
   qualified
   professionals if
   affirmative action is
   eliminated.

DEVELOPING A CONVINCING VISION

A brief provides you with a set of fully developed arguments. But, as Karl Llewellyn observed about lawyers arguing before appellate courts, something more than fully developed arguments is required. He said that while courts accept a duty to the law, they also hold a vision of justice, decency, and fairness. So the obligation of a legal case is to combine what Llewellyn calls a technically sound case on the law (which the other side will probably also have) with a convincing vision that will satisfy the court that "sense and decency and justice require . . . the rule which you contend for. . . . " He says:

> Your whole case must make *sense*, must appeal as being *obvious* sense, inescapable sense, sense in simple terms of life and justice. If that is done, a technically sound case on the law then gets rid of all further difficulty: it shows the court that its duty to the Law not only does not conflict with its duty to Justice but urges along the exact same line (182).

Reread his statement. Notice that it is the vision that moves the decision maker in your direction, while the arguments merely dispel doubts that the vision is correct and provide a rationale for its promulgation.

What is sensible, just, decent, or right is a function of the world view of the decision makers. To make a case is to engage and shape that world view on behalf of your cause. As Richard Rorty says, truth, goodness, and beauty are not eternal objects that we try to locate and reveal as much as artifacts whose fundamental design we often have to alter ("Philosophy" 143). Rorty believes that we satisfy our burden of proof by offering "sparkling new ideas, or utopian visions of glorious new institutions. The result of genuinely new thought . . . is not so much to refute or subvert our previous beliefs as to help us forget them by giving us a substitute for them" ("Is Derrida" 108–09).

Robert Branham says that policy propositions necessitate imagination "of the alternative worlds in which the proposed actions would operate." They entail a comparison of alternative visions of the future emerging from policy alternatives. "At minimum," he says, "debaters must articulate a vision of the future world in which the plan exists and a future in which it does not" (247). Review the discussion on storytelling in chapter 2 to see what it means to articulate a vision.

Learn the Decision Makers' Vision

In our discussion of critical appraisal in chapter 2, we explained the role of narratives, scripts, and scenarios in evaluating argument. We said that decision makers evaluate arguments in terms of their personal vision. To make a convincing vision of your case first requires an understanding of the vision of your proposition now held by the appropriate decision makers.

People on both sides of the affirmative action debate share a vision of an America where everyone is judged on the basis of their individual merits, and race, gender, or ethnicity play no part in the equality of opportunity. At that point, however, the visions separate. One vision is of America, the land of individual opportunity, with nothing standing between you and the presidency but your abilities and ambitions.

Another vision is one of America where white men dominate and where without the force of law, others will never have an equal chance for success.

That vision includes the fact that there has never been a president who was not a white man. No matter which vision your decision makers hold, they will likely dismiss arguments predicated on visions they find ridiculous.

Some people find a vision of heaven in which angels wear white robes and wings and play harps unbelievable while others take it quite seriously. It is prudent to sound out decision makers on their vision before trying to attach your case to one.

Tell the Story of Your Vision

The "oldest living Confederate widow" tells us that "Stories only happen to the people who can tell them" (Gurganus 256). Reality rests upon the stories we take as accurate characterizations of the way things truly are. Visualization serves to intensify the feelings of the decision makers toward your proposition; it vividly projects them into a state in which your proposed decision is effectively in operation (Gronbeck, *et al.* 128). When you tell the story of your vision, you make your proposed decision real.

Telling the story of your vision allows you to take your decision makers on a trip through time. Wayne Beach says people regularly engage in "time-traveling" in their communication through the medium of telling stories, or "storifying," as he calls it (1). To make sense of the future, we must often turn to the past and consider the present, says Beach.

In legal contexts, decisions almost always turn on a characterization of the past: did the accused run from the murder scene; was the contract actually agreed to by all parties even though it had not been signed; was the car exceeding the speed limit at the time of the accident?

To make a sound policy decision, as in the question of affirmative action, decision makers must be taken on a trip through past American history, and then given a vision of the future as it would function under the proposition. The more effectively these stories are told, the more real the vision will be and the more motivated the decision makers will be to support your proposition.

Consider an Example

A member of the U.S. House of Representatives submitted a bill (proposition) asking that the Custer Battlefield National Monument in Montana be renamed the Little Bighorn National Battlefield Park and that a Native American memorial be erected. He had prepared his case carefully, but he also had to address a well-established vision of what happened between people coming to live in North America from the sixteenth century on and those who were already living there. Unless he could inspire members of Congress with his new vision, his proposition stood little chance of passing.

Randall Lake observes that contemporary civilizations make themselves legitimate by grounding their origins in historical processes, and that is the case in the United States today. Lake says there is a powerful and well-developed Euramerican narrative in place that renders Native Americans relics of the past and thus absent from the present and irrelevant to the future. In brief, the Euramerican narrative follows a "time's arrow" metaphor, suggesting events moving in a line from past to present to future. The Europeans arrived in North America, encountered a savage that had to be "civilized" and "saved," and ultimately produced a "vanishing red man." In this vision, the Battle of the Little Bighorn is merely an anomaly, a glitch in the steady movement toward the inevitable triumph of the Europeans. So it makes sense to honor Custer, a martyr in a great cause. Since the Native American has vanished, there is no point in a memorial.

Those who would sustain a case for a Native American memorial must take the decision makers on a time-traveling expedition to establish an alternate vision to the time's arrow notion. They offer a "time's cycle" vision instead. Tribal life, says Lake, moved not along a linear chronology but in a cyclical pattern associated with the seasons and cardinal directions: the circle, not the line, is important. Thus, there is no beginning or end, but a constant cycling. We approached a young boy at the Taos Pueblo one time and asked, "How old are you?" He replied, "I do not measure my life with numbers."

In the Native American vision, the cycle now comes around to memorializing *all* those who fought at the Little Bighorn. The proposition to change the name of the memorial was proposed by then U.S. Representative Ben Nighthorse Campbell of Colorado (he shortly became a U.S. Senator), whose great-grandfather fought against General George Armstrong Custer and the Seventh Cavalry at Little Bighorn River. In his vision, Native Americans did not vanish and become irrelevant, they have been here all along and were just made invisible by the Euramerican story.

Ben Nighthorse Campbell, by his very presence in the U.S. House of Representatives, represented the circle—what goes around, comes around—a Native American, whose ancestor fought and defeated Custer, stood before the nation as a symbol that there is no vanishing red man. The case would have been infinitely weaker had it been argued by a Euramerican.

The Congress chose Campbell's vision: a Little Bighorn National Battlefield Monument (Public Law 102–201), with monuments to both sides, such as we have at sites of Civil War battles. The once invisible army that attacked Custer appears now as the victor in the battle.

COMMUNICATION TO SPECIFIC DECISION MAKERS

Preparing a brief and a vision of the case are part of the overall planning and strategy in case building. They represent the vital research phase. However, each time a specific decision making context is encountered, a specific adaptation of the case must be made. Is the case to be presented in writing, orally, or both? Will others present counterargument? What format of argument will be followed: discussion, presentation, debate, negotiation, mediation? What sphere-based rules apply? Will a decision be made immediately or after deliberation?

What Are the Communication Constraints?

Having done all the research on your case, there is a powerful temptation to present everything you have at every opportunity. Lawyers once wrote such long briefs that the appellate courts set page limits. In almost every situation, time limits will apply, even if only by implication. The important point to remember is this: say what you need to say to make your point, and no more. Do not expect the decision makers to hear or read volumes of material and select what is most relevant to them. It is your job to do the selecting and to make the difficult decision to leave out much material that is good but not the best for this group.

Use different media effectively. Because some people feel more comfortable writing their case than presenting it orally, they choose to bypass oral presentations. The reverse is also true. It is a mistake to presume that writing or speaking alone is as effective as a combination of the two plus any other appropriate nonverbal means, such as charts, graphs, films, models, slides, or transparencies. Each medium of communication can serve a role in making a case and should be used.

What Counterargument Will Occur?

In formal debates like trials or legislative deliberations, speakers are followed by someone taking another point of view and likely to refute what has been said before. In other situations such direct advocacy may be avoided. There are times when a speaker has been invited to present a case, only to learn later that others have also been invited to present alternate cases. On some television magazine programs such as *60 Minutes*, people are interviewed individually, and later their remarks are edited together to make the interview appear to have been a debate.

The presentation of a case must be adjusted to meet the needs presented by counterargument. The more powerful, direct, and sustained the counterargument, the more carefully the case must be adjusted to withstand such criticism, to bolster weakened points, and to engage in counter-refutation. If there is to be such direct counterargument, it is important that you know that in advance, secure specific permission to respond to the attacks, and come prepared with backup support.

What Argumentative Format Will Be Used?

Veteran advocates do not walk into a decision making situation without plenty of advance notice of the order of the speakers, how long they will speak, how frequently they will speak, what the agenda will be, how the physical surroundings will be set up, what materials will be appropriate, who will attend, and so forth. Read the history of debates among candidates for major political office to see how much attention they pay to such details.

Lawyers, using their image of courts as a model, often walk into an arbitration only to discover the rules are quite different. They raise objections to witnesses and evidence, they demand recesses or postponements, they try to speak at great length, only to be told by the arbitrator that it is not done that way here. Arbitrations are informal: people sit around a table and discuss a problem. The arbitrator may not admit certain evidence or may admit evidence that would be rejected in a court. Formal speeches are rarely made, and an effort is made to keep the proceedings short and simple. Lawyers who do not bother to learn these differences tend to make a poor case presentation.

Political candidates carefully work to keep "debates" more on the order of press conferences in which a panel of reporters alternate in asking questions. They toss coins to see who speaks first and last, because they know these are important speaking positions. They like to turn a reporter's question into an opportunity to make a short speech rather than answer the question, and they earnestly avoid any direct interaction with each other that might force them to address specific issues while on the defensive.

In business presentations, it is often the case that day-long sessions will be scheduled with one presenter after another coming to the front. It is also common in business presentations to use many transparencies and an overhead projector in a darkened room. This means that unless you are one of the first presenters, your audience is likely to be lulled into a soporific stupor by the time your turn comes. If you follow the pattern of all the others, you will be unlikely to make much of an impression.

To bring the decision makers back to life, it will be necessary for you to violate the established pattern. It may be smart to turn up the lights, turn off the projector, and talk directly to the audience. Using other forms of visual aids such as videotape or handouts may also help. The important point is this: do not let obedience to an established pattern work to your disadvantage.

As we said earlier, in some situations direct advocacy of a case is considered in bad taste. When the format is more on the order of investigation, analysis, or general discussion, it may be necessary to get your case across indirectly while paying plenty of consideration and deference to other points of view.

What Are the Rules of the Sphere?

From among the mass of argument and support for your proposition, some will be quite inadmissible in certain spheres. Admissibility is most clearly defined in law, where some arguments, witnesses, documents, or comments simply will not be heard. On the other hand, many scholars become disturbed when their scientific research is presented in court in abbreviated form, without the careful documentation required in science. Many legal arguments would never survive scholarly scrutiny. Of course, a scholarly argument that wins praise in one discipline might be considered nonsense in another discipline.

What counts as the starting point for argument and what counts as proper support will vary from sphere to sphere. In selecting your specific case for presentation, you must know what rules apply. A corporation may make a decision based on solid arguments within its context that would never win the adherence of government regulators. One case would have to be defended before company executives, with quite another ready for presentation before a regulatory agency. This is not to say that the company is being two-faced or devious; it merely recognizes that arguments and support that lead to a business decision may need to be combined with different arguments and support adjusted to another sphere. Amateurs at case making frequently argue successfully before their supporters and then expect the same case to be as effective in convincing neutrals or opponents.

How Will the Decision Be Made?

Rarely does a single case presentation lead to immediate decision. Typically, some time passes between argumentation and decision making. The questions for case selection are how much time will pass, how many other deliberations will take place, how much of the ultimate decision will be made outside your presence?

The more time that will pass between your case presentation and the decision, the more your case must be designed to make a lasting impression. A complex case with many claims may be effective for relatively short-term recall, but the more time that will pass, the more the case must be encapsulated in a few memorable points that will stay in decision makers' minds.

It is here that vision, language, and focused argument come together to make powerfully memorable arguments. Few remember the legal intricacies of Justice Holmes's argument in Schenck v. United States but many firmly "know" the prohibition against "falsely shouting fire in a theatre and causing a panic." He boiled his case down to a memorable statement that was combined with another: this speech act would present a "clear and present danger," which government has a right to punish, and thereby made a case for an interpretation of the First Amendment to the U.S. Constitution that retains currency more than three-quarters of a century later.

The more deliberations that will occur prior to the decision, the more your case must be designed to endure close scrutiny. If you have weaknesses that are sure to be exposed, it makes sense for you to bring them up first, acknowledge them, and then show why they do not fatally damage your case. Use a two-sided approach, giving full credit to other proposed decisions while showing clearly why they are not the best, and use more neutral language, as discussed in chapter 15, which is unlikely to offend anyone.

What Critical Values Will Be Applied?

Because different demands will be placed on your case as you move from one context or sphere to another, it makes sense to pay attention to the way each set of decision makers approaches the decision task. We will identify five generic values usually relevant to decision making that can guide your analysis of each situation.

Clarity It seems belaboring the obvious to say your case should be clear to the decision makers, but clarity is tricky. Language meaning, as we explain in chapter 15, is socially based. If you ask people, "Is what I have said clear?" they may say it is when their understanding is not at all what you hoped it would be. What you need to understand is what interpretative strategies are typical of these decision makers, and then try to express your case so that it will be clear in a joint sense—satisfying you and them.

Significance   What is highly significant to you may be less so to your decision makers. We all have hierarchies of concerns. For example, if someone asks you if world peace is significant to you, you may say it is, but not significant enough to donate money to the cause or attend a conference. When presenting a case, it helps to have an idea of where your significance coincides with that of the decision makers.

Relevance or Salience   One way you can decide what parts of your brief should be presented to a particular set of decision makers is by learning what is relevant to them; what is salient at the moment. In the debate over affirmative action, we have included an issue related to legality or constitutionality. While everyone is probably concerned with that issue, its relevance is most likely to be found within the legal system. People may say that they certainly want to act within the law, but that question will not become salient unless and until the courts take up a case in which that question will be considered.

Inherency   Decision makers might agree with the substance of your case but feel unmoved to action because they do not believe you have identified inherent problems—problems so deeply embedded that action is required. Many people believe that persistent deficit spending by Congress is inherent to the system such that it will be eliminated only by an amendment to the Constitution requiring a balanced budget. Others, however, reject that inherency. They say that deficits may be a problem, but we already have the ability to deal with them short of rewriting the Constitution. Try to learn how your decision makers perceive your concerns in relation to inherency.

Consistency   Gidon Gottlieb says, "One of the demands of rationality most often emphasized is the requirement of consistency" (171–72). "In our culture . . . there is a clear notion that the charge of inconsistency is a winning argument" (Sillars 3). Unfortunately, one person's consistency is another's confusion as different argument elements are identified as needing to be consistent with one another. While you will want your decision makers to believe your case is consistent, it will be important for you to learn their standards of consistency.

What Sequence of Claims Is Most Appropriate?

Remember, the purpose of a case is to generate adherence to your proposition by the immediately appropriate decision makers. That means the series of claims included in the case must combine to move the decision makers from where they are to where you want them to be. If you propose to coworkers after a particularly tough job, "Let's order in pizza for the whole crowd," and everyone agrees, your case is made. If, however, your proposition stipulates that the boss pay for the pizza and the boss does not cheer, you need to make a more elaborate case. The boss clearly agrees everyone should get pizza but is reluctant to pay, so what set of claims could you make to get the boss to pay? How should you sequence those claims? There are many different patterns by which cases may be structured, and the same case might usefully be structured differently for different decision contexts. We will illustrate a few of the most commonly used patterns.

Chain of Reasoning   You might use a series of claims that starts with ones on which the decision maker is virtually certain to agree (identify a starting point) and move in small steps of adherence to the proposition itself. In the pizza case, it might look like this:

> CLAIM ONE (a starting point): The boss wants workers who are highly productive. This should elicit an immediate "yes" from the boss. In fact, this case pattern has been called the "yes, yes" format because its power lies in securing an increasingly encompassing series of affirmations from the decision maker. It may be used in direct interaction or may be used rhetorically.
>
> CLAIM TWO (still virtually a starting point): Happy and satisfied workers are the most productive.
>
> CLAIM THREE (starting to draw the boss toward the proposition): Workers who are given treats when they do good work are happy and satisfied. The boss can see the pattern now moving inexorably toward the proposition, but affirmation of the previous claims makes it hard to pull out now.
>
> CLAIM FOUR (starting the curve toward the plate): This group has just finished doing a good job.
>
> CLAIM FIVE (this is the kicker): Now is the time for a treat as an investment in higher productivity by this work force.

Problem-Solution   A common approach to case structure is a problem-solution format. It is widely used in journalistic writing and policy decision making. One of the most enduring formats for public speaking, called the *motivated sequence*, rests on this pattern. Bruce Gronbeck and colleagues claim that it approximates the normal processes of human thinking and will move an audience toward agreement with a speaker's purposes. They describe the following sequence of claims:

> ATTENTION: An opening claim aimed at generating the active involvement of decision makers
>
> NEED: A claim that identifies a condition in need of correction
>
> SATISFACTION: A claim that identifies a way the condition can be corrected
>
> VISUALIZATION: A claim that sets forth the vision of the case: the world in which the condition is corrected through the proposed method
>
> ACTION: A claim that calls for specific measures to put the proposed action into being (183)

The end of a century presents an excellent occasion for problem-solution cases, because people seem uneasy about the future during such times. To convince us to subscribe to *TaiPan*, an investment publication, here is the motivated sequence that was used in a Summer 1995 special edition sent to potential subscribers. It will quickly become obvious that the rhetorical style of this publication is exaggeration bordering on the humorous, but their intent is quite serious.

ATTENTION: **The 20th Century is Dead.** It died on November 8, 1994, when the Republicans took control of Congress. In what they call the, "Special Millennium Fever Edition," the publishers tell us that this is the twilight of the United States as we have known it, "There's a certain madness in the air as the year 2000 draws near. It's millennium fever, and whether we see the second coming or just a lot of hoopla, things will change at an alarming rate. **Are you prepared? Read on . . .** " They have our attention.

NEED: There will be, say the publishers of *TaiPan*, eleven major events and trends that will change life forever. They include (1) "invisible wealth"; (2) "Super flus," "deadly bacterias," "mutant viruses and famine fungus"; (3) "hot stocks"; (4) "poor white collar people"; (5) "new enclaves of wealth and power"; (6) "being there walls" (video technology); (7) "technological breakthroughs that will knock your pants off"; (8) "earth-shaking profits from the big one" (earthquakes and natural disasters); (9) "poor bastards" (inner city poor); (10) "smart wars"; and (11) "Democrats will reinvent themselves as libertarians." All these changes can either leave us behind and in danger, or we can take steps now to avoid disaster. There is clearly a need to do something.

SATISFACTION: Fortunately, *TaiPan* can meet our needs, because, as their past success in forecasting the future has proved, if you can anticipate the future, you can turn it into success rather than failure:

You need a strong grasp of what is already happening and the ability to look into the future—to foresee what can happen *before* it happens to you.

Inside [the investment publication], you'll find ways you can grasp the future profits now. And you'll find a whole new strategy for understanding the seemingly "random" nature of events.

VISUALIZATION: The picture the publisher wants to generate is of a world that is in chaos with great danger for anyone who is not prepared. Of course, the way to make your way through this treacherous world is to subscribe to *TaiPan*, and then all will be well. Here is the word picture:

As the year 2000 draws ever closer, people will claim they've seen Jesus, that they've seen aliens, that they've seen the Devil himself. Historically, at moments like this, stock markets crash, mass-suicide cults become popular, the Virgin Mary makes an appearance in various Catholic countries, and for a time "the madness of crowds" takes over.

But a few stand calmly—and prosper— in the middle of this madness.

ACTION: *TaiPan* offers a no-risk offer with a free bonus. All you need to do is fill out the order form, give your credit card number, and you will receive a subscription that you can cancel anytime in the first 90 days if you are not 100% satisfied. Additionally, you will receive a free 100 page *Annual Forecast Issue* bonus. All this for only $79.95 for one year or $139.95 for two years.

As we said at the start of this example, it is easy to laugh at the exaggerated claims and intense language used to attract subscribers. However, *TaiPan* has been sending out material like this for several years, seems to be making money, and must have a good idea of what their target audience will accept as reasonable.

In chapter 3, we speak of a stock issues case that asks, is there a need for a change; is there a practical plan to meet that need; is the plan advantageous? This case format is essentially the same as the problem-solution one just described.

Criteria   A case pattern particularly well suited to propositions of value is one that essentially involves three steps:

1. Establish adherence to a set of criteria.
2. Establish adherence to claims of fact relevant to the criteria.
3. Use the criteria to gain adherence to a value judgment about the factual claims.

Robert Pear and Erik Eckholm illustrate the criteria case structure in a discussion of physician ownership of profit-producing medical facilities and equipment. They cite the argument of Dr. Arnold S. Relman, editor of the *New England Journal of Medicine.*

CRITERIA CLAIM: "When you earn money by referring to a facility where you are an investor, you're just using your patient as a economic commodity." Relman thus claims that one criterion [measure or test] of improper behavior on the part of physicians is whether a patient referral produces a profit that involves a conflict of interest such that the action is more for greed than for good health.

FACTUAL CLAIMS: Pear and Eckholm claim (1) there has been a rapid rise in ownership of magnetic resonance imaging (MRI) machines by physicians who use them as a diagnostic tool; (2) ten percent of physicians have invested in businesses to which they refer patients; (3) physicians who share ownership of laboratories and other health care businesses order more services than other physicians.

VALUE-JUDGMENT CLAIM: Since each of these factual claims identifies an instance in which the referring physician will earn more money with more referrals, this behavior is improper.

The final claim uses the criterion established first to make a judgment on the factual claims. The case structure is effective by separating a criterion or principle of value to which adherence can be gained in the abstract, and only then applying it to a specific case for which adherence to a value judgment is sought.

The criteria format can work with propositions of policy and fact as well. In the physician example, some advocates have gone on to argue for laws that prohibit physicians from referring patients to business ventures in which they have a financial interest. The case would merely add one more step:

> POLICY-ACTION CLAIM: Since that which is improper should not be allowed, government should legislate against physician referral to business ventures in which they have an interest.

To use this pattern for a proposition of fact, one simply first establishes the criteria for what counts as fact and then advances the factual claims that show consistency with the criteria. In a debate over dinosaur DNA, opposing sides in the discussion used this type of case.

Scott R. Woodward, microbiologist at Brigham Young University, reported in an article in *Science* that he has extracted DNA from the bones of a dinosaur. His argument is straightforward:

> CRITERIA: (1) If you extract material from dinosaur bones, what you find is, in fact, from a dinosaur. (2) If the genetic sequence observed is different from any other sequence ever studied, it is from a dinosaur.
> FACT CLAIM: The gene fragments actually came from the bones of a dinosaur, and they are unlike the thousands of gene fragments that the research team has studied in the past. So, it is dinosaur DNA that has been found.

Those who disagreed with the scientist's case made a similar argument.

> CRITERIA: Marc W. Allard and his colleagues at George Washington University argued that since the nearest modern relatives of dinosaurs are birds, not mammals, dinosaur DNA must resemble bird DNA.
> FACT CLAIM: In fact, the DNA under study showed great similarity to living mammalian genes, not birds. So, the DNA could not be from a dinosaur. It probably came, they claimed, from some mammal, even human, that had contaminated the 80-million-year-old-bones ("Was It A Dinosaur?").

CONCLUSION

Case building rests on thorough research and preparation. Before you are ready to support any proposition, you should have worked through the steps in critical decision making and have a wide appreciation for the problem and the various alternatives. You should phrase your proposition to express your position clearly in relation to the particular decision context or sphere at hand. And you should fully understand the status of presumption and burden of proof for each set of decision makers.

A full brief that surveys the various decision contexts, notes the uncontroversial matter, states potential issues, and then outlines all available arguments alongside potential counterarguments should be prepared well in advance of decision making. At the same time, a convincing vision of the case that will help drive home your position and make it memorable should be conceived. Finally, a specific case presentation must be prepared for every set of decision makers to whom it is to be presented. Three possible sequences of claims in a case are: chain of reasoning, problem-solution, and criteria.

PROJECTS

4.1 Interview a politician, scientist, lawyer, or business person. Ask your specialist how a case is made within the specialty. Ask to see a sample of one used in the past.

4.2 Prepare a case for any proposition.

4.3 Exchange cases with another member of the class and prepare a critique of the case you recieve while the other person does the same with yours. Then get together and talk about how each of you could improve your cases.

4.4 Volunteer to work on a political campaign or an effort to pass a piece of legislation. Keep a journal of how arguments are put together in case formats. Write a paper reviewing your experience.

4.5 Look in the *Congressional Record* for a place where a major bill is being debated. Based on what is said in the arguments, identify the case being defended on both sides and write it out in outline form. Then, comment on what type of case it is and how well suited it is to a set of Congressional decision makers.

REFERENCES

Adanan and Constructors. 115 *Supreme Court Reporter*, 2097 (1995).

Beach, Wayne. "Temporal Density in Courtroom Interaction: Constraints on the Recovery of Past Events in Legal Discourse." *Communication Monographs* 52 (1985): 1–18.

Branham, Robert. "Roads Not Taken: Counterplans and Opportunity Costs." *Journal of the American Forensic Association* 25 (1989): 246–55.

Campbell, John Angus. "The Polemical Mr. Darwin." *The Quarterly Journal of Speech* 61 (1975): 375–90.

Gottlieb, Gidon. *The Logic of Choice*. New York: Macmillan, 1968.

Gronbeck, Bruce E., Raymie E. McKerrow, Douglas Ehninger, and Alan H. Monroe. *Principles and Types of Speech Communication*. New York: Harper, 1990.

Gurganus, Allan. *The Oldest Living Confederate Widow Tells All*. New York: Ivy, 1989.

Jaehne, Dennis. "Administrative Appeals: The Bureaucratization of Environmental Discourse." Diss. U of Utah, 1989.

Lake, Randall A. "Between Myth and History: Enacting Time in Native American Protest." *The Quarterly Journal of Speech* 77 (1991): 123–51.

Lively, Kit. "A Jolt From Sacramento." *Chronicle of Higher Education* 9 June 1995: A 25+.

Llewellyn, Karl N. "The Modern Approach to Counseling and Advocacy—Especially Commercial Transactions." *Columbia Law Review* 46 (1946): 167–95.

Pear, Robert, and Erik Eckholm. "When Healers Are Entrepreneurs: A Debate Over Costs and Ethics." *New York Times* 2 June 1991: 1+.

Rorty, Richard. "Philosophy as a Kind of Writing: An Essay on Derrida." *New Literary History* 9 (1978): 141–60.

———. "Is Derrida a Transcendental Philosopher?" *Yale Journal of Criticism* 2 (1989): 207–15.

Schenck v. United States (249 US 47, 1919).

Shannon, James. *Texaco and the $10 Billion Jury*. Englewood Cliffs, NJ: Prentice-Hall, 1988.

Sillars, Malcolm O. "Values: Providing Standards for Audience-Centered Argumentation." *Values in Argumentation*. Ed. Sally Jackson. Annandale, VA: Speech Communication Association, 1995: 1–6.

TaiPan. Summer 1995.

"Was it a Dinosaur?" *Chronicle of Higher Education* 7 July 1995: A6.

Whately, Richard. *Elements of Rhetoric*. Ed. Douglas Ehninger. Carbondale: Southern Illinois UP, 1963.

"Why You Should Pay $349 For This Radio." *New Yorker* 10 July 1995: 11.

5

Analysis and Case Building in Law

Key Terms

trial	story model
judges	prima facie
jury	brief
stare decisis	appeal
syllogism	appellate argument
law	presumption
analogy	burden of proof
relational structuring	decision
temporal structuring	trial impact

Much of the analysis and case building practiced in a wide spectrum of spheres can be traced back to practices in law. For thousands of years, people seeking justice have understood the importance of identifying issues, clearly stating claims, and putting together cases. Knowing this, those working in other spheres have often borrowed concepts and procedures from the law to guide their own argumentation. For this reason, we have chosen legal-oriented spheres as models to illustrate analysis and case building.

While the Western legal tradition has a body of common argumentative practices that allows us to talk about it as a sphere, in practice there are many legal spheres or subspheres. For example, legal argumentation within the federal system has rules and procedures that differ from those prevailing in the several states. And practices of argumentation in the law can vary substantially from one state to another, one locale to another, and even one judge's courtroom to another.

Furthermore, argumentation in law can vary according to the kind of case. Criminal cases call for argumentative practices that are different from those in civil cases. In criminal cases, for example, the argument must meet a greater burden of proof (beyond a reasonable doubt) than that required of arguments in civil cases (by a clear preponderance of evidence). And even within these broad concepts, analysis and case building in, say, a murder case can be different from that in a narcotics case. And analysis and case building in patent law, tax law, estate law, divorce law, labor law, environmental law, and torts (such as acts of negligence leading to personal injury) are quite different in many respects. Argumentation at the trial level is profoundly different from that before appellate courts.

So as we begin this chapter, we call your attention to the fact that while our example is fairly representative of analysis and case building within the legal sphere, it cannot be taken as directly applicable in all instances. It is only through experience that lawyers learn the subtle differences.

We have chosen a real case as the vehicle for discussing legal analysis and case building. While we fictionalize the names, most other aspects of the case are presented just as they occurred. The chapter is divided into two parts: the trial and the appeal. Because this case had an ambiguous outcome, as we will explain, you may want to simulate the trial in class to determine your own verdict.

THE TRIAL

John Howard Avery was charged with rape under Utah Code Ann. Sec. 76–5–402 (1991), in the Third Judicial District Court in and for Salt Lake County, the Honorable Brennan White presiding. The charge resulted from a complaint by Alberta Meyer that Avery had sexual intercourse with her without her consent. The Utah code states:

1. A person commits rape when the actor has sexual intercourse with another person without the victim's consent.
2. This section applies whether or not the actor is married to the victim.
3. Rape is a felony of the first degree.

Analysis Through Critical Decision Making

You will recall from chapter 3 that analysis should rest on the steps in critical decision making. The first opportunity for this came when the prosecuting attorney learned of Ms. Meyer's claim. The question was whether or not her story was credible enough to warrant filing charges. Was it likely to convince a jury? Here is her story as reported in the appellate brief prepared by the attorney general of Utah:

> Alberta Meyer first met defendant John Howard Avery in early August, 1993. Approximately a week later on August 12, 1993, they attended a wedding reception together. After the reception, [they] went to a club known as Casablanca. Throughout the evening they were friendly and even affectionate toward one another. Displays of affection consisted of brief hugging and some kissing, but there wasn't anything pushy, presumptuous or forward. They also danced and Avery ordered drinks for the two of them.
>
> Avery also spoke with some of his friends while at Casablanca whom he said he had been involved with in drug trafficking years ago. When Alberta asked defendant about these friends, he told her that they were people who were drug traffickers—dealers.

Shortly before Casablanca closed, Tony Olivera, a friend of defendant who worked at the club, invited defendant and Ms. Meyer to attend a party at his home after the club closed. They left Casablanca at approximately 1:00 to 1:30 a.m. as it was closing.

Defendant and the victim were the first to arrive at the party, along with Gale Crockett and his companion that evening, Katherine Oberer. During the party, defendant and the victim continued to be affectionate, much as they had been while at Casablanca. Although drinks were served at the party, neither defendant nor the victim consumed any alcohol while at the Olivera residence.

As other people began to arrive, defendant spoke with Gale Crockett. The victim sat down on the couch near them and defendant then sat down next to her and kissed her. Mr. Crockett and Ms. Oberer then were "going to light a bowl up," but Mr. Olivera told them not to smoke marijuana in his house and to go outside on the balcony, and they complied. Neither Gale Crockett nor Katherine Oberer saw the victim or defendant again that night.

Ms. Meyer asked Mr. Olivera where the restroom was, and he indicated that it was down the hall. Defendant said he also had to use the restroom, and so the two proceeded down the hallway. As the victim was going into the bedroom to use the main bathroom, defendant grabbed her and pulled her into the other restroom. Defendant closed the door, pushed the victim into the corner and started to undress her. The victim stated that she told defendant to stop and resisted his advances. Defendant relented only after other people started knocking on the door to use the restroom. The victim testified that she did not tell others at the party about what happened in the restroom because she thought defendant just had too much to drink; wanted to see how far he could go.

[Avery and Meyer] then went into the master bedroom where they spoke with Mr. Olivera. The defendant then used the restroom and [Meyer] continued to speak with Mr. Olivera until he was called away. Defendant came out of the bathroom, looked around the bedroom, down the hallway, closed and locked the bedroom door, and turned the light off. Defendant then went over to the bed where the victim was sitting and pushed her backward onto the bed. Despite the victim's repeated protestations, defendant proceeded to undress her. The victim testified that defendant told her to "shut up" and that she "would enjoy it."

The victim stated that she continued to resist defendant's advances, and defendant threatened to have Gale Crockett and his other friends help him rape her if she resisted or cried out for help. She stated that defendant told her, "they'll hold you down and they'll want their turn. And the only way you'll leave here is in an ambulance." The victim was afraid to scream because she did not know anybody at the party and didn't want to call his bluff. Defendant then forced the victim to have sexual intercourse.

Knowing that Utah law allows a person to be convicted of rape solely on the testimony of the victim, the prosecuting attorney could have filed charges after hearing only Ms. Meyer's statement. However, critical decision making processes mandate a survey of the range of objectives and values implicated and a canvass of a wide range of alternative decisions. In this case, as in many others, there is always the possibility that anger, jealousy, revenge, or other motives may move someone to make false charges. It makes good sense to see how the story checks out.

In an interview with Mr. Avery, the prosecutor heard another version of the story. Avery did not deny most of what Ms. Meyer said, including the fact that they had sexual intercourse. But Avery claimed that Ms. Meyer had been very affectionate all night long, at the bar and at the party, she had encouraged him, and there were people who had observed her encouragement right up to the time they went into the bedroom. According to the Utah Supreme Court, this is what Avery claimed:

> He testified that he entered the restroom first and Meyer followed him in and initiated the sexual conduct. When people began knocking on the door, he suggested that they find a more appropriate place to continue. She agreed, and they went into the master bedroom. While in the bedroom, they spoke with Olivera. Avery asked Olivera if he and Meyer could use the room. Olivera agreed, left, and closed and locked the door behind him. Avery and Meyer then began to have sexual intercourse. Avery stated that they discussed birth control and he agreed [but failed to carry out his agreement]. His failure caused Meyer to become very angry. When defendant took her home, she was still upset.

Still following the mandate of critical decision making to search for new information and criticize alternatives, the prosecuting attorney then interviewed Jackie Sheraton, a friend of the victim's, who said that on the morning after the party (it was close to dawn when Meyer got home), Meyer told her about the rape. She said that Meyer was "distraught, confused, and kept saying something had happened and it was very wrong." Ms. Meyer then went to the hospital where a Code R (a test to verify sexual intercourse) was performed.

Within a few hours of the rape, Ms. Meyer reported it to the police. Jeff Sorensen, a police officer, said that he questioned Meyer after she reported the rape and her story told to the prosecutor was consistent with what she told him on the morning after the incident. Mr. Olivera told the prosecutor that he did not remember having a conversation with Avery about his using the bedroom, nor did he remember closing and locking the bedroom door.

Since Ms. Meyer's story seemed to be supported by other witnesses and evidence with sufficient force to warrant the selection of a proposition (in law, a charge), the prosecutor decided to go forward with the case. He had to build a prima facie case for the charge selected. Criminal codes are so complex and varied that prosecutors have a wide range of latitude in selecting the charge or proposition they intend to advance. Obviously, they try to choose the charge that seems most appropriate to the alleged facts, but they do so with an eye on what they believe they can realistically support in court.

The prosecutor might have chosen a less serious felony or a misdemeanor with lighter penalties, which a jury might find easier to accept. Forcible sexual abuse, for example (Utah Code Ann. Sec. 76–5–404 (1990)), is a second-degree felony. It is defined as follows:

> A person commits forcible sexual abuse if the victim is 14 years of age or older and, under circumstances not amounting to rape, object rape, sodomy, or attempted rape or sodomy, the actor touches the anus, buttocks, or any part of the genitals of another, or touches the breast of a female, or otherwise takes indecent liberties with another, or causes another to take indecent liberties with the actor

or another, with intent to cause substantial emotional or bodily pain to any person or with the intent to arouse or gratify the sexual desire of any person, without the consent of the other, regardless of the sex of any participant.

This would be an easier charge to prove, and its lighter penalty might be more appealing to jurors. In this case, however, the prosecutor decided to claim that John Howard Avery was guilty of rape, a proposition of fact and law (value).

Decision Makers in the Legal Sphere   Legal arguments must satisfy two quite different kinds of decision makers. In that sense, law can be called a "multi-layered and multi-faceted" sphere (Newell and Rieke 212). The first group of decision makers consists of judges, and the second consists of jurors. There is actually a third set of decision makers, appellate judges, whom we will discuss in the second half of the chapter. As we will explain, their criteria for assessing arguments are essentially the same as trial court judges.

Judges are trained in the law and are charged with the responsibility of assuring that lawyers' arguments satisfy the law in such areas as these:

1. Whether a particular court has jurisdiction over the case
2. Whether the case has been properly brought before the court
3. Whether a prima facie case has been advanced
4. Whether certain testimony and physical evidence can be properly admitted
5. Whether the trial has operated within the demands of due process of law
6. How the jury is to apply the law to their decision on the facts.

Jurors, on the other hand, have the singular task of determining the facts: what happened in the case with which the court is concerned. In this case, they will have to decide which story to believe about the alleged rape. Lawyers will need to address both sets of decision makers and satisfy their quite different demands on their arguments.

Forms of Argument in the Law   Just as there are two kinds of decision makers in the law, there are two broad sets of argument forms required to satisfy the decision makers. Judges demand arguments that use such warrants as these suggested by former Justice of the U.S. Supreme Court Benjamin N. Cardozo:

1. Past court decisions (the common law) that have set precedents (*stare decisis*)
2. Federal and state constitutions
3. Federal, state, and local statutes
4. History, custom, or tradition
5. Legislative intent
6. The pragmatic effect of decisions (51–180)

The arguments are usually structured along the lines of a logical syllogism as we describe in chapter 2. The basic format is this:

Major Premise: This is the relevant law. . . .

Support:	One of the six warrants above.
Minor Premise:	The facts of the present case are embraced within those contemplated in the law.
Support:	The jury's findings of facts in comparison with the facts of similar cases already decided.
Conclusion:	This case should be decided according to the law stated in the major premise.

When attorneys argue issues of law (value) as we have just described, they address themselves exclusively to the judge. Most often, the jury is dismissed so that they do not hear these arguments.

The judge will evaluate the arguments according to the criteria suggested by Justice Cardozo, with the strongest attention being given to previous cases that involved issues like the ones now before the court. If one side can find a case decided by the highest legal authority in America, (see argument by authority in chapter 6) the Supreme Court of the United States, where the facts are almost exactly the same as this case, and where the court set down a specific test stating the criteria by which the ruling is to be applied, the judge is likely to give it a high evaluation.

This is reasoning by *analogy* as we will explain in chapter 6. One or more cases are presented as essentially the same as the present case to the end that the present case should be decided the same way the previous cases were decided.

The argument is strengthened by the authority of the court that made the decision. Decisions by courts in other states are considered, but are not given as much authority as decisions made by courts in the state where the case is being tried, or by the Supreme Court of the United States.

Even when arguments are presented to the jury, they must continuously satisfy the requirements of the law. And the sequence of evidence (witnesses, documents, physical evidence, expert testimony) also tends to conform to the legal structure. Yet, the jury as relevant decision makers, have no experience or knowledge of the law. So, attorneys must also structure arguments for them in the form of a good story, as we describe in chapter 2, or a retrospective convincing vision as discussed in chapter 4.

This means that jurors are exposed to arguments involving *relational structuring*, how the evidence relates to claims in the legal structure we have just described, and *temporal structuring*, how events of the conflicting stories are ordered in time. This involves coming up with a scenario that puts people, motives, causes, and effects into a satisfying structure (Schum).

The jurors conceive of the trial in terms of causal relationships—who did what to cause this? They put these causal arguments into the context of a story with a beginning, middle, and end. The jurors' stories include episodes or scenes embedded within the major story line of varying levels of significance. At the time of the verdict, juries construct a common story with episodes that match the requirements of the law as given in a judge's instructions to the jury (Hastie, Penrod, and Pennington).

The story model used by juries, which, therefore, identifies the argument form to be used by attorneys, contains three stages:

1. Put the trial evidence into meaningful structure through the addition of jury members' own sense of reality.
2. Specifically identify the requirements of the law in relation to possible verdicts.
3. Go back and revise the story in number one so that it satisfies the requirements in number two (Pennington and Hastie).

The jury, therefore, evaluates arguments by testing them against their sense of how people behave and how events reasonably take place. Then they test the story against their understanding of the law. If they can find a sensible story that correlates with the expectations of the law, they have their verdict.

With this understanding of the two kinds of decision makers who must be satisfied and the argument forms they use to evaluate arguments, we can now turn to the case building stage of this trial.

Building the Case

In law, a *prima facie* case is one that presents arguments that affirm all the essential elements of the proposition. To find what those elements are, a prosecutor looks to the wording of the law and the language of appellate courts in interpreting it. In Utah in 1991, a charge of rape required affirmation of two essential issues:

1. Did sexual intercourse occur between Avery and Meyer?
2. Did sexual intercourse occur without Meyer's consent?

The prosecutor had to work within the legal demands set and enforced by the trial judge and possibly by one or more appellate courts, but not behave in such a dry, legalistic manner as to lose the support of the jury. Because society puts the burden of proof on the state, the prosecutor must present arguments to answer yes to both these essential elements while developing a convincing vision around which the jury could construct its story.

In this instance, there was a good deal of uncontroversial matter (see chapter 4). Avery did not deny that sexual intercourse had occurred. Although the prosecutor had to put evidence in support of that fact into the record to satisfy the appellate court, there would be no problem with it before the jury. So the only potential issue the prosecutor could foresee was whether Meyer had given her consent.

What counterarguments could be anticipated? When informed of the charges against him, Avery immediately found a lawyer, Morris Medford, to defend him. He paid him $9,000, told him his side of the story as we have already reported, and gave him the names of people who could give testimony to support his version. He mentioned Gayla Harrison, the bartender at Casablanca, who could testify that Meyer had been affectionate and quite willing while they were drinking and dancing together. He also identified Katherine Oberer and Omar Ortiz, who had been at the party. Avery said they would testify that they saw Avery and Meyer "engaging in kissing, fondling and other intense sexual play." Ms. Oberer would say she saw them "making out" quite passionately on the couch for 10 or 15 minutes before they went to the bedroom. Medford said he would proceed to prepare a defense.

Let's see how the prosecution's trial brief anticipating the counterarguments of the defense might have looked.

Prosecution's Trial Brief

I. Avery and Meyer had sex.

    A. Meyer testifies so.
    B. Avery agrees.
    C. Hospital test confirms.

II. Meyer did not consent.
    A. Meyer says so.
    B. Tony Olivera denies he gave permission to use the bedroom.
    C. Jackie Sheraton says Meyer was distraught, what happened was wrong.
    D. Jeff Sorensen says Meyer's story at trial is consistent with what she said the morning after the incident.

I. Defense does not deny this claim.

II. Meyer did consent.
    A. Avery says so.
    B. Avery says Olivera gave permission to use the bedroom.
    C. Gayla Harrison says Meyer was affectionate and willing.
    D. Katherine Oberer says they were passionate on the couch.
    E. Avery says she's just angry over a careless birth control method.

What convincing vision of this case could the prosecutor develop? The jury's presumptions had to be considered. How would they view the events? A woman going to the apartment of those identified as drug traffickers whom she did not know, with a man she had only recently met, could be viewed by ordinary people in a conservative state like Utah as asking for trouble. If the jury additionally understood her behavior as having been sexually promiscuous, they might well believe Avery.

How does the prosecutor begin the opening statement, in which the convincing vision of a legal case is set out, so as to portray Ms. Meyer as a victim, not a willing participant? Let's listen to what the prosecutor might have said.

Jackie Sheraton was half awake, trying to convince herself to get up, when she heard her doorbell ringing and ringing. Angry at such impatience at 6:00 a.m., she shouted through the door, "Who is it?" All she heard were incoherent sobs. Now frightened at what was going on outside, she looked through the peephole in the door. She saw her friend Berty Meyer, tears washing through mascara making her face appear ghostly, collapsing against the door.

Later, after a cup of coffee and lots of comforting talk, during which Berty had seemed distraught, confused, saying over and over again that something had happened and it was very wrong, Jackie learned that Berty had been a victim of acquaintance rape. Jackie knew about this; she had read about the fact that most rapes are committed not by strangers who leap out from behind bushes but by those who are friends, family, or dating partners. She knew that just because a woman agrees to date a man it does not follow that she is willing to have sex with him, but men don't always behave according to this rule.

Jackie urged Berty to go to the police, but Berty said, as Jackie will testify, she was afraid everyone would think she was a slut, that she would be put through embarrassing and demeaning attacks. Like so many victims of acquaintance rape, she wanted to pretend it never happened. But finally, Jackie convinced her that if women don't take the initiative to come forward and see that rapists are punished, there will just be more silent victims.

John Howard Avery does not deny that he had sexual intercourse with Berty. But he will ask you to believe that Berty willingly had sex with him, went home at dawn, and then went to the home of her friend Jackie on the point of collapse, resisting the idea of making a police report until finally accepting Jackie's arguments, and then agreeing to go to the hospital for a test and then on to the police for their interrogation just because she was angry over the way he made love. He will ask you to believe Berty gave her consent and then decided to charge rape because he did not keep his word on a method of birth control.

Because the charge of rape turns almost completely on the word of the victim, it is important that the prosecutor make that word as credible as possible. Giving the jury the first impression, which is the most powerful and lasting (Rieke and Stutman 109–13), of Berty in tears, collapsing on her friend's doorstep, will shape the way they hear all the other testimony. As long as they hold the vision of her as victim, they will probably discount testimony of her affectionate behavior earlier in the evening. After all, kissing and hugging do not amount to an invitation to have sex.

At the trial, the prosecutor laid out the case; defense attorney Morris Medford cross-examined Meyer to challenge her story, called Avery to the stand to give his version, and called Gayla Harrison, who told the jury how affectionate the two had been at the bar.

Medford had not interviewed Harrison before the day of the trial, nor had he made contact with any of the other witnesses Avery had suggested. Avery was convicted of rape and was sentenced to an indeterminate term of five years to life in the state penitentiary.

THE APPEAL

Avery dismissed Mr. Medford as his attorney, hired another one, and appealed his conviction on the grounds that he had received ineffective assistance of counsel.

We must now consider a different form of analysis and case building as it occurs before appellate courts. Now, of course, the presumption and burden of proof have shifted. Until his conviction, Avery was presumed innocent, and the burden of proof rested on the state. It was the state that had the obligation to advance and defend a prima facie case. With conviction, presumption shifts: Avery is held guilty of rape unless and until he advances a prima facie case to show that his conviction should be reversed or that he should receive a new trial. We will outline his brief first, then give the state's response.

Appellate Brief

At the appellate level, analysis turns to questions of law found in six sources of law mentioned on page 95. Particular attention is given to constitutions, statutes, and, most predominantly, the published decisions of appellate courts. This process resembles the brief discussed in chapter 4. In an appellate brief, lawyers are usually required to establish their case in the following order.

Statement of Jurisdiction   The appellate court must be satisfied that it has jurisdiction over the case. A reference to the Utah Code Ann. Sec. 78–2–2(3) (h)(i)(Cum. Supp. 1989) satisfied this requirement.

Nature of Proceedings   The court wants to know the history of the case. They are told that this is an appeal from a conviction and final judgment entered against the appellant in the Third Judicial District Court, where the appellant was convicted by a jury of rape.

Statement of the Issue Presented on Appeal   The brief must identify the point of law on which the appellant asks appellate consideration. Specifically, it argues that the law guarantees a defendant effective assistance by trial counsel, and Avery did not receive that from lawyer Morris Medford.

Applicable Constitutional Provisions, Statutes, and Rules   To call attention to the applicable constitutional provisions, statutes, and rules, the brief cites the Sixth and Fourteenth Amendments to the U.S. Constitution and Article 1, Section 12 of the Utah Constitution, all of which refer to one's right to a speedy public trial by an impartial jury under conditions of due process of law and representation by counsel.

Statement of the Case   The appellant states that his lawyer's failure to interview all the potential witnesses, his failure to interview Avery and Ms. Harrison, whom he called as witnesses, until the day of the trial, and his failure to call other witnesses to testify constitute failure to render effective assistance by trial counsel, guaranteed by the constitutional provisions cited. In essence, Avery accused his lawyer of failing to conduct critical decision making procedures and thus a failure to build and present an effective case.

Statement of the Facts   The brief reviews the story of the trial as we did on pages 97–99.

Summary of the Argument   The brief reviews the claims of ineffective counsel and concludes that the appellate court should reverse the trial court and order a new trial, because Avery's conviction was unfair. He might not have been convicted had he been effectively represented.

Now comes the main section of an appellate brief.

Argument   What is required to make a prima facie case on appeal? The lawyers turn to precedent—judicial decisions on previous cases with similar fact situations. In the United States, appellate courts generally follow a rule of *stare decisis,* which commands the court to let previous decisions stand and not upset that which is settled. So if the advocate can convince the court that this case is like prior cases already decided, that will constitute powerful support.

In our earlier discussion of arguments to judges, we said that attorneys try to find a case (or cases) meeting these demands:

1. Decided by the U.S. Supreme Court, the most powerful legal authority available
2. Dealing with a fact situation very close to the present case (analogy)
3. Where there is a clear statement of the rule (criteria for decision) to be followed.

Appellate courts evaluate arguments according to these criteria along with judging the extent to which the rule makes sense in this case. The greater the legal authority, the more analogous the previous case(s), the clearer the rule of law or test, and the more clearly the rule seems to make good law, the stronger the argument will be in the eyes of most appellate judges.

The appellate justices' job of argument evaluation is made difficult in proportion to the strength of the other side's arguments. When the arguments are similarly strong, which is not uncommon, the decision may turn primarily on the question of which decision makes the best law—produces the most just decision—in this instance. See if you think the following argument meets those criteria.

In a case decided by the United States Supreme Court, Strickland v. Washington, the essential elements (the criteria for decision or the test) of a case on ineffective assistance of counsel are set forth. The court identifies these issues:

1. Whether counsel's performance was defective. This requires a showing that counsel made errors so serious that counsel was not functioning as the "counsel" guaranteed the defendant by the Sixth Amendment to the U.S. Constitution.
2. Whether the deficient performance prejudiced the defense. This requires showing that counsel's errors were so serious as to deprive the defendant of a fair trial, a trial whose result is reliable.

The Utah Supreme Court decided, in State v. Verde, that Utah courts are to decide ineffective assistance of counsel claims by applying Strickland's two issues. Then the brief goes on to provide a discussion of legal interpretations of these and other cases so as to show their relevance to this case.

On the question of presumption, the brief reminds the court that at trial, presumption favored Avery. It would not have been necessary to prove that Meyer gave her consent, only that there is reasonable doubt that she did not.

So the argument comes down to this: Did Medford's failure to interview witnesses prior to trial, and his failure to call more witnesses to testify, constitute ineffective counsel? Might the jury have entertained a reasonable doubt about Meyer's story if they had heard other witnesses or more effective testimony?

Avery's arguments, therefore, make these responses to the essential elements.

I. Counsel's performance was defective. Medford failed to interview his witnesses before the day of the trial, and he failed to call witnesses who could have strengthened his case.
   A. He chose to call Gayla Harrison to testify to the fact that Meyer had been affectionate with Avery, and she did that with regard to the time they were at Casablanca. But it was only shortly before the trial that Medford learned that Harrison did not attend the party and could say nothing about their behavior there. So Medford learned that he lacked any evidence about their behavior at the party too late to call other witnesses. Had he interviewed Harrison earlier, he would have had time to call other witnesses.
   B. Avery gave Medford the names of other witnesses, particularly Oberer, who could have testified that Meyer was affectionate and "made out on the couch" with Avery for 10 or 15 minutes before they went into the bedroom. Medford failed to call them.
II. Deficient performance did prejudice the defense.
   A. If Medford had interviewed the witnesses Avery supplied, he probably would have called them.
   B. If the other witnesses had testified, they would have shed reasonable doubt on Meyer's claim of rape. Her 10 or 15 minute "making out" session on the couch could well have created a reasonable doubt in the minds of the jurors.

The Attorney General's Response

The Attorney General of Utah, arguing as appellee, denied the claim of ineffective assistance by counsel. The state claimed that Avery did not give the names of potential witnesses to Medford in enough time for him to check them out, that Avery was not communicative with Medford, and that Medford's decision not to call former drug traffickers as witnesses was within the range of what reasonable attorneys would have concluded. Furthermore, the state argued that Avery's story was so patently false that no amount of testimony about Meyer's behavior would have put the jury into a state of doubt. Finally, there were inconsistencies in Oberer's statement about "making out" that did not even fit with Avery's story.

The Appellate Decision

The Utah Supreme Court agreed with Avery. They said this:

> If counsel does not adequately investigate the underlying facts of a case, including the availability of prospective defense witnesses, counsel's performance cannot

fall within the "wide range of reasonable professional assistance." This is because a decision not to investigate cannot be considered a tactical decision. It is only after an adequate inquiry has been made that counsel can make a reasonable decision to call or not to call particular witnesses for tactical reasons. Therefore, because defendant's trial counsel did not make a reasonable investigation into the possibility of procuring prospective defense witnesses, the first part of the Strickland test has been met.

In the instant case, the second part of the Strickland test has also been met. If called as witnesses, several of the people would have testified to the amount of consensual physical contact that occurred between Meyer and Avery at Casablanca. The most important witness would have been Katherine Oberer, who had the opportunity to observe the couple both at the club and at the party, where, according to Meyer, the rape occurred. This testimony is important for the reason that it reflects upon the credibility of Meyer, because Oberer's testimony, although not completely consistent with Avery's testimony, contradicts several aspects of Meyer's testimony. This is important in the instant case because Meyer's testimony is the only direct evidence of Avery's guilt.

In reviewing this testimony, it is important to note that because it affects the credibility of the only witness who gave direct evidence of defendant's guilt, the testimony affects the "entire evidentiary picture." It should also be noted that although it is undisputed that a person can be convicted of rape solely on the testimony of the victim, the State's case rested upon the testimony of one person. There is no independent physical evidence that supports or contradicts Meyer's testimony. The conviction, therefore, is not strongly supported by the record. There is reasonable probability that if these witnesses had been called at trial, the outcome of the trial would have been different. Since both parts of the Strickland test have been met, we hold that Avery was denied his constitutional right to effective assistance of counsel.

Reversed and remanded for a new trial.

If you review the criteria for a judicial argument, and then read the opinion in the light of those criteria, you will see that their argument followed the criteria closely. Arguments presented by attorneys to judges and the arguments judges use in reporting their decision or opinion conform to the same set of criteria.

In this case, because the Strickland rule was well established, the appellate court finally made its decision on the extent to which the facts of this case met the test. In that sense, it was the good story or vision the appellate counsel could communicate of *how the trial might have been conducted by an effective counsel* that was crucial in deciding the case.

The Impact of the Trial

A great deal of time and money was spent on this criminal trial, only to result in an appellate court's decision that it had to be done all over again. The court would not allow a defense lawyer to fail to perform effective analysis and case building that resulted, or may have resulted, in his client being convicted and sentenced to five years to life in the penitentiary. This case serves as an excellent illustration of the importance of analysis and case building in law.

In particular, the case illustrates how following the steps of critical decision making will guide you to effective argumentation. Notice that the Utah

Supreme Court finds that a decision not to engage in these steps, as Avery's first lawyer did, can never be a strategic choice. In argumentation, strategic choices of how to build and present a case must rest on the fullest possible knowledge of the relevant claims, facts, values, issues, and potential propositions.

Counterarguments or defense cases cannot rest on inadequate analysis. It may well have been that the prosecutor shifted presumption at the very beginning of the trial by communicating a convincing vision of the case that Meyer was a victim of rape, not a willing sex partner. So the defense lawyer had to have available the strongest possible support for a counterargument.

By the time the defense put its witnesses on the stand, the jury may well have developed a presumption in favor of conviction. As we said earlier, when skill at argumentation and communication are equal, the side that has done the best analysis and case building based on the best research will probably prevail.

The prosecutor was faced once again with the prospect of a rape trial against Mr. Avery. Ms. Meyer was willing to go through it once more. But Avery had already spent a total of about 22 months in prison, and the prosecutor did not relish the idea of a new trial. A plea bargain was struck: Avery entered a guilty plea to forcible sexual abuse, and the court credited him with the time already served and set him free on parole. If there had been a new trial, though, you can bet Avery's lawyer would have taken the case quite seriously.

CONCLUSION

We have examined the law as a general sphere of argument in relation to a specific trial from start to finish. The importance of thorough analysis based on the steps in critical decision making is emphasized at the trial level and in the appellate court opinion.

The two types of decision makers in the law, judges and jurors, have been discussed in terms of the argumentation that must be adapted to their special criteria. Judges demand a relational structure in which claims, evidence, and law are logically displayed. Jurors respond best to a good story that provides a temporal structure. That helps them form an image of the characters, motives, events, and causes that will form the fact situation of the case.

We have illustrated the format for a trial brief and an appellate brief, indicating how they are quite different. Finally, we have noticed how appellate courts structure their opinions along the same argumentative structure that is used by attorneys in arguing the case.

PROJECTS

5.1   Go to your local courthouse—municipal, county, state, or federal—and spend at least two hours watching a trial. Courts are completely open to the public; you do not need permission. Write a report on the argumentation you observed.

5.2 Interview a lawyer to learn about the particular characteristics of legal argumentation. Write a report on the interview.

5.3 Ask a lawyer to allow you to copy the briefs from a recent appeal. You may need to call different firms to find one. Then analyze the briefs and write a report commenting on the argumentative forms.

5.4 Read the written opinion of an appellate court. You can find them in the library in *United States Reports* and other similar publications the reference librarian can point out. Write an analysis of the argumentation of the judges.

5.5 Select a book that documents a particular legal case, real or fictional, for example: Rodney A. Smolla, *Jerry Falwell v. Larry Flint*. New York: St. Martin's, 1988; or Scott Turow, *Presumed Innocent*. New York: Warner, 1987. Write a paper describing the process through which legal arguments are developed and presented by lawyers and tested by a jury.

REFERENCES

Cardozo, Benjamin N. *The Nature of the Judicial Process*. New Haven: Yale UP, 1921.

Hastie, Reid, Steven Penrod, and Nancy Pennington. *Inside the Jury*. Cambridge: Harvard UP, 1983.

Newell, Sara E., and Richard D. Rieke. "A Practical Reasoning Approach to Legal Doctrine." *Journal of the American Forensic Association* 22, (1986): 212–22.

Pennington, Nancy, and Reid Hastie. "Evidence Evaluation in Complex Decision Making." *Journal of Personality and Social Psychology* 51 (1986): 242–56.

Rieke, Richard D., and Randall K. Stutman. *Communication in Legal Advocacy*. Columbia: U of South Carolina P, 1990.

Schum, David A. "Argument Structuring and Evidence Evaluation." *Inside the Juror*. Ed. Reid Hastie. Cambridge: Cambridge UP, 1993: 175–91.

State v. Verde, 770 P.2nd 116 (Utah 1989).

Strickland v. Washington, 466 US 668, 104 S. CT. 1052 (1984).

6

The Nature of Arguments

Key Terms

grounds
warrant
backing
qualifier
rebuttal
reservation

argument by generalization
argument by cause
argument by sign
argument by analogy
argument by authority
guidelines for analysis

You will find argumentation used in all spheres of life. Argumentation can be seen in the philosopher's careful step-by-step pursuit of a single claim with all of its ramifications. It can be found in the give-and-take debate of a corporate boardroom or the state legislature. It is found in your everyday conversations with others. Given such a wide variety of situations, it is impossible to explain a single system for understanding argumentation. It is different from sphere to sphere but there are also similarities that we will begin to examine in this chapter.

In western culture everyone is expected to give reasons to justify their claims. If a judge simply said to a defendant, "I think you are as guilty as sin and I intend to lock you up and throw away the key," the judge would be making an argument about the defendant's moral state and what should be done about it, but it would be a legally unacceptable argument. So, the decision must be based on evidence and reason within certain carefully defined limits. While the standards of reasonableness will differ from sphere to sphere, all will have standards by which decision makers will expect arguers to act. Even conversational argumentation has its standards of reasonableness (Jackson and Jacobs).

A second similarity in the nature of reason giving is in the types that arguments may take. Certain spheres will emphasize one type of argument over another. In the Judeo-Christian tradition, the emphasis is on reasoning by analogy from sacred text as authority to contemporary understandings and actions. Scientists argue for general principles from observing natural phenomena. Lawyers argue from legal statutes, customs, and precedents, but taken together, all use a limited number of argument types.

A third similarity among these argument spheres is that the argument types can all be examined using a single model. This model provides you with an analytical tool for judging the reasonableness of an argument. In chapter 3

we discussed how you might analyze a controversy to find the important issues. In chapter 4 we explained how these issues can be built into an organized system of arguments: a case. In this chapter we will show you how each
argument can be examined through the Toulmin model of argument, the major types of arguments, and some principles for developing your own arguments and examining the arguments of others.

THE MODEL OF AN ARGUMENT

In this chapter we will look intensively at individual arguments using a modification of a model developed by Stephen Toulmin (1958 iii) to help you understand the parts of an argument and their interrelationships. The model we are
using is useful to analyze an argument. But do not be confused by it. It does
not represent the order in which you should organize your argument. Depending on the decision makers, you may choose to leave some parts out or
organize differently than we describe it here. The model explains all the parts
you might use and provides a basis for analyzing an argument.

Here is a summary of an argument that has been made about the influence of dams on America's rivers:

By 1980 nearly all of the good sites for dams on America's rivers had been
developed. But "public resistance to the enormous costs and pork-barrel smell
of many dams, and a developing public understanding of the profound environmental degradation that building dams can cause" are more important in
the rising opposition to building dams on the nation's rivers. Four dams have
converted 140 miles of the lower Snake River "from healthy river ecosystems
to impoverished reservoirs." Of the 600 miles of the Columbia between the
dam nearest the ocean and the Canadian border, only forty-seven miles of
river have remained in their natural state. For more than 250 miles below
Glen Canyon Dam the Colorado River is "essentially dead."

These dams have seriously damaged the Salmon migrations and require
expensive barging of small salmon on their way to the ocean. The number of
wild salmon migrating up the Snake has fallen from up to 200,000 each year to
under 200. Dams alter waterflows, causing temperature changes that seriously
impact all the species of flora and fauna in the river. Using dams to regulate
America's rivers may have benefits of hydroelectric power, river transportation, irrigation, and flood plain management, but the ecosystem has been
damaged almost beyond repair (Devine).

Let's look at this argument and see what its parts are and how they are put
together.

Claim

In the second sentence, and most clearly in the last sentence, you find the
claim. It is a value claim:

(Claim)   Dams have damaged the ecosystem almost beyond repair.

Grounds

But, a claim alone is only an assertion. To make a claim believable, one must have a reason. The arguer must provide *grounds, a statement made about persons, conditions, events, or things that says support is available to provide a reason for a claim*. In this argument the grounds for supporting the claim are a series of subclaims of fact:

(Grounds) ————————————————▶ *(Claim)*

The ecosystem of rivers with dams on them has been damaged by water temperatures and flow changes that have affected all the flora and fauna.

[Therefore] Dams have damaged the ecosystem almost beyond repair.

Warrant

To make this a good argument, the grounds must have a basis for justifying the claim. There must be a *warrant, a general statement that justifies using the grounds as a basis for the claim*. It is the warrant that makes the movement from grounds to claim reasonable. In many, perhaps most arguments, the warrant is not stated, it is implied. In this case it is stated several times.

(Grounds) ————————————————▶ *(Claim)*

The ecosystem of rivers with dams on them has been damaged by water temperatures and flow changes that have affected all the flora and fauna.

[Therefore] Dams have damaged the ecosystem almost beyond repair.

(Warrant)
[Since] Dams cause these changes.

Backing

For some people claims, grounds, and warrant is all an argument would need. They would accept the reasoning and find the claim acceptable. Others, however, particularly on controversial questions, would want more. They would require backing for either the grounds or the warrant. *Backing is any support (specific instances, statistics, testimony, values, or credibility) that provides more specific data for the grounds or warrant*. In this case examples provide specific backing for the grounds and the warrant is backed (although unstated) by the value of nature.

(Grounds) ————————————▶ *(Claim)*

The ecosystem of rivers with dams on them has been damaged by water temperatures and flow changes that have affected all the flora and fauna.

[Therefore] Dams have damaged the ecosystem almost beyond repair.

(Backing)
The Salmon River
The Columbia River
The Colorado River

(Warrant)
[Since] Dams cause these changes.

(Backing)
Value of nature

Qualifier

To be reasonable, an argument must have a claim and grounds for that claim, and the link between the two must be justified by a warrant. Sometimes grounds or warrant must have backing, depending on the level of questioning by decision makers. Sometimes, you have to look very carefully at the claim to see how much is being claimed. Some claims will have a *qualifier, a statement that indicates the force of the argument.* As we noted in greater detail in chapter 1, words such as *certainly, possibly, probably, for the most part, usually,* or *always,* show how forceful a claim is. The qualifier in this case, "almost," is limited but still indicates a forceful claim.

(Grounds) ————————————▶ *(Claim)*

The ecosystem of rivers with dams on them has been damaged by water temperatures and flow changes that have affected all the flora and fauna.

[Therefore] Dams have damaged the ecosystem almost beyond repair.

(Backing)
The Salmon River
The Columbia River
The Colorado River

(Qualifier)
Almost

(Warrant)
[Since] Dams cause these changes

(Backing)
Value of nature

Rebuttal and Reservation

The actual strength of this argument has to be judged as well by possible *rebuttal, the basis on which the claim will be questioned by decision makers,* thus requiring of the arguer more or less support, or more or less qualification. In this case the main rebuttal is identified as the advantages to dams. You recognize that the clash over this claim will probably not be over its correctness but over its relative importance.

Sometimes arguers will have a *reservation, a statement of the conditions under which the claim would not apply.* There is no reservation here but there might have been if, for instance, the arguer had said "Dams have damaged the ecosystem almost beyond repair *in the western states.*" Since there is no reservation the arguer has the burden of proving this is a national problem.

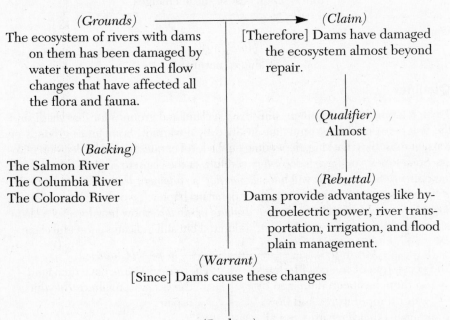

(Grounds) ⟶ *(Claim)*

The ecosystem of rivers with dams on them has been damaged by water temperatures and flow changes that have affected all the flora and fauna.

[Therefore] Dams have damaged the ecosystem almost beyond repair.

(Qualifier)
Almost

(Backing)
The Salmon River
The Columbia River
The Colorado River

(Rebuttal)
Dams provide advantages like hydroelectric power, river transportation, irrigation, and flood plain management.

(Warrant)
[Since] Dams cause these changes

(Backing)
Value of nature

Not all arguments are the same. Some will be found reasonable without backing. Some parts will not be stated, some will be carefully developed. Some claims will be subject to significant rebuttal, others to little. Some warrants will be specific; others will be vague. You will find some arguments much easier and others more difficult to diagram than this one on dams on America's rivers. However, the Toulmin model should help you evaluate the argument when someone asks, "Is this argument reasonable?" It will be the basis for examining the problems with arguments in chapter 13, (Refutation

---

THE PARTS OF AN ARGUMENT

Claim: A single statement advanced for the adherence of others

Grounds: A statement made about persons, conditions, events, or things that says support is available to provide a reason for a claim

Warrant: A general statement that justifies using the grounds as a basis for the claim

Backing: Any support (specific instance, statistics, testimony, values, or credibility) that provides more specific data for the grounds or warrant

Qualifier: A statement that indicates the force of the argument (words such as *certainly, possibly, probably, usually,* or *somewhat*)

Rebuttal: The basis on which the claim will be questioned by a decision maker

Reservation: A qualification of the original claim that answers a rebuttal

---

by Fallacy Claim). It will also be useful to you in understanding the different types of arguments.

TYPES OF ARGUMENTS

In chapter 2 we identified the commonplaces of arguments: those principles that are used to generate starting points of argumentation. Among the commonplaces were certain principles of reasoning: generalization, cause, sign, analogy, and authority. These constitute the basis for most arguments. The purpose of this chapter is to look at those principles more carefully to see how they are applied in all but the most specialized situations and how they differ in the nature of their grounds, claims, and warrants.

There is no natural superiority of one type of argument over another. However, their relative usefulness will vary from sphere to sphere. Authority is a crucial form of argument in religion, but is almost useless in science. Analogy, a strong force in political argumentation, is frequently considered suspect by social scientists. The economist may consider a sign argument useful but not nearly so useful as does the weather forecaster. Nonetheless, each type of argument has its use and the chances are that not a week goes by that you do not use them all.

Argument by Generalization

Generalization, or rhetorical induction, is an argument in which a series of like instances are assembled to show the existence of a general principle. A good example is a public opinion poll. For instance, a 1995 *Time/CNN* poll claimed that 44 percent of adult Americans were very concerned and 25 percent fairly concerned about the amount of violence depicted in movies, TV, and popular music. But they didn't ask all adult Americans; they asked a sample of 600 and reasoned that they could generalize about all Americans from that group ("Unpopular Culture").

(Grounds) ───────────────────────▶ *(Claim)*
69% of the sample of adult Ameri-   [Therefore] 69% of all adult Ameri-
    cans asked say they are con-   cans are concerned about vio-
    cerned about violence depicted   lence depicted in the media.
    in the media.

(Warrant)
[Since] The sample
represents the nation

Generalizations also can be made from individual incidents. Deborah Cramer argued that the Georges Bank, "One of the world's most prolific fishing grounds, . . ." is "nearly empty of fish." She supported this generalization with these examples:

1. Instead of catching "217 million pounds of cod, haddock, and yellowtail each year," the 1993 catch was only 66 million pounds and less in 1994 and 1995.
2. Instead of catching 20,000 pounds of halibut a day, catches are now "so rare that regulators don't even keep statistics on them."
3. In 1842 the redfish caught yearly out of the Gulf of Maine peaked at 130 million pounds. Today the fishery is wiped out (22–24).

(Grounds) ───────────────────────▶ *(Claim)*
Depletion on the Georges Bank   [Therefore] The Georges Bank,
                                           "one of the world's most pro-
                                           lific fishing grounds, . . . is
(Backing)   nearly empty of fish."
Cod, Haddock, yellowtail, halibut,
    and redfish.

(Warrant)
[Since] The depleted fish constitute
the Georges Bank fishery

You will note that this argument contains a qualifier, "nearly empty of fish." But "nearly empty" is still a very forceful claim. Therefore, it requires strong grounds to cause decision makers to accept it.

Argument by Cause

In Western culture we tend to believe that people, things, and ideas cause events to take place. If there is inflation in the economy, then the President or Congress are believed to have caused it. If you don't feel well, you expect a physician to tell you the cause. An argument by cause can reason from cause to effect or from effect to cause.

In an argument from *cause to effect* the grounds function as a cause for the claim. For instance, James Q. Wilson, UCLA Professor of Management, in his 1995 speech "What To Do About Crime" builds his whole speech on the examination of "root causes." He argues against the warrant that poverty is the root cause of crime. That very common argument looks like this.

(Grounds) ────────────────▶ *(Claim)*

Poverty has increased in America today. | [Therefore] crime has increased in America.

(Warrant)
[Since] Poverty is the cause
for crime.

Wilson argues:

> There is only a very weak relationship between crime and unemployment or the business cycle. There are many good reasons for trying to do something about poverty and providing jobs, but ending crime is the worst possible reason. Indeed, much of the increase in crime around the world has occurred at a time of enormous gains in national prosperity and national well being, so much so that in this century, unlike the previous century, the crime rate has become unhinged from the business cycle (375).

He argues that increased poverty was the cause of increased crime in the 19th century but not the cause in the twentieth. Wilson argues that the "root causes of crime . . . are family and neighborhoods. . . . There are now data that show any fair-minded observer rather conclusively that after controlling for income, and for every racial and ethnic group, children raised in single-parent families headed by never-married young women, are materially worse off in terms of school achievements, delinquency, emotional problems" (375). So, for Wilson the argument is as follows:

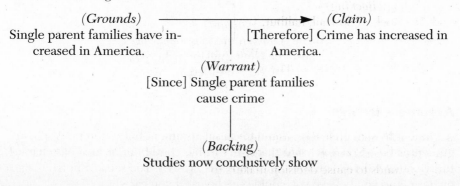

(Grounds) ────────────────▶ *(Claim)*

Single parent families have increased in America. | [Therefore] Crime has increased in America.

(Warrant)
[Since] Single parent families
cause crime

(Backing)
Studies now conclusively show

In *effect to cause* reasoning the grounds function as the effect of the claim. When people find that something is a problem they seek to find a cause for it. This is substantially the basis of medical diagnoses. You have a headache and you wonder about cause: "Was it something I ate?" "Stress?" "Lack of sleep?" "A problem with my eyes?"

(Grounds) ————————————→ *(Claim)*
I have a headache.   [Therefore] I have been under too
                               much stress.

(Warrant)
[Since] Stress causes
headaches

Or in the case of James Q. Wilson's argument about crime:

(Grounds) ————————————→ *(Claim)*
To control the increasing crime rate   [Therefore] We must find a way to
                                        provide a traditional family at-
                                        mosphere to "single-parent
                                        families headed by never-
                                        married young women."

(Warrant)
[Since] Single-parent families
cause crime

Remember the earlier argument by generalization about the depletion of the Georges Bank fishing grounds? Later in that same article, Deborah Cramer proposes a solution to the problem by arguing from effect to cause.

She argues that the only way to save the New England fisheries is with quotas that are enforced (26).

(Grounds) ————————————→ *(Claim)*
To preserve New England fisheries   [Therefore] Quotas must be set and
[and return them to adequate   enforced on the fishery.
productivity]

(Warrant)
[Since] Only enforced quotas will
cause the New England fishery
to be preserved.

Argument by Sign

Argument by sign is closely related to causal argument but different. A sign argument is based on a warrant that every thing, condition, or idea has characteristics that will tell you whether or not it is present. You see a "For Sale" sign on a car, and you believe you could buy the car if you cared to.

As we mentioned earlier, sign argument is probably best known by its legal name, argument from circumstantial evidence. Remember the O. J. Simpson trial? There were no eye witness reports of his presence at the murder scene. There was no weapon entered into evidence. The prosecution's case against him in the murders of Nicole Brown, his ex-wife, and Ronald Goldman, a friend of Nicole Brown, was based on finding his blood and hair at the scene and their blood at his home and in his car, of finding bloody footprints and a glove at the scene, as well as a bloody glove and socks at his home that appeared to match some he had owned. All of these grounds were used as signs to argue that he committed the murders.

(Grounds) ⎯⎯⎯⎯⎯⎯⎯⎯▶ (Claim)

O. J. Simpson's blood, hair, and gloves were at the murder scene.

Victims' blood was at his home and in his car.

[Therefore] O.J. Simpson murdered Nicole Brown and Ronald Goldman.

(Backing)

Numerous expert witnesses

(Warrant)

[Since] These signs connect O. J. Simpson to the murders.

Weather forecasts are sign arguments. A ridge of high pressure is a sign that there will be no rain or snow, while low pressure or unstable upper level disturbances are signs that rain or snow may develop. For many years the American bald eagle was rarely seen. Consequently, the bird was placed on the Endangered Species List. In recent years they have been seen in greater numbers in more places: a sign they are no longer endangered.

It is important to differentiate causal and sign argument. The shortage of bald eagles was a sign that they were endangered, but, it was not the cause. The cause most argued was the pesticide DDT that got into the eagle's systems and made them unable to reproduce. The causal link was strengthened when eagles increased after the use of DDT was outlawed. A sign is not necessarily a cause, and vice versa.

Argument by Analogy

In arguing by analogy you compare two situations that you believe have the same essential characteristics and reason that a specific characteristic found in one situation also exists in the analogous situation.

It has been traditional to differentiate between literal and figurative analogies. The literal analogy is presumed to be based on factual comparisons of situations and the figurative analogy is based on more fanciful relations. No two situations can be *literally* alike. However, some comparisons are more material than others. The most important factor for you as an arguer, how-

ever, is not the materiality of the cases but how the decision makers will see
the quality of the relationship argued.

Robert Reich, President Clinton's Secretary of Labor argues that the
United States has a big income gap. "The top 5 percent of Americans earn
more than 48 percent of our total national income. The bottom 20 percent of
Americans earn 5.7 percent." " . . . Shaquille O'Neal and I average [about] six
feet tall, but that doesn't tell you much about who has the height and how
much of it." Shaq is seven feet one inch tall while Reich is only four feet ten
inches (Greer 5).

(Grounds)	*(Claim)*
The top 5 percent of Americans earn 48 percent of the national income while the bottom 20 percent earn 5.7 percent. O'Neal and Reich average about six feet tall but O'Neal is seven feet one inch and Reich is four feet ten inches.	[Therefore] Average income figures do not reflect the reality of income distribution in America.

(Warrant)
[Since] The statistical average
of the top 5% and the bottom 20 percent
of wages earned is analogous to
averaging O'Neal and Reich.

While the comparison of the economy with the height of the two men
seems like a figurative (even fanciful) analogy, the comparison of the statistics
might not be. Again, the question is, is it believable to decision makers?

Anthony M. Platt argues against proposals to end Affirmative Action laws.
Such proposals are based in part on the claim that "the worst excesses of racial
discrimination have been eliminated." Platt argued that is not true with a series of arguments by analogy:

1. "Some 750,000 Black Americans, mostly men, are incarcerated every day
   at a rate of imprisonment that is higher than for Black South Africans."
2. "Urban black communities suffer a public-health crisis that is comparable
   to many third world countries."
3. "Millions of Americans live in segregated, prison-like, public-housing
   projects and attend public schools which, in many cities, are as segregated
   and as third-rate as they were in the 1950s."

(Grounds)	*(Claim)*
Imprisonment same as Black South Africa Public health comparable to third world Housing and schools like the 1950s	[Therefore] current status of African Americans is "one of misery."

(Warrant)
[Since] Black South Africa, third world
countries, and the United States of the
1950s are analogous to today.

Argument from Authority

In Chapter 10 we will discuss how your credibility can support the adherence decision makers give to your argument. Even persons of high credibility, however, frequently use the credibility of others to argue a claim. In argument from authority you argue that a claim is justified because it is held by a credible person; ordinarily someone other than yourself. The most common way of presenting such an argument is to cite an authority.

There has long been an argument in this country over whether or not the wide availability of guns is a stimulus to violence. At the time of the bombing of the Alfred P. Murrah Federal Building in Oklahoma City in 1995, Michael Kramer argued that guns are a stimulant to violence. He quoted an emeritus professor of psychology at the University of Wisconsin, Leonard Berkowitz, in making his argument by authority. "The finger pulls the trigger, but the trigger may also pull the finger. It's not just that having a gun is a convenient way of settling an argument. The weapon itself is a stimulant to violence."

(Grounds) ————————————▶ *(Claim)*
U of Wisconsin psychology profes-   [Therefore] A gun is a stimulant to
   sor Leonard Berkowitz says   violence.
   that possessing a gun is a "stimulant to violence."

(Warrant)
[Since] Professor Berkowitz is an
authority on the subject.

(Backing)
Berkowitz has studied the role of
weapons in human behavior for
forty years.

The warrant of authority is crucial to the success of this argument. The decision makers must believe that Berkowitz is an authority, that is why Kramer mentions his years of experience. Such authority might also be argued based on an organization rather than an individual. The findings of government and independent agencies like the Census Bureau or the Brookings Institute may also be used in argument by authority.

There is another kind of argument from authority that is considered more questionable. It is called *bandwagon* or *ad populum*. It says that a claim is a good one because people believe it. Although it is considered a fallacy by many, its acceptability depends on the sphere in which it is used. In science, for instance, an argument that most people believe there is global warming so it must be true, is unacceptable. However, in a democratic society it is a powerful kind of political argument. It rests on the authority of majority opinion, a strong political value. While the National Rifle Association and many politicians argued in 1995 for a repeal of the law to ban the sale of certain assault weapons, a *Time/CNN* poll indicated that 69 percent of gun owners support the ban on assault weapons ("What Gun Owners Think"). This is a powerful political argument because it argues that a majority of those who might be expected to oppose the ban actually support it.

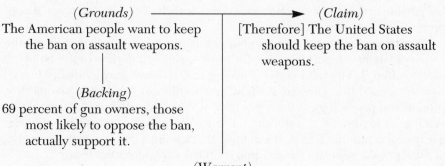

(Grounds)
The American people want to keep the ban on assault weapons.

(Claim)
[Therefore] The United States should keep the ban on assault weapons.

(Backing)
69 percent of gun owners, those most likely to oppose the ban, actually support it.

(Warrant)
[Since] The views of the American people should be law

THE ANALYSIS OF ARGUMENTS

You can see from the examples we have discussed in explaining the types of arguments, that people do not organize their arguments exactly according to our model or any other model. That is because arguments are aimed at decision makers who know things about the subject, share values and credibility assumptions that the arguer need not mention, and respond to language structures that change the order of the model in actual use.

Consequently, the Toulmin model is a useful analytical tool to check your own arguments and the arguments of others for the kinds of problems discussed in chapter 13. In this section we will explain some of the characteristics of arguments that make the application of the model difficult, and then some guidelines for using the model to help you analyze an argument.

Characteristics of Arguments

Arguments are difficult to analyze, but if you recognize why that is the case it will help you to use the model more effectively. They are difficult because they usually have parts missing, the order of the parts may vary, and they may overlap with one another.

Parts Missing Most arguments have parts left out. If the arguer believes the decision makers accept the grounds, then he or she will sometimes provide no backing as is the case of the argument by analogy about the state of African Americans on page 116. Warrants are frequently omitted because they are clearly implied by the other statements the arguer makes. An example of this is the argument about violence in movies, TV, and popular music on page 112.

It is not the lack of a stated warrant that poses a problem for decision makers. The warrant is clearly implied. The real concern is on the level of adherence the decision makers give to the implied warrant.

In the argument by James Q. Wilson on page 113, he mentions what data show but he gives no specifics on those data to establish that single-parent families are the cause of crime. Do the decision makers believe that these data exist? Do they trust that he knows the data? The unstated warrant assumes that they do.

Sometimes even claims are not stated. This is particularly true of argumentation that follows a strategy of telling stories. You could tell stories about people who defended themselves from assault by having a weapon in their possession without ever stating the claim that people should carry a weapon for self protection. The claim is not stated but the decision maker knows that is the claim because the overall orientation of the argument clearly implies it.

Order in Arguments   Arguments do not necessarily follow the order: grounds, warrant, claim. Indeed, they most frequently, and clearly, begin with the claim.

James Q. Wilson argues against poverty as a root cause for crime on page 113 by stating his claim first: "There is only a weak relationship between crime and unemployment or the business cycle." That is also true of Deborah Cramer's argument from effect to cause on page 114: "To preserve New England fisheries, it will be essential to set quotas. . . ."

On the other hand, either one might have decided to present the grounds first. For instance, Deborah Cramer might have told of the decline in production of cod, haddock, yellowtail, halibut, and redfish just before making the claim that the Georges Bank has been depleted of fish. Such an approach is the standard of argumentation in the sciences and social sciences where the grounds are always developed first and the claim then developed from those grounds. Such an approach is seen by many as objective. The arguer wants to imply that the evidence is studied before a claim is made though it is, of course, an argumentative strategy. The arguer knew the claim all along but chose to delay revealing it to decision makers.

Overlapping Arguments   Frequently, two or more arguments are developed in the same paragraph because the arguer sees them as linked. That is the case of the argument about the status of African Americans on page 116. Anthony M. Platt claims that the current status of African Americans is "one of misery" but we have, for convenience sake, combined three analogies here: one with South Africa, one with third world countries, and one with the United States of the 1950s. James Q. Wilson on page 113 argued that families and neighborhoods are the cause of crime. These two claims should be analyzed separately and then together to see how well he develops the argument. If you did that you would discover that he never supports the claim about neighborhoods.

Guidelines for Analyzing Arguments   •

Frequently, arguments are linked to one another, their parts do not appear in any particular order, and parts are left out. Consequently, you may have trouble seeing in an article, television commercial, or speech what an argument is and what its parts are. Here is a useful sequence of guidelines for analyzing an argument:

1. Discover and state the claim or claims. What is it the arguer wants you to believe, value, or do? Claims may appear anywhere in the argument but most likely at the beginning or the end.

2. Look for the subclaim of the grounds. It can best be determined if you know the claim first and then ask yourself "On what basis am I supposed to give adherence to the claim?"

3. Look for the warrant. Since it will most frequently be the part omitted, it will be the most difficult to find. But if you know the claim and the grounds you can find even an unstated warrant because it is the statement that would justify the movement from grounds to claim. If stated it will frequently be identified by words such as *for, because, since*.

4. Examine the warrant to determine the kind of argument you are analyzing. Look back over the examples we have used and you will see it is the warrant that identifies the kind of argument by identifying the commonplace (or principle) behind it. Here are a few of the warrants we have used:

   "The sample represents the nation. . . ." [generalization (representative, comprehensive, overall)]

   "Single parent families headed by never-married young women cause crime." [cause (effect, generate, because, lead to, result in)]

   "These signs indicate that O. J. Simpson committed the murders." [sign (indication)]

   "Black South Africa, third world countries, and the United States of the 1950s are analogous to the United States today." [analogy (parallel, like, alike)]

   "Professor Berkowitz is an authority on the subject." [authority (expert, knowledgeable, trustworthy, skillful)]

5. Look for backing (evidence, values, credibility).

6. Look for qualifiers. What limits are put on the claim? Look for words like *usually, sometimes*, and *frequently*, which modify the force of the claim.

7. Look for refutation and reservation. Given the argument you have diagramed, to what potential rebuttal has the arguer adapted the claim?

8. Evaluate the quality of the argument by asking how well the elements of the argument adequately meet decision makers' possible rebuttals.

CONCLUSION

Arguments appear in a wide variety of situations, and they differ in their nature from one context to another. Yet all arguments can be diagramed by a variation of the Toulmin model, which illustrates how a claim can be justified only by showing that there are warranted grounds for it. In addition, grounds and warrants may need backing; claims may need to be qualified and stated with a reservation to avoid rebuttal.

Although the model provides a basis for the analysis of all arguments, not all arguments are alike. Certain types of arguments (commonplaces) can be observed. Argument by generalization attempts to draw a general claim from a series of instances. It is a rhetorical induction, the argument form closest to pure induction. Arguments may claim cause and effect relationships either of cause to effect or effect to cause. They may claim the existence of one condition as a sign of another. Arguments may claim that one condition is analogous to another, and they may be warranted by the credibility of an authority.

The Toulmin model is an analytical tool. People do not organize their arguments according to the model because decision makers already know something about the subject. So, with most arguments, parts are missing, the order is different than the model, and arguments overlap. To analyze such arguments, first start by stating the claim(s) and then find the grounds. Once this is complete, you should be able to find the warrant (frequently unstated) that justifies the supporting relationship between grounds and claim. This should also tell you what kind of argument is at hand.

Finally, take notice of the materials that serve as backing, qualifiers, refutation, and reservation. These pieces of information will permit you to evaluate the quality of the argument for the decision makers.

PROJECTS

6.1 Bring to class one example of each of the types of arguments. Look for these in contemporary publications such as newspapers, magazines, and advertising flyers. Be prepared to explain each argument by relating its parts to the Toulmin diagram. Your instructor may assign different types of arguments to different class members.

6.2 Videotape television commercials. Choose two or three about similar products (e.g., automobiles, breakfast cereal, laundry soap, toothpaste). Write a short (no more than three-page) paper in which you compare the nature of the arguments used and comment on which is most likely to get your adherence.

6.3 In class, engage in direct-clash debates in which one person advances a specific argument and another responds to it. What are the main disagreements? What problems does each person identify in the other's arguments?

6.4 Prepare a short speech (a minute or two) in which you support a single claim of fact or value. Use at least two different types of arguments.

6.5 Find a short argument (a letter to the editor is usually a good example) and follow the eight steps to analyze the arguments in it.

REFERENCES

Cramer, Deborah. "Troubled Waters." *Atlantic Monthly* June 1995: 22–26.

Devine, Robert S. "The Trouble With Dams." *Atlantic Monthly* Aug. 1995: 64–74.

Greer, Colin. "We Can Save Jobs." *Parade* 21 May 1995: 4–5.

Jackson, Sally, and Scott Jacobs. "Structure of Conversational Argument: Pragmatic Bases for the Enthymeme." *Quarterly Journal of Speech* 66 (1980): 25–65.

Kramer, Michael. "Why Guns Share The Blame." *Time* 8 May 1995: 48.

Platt, Anthony. "Rigging the Game for Racism." *California Journal* June 1995: 15.

Toulmin, Stephen. *The Uses of Argument*. Cambridge: Cambridge UP, 1958.

Toulmin, Stephen, Richard D. Rieke, and Allan Janik. *An Introduction to Reasoning*. New York: Macmillan, 1984.

"Unpopular Culture." *Time* 12 June 1995: 26.

"What Gun Owners Think: A Special Time/CNN Poll." *Time* 29 May 1995: 20–21.

Wilson, James Q. "What To Do About Crime." *Vital Speeches of the Day* 1 April 1995: 373–76.

7

Support: Evidence

Key Terms

example	sphere dependence
hearsay evidence	hypothetical example
reluctant evidence	negative evidence
statistics	documented evidence
testimony of fact	assertion
testimony of opinion	expert evidence

It should be clear from the previous chapter that an argument is a series of subclaims that support a claim and if decision makers find these, and the connections among them, reasonable they accept the argument for the claim. Each of those subclaims serve as what we will call support for the claim. In addition, sometimes a subclaim has backing that also supports it and, therefore, the claim.

For you to understand the nature of support in argumentation we will examine a highly controversial issue in American politics: gun control. Those who argue for greater restrictions on the private ownership and use of firearms argue that police statistics show that guns are the major source of the contemporary increase in violent crime. They point to the increase in students taking guns to schools. They use estimates by researchers that by the year 2003 the annual number of firearm deaths will be greater than automobile accident deaths. They argue that state records show that gun restrictions under the Brady Bill have kept guns out of the hands of felons and mentally unstable people. Additional restrictions, they say, will further stem the violent atmosphere in America.

Those who oppose restrictions on gun ownership and possession argue that it is a basic right protected under the second amendment to the Constitution. They say that the National Rifle Association opposes such restrictions because it wants to protect people's natural rights. Total violent crime, they say, is highest overall in states that are more restricted according to the FBI Uniform Crime report. Guns are needed so that the law abiding citizens may protect themselves and, they say, guns don't commit crimes, criminals do. Lenient judges and plea bargaining attorneys who put criminals out on the street are the problem, not guns in the hands of honest citizens.

In these arguments for and against gun control we can see that support (backing) is available in three forms: evidence, values, and credibility. The arguer chooses which to use and emphasize.

CREDIBILITY: Are organizations like the FBI, police agencies, cited researchers, and the NRA, trustworthy? Are they competent to judge the situation? Is the maker of the original argument credible?

VALUES: How important is the control of violence? Is gun ownership a constitutional right? A natural right? How important is self protection?

EVIDENCE: Are there increased examples of children taking guns to school? How good are the statistical projections on firearm deaths? What is the relationship between restriction and violent crimes?

When decision makers ask these questions they are asking for backing for the grounds and warrants of the arguments generated by the controversy. The next three chapters deal with these three types of support: credibility, values, and evidence. This chapter will examine evidence in the form of examples, statistics, and testimony. In chapter 9 we will examine values as support, and in chapter 10 we will see how credibility supports a claim.

Evidence, as we will use the term in this chapter, is *the support for a claim that the arguer discovers from experience or outside authority: examples, statistics, and testimony.* As we stated in chapter 2, different spheres have different definitions of what counts as evidence and which forms have the most significance. In some spheres, evidence plays an extremely important role while in others values and credibility are more important. However, there is substantial empirical data and centuries of commonsense observation to support the idea that most decision makers are influenced by evidence to justify its study and use.

FORMS OF EVIDENCE

Evidence (examples, statistics, and testimony) supports a claim in such a way as to cause the decision maker to give adherence to that claim. Evidence need not be a part of the spoken or written argument in order to contribute to adherence, however. The simplest form of an argument is the statement of a claim: an assertion. Assertions are not usually considered good arguments, but they can gain adherence when decision makers already know the evidence.

LISA: Pick me up at 5:00 so we can get to Carl's early and make sure we get to the game on time.

BOB: Okay, Carl is always late so that's a good idea.

Lisa's assertion receives instant adherence from Bob because of previous experiences with Carl's tardiness. If called upon, Lisa could provide examples such as the time they were late for the barbeque or Lynn's birthday party. The specific instances are in the mind of the decision maker and, thus, stated evidence is unnecessary.

In addition, the arguer cannot ignore evidence in the minds of the decision makers that runs counter to the argument. The unstated negative evidence in the minds of the decision makers must be met as surely as the evidence of an outspoken opponent. Although the emphasis in this chapter is on the way in which you may strengthen arguments through the use of evidence, you should always consider possible responses to unstated evidence held by decision makers.

Example

Examples may refer to *an undeveloped instance used in an argument by generalization*. An extended example, or *illustration,* usually means *an extended instance that illustrates a general principle* (Perelman and Olbrechts-Tyteca 357). Murray Weidenbaum argues that while Congress and the President can't agree on a health care program for the nation, one is developing with the growth of health maintenance organizations. He cites five examples: Michigan, New York, St. Louis, South Carolina, and Southern California (382–83). A lengthy description of how the pharmaceutical companies and distributors are being forced to merge because of economic forces serves as an illustration of the principle of the economic forces reforming health care.

Examples aim at confronting others with what they will accept as bits of reality, things that happened. One of the most compelling and probably most commonly used examples occurs when you remind others of their own experiences.

Remember our earlier example of the argument of Bob and Lisa and the examples they might have used to support their claim about Carl? Those examples were of their own experiences. Such examples abound in interpersonal argument.

Let's go backpacking this summer. We had such a great time last year on the Kern Plateau and the Wind Rivers.

Let's go see the new Tom Hanks movie. I really liked him in *Forrest Gump.*

Don't buy beets. I've never had beets cooked a way I like them.

Even in public argument you might be arguing in class about a proposed change in the university registration system. You could use compelling examples from your classmates' or your own experiences.

George Allen, Governor of Virginia, uses examples of three families that he believes are typical of decision makers to personalize his argument for a cut in government spending and taxes:

This evening, three families traveled from different regions of Virginia to see their General Assembly in action. Those families—the Morgans, the Pittmans, and the Fritzs—are here in my office tonight instead. . . .

Just as I did, General Assembly members will have to decide for themselves: Is spending nearly $100,000 a year to operate a yacht *more important* than a tax cut for folks like Tom and Sharon Morgan? I sided with the Morgans, who are from Northern Virginia and have just put three children through college.

Is spending 25,000 taxpayer dollars to buy plaques for a fishing tournament *more important* than allowing families like Al and Teresa Pittman to keep more of their hard-earned money? I chose the tax cut for Al, a Norfolk policeman, and Teresa, a homemaker, because they are struggling to raise their four children.

And, is spending 120,000 of taxpayer dollars researching the merits of additional trees in cities *more important* than reducing the tax burden on Virginians like Dennis and Alice Fritz? I decided my priority was Dennis, an insurance agent, and Alice, an elementary school teacher, in Southwest Virginia. The Fritzs are working hard to provide for their three little girls (431).

In chapter 2, we described how good stories function in argumentation. Each example, and particularly extended examples, need the characteristics of good stories. The story should ring true for the decision makers. The illustration must have characters, action, motives, and outcomes that make sense to them. In the case of your possible classroom argument about a change in student registration, you might ask students to create their own stories. The scenario of long lines, faulty telephone instruction, failure to get classes, preferences for others, and payments that must be made just before pay day, is a "story" that rings true to them.

In most public argumentation and many interpersonal argumentative situations, the specific instances you use will be outside the experience of the decision makers. Indeed, they will most frequently be outside your experience. In those situations it is important to make the specific instances as believable as possible, to make them seem real. Specificity of details and the citation of trustworthy sources promotes the idea that the instances are real because they can be verified by the decision makers.

For instance, Tim Crothers, writing in *Sports Illustrated* argues that the owners of professional sports teams, "using everything from subtle implications to outright threats, wheedle or blackmail communities into meeting their demands" (78). He provided a list of 39 hockey, football, basketball, and baseball franchises considering a move unless they get new facilities. That's 39 examples out of 109 franchises. He provided ten extended examples such as the New Jersey Devils' move to Nashville, and the move of the Québec Nordiques to Denver.

He developed the examples of the then Los Angeles Raiders. "Owner Al Davis," he said, is "the patron saint of stadium extortion." Davis had moved the Raiders from Oakland to Los Angeles. Then he threatened that if Los Angeles didn't build a new stadium he would move the team back to Oakland, which he did. "For a few dozen skyboxes," said Crothers, "Davis would pledge to move to Mogadishu" (80).

Sometimes an extended example will be used as the unifying backing for an argument. Sigrid Bathen used the story of Danny Balfour, a California six-year-old foster child who had been in at least seven foster homes and was "beaten to death by his foster father" to argue that California has a "sorry history of services to children—services which, by all accounts are getting worse, progressively more poorly funded, and less accountable either to taxpayers or the children and families they are designed to help" (24). Other examples are mentioned to support the idea that Danny Balfour's case is representative, but it is from his case that the details of support are provided.

A special kind of specific instance, called the *hypothetical example*, is used where real examples are not available or when the available real examples are not close enough to the decision maker's experience. It is important that a hypothetical example be perceived as equivalent to a real example. That is, it must have the characteristics of a real example.

Here is a hypothetical example that you might use to illustrate the problems of auto repair ripoffs:

> Here's a not very far fetched description of what you might be involved with. You take your Ford Probe in for repairs; there's something wrong in the engine or transmission, it's making a lot of noise that it didn't make before. You learn that the repair should take about ten hours and the charge is $30 an hour. The bill is $300 for labor. Sounds like simple arithmetic, right? Wrong! The actual work took only seven hours and that should save you $90. But, the service manager tells you they go by the *Flat Rate Manual* that says this repair should take ten hours to do so you pay for ten hours of labor, even though it took only seven.

Statistics

Statistics are essentially a numerical compacting of examples. Statistics provide a means for talking about a large number of examples without citing every one. These means of compacting examples are found in various forms in argumentation: raw numbers, central tendencies, probabilities, and trends.

Raw Numbers   Some statistical references are clearly intended to emphasize significant numbers of examples. When an argument surfaced over non-profit organizations that "skirt the grey areas of tax laws to raise millions of dollars while at the same time maintaining their tax-exempt status," two examples were given using raw numbers.

The American Association of Retired Persons raised "over $173 million in business ventures" and the National Rifle Association makes $14 million ("Making Money the Nonprofit Way"). Alex Taylor III noted that there was a decline in new car sales and an increase in used car sales. Why? Because when "1.5 million two- and three-year old cars come off lease" a dealer "will sell you an off-lease 1993 Taurus for about $13,500 v $17,500 for the 1995 model" (30).

There are a number of points worth observing about these examples of raw numbers. First, the raw numbers are rounded off to make them easier to understand without essentially damaging their accuracy: The AARP raises over $173 million and the NRA makes $14 million. These are not exact but rounded numbers. Second, the statistics are compared with other possibilities so the decision maker can tell, not just that the 1993 Taurus costs less than a 1995, but how much less: "$13,500 v $17,500."

Comparison is strongly influenced by the statistical measure you use. For instance, in 1995 when some argued that the United States was spending too much money on foreign aid, the statistics showed that the United States was second only to Japan in the dollars spent on foreign aid (Japan $11.3 billion,

United States $9.7 billion). However, as a percentage of the nation's gross national product the United States was last among developed nations with 0.15 percent. Twenty other countries had a greater percentage of their gross national product in foreign aid led by Denmark, Norway, and Sweden with 1.03 percent, 1.01 percent, and .98 percent ("Soft Touches").

One adaptation of statistics that none of these arguments used because they are national arguments, but one you should consider, is to localize or personalize statistics. For instance, what price comparison on the Taurus could you get by calling your local Ford Dealer? Statistics must be rounded and compared for easier comprehension of their magnitude, and perhaps localized and personalized for greater impact.

Central Tendency   Some statistics go beyond raw numbers to provide some indication of what is normal in a larger population. Central tendencies are frequently called averages. The following argument uses averages to claim that college and university salaries discriminate against women:

> Current average salaries for assistant professors is about $40,000 and full professors average about $60,000. Few women have reached the rank of professor, and those that do earn less than men. Male full professors average $62,380 but women average $55,080, according to 1993–94 figures compiled by the American Association of University Professors. The same kinds of differences exist among associate and assistant professor. Women assistant professors earn an average of $36,320 compared with male assistant professors who average $39,060 (*Annual Report*, 18).

It's true that fewer women are in the hard sciences where the better salaries are, but that doesn't account for all of the problems. Martha S. West of the University of California, Davis, points out that in 1981–82, 27 percent of full-time faculty were women though 35 percent of all Ph.D.'s were earned by women. "By 1993–94, 31 percent of faculty were women, but the percentage among women earning doctorates had increased to 47 percent. The gap between these two figures has doubled from an 8 percent difference to a 16 percent difference twelve years later" (27). Furthermore, women are found in larger percentages in the lower paying institutions. Public two-year colleges employ almost 38 percent women while private research universities employ slightly less, and public research universities slightly more, than 20 percent (27).

Statistical Probability   In chapter 2, we talked about various meanings of the word *probability*, and statistics can represent one of them. D. Stanley Eitzen argues that "the higher the unemployment rate in an area, the higher the crime rate." At age 11 African American and white youths are equally likely to commit violent crimes but African Americans in their late twenties are "four times more likely to be violent offenders." But, employed African Americans and whites in their late 20s "differ hardly at all in violent behavior" (70). The numbers are based on a concept of probability called *frequency*. Essentially, the "equally likely" and the "four times more likely" say that when measured over many instances, the results will be the same as pure chance (as in flipping a coin) or four times greater than pure chance.

The statistics are an expression of the frequency with which events occur by pure chance, or the likelihood that something exceeds pure chance. That is, pure chance would predict that, say 30 percent of the population will get cancer by the time they are 70 years old, but if they smoke, their likelihood exceeds pure chance by a significant factor. Or, pure chance would predict that African American and white youths would commit the same percentage of violent crimes. Four to one is a significant movement beyond pure chance. It's the same thing as saying you have a pure chance likelihood of hitting 21 in a blackjack card game of, say, less than 10 percent, but you can exceed chance if you remember all the cards that have been dealt so as to know the cards yet to be dealt, and then adjust your betting accordingly. That's why casinos have resorted to dealing from a shoe containing far more than the usual 52 card deck: it's a lot harder to memorize what has been dealt.

One of the problems of judging by statistical probability is the problem of deciding what probability is significant. The Delaney Clause of the Federal Food, Drug, and Cosmetics Act establishes a zero tolerance rule for judging additives in processed foods. Here is an argument against zero tolerance and for a higher probability requirement.

Delaney allows no additive in processed foods that research has shown may induce cancer in laboratory animals—zero tolerance. "Pesticides are considered additives if they concentrate at all in the food during processing. Furthermore, under Delaney a substance can be defined as inducing cancer even if the incidence only happens at high doses, causes only benign tumors or despite negative results from other animal-feeding studies" (Thompson 13).

Statistical Trends   Many times statistics are used to compare the nature of a situation over time to discover the trend that might indicate its magnitude and potential. Jacqueline M. Graves observed that the number of Native Americans "has grown the fastest [of all ethnic groups] without immigration from 1970–1990." Their percentage of the total population of the United States rose from .04 percent in 1970 to .08 percent in 1990. It doubled. This statistical trend, she argued, has not been caused by increased birth rate but by "the astounding success of casino gambling on Indian reservations." People who had not acknowledged their tribal membership before are claiming it now.

Another survey uses the trend among high-achieving teens (as measured by those in *Who's Who Among American High School Students*) as a sign that such teens "may actually be leading healthier, happier lives than those led by teens 25 years ago." Compared to 1972 marijuana use in 1994 was down from 27 percent to 10 percent. Sexual activity remained the same, but "contraceptive use among sexually active teens climbed from 51 percent in 1971 to 91 percent in 1994. Moreover, 68 percent had a happy family life, up from 59 percent in 1971" ("Maybe Kids Are OK After All").

The article on Native Americans is based on census data accumulated every ten years from 1900 to 1990. It shows a steady increase in Native Americans from 1950 to 1990. Thus, a trend is a more reasonable explanation than it is in the second case. The teen sex data is based on a small percentage of high school students and it only compares two years. While the differences may be significant, they do not establish a trend—only a change that might be reversed in a subsequent year. Trends require more points of steady change.

So, statistics are compacted examples that sometimes appear as raw numbers, are sometimes averaged, frequently rounded off, always compared, if they are to have maximum force for decision makers. From the point of view of evidence, however, you must remember that no matter how much counting and predicting has gone into statistics, they still rely on the response of the decision makers to have value in argumentation. Lots of people acknowledge the statistical relationship of smoking to cancer and heart disease, for instance, but do not apply them to themselves.

Testimony

Testimony is the statement of another person or agency that is used to support a claim. It may be used with examples or statistics as backing for the grounds of an argument. It may also serve, as we noted in chapter 6, by itself as the grounds for an argument by authority. Testimony adds the credibility of its source to the grounds or warrant of an argument.

Traditionally, testimony has been divided into two types: *testimony of fact* and *testimony of opinion*. Obviously, all testimony represents the opinion of the person or agency cited. However, testimony about facts that provide examples or statistics is seen by many as stronger than testimony that only expresses the opinion of the source. Indeed, there is a general view among the researchers in this area that example and statistical evidence is more powerful than opinion evidence (Reinard 38–40). This is in line with the commonsense notion that testimony of fact is preferable to testimony of opinion.

Testimony of fact adds to examples or statistics the credibility of the source of the testimony. Jerry Jasinowski, President of the National Association of Manufacturers, argued before the World Economic Forum in 1995 that "American manufacturing has, by a broad collection of measures, become number one."

> America is number one in the global competitiveness battle. That's not just my claim. It is the assertion of the 1994 World Competitiveness Report put out annually by the prestigious World Economic Forum.
>
> America is number one in exports. Our double digit rate of export growth exceeds our competitors. In 1994 we sold half a trillion dollars worth of goods overseas. According to world-renown management expert Peter Drucker: "The most important event in the world economy in the late 1980s was the boom in United States manufacturing exports. . . . The export boom was unprecedented in American history, and indeed, in economic history altogether."
>
> America is number one in productivity. A Brookings Institution study found that productivity in German manufacturing was 86 percent of that in the United States while Japanese productivity was an even lower 78 percent (348).

Here is a case where the testimony comes from the organization he is speaking to (The World Economic Forum), a highly respected management scholar (Peter Drucker) and, perhaps, the most highly respected American private source (The Brookings Institute). This testimony makes his a powerful argument and illustrates how a variety of sources may be used.

The distinction between testimony of fact and opinion that was noted may not be as great as it might at first seem. The testimony of these three sources are statements of fact, but the facts as they have come to see them. But all these pieces of testimony represent opinion. The crucial question for you as you use testimony is whether it will be perceived as fact and not "just opinion." That judgment will depend on the credibility of the source and the specificity with which that source develops the information.

The distinction between the two types of testimony is very important to certain specialized spheres of argumentation such as the law. A witness may testify to seeing the defendant enter the house at about 9:20 p.m. and leave about 10:15 p.m. carrying a suitcase. However, if the witness thinks the suitcase was full of valuables, that is opinion and not considered evidence by legal standards.

Some of the biases of these specialized spheres have been incorporated into our general practices. For this reason we test factual testimony by asking about the testifier's experience, access to direct perception of the facts, and expertise on the matter at hand. As a general principle, good factual testimony comes from an expert source with direct knowledge. That source carefully delineates the fact testified to from its own and other's opinions. Even so, you must remember that the source is only testifying *about* facts and any time a human is involved, so is opinion.

GENERAL PRINCIPLES FOR THE USE OF EVIDENCE

To set down specific principles for the use of evidence is difficult because the decision makers addressed are so important in determining the believability of an argument. However, some principles have evolved that are generally accepted by most persons in our society. These principles serve as reasonable standards for tests of evidence. They help you to see the difference between forceful and questionable evidence.

Use Representative Instances

This is another way of saying that you should choose the best examples available to prove a generalization. Remember the use of examples of Murray Weidenbaum on page 125? He argues that the American health system is moving toward a new arrangement based on five examples each from a different major region of the country (Michigan, New York, St. Louis, South Carolina, and Southern California) that have become dominated by health maintenance organizations. His specific instances seem representative of what is going on in health care generally. The examples represent a significant proportion of the health care business.

There is no mathematical formula for judging representativeness, although specialists in survey research have standard rules they follow. Ultimately, the key question is, to what extent will decision makers believe that these examples are representative and, therefore, reason enough to warrant adherence?

Use a Sufficient Number of Instances

To form a satisfactory generalization, enough examples must be provided to convince others that the argument is believable. There is no magic number for the amount of evidence needed, but there is a long standing "rule of three." Where a claim is in contention, use at least three examples. It is clear, however, some evidence is useful even when the decision makers already agree to the claim. It also is clear that the argument is seen as more powerful when more high quality evidence from multiple sources is added. But, large amounts of evidence that is perceived as of low quality weakens an argument (Reinard 40).

On page 126 we noted that Sigrid Bathen used the story of Danny Balfour to argue that California has a "sorry history of services to children" and that this condition is getting worse. Is this one example significant enough or are more significant examples needed? The number of instances may influence the qualifier. In this case, if there are not enough instances to convince decision makers that this *typically* happens she may have to argue that it *sometimes*, or *too often* happens.

Account for Negative Instances

Particularly with knowledgeable decision makers you make a mistake if you fail to account for instances that do not support the claim. Remember Governor George Allen's examples of the Morgans, the Pittmans, and the Fritzs who would receive tax cuts because the state would no longer operate a yacht, provide plaques for a fishing tournament, or study the merit of trees in a city? But what if an opponent of his budget cutting plans were to argue that these were minor examples of budget cutting and that he does not justify larger cuts in human services or education? And what if the opponent were to argue that these three families are not typical of the many other families who would lose benefits? He would have to counter such negative instances.

Speakers or writers who fail to account for negative instances of which a receiver has knowledge will lose credibility. Even with people who do not know the negative instances, some acknowledgement of them may strengthen an argument because it makes the arguer seem more trustworthy.

Give the Value Characteristics of Instances

It is important to let the receiver know what value judgments apply to the example. Phrases like, "The *best* example of the failure of our government to resolve important problems is the budget deficit," "that 54 percent of all high school seniors have smoked marijuana is a *good* example of the widespread use of drugs," "A *recent* example of press censorship occurred in the *New York Times*," "The war in Bosnia is a *good* example that Americans do not want to be involved in foreign wars," or "A *typical* example of the efforts to clear up water pollution is the activity on the Connecticut River" help to give decision makers a more specific idea of the value the arguer puts on the example.

Make Instances Seem Real with Details

People tend to give greater adherence to more specific examples (Kline 412). Even hypothetical examples should be given the characteristics of real examples. Suppose you were to argue for new traffic regulations and develop a hypothetical example to explain how traffic congestion can be a serious imposition that needs new regulations. That hypothetical example might be stated like this: "Suppose you start home tomorrow night and find yourself in a massive traffic jam that delays you, and you miss an important appointment." Your example would be better if given the characteristics of a real example of streets and freeways your decision makers know: "Suppose as you leave work at 5:00 tomorrow night you turn onto the freeway at the Temple Street on-ramp. All that is needed to close down the Hollywood Freeway is one car out of gas just beyond Silver Lake Boulevard and there you are, stuck for hours in the sweltering heat, missing your important appointment."

Use Decision Makers' Experience

Although you should provide enough examples to support your claim with decision makers, the other side of that coin is also important. The tedious repetition of examples for people who already know them can injure the effectiveness of an argument. Therefore, you should remind decision makers of what they already know in support of your case. Phrases such as "as you already know," "your own experience has shown," and "as you learned last week" help strengthen your case.

Use Current Examples and Statistics

Clearly, the most up-to-date information is superior to less current information in assessing the present situation. Even for historical study, current information should be more useful because historical evidence is frequently cumulative. That is, every new piece of information makes the previous idea clearer. Also, more recent statistics may be more useful in historical argument because more sophisticated statistical measures have been employed.

Use Reliable Sources for Instances and Statistics

Avoid the bias of the source. This is important, not only because of the danger of drawing a less accurate generalization, but because such bias, when recognized, will damage the argument. Even though it is sometimes possible to win adherence through the use of biased sources that some decision makers do not recognize as biased, it is not wise to do so. Evidence from such sources can only be successful in seeking short-term adherence. Even persons who initially gave adherence will learn from others of the biased sources and, in the long term, remove adherence. Such a discovery could weaken your credibility with them on many claims.

Even information that is not biased but *appears* to be from a biased source is poor evidence because of others' reactions. An aspirin company offers a free booklet that they claim explains about aspirin. You have no way of knowing whether the information provided is accurate but you may distrust it because it is offered by a source potentially biased by its own commercial self-interest.

For each example or statistical study that you take from someone else, ask yourself the extent to which that source is biased and the extent to which it may appear biased to others. Federal Government agencies such as the Bureau of Labor Statistics are generally regarded as unbiased. Research foundations supported by private companies have a variety of levels of confidence attached to them. For instance, the statistics on petroleum imports collected by *Petroleum Supply Annual* are acceptable. However, research by the American Tobacco Institute is not. Though both may be quite objective, the petroleum industry needs accurate information to do its work while the tobacco industry, under fire from health agencies, is not perceived that way. Bias should be carefully considered because it can have a serious influence on the extent to which decision makers are willing to adhere to an argument.

Carefully Consider Statistical Measures

For our purpose, statistical measures basically answer the question: How typical are the examples? Darrell Huff in the book *How to Lie With Statistics*, presents many of the problems of statistical argument in everyday language.

One could spend a lifetime of study and become an expert in statistical argument and its errors. For the moment, however, the following are a few of the mistakes that need to be avoided.

"The Sample with the Built-in Bias"   If you asked your classmates what they thought about the federal ban on assault weapons and they approved it by a vote of 15 to 5, that would be impressive, but if 10 others had refused to answer your question, you might have a built-in bias for which you were not accounting. Thus, the potential actual split was 15 to 15 or 25 to 5. The real proportions could be as great as 5 to 1 or as little as dead even. Also, suppose some of the people who opposed the ban did so because they thought it was not strong enough. That would give you another built-in bias.

"The Gee-Whiz Graph"   Graphic representation of statistical data can provide a visual clarification. It can also mislead. All graphs should be carefully examined to be sure that they provide information in a form that reflects the best interpretation of the data. Figure 7.1, page 135, and 7.2 on page 136 are graphs of the annual number of violent crimes in the United States between 1983 and 1992. The

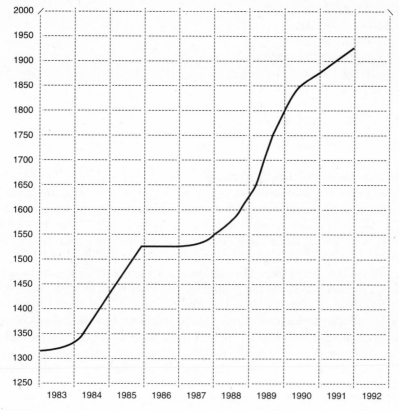

FIGURE 7.1
Violent Crimes in America, taken from *Statistical Abstract, 1994*. p. 198

figures could be graphed in many ways. What do these graphs show? Is there a steady and significant growth in violent crime over the period? Is the growth relatively flat until 1987? Would 1993 or 1994 rates (they dropped) help you understand the meaning of this graph? Remember that graphs such as these are arguments, and they are no better than the analysis and evidence that goes into them.

"The Well-Chosen Average"   *Average* is a popular term standing for some measure of central tendency in data, but there are many ways of measuring it. One such measure is a *median*. It represents the point above and below which 50 percent of the items fall. A second is a *mode*, the figure that appears most frequently. The third is the *mean*, an arithmetic average and the term most correctly applied to the term *average*. The mean is found by dividing the number of items in a series into the total of all the items.

It's salary negotiating time at the place where you work, and the company president says that you shouldn't expect much of a raise because the average salary at this company is $20,000 a year, and you already earn that. The average in this case is the mode. You check it out and find that the median salary is $30,000 and the mean salary is $57,000. Here are the salaries:

$450,000 × 1
$150,000 × 1
$100,000 × 2
  $57,000 × 1   Mean
  $50,000 × 3
  $37,000 × 4
  $30,000 × 1   Median
  $20,000 × 12 Mode

Has your employer chosen the measure of central tendency well?

"Much Ado About Practically Nothing"   There are groups in higher education who undertake the task of determining the quality of graduate programs in various disciplines. One hears the statement, "We are one of the top five communication [or psychology or political science] departments in the country." Statistical reports are published showing the relative ranking of all graduate programs by specialty. They make an impressive display, and people use them in arguments. The problem is that the data are gathered by randomly sending questionnaires to people in the discipline who may have only limited knowledge of work in all the institutions to be considered. The results do not control the bias in favor of the department the largest number of surveyed faculty graduated from, bias toward schools with certain popular approaches to the field, bias in favor of larger schools, and the long time between periods of productivity in a department and when they become part of its reputation. Those who understand this may well see the data as "much ado about practically nothing."

Use Comparison to Clarify Statistics

We noted earlier in the discussion of statistics that they can be more useful if compared. If you lived in Albuquerque, New Mexico, you could argue that your state and local tax burden is low for a family of four with a $50,000 a year

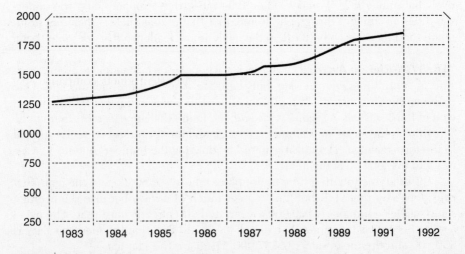

FIGURE 7.2

income. It averages only $6,900 according to the *Statistical Abstract of the United States*. But, $6,900 sounds like a lot of money, almost 14 percent of income, to some people. It would be best to compare it with other cities like Des Moines, Iowa, $8,200; New York, $13,200; Philadelphia, $15,200; or Bridgeport, Connecticut, $18,800 to show that the Albuquerque tax burden is the lowest surveyed in the Bureau of Census figures (310).

If you wanted to argue that government projections for the fastest growing occupations in the country show that those occupations are in the health care area, you might cite these examples by the Bureau of the Census: Home health aides are expected to increase 138.1 percent by the year 2005, human service workers 135.9 percent, physical therapists 88 percent, and occupational therapists 78.1 percent. Those percentages look impressive but they become even more impressive when compared to some that are estimated to decline in the same period: Machine operators—32.8 percent, telephone installers—50.3 percent, equipment operators—60.2 percent, and frame wirers—75.3 percent (411).

Base Testimony on Credibility Measures

The purpose of testimony is to provide credibility to a claim by adding a second person or agency to its support. The trustworthiness and competence of the source of the testimony is essential to its effectiveness. We discuss credibility in greater detail in chapter 10. We will make only a few comments here.

Before you accept testimony, ask yourself if the person was in a position to know, either as an observer or with the expertise to make an intelligent observation. Ask if the source of the testimony has anything personal to gain by the acceptance of the facts testified to. Ask if this is first hand knowledge or just a testimony about someone else's testimony.

A more specific source will add greater force than a vague one. Reports in the press are often attributed to unnamed or unknown sources, and readers have trouble assessing credibility. For instance, Tom Lealos argues that the two-year study and Draft Environmental Impact Statement on the California Spotted Owl Habitat by the U.S. Forest service "is nothing less than bureaucratic arrogance, prompted by fear of litigation from an environmental community that has historically misinterpreted the original intent of the laws. . ." (8). Decision makers might ask, "Who is Tom Lealos?" When they learn that his views are published in the newsletter of a forest products company, his opinion would usually be judged as biased. Using the evidence he cites to support the argument would be stronger than his testimony.

SPHERE DEPENDENCE OF EVIDENCE

Evidence may be evaluated differently depending upon the sphere in which the argumentation occurs. The evidence necessary to provide grounds or backing for a claim may well change as the sphere of argument changes. Sphere dependence in evidence does not merely mean that some evidence will be accepted in one sphere and rejected in another, but also, that one kind of evidence may be used in two spheres but valued more in one than in the other. We will note some of the more common cases of sphere dependence of evidence.

Hearsay Evidence

Legal practice does not lend credibility to *hearsay evidence*, that is, testimony a person might give about a statement made by another person. It is usually not admissible. Only what that person directly observed is admissible. The law makes this provision because only statements from witnesses who can be held responsible are accepted. But in politics the reverse is frequently the case. When reporters say that the President of the United States (or even a "usually reliable source") told them something, it has a potential for developing a greater adherence to their arguments than if they claimed they observed it themselves.

In politics, ideas are frequently tried out on the public without requiring the arguer to be responsible for them. In addition to a "usually reliable source," you may hear of an idea that was attributed to someone ("The Secretary of State is said to have told the President of Pakistan. . . ."). These are not as strong as a direct quotation, but they are still acceptable because of the sometimes circumspect tradition of political argument.

Ordinary and Expert Evidence

A similar situation exists in the difference between *ordinary* and *expert* testimony. In most professional spheres the expert is preferred. In humanistic scholarship a philosopher, such as Plato, John Locke, or Karl Marx, is preferred over the observations of ordinary people. In literary criticism Jane Tompkins, Catherine Belsey, or Thomas Eagleton are expected to be more perceptive about literature than college students. In interpersonal argument people probably trust people they know better than they trust strangers. You may trust your friends to recommend a movie more than the expert critic in the local newspaper. You believe your friend "knows what you like."

Expert evidence for the behavioral social scientists is not a matter of differences in testimony. They frequently survey ordinary people so the testimony is ordinary, but the means to draw conclusions from it is not. Behavioral social scientists draw their conclusions about human behavior through an elaborate system of statistical calculations. So, the evidence becomes not just a collection of instances, but a complex expert statistical demonstration.

There is an interesting situation involving expert and ordinary testimony in the court of law. Lawyers make a distinction between ordinary witnesses and expert witnesses and the legal system has careful distinctions as to when each is most acceptable. But, as far as jurors are concerned, little distinction is made between ordinary witnesses, expert witnesses, and other members of the jury who can say, "Well, I have been there myself, and believe me, this is how things are done." In fact, other jurors may be the most powerful source of testimony (Hawkins).

Reluctant Evidence

Reluctant evidence, from those who are antagonistic to one's purpose, has long been considered the best evidence in public debates. In a court of law witnesses are under oath and required to testify against their own interests. In public argument a person's argument may be quoted by an opponent to attack the claim and make the person seem to have extreme views.

At one point in the public debate over abortion, those who favored a "pro-choice" view argued that the "pro-life" forces wanted to restrict, not just abortion, but all reproductive freedom, including birth control. A Planned Parenthood brochure features eight quotations from opponents with the question: "Do you want people like these in charge of *your* reproductive freedom?" One quote, for instance, is from Randall Terry, Executive Director of Operation Rescue, "I don't think Christians should use birth control. You consummate your marriage as often as you like—and if you have babies, you have babies. . . ." These eight quotations from pro-life spokespersons serve to make them appear to be at the far fringe of the pro-life movement ("Listen"). The issue is abortion but the evidence, while not reluctant when stated, is used to weaken the pro-life argumentation by associating it with opposition to something most decision makers support: birth control.

Negative Evidence

Negative evidence, or the absence of evidence, is used in all spheres of argument, but it is used differently in different spheres. It is frequently used in historical scholarship. A historian who finds no evidence of women doctors, lawyers, or professors in early America will claim from this negative evidence that the professions were male dominated.

Social scientists use negative evidence in the form of the null hypothesis. They try to prove that the data may be attributable to sampling error. When they cannot prove this null hypothesis, they believe that the reverse—the hypothesis is true. So, a researcher who cannot prove that children do not grow more violent from seeing violence on TV (the null hypothesis) believes that they do (hypothesis).

Negative evidence is used in international relations. For example, the leaders of China tell the world community they deserve trust and respect, yet others cite the evidence of human rights violations to argue that the Chinese have not changed. When most favored nation trading status is extended to the People's Republic of China, human rights advocates attack the decision based on a lack of (negative) evidence. People asked for evidence of change before the United States resumes normal relations. Lack of such evidence served as grounds for the claim that sanctions should be enforced against China.

Documented Evidence

In law and in most scholarly fields of humanistic inquiry (e.g., literature, philosophy, history, theology) there is a clear bias for documented over undocumented evidence, perhaps because written or recorded evidence seems more permanent.

Traditional historical scholarship provides a reasonable example of this emphasis. There is such a bias toward documents that elaborate methods have been defined by students of historiography to determine which documents are best and how they should be interpreted. For historians, for instance, there is a strong preference for "primary sources"—original documentary evidence. At the same time, there is a strong reservation about "secondary sources—interpretations of evidence or events. This preference is related to the historian's interest in objective historical reconstruction (Wise 59).

Documented evidence for historians has also meant documents that came from official sources or from the reports of well-educated and, presumably, more knowledgeable people. In recent years there has been a growing interest in what has been called social history that tries to define how ordinary people were responding to events. Consequently, such persons have been interviewed (what is called oral history) and these interviews, along with diaries and letters, have been accorded greater weight. Still, there remains a strong bias for documented versus undocumented evidence.

Assertion and Evidence

Testimony as evidence means, as we indicated earlier, the testimony of someone *other than* the person making the argument. However, studies of arguments in conversational discourse reveal that people do use their own authority as grounds for claims (Willbrand and Rieke 419–23).

Children argue by assertion more frequently than adults. However, the examination of the arguments of well-known adults shows that they use assertion frequently. Sometimes such assertions gain the adherence of decision makers because they trust the person making the assertion.

Arguing by assertion is a questionable practice in any situation where the arguer does not have unquestioned credibility. However, Senator Mark Hatfield of Oregon, because he is a Republican Senator and conservative Christian, may not need evidence when he argues against legalizing public prayer in the schools.

> I must say very frankly that I oppose all prescriptive prayer of any kind in public schools. Does that mean that I am against prayer? No. It does not mean that at all. I am very strong in my belief in the efficacy of prayer. But I must say that there is no way [the Senate] or the Constitution or the President or the courts could ever abolish prayer in the public schools. That is an impossibility. Prayer is being given every day in public schools through this country—silent prayer, personal prayer that in no way could ever be abolished even if we wanted to.

Hatfield has no evidence to support his assertions but his argument may be accepted because of his conservative credentials and his status. So, if the people hearing the claim accept the credibility of the person advancing the claim, assertion may function as if evidence is attached. It is a practice to be cautioned against because, for most people in public situations, assertion without evidence will not gain adherence.

Thus, each sphere will have its own interpretation of the degree of reliance than can be put into evidence: expert or ordinary, original or hearsay, willing or reluctant, positive or negative, documented or undocumented, substantial or asserted. There may be some general bias for one or the other in each of these pairs. You will do best to think clearly about the standards of the sphere in which you undertake to argue before you select the evidence you will use.

CONCLUSION

Arguments may be supported to gain decision makers' adherence using evidence, values, and credibility. *Evidence*—the traditional term for examples, statistics, and testimony—is the subject of this chapter.

Examples may be used to develop a generalization or illustrate a general principle. They can be real instances or hypothetical ones. Statistics provide a means for compacting examples, for talking about a large number of specific instances at one time. Statistical measures provide the basis for averaging and comparisons. Such measures can be simple or highly sophisticated. Testimony about fact or about opinion is a means of adding credibility to a message.

A number of general principles guide you in using examples, statistics, and testimony. All are based on the inclination of the decision makers, but the principles provide general guidelines:

1. Examples should be representative.
2. Examples should be in sufficient number.
3. Negative instances should be accounted for.
4. Value characteristics of examples should be given.
5. Detail should be given to make examples seem real.
6. The decision makers' experience should be used.
7. Examples and statistics should be current.
8. Examples and statistics should come from the most reliable sources.
9. Statistical measures should be carefully considered.
    a. Avoid the "sample with the built-in bias."
    b. Avoid the "gee-whiz graph."
    c. Avoid the "well-chosen average."
    d. Avoid "much ado about practically nothing."
10. Statistics should be made clearer through comparison.
11. Testimony should be based on credibility measures.

Some forms of evidence are sphere dependent; that is, they have different values depending on the sphere in which they are used. Hearsay evidence is suspect in a court of law but quite acceptable in political argumentation. Many fields regard the expert witness as superior to the ordinary witness, but this is not true for social scientists interested in human behavior or for interpersonal argument. Reluctant testimony depends for its value on the extent to which its author is clearly perceived to be reluctant. Negative evidence is useful in international relations but not in scientific argument. Documented evidence is preferred in most scholarly fields and in religion.

PROJECTS

7.1 Deliver a short argumentative speech in which you state a single claim and support it with specific instances, statistics, and testimony.

7.2 Carefully observe about ten television commercials. To what extent do they use support as we have discussed it in this chapter? Are there differences among commercials? Which are more convincing to you? Why? (Remember the supporting materials discussed in this chapter are not the only causes of adherence.)

7.3 Write a short paper evaluating the support in a contemporary argumentative essay or editorial.

REFERENCES

Allen, George. "State and Local Government Relationship." *Vital Speeches of the Day* 1 May 1995: 429–34.

"Annual Report on the Economic Status of the Profession 1993–94." *Academe* Mar./April 1994

Bathen, Sigrid. "The Future for California Children." *California Journal* June 1995: 22–27.

Bureau of the Census. "Civilian Employment in the Fastest Growing and Declining Occupations: 1992 to 2005." *Statistical Abstract of the United States, 1994.* 114 ed. Washington, DC 1994: 411.

Bureau of the Census. "State and Local Taxes Paid by a Family of Four in Selected Cities, 1994." *Statistical Abstract of the United States, 1994.* 114 ed. Washington, DC 1994: 310.

Crothers, Tim. "The Shakedown." *Sports Illustrated* 19 June 1995: 79–82.

Eitzen, D. Stanley. "Myths, Facts, and Solutions." *Vital Speeches of the Day* 1 May 1995: 469–72.

Graves, Jacqueline M. "More Americans Are Going Native." *Fortune* 26 June 1995: 30.

Hatfield, Mark O. "Remarks on a School Prayer Amendment to the Improving America's School Act, 1994." *Congressional Record* 27 July 1994: S9894.

Hawkins, J. "Interaction and Coalition Realignments in Consensus Seeking Groups: A Study of Experimental Jury Deliberations." Diss. U. of Chicago, 1960.

Huff, Darrell. *How to Lie With Statistics.* New York: Norton, 1954.

Jasinowski, Jerry. "America's Manufacturing Revolution." *Vital Speeches of the Day* 15 Mar. 1995: 348–52.

Kline, John A. "Interaction of Evidence and Reader's Intelligence on the Effects of Silent Message." *Quarterly Journal of Speech* 55 (1969): 407–13.

Lealos, Tom. "Bureaucratic Arrogance." *The Timberline*. Terra Bella, CA: Sierra Forest Products, April 1995: 8.

"Making Money the Nonprofit Way." *U.S. News and World Report* 26 June 1995: 19.

"Maybe Kids Are Okay After All." *U.S. News and World Report* 26 June 1995: 20.

Perelman, Chaim, and L. Olbrechts-Tyteca. *The New Rhetoric*. Notre Dame, IN: U of Notre Dame P, 1969.

Planned Parenthood. "Listen to the Anti-Choice Leaders—Then Help Us Stop Them Before It's Too Late." New York, 1989.

Reinard, John C. "The Empirical Study of the Persuasive Effects of Evidence: The Status After Fifty Years of Research." *Human Communication Research* 15 (1988): 3–59.

"Soft Touches." *Time* 5 June 1995: 20.

Taylor, Alex III. "Driven Only On Sunday." *Fortune* 26 June 1995: 30.

Thompson, Kevin. "The AntiClause." *California Farmer* Jan. 1995: 12+.

Weidenbaum, Murray. "A New Look at Health Care Reform." *Vital Speeches of the Day* 1 April 1995: 381–84.

West, Martha S. "Frozen in Time." *Academe* July/Aug. 1995: 26–29.

Willbrand, Mary Louise, and Richard D. Rieke. "Strategies of Reasoning in Spontaneous Discourse." *Communication Yearbook*. Ed. James A. Anderson. Newbury Park, CA: Sage: 1991: 414–40.

Wise, Gene. *American Historical Explanations: A Strategy for Grounded Inquiry*. Minneapolis: U of Minnesota P, 1980.

8

Argument and Evidence in Science

Key Terms

quantitative sciences
natural order
claims of fact
empirical
peer
generalization
abduction
hypothesis
theories

conditional cause
sign
model
homology
review authority
grounded claims
specific instances
statistical probability
testimony

For many people scientific methods stand as the most competent way to understand what is going on in the world. Scientific standards for evidence and argument are held up as the way to understand what the natural world is like. Arguments that fail such tests are easily disregarded, not only by the scientists who work in the sphere, but by lay persons as well. The sphere of science has great credibility in our society, and an examination of its understanding of evidence and argument will provide insight into the standards people frequently seek in public arguments.

First, let us define *science*. There are, after all, terms like *physical science*, *human science*, *political science*, *creation science*, and so on. There is the distinction made by many between "quantitative" and "qualitative" science. What we will examine here are the *quantitative sciences: those disciplines and individuals who use the physical sciences as a model and mathematics as a foundation to develop explanatory theories of how physical, biological, and human entities function.* We mean to exclude from this sphere any humanistic (literary, historical, philosophical) study and any study that goes by the designation science (sometimes called qualitative analysis) that aims to understand individual phenomena.

The sphere of quantitative science can sometimes be identified by academic departments (e.g., physics, chemistry, geology, biology) in the physical and biological sciences. But many academic departments in the social sciences have some faculty members who are oriented to the quantitative while others are more qualitative in their research (e.g., anthropology, communication, political science, sociology). There is even some study frequently associated with the humanities that is quantitative, linguistics, for instance. The science that we discuss in this chapter is the quantitative, and it ranges over a wide variety of fields with the physical sciences as its model.

We also need to distinguish between what we call *scientific argumentation* and the political argumentation that is frequently associated with science. Scientists may be motivated to see to it that federal funding goes to their particular research. In addition, they may argue before public agencies for certain policy options. They may even argue that particular scientists are not competent or have falsified data. These are all part of a political role that scientists frequently play. This political role of scientists is illustrated in their public arguments over smog laws, restrictions on secondhand smoke, child safety restraints in automobiles, and a host of other policy matters.

We propose to examine not this significant political role of scientists but how scientists argue as scientists: What kind of argument and evidence will they most admire in the scientific journals, research papers, and grant applications? We look at how scientists are supposed to argue, though they sometimes do not.

The values of scientific study, as we will explain in greater detail in chapter 9, begin with the value of discovering order in nature through empirical and modeled rational (mathematical and logical) means. This natural order is first engaged through observation (empiricism). These observations are represented through agreed-upon procedures in numerical forms of evidence that support claims of proposed fact, called *hypotheses*.

Even if the natural order cannot be directly observed (i.e., you cannot observe a quark, a neutron, or an attitude) scientists still require that there be empirical adequacy. That is, the signs of the phenomenon must be observable. The procedures for finding these claims of fact must be clearly defined so that they may be replicated or questioned. These claims of fact are linked together to provide theoretical propositions of explanation. Such propositions are in turn used to predict another specific situation that has not been observed.

From this perspective a theory about how dinosaurs became extinct is built from careful observation of fossil and sedimentary remains. It is stated in claims of fact combined with other claims of fact already acknowledged to provide a proposition of cause. In the same way, a scientist could argue that the same causes will function in the future on another phenomenon that can never be directly observed. The same assumption, of the ability of theory to predict, holds for theories about gene structure, compliance gaining among humans, or social structure.

The case of the extinction of the dinosaurs is a useful place to begin because it is probably easier to understand than many of the more complex issues of physics or chemistry and because of the wide interest in dinosaurs today.

Dinosaurs existed on the earth for approximately 130 million years; the descendants of creatures that probably first crawled out of the swamps 400 million years ago. But, while not the oldest creatures on earth, they lasted longer than any other through the Triassic, Jurassic, and Cretaceous periods.

By contrast, humans are probably only 100,000 years old, and Mammalia has dominated the land ecosystem for only 70 million years. During the period of dinosaur dominance, no mammal was larger than a cat, so dinosaurs not only existed for 130 million years, they dominated the world. Dinosaurs are most closely related to birds and to mammals, not to reptiles as was commonly thought. Crocodiles or alligators existed before dinosaurs, and although they share some characteristics, they are not warm-blooded as dinosaurs were (Bakker 15–25).

At the close of the Cretaceous period, all dinosaurs died in what has been metaphorically referred to as a "mass murder." There have been many theories about how this happened: some proposed causes include substantial temperature and climatic changes, poison from new plants, new mammals that ate dinosaur eggs, or the effect of cosmic rays (425). In recent years two theories have been dominant.

The most powerful theory is that a massive asteroid (or asteroids) hit the earth and created at least the Chicxulub Crater in Mexico's Yucatan, and a worldwide dust cloud that blotted out the sun, killing off plants and animals. The second theory found the cause in big volcanic eruptions.

In the 1990s a third theory was devised that united these two. Its basis is in a belief that a huge asteroid hit the earth "with the force of millions of hydrogen bombs," creating shock waves that came together at the other side of the planet (the antipode) heating and breaking the ground and triggering huge volcanic eruptions (Broad).

Thus, there are three theories that are being seriously considered for an explanation of the end of the dinosaurs. For each, the argumentation forms around a proposition of fact: e.g., a giant asteroid hit the earth blotting out the sun and killing many plants and animals. The nature of the controversy among these three theories explains many of the conditions of scientific argument and evidence.

THE TRADITION OF ARGUMENTATION IN SCIENCE

There are several ways that the dinosaur debate helps to define the tradition of argumentation in the science sphere. Four of which serve as a preliminary definition of scientific argumentation. They are that science (1) deals in claims and propositions of fact; (2) searches for truth over personal gain; (3) reveals results that are complete enough to test; and (4) establishes theory that changes slowly.

Claims of Fact

First, traditional scientific argument, in its central concern, argues claims and propositions of fact. Stephen Toulmin, et al. identify four "broad and familiar issues" of science:

1. What kinds of things are there [or were there] in the world of nature?
2. How are these things composed, and how does this make-up affect their behavior or operation?
3. How did all these things come to be composed as they are [or were]?
4. What are the characteristic functions of each such natural thing and/or its parts? (315)

In the case of dinosaurs, one must deal with issues like (1) Did they exist? (2) Were they warm-blooded? (3) Were they destroyed by volcanic action? (4) Do asteroids create clouds of dust? and (5) Can clouds of dust block the sun enough to kill living things? All these issues must be answered by claims of fact. In the case of the dinosaurs there aren't any policy questions that might come up except for the issue of who should get the grant money to continue research, but that is not always the case.

In 1989 two chemists, Stanley Pons and Martin Fleischmann, announced that they had discovered cold fusion. Pons and Fleischmann presented claims of fact, but scientists criticized them for going beyond claims of fact to claims of policy.[1] The two scientists, and their supporters, dramatized their findings by going public and talking about the implications for future American policy (cold fusion would provide an inexpensive source of energy without nuclear waste or the threat of nuclear explosion). Their procedure would cost no more than $1,000; conventional magnetic fusion and laser pellet approaches would cost hundreds of millions of dollars ("Cold Fusion Could" 62).

In this, they were making nonscientific arguments, and many in the scientific community were quick to criticize them for it. Policy is the issue when scientists testify before government bodies. However, dinosaur extinction, cold fusion, or any other scientific question is limited to fact, and policy is outside its sphere of jurisdiction.

Search for Truth over Personal Gain

Many regarded as premature and unorthodox Pons' and Fleischmann's announcement of their claim to cold fusion. The scientists stated they made their announcement to establish their claims and file patents before Brigham Young University physicist Stanley Jones could publish his claim to similar, though more modest, results (Close 82).

Scientists are not supposed to act for personal gain. Yet public identification of discoveries has been, since the early eighteenth century, the basis on which scientific achievement is credited (Gross 90). Robert K. Merton identified the "paradox at the heart of the scientific enterprise," years ago:

---

[1]Jeanine Czubaroff has argued that theoretical models and research programs are policies and scientific questions can be examined, therefore, as policy following the stock issues of policy discussed in chapter 3. Her argument is an interesting one and well worth examining. However, scientists do not think they are arguing policy and our purpose here is to explain how the sphere of scientific argument is seen by its practitioners.

While the general progress of scientific knowledge depends heavily on the relative subordination of individual efforts to communal goals, the career progress of scientists depends solely on the recognition of their individual efforts (Gross 89).

The paradox has always been there, yet scientists are expected to have their work subject to *peer review* in which evidence and argument is tested by the scientific value of developing new knowledge, not the professional advancement of the scientist.

Testable Results

Science exists, according to its own rules, in an atmosphere of the free exchange of ideas, and to withhold information inhibits scientific progress. Probably most important, this argument calls attention to the fact that science is not a collection of observations or theories. Science is a comprehensive system of empirical knowledge building. So, the theory revealed, the methods followed, and the evidence used are all part of a comprehensive system. The results of each paleontological study that point to one theory or another about dinosaurs are printed in scientific journals such as *Science, Nature, New Scientist,* and *Technology Review.* Specific details of how the claims were supported and argued are provided so that others can test the findings.

In 1993 Virgil L. Sharpton and his group claimed that their tests showed that the Chicxulub Crater in the Yucatan (so clearly at the center of the asteroid impact theory) might be as much as twice as large as previously thought. Such an impact would considerably strengthen the theory and make it almost certain.

Then, in 1995, A. L. Hildebrand and his group, using essentially the same data, came to the conclusion that the original diameter estimated at 180 km is correct. How could such a discrepancy exist? When one looks at the craters on the moon they look to be very clearly defined. But in actuality, craters are quite irregular and have a series of rings caused by the aftermath of the impact. So, it is difficult to determine which ring is the impact ring. The diameter of the Chicxulub Crater is particularly difficult because it is buried by up to a kilometer of sediment. Hildebrand, et al. supplemented the original data base with five new measurements (Melosh). Testing is sure to continue until the scientists are convinced of the high probability of the correct size or until it is decided that some other factor (such as the presence of iridium) is a better indication of crater size.

Established Theory Changes Slowly

A theory evolves slowly over time according to Stephen Toulmin. Even Thomas Kuhn, who used the term "scientific revolution" to characterize major changes in theory, agrees that there is no sudden overturning of theory (Suppe 135). The replacement of Newtonian physics by the theory of relativity did not come suddenly when Albert Einstein said "$E = mc^2$." There was a continual building of the theory as one anomaly in Newtonian physics after another was found. Newtonian mechanics were being dismantled for many years before Einstein. Likewise, the theory of evolution had been around for some time before Charles Darwin. He provided evidence and the unifying explanation and got credit for it. That is not to say that these were not "scientific revolutions" but rather that they were theoretical statements that built on, and made sense of previous theory and findings.

The theory of a giant asteroid striking the earth, causing shock waves, and producing significant volcanic action at the antipode is attractive. It is attractive because it is based on scientific evidence like the Yucatan Crater and the massive volcanic action in what is now India, and because it relates the two theories and does not radically change any of the established findings. Physicist Mark B. Boslough of Sandia Laboratories, who had led a group in a computer simulation to see what the consequences of such an impact would be, told a *New York Times* reporter that much more research has to be done but, "it's hard not to like the story" (Broad C10).

Scientists observe physical, biological, human, or social phenomena for factual claims. These claims are combined with existing knowledge to form theories that serve as general laws or rules about the natural condition. The theories develop in a system of peer review where others can see the claim, the evidence, and the method of argumentation and test them to confirm or deny. Since theories are built up of many subtheories and empirical confirmations, they are not, according to scientific tradition, easily overturned. New major theories are slowly infused into the system until, at some point, there is a realization among scientists, that a crisis exists and they need a new theory to account for all the contradictions in the original theory. With this clearer understanding of scientific argument we will look more carefully at the roles that the different types of argument (chapter 6) and forms of evidence (chapter 7) play in it.

SCIENTIFIC USE OF ARGUMENT TYPES

All five of the types of arguments discussed in chapter 6 appear in scientific argument: generalization, cause, sign, analogy, and authority. The first three, particularly cause and sign, are the most important. In addition, scientists apply each of these types by their own rules based on empiricism, logic, and mathematics.

Argument by Generalization

In one sense, all scientific argument is by generalization. The goal of such argument is to make observations that will explain a class of phenomena. Those explanations generalize about how individual cases behave or about what properties individual cases have in common. Until well into the nineteenth century, using induction or experiments to form generalizations that would serve as theories to explain the natural world was the dominant tradition of science known as baconianism after Francis Bacon, its chief architect (Campbell 500). Generalization in modern science functions by what C. S. Peirce called *abduction*. As John Lyne explains it:

> If a given generality were true, the reasoning goes, then many particulars would be expected to turn out a certain way; if those particulars turn out in the predicted way, then the generality *may be* true. As more particular cases turn out in the predicted way, confidence in a general theory builds. . . . By statistical induction, one establishes what [the] percentage, or probability, is (184).

So the scientist begins with a hypothesis formed from limited cases. This hypothesis *may be* a valid generalization. But, the generalization must be tested for what it might be expected to show. To some extent this is a matter of replication.

Other confirmation is based on what could be expected. The original basis for the asteroid hypothesis was based on the research of geologist Walter Alvarez from the University of California, Berkeley. He and a team from the Lawrence Berkeley Laboratories, including his father Nobel Laureate Physicist Luis Alvarez, found a large amount of iridium in a 66 million-year-old layer of rock in Italy in 1977. Iridium is found at the core of the planet and from extraterrestrial objects hitting the earth. He and the group from Berkeley were thus able to tie the demise of the dinosaurs to the impact of a six-mile-wide asteroid. The theory was not new but Alvarez had evidence, and substantiating evidence has accumulated since then around the world (Lessem 190). So, more and more evidence of iridium is taken to mean that the asteroid hypothesis has become an established theory.

While part of the process of making the generalization acceptable, such tests are not argument by generalization themselves, but argument from sign as we will explain shortly. The purpose of scientific argument is to build theories that will provide the scientific community with the most rational explanation of the natural order. This requires that extensive experimentation and evidence be assembled, but generalization is only part of the process. Perhaps more important is the examination of anomalies in the theory that might question it. Toulmin, et al., provide a useful example from weather forecasting:

> Weather forecasting, for instance, presents some serious challenges to science, to find ways of squaring the observed course of meteorological events with the accepted principles of physical science. But that does not mean that scientists feel any responsibility for explaining every last day-to-day or minute-to-minute change in the weather. Presumably such changes are brought about in a perfectly intelligible way by some minor local fluctuation in the atmospheric conditions, but normally no real scientific interest will be served by tracking down exactly what that fluctuation was. Only if a *significant* anomaly can be demonstrated—for instance, a storm that blew up "out of nowhere" under atmospheric conditions that apparently ruled out such a possibility—will there be a genuine *scientific issue* to face (319).

Argument by generalization is, on the face of it, crucial to science. The generalizations (theories) require testing to make them more powerful. That testing is not always by replication. It will more often rely on the next two kinds of argument, cause and sign.

Argument from Cause

The assumption of science is that there is order in nature and that order is held together by cause and effect relationships. High- and low-pressure changes cause changes in the weather. Changes in the social order cause changes in the way individuals live their lives.

When paleontologists discovered that there was a point in the strata of the earth when there were fossil remains of dinosaurs, and then when there were none, they became interested. They concluded from this phenomenon that about 65 million years ago dinosaurs died out rather suddenly. An important question then became why. What caused this phenomenon? Scientists assume that differences can be explained, so the search for cause is perhaps the most important scientific argument. "In one form or another, . . . causal relationships represent the most common scientific argument advanced" (Anderson 9).

Usually, in the physical and biological sciences, a cause comes before the effect and is both necessary and sufficient for the effect to occur. Thus, the cause must always be there. A cause is sufficient if no other factor is necessary. It takes combustion, fuel, and oxygen for there to be fire. These three together are necessary and sufficient cause for fire. Fuel alone, however, is a necessary but not a sufficient cause. The force of a scientific argument is determined by the extent to which necessity and sufficiency approach certainty.

This requirement of approaching certainty poses an increasing problem in all sciences, but particularly in the human sciences. No cases of human behavior meet certainty standards. Consequently, the human sciences use a more open statistical probability as the basis for judging cause, called a *conditional cause*. The claim is the best explanation, but it is conditional because it is supported at a statistical level that admits of some evidence to the contrary. Beatrice Schultz studied several variables to see how persons who were trained in argumentation would evaluate themselves as leaders in decision making groups compared with the self-evaluation of those who had not been so trained.

> Self-ratings for argumentative trainees and other participants were compared by t-test, with results showing that trainees perceived themselves as significantly more self-assured (t = 2.78; df 36; p <.01), more goal-oriented (t = 2.65; df 36; p <.01) more quarrelsome (t = 2.85; df 36; p <.01) and in the direction of significance for summarizing (t = 1.81; df 36; p = .08). Untrained participants did not significantly alter their ratings after the second session (560).

Before the training there was no difference between the experimental group and the control group, but after the experimental group was trained, they showed a significant difference in the perception of their leadership qualities versus the control group. The only difference between the two was the training that became the necessary and sufficient cause for the change. How well do we know that? Consider one leadership characteristic: "self-assured (t = 2.78; df 36; p < .01).” A *t-test* is a statistical procedure to compare the means of two groups. The *t* value of 2.78 with the recorded degrees of freedom (df36) tells the researcher that chance alone was unlikely to be the source of the difference they found; probably less than one time in a hundred.

If the design of the experiment was perfect, the elimination of chance as an explanation should leave only the “treatment” (training) as the cause. But this experiment does not prove that the training caused everyone to change as would be expected in a traditional understanding of cause. As a matter of fact, some changed, some did not, and a few probably regressed. Statistically, however, the total group changed. Change is dependent on some unknown characteristic so there is cause but the cause (training) is conditional.

Remember, however, what we noted earlier: no science is immune from this problem. Penicillin causes an allergic reaction in some small percentage of the population. Even the physical sciences have margins of error. The Challenger spaceship disaster was caused by an O ring that failed when the temperature fell below 53°F, the minimum for which the engineers had tests (Gouran 439). A decision was made to go ahead with the launch even when the temperature fell below that level. Dennis Gouran explains that the odds were against failure in that technological system. However, as the tragedy illustrates, this conditional cause could not predict an individual case—only a probability.

Scientists look for the necessary and sufficient causes of phenomena. There is always some question, but certain causal relationships, particularly in the physical and biological sciences come closest to producing the ideal relationship between cause and effect. For much of science a conditional relationship is the best that can be expected. This is particularly true of the human sciences, but it is a growing reality even in physics.

Argument from Sign

A major way to test a theory is to look for observable phenomena that the theory predicts would be there. All of the theories of dinosaur extinction are developed by sign argument. Because they are propositions of past fact the evidence, fossil remains, strata of rock, iridium, craters, and volcanoes all are signs of what happened. Even Sandia Laboratory’s computer model of the effect of a large asteroid colliding with the earth is a sign of what happened in the physical world.

How does a biologist associate a particular plant or animal with a particular biological order? Given our everyday observation of mammals (people, dogs, cats, and so on), our common sense would not put whales in the class Mammalia. They are vertebrate animals that have self regulating body temperature, hair, and, in females, milk-producing mammae. These are all signs that are used to define mammals. In chapter 15 we will discuss definition in greater detail. For now, you can think of any definition as an argument from sign. A whale is a mammal if it has the signs used to identify a mammal.

The argument from sign becomes particularly crucial in an argument in the human sciences. All survey research is a sign argument. The sample of the population is taken as a sign of the whole population. It is also an important part of experimental research in the social sciences. For instance, Cynthia Hoffner and Joanne Cantor wanted to find out what factors affect "children's enjoyment of a frightening film sequence." They studied 5- to 7-year-olds and 9- to 11-year-olds. The children viewed a sequence from *Swiss Family Robinson* in which two brothers encounter a snake. The researchers varied the introduction and the ending to provide either a threat or happy circumstances.

First, note that a video of the Robinson boys encountering a snake is taken to be a sign of a frightening film sequence. After viewing the sequence the children were asked if they felt happy, scared, or just okay. They were also asked a number of questions such as how worried, scared, and so on, they were. Note that what the children said is taken as a sign of what they actually felt.

In addition, Hoffner and Cantor monitored skin temperature and heart rate to measure the children's "residual arousal to enjoyment." Here is one example of their sign argument on this subject: "Skin temperature changes accompany peripheral vasoconstriction, which is a measure of [sign of] sympathetic arousal" (46–48). We have simplified the procedure they used, but it should be clear that sign argument is used at every stage of the study's design.

Social scientists cannot show you "enjoyment" or "frightening," nor can they show you an "attitude," "violence," "communication conflict," or "deception." They must test their theories against things, events, or behaviors that are signs of those abstract concepts. We have talked about schemata that some psychologists believe guide people's mental processes. However, no one has ever seen schemata, held them up to the light, or poked them with a finger. So what makes the concept believable? Schemata are accepted because numerous studies using outward signs point to the existence of such organizing principles.

Argument by Analogy

Generalization, cause, and sign are the principal means by which scientists argue, but argument by analogy serves an important function also. There are two distinct phases to scientific argument: one is to provide an explanation of a phenomenon, the other is to build an empirical argument that can be tested. The first uses analogy extensively, the second only in very careful ways.

In one sense all argument is by analogy, because claims are made that are not the same as the incidents, things, or beings on which they are based. A series of examples can be thought of as analogous to the generalization it produces, or a sign can be seen as an analogy for what it represents.

Physicist Roger S. Jones uses a simple example of the basic scientific activity of measurement. To measure the length of a table top, he says:

> All I need do is decide between which two marks on the meter stick the right end of the table lies. . . . In practice, deciding whether two points are coincident boils down to making judgments about the distance between two points. Point A on the table and point B on the meter stick cannot literally be coincident, for two objects cannot occupy the same place at the same time (21).

In that sense, even measurement is an analogy.

Scientists acknowledge this as a condition of their knowledge and except for a few (like Roger Jones) argue there is a natural order about which they can develop knowledge claims even though measurement is not exact.

Analogy serves in this system as an explanation. There are quarks in physics, DNA in genetics, universes in astronomy. There are spirals of science, sound waves, attitudes of people. These serve as ways to explain phenomena that cannot literally be identified.

There is the analogy of mathematics, in which the rules of mathematics are used as a model of the natural world. Gene Shoemaker of the United States Geological Survey estimates that "an asteroid more than six-tenths of a mile in diameter will hit earth once every 40 million years" (Lessem 293). From this generalization you could reason by analogy that the earth is overdue for an impact that might kill three-fourths of all living things as it perhaps did 65 million years ago in the time of dinosaurs.

Such argument by analogy includes, of course, metaphor and models (Leatherdale 1). Your biology textbook has a model of DNA. It doesn't look like DNA, but it is a way of explaining that genetic phenomenon by analogy.

In the scientific tradition we are examining here the use of analogy, while useful as explanation, is not as useful in making an empirical argument. Because scientists try to understand the natural world there is a problem with the comparison of two things that are not the same. This would be particularly true of the figurative analogy, as in the example (in chapter 6) in which Labor Secretary Robert Reich compared the income gap in the United States to the difference in his height (four feet ten inches) to Shaquille O'Neal (seven feet one inch). However, even the so-called literal analogy (the one we used comparing the conditions of African Americans in this country to South Africans and residents of the third world countries) would be suspect because they have at least as many differences as similarities. Such an argument would be treated more like the unscientific building of a theory (generalization) from a single example and then claiming to apply it in another case.

While not as forceful a scientific argument as the three we discussed before, analogy is argued, particularly in the biological sciences. The term used for an analogous relationship in biological sciences is *homologous,* which means there are extensive similarities of structure and evolutionary origin between two biological entities. In genetics, for instance, homology means having the same linear sequence of genes as another chromosome. So before a biologist can claim an analogy (homology) between the arm of a human and the flipper of a seal, detailed evidence and generalizing is necessary.

John Lyne and Henry F. Howe use the example of E. O. Wilson who moved far from his own area of expertise as an entomologist ("his publications prior to 1971 concern such topics as chemical communication among ants and castes within insect societies"). In 1975 Wilson wrote *Sociobiology: The New Synthesis.* In it, and subsequently, he and his followers argue for the existence of genes for moral principles such as "altruism" (Lyne and Howe 136–40). Lyne and Howe criticize Wilson because sociobiology reveals a "superficial relationship." To say, for instance, that "certain human behavior is 'like' a certain baboon behavior" provides a basis for an analogy in public argument but not the homology necessary to a geneticist (142). It is probably most significant that sociobiology has had considerable popularity outside biology in the public sphere. Arguers in the public sphere hold analogy to less rigid standards than scientists do.

On the other hand, scientists interested in the effect of carcinogens on rats believe there is a homology between rats and humans. To develop statistical analyses of the effects of smoking and cancer on humans where large amounts of tars and nicotines must be ingested in a short period of time, rats are used rather than humans. Decisions are made about amounts necessary and periods of time based on assumptions about comparative body weights. More important is the basic assumption that humans and rats are homologous. That is, the analogy is based on extensive similarities of structure and evolutionary origin between rats and humans.

Unless a very strong analogy (homology) can be established, argument by analogy in science looks more like generalization. It serves as an explanation of a phenomenon.

Argument from Authority

By the usual rules of scientific argumentation, argument from authority is not an acceptable form. Recall our earlier argument that traditionally, scientific advance subordinates individual effort to the search for knowledge. Individuals have their names attached to theories (Haley's Comet, Heisenberg's uncertainty principle, Newton's laws, Darwin's theory) and scientists recognize the outstanding achievements of others with the Nobel and other prizes. However, in the presentation of scientific arguments in scholarly papers and journal articles, you will not find the argument "X is true because Y said it."

Of course, each scientific paper includes a review of the literature in which the scientist identifies the significant findings to date and shows how the current research fits with it. The review of the literature gives the appearance of argument from authority because the most significant contributions must be by the most authoritative researchers. However, the argument advanced in the review of the literature is about the findings and theories of the research. The authority of the author is secondary.

There is also the authority of established theories. Earlier we noted that Pons and Fleischmann, E. O. Wilson, and Robert T. Bakker (who argues that dinosaurs were "done in by pests and pestilence" [443]) take on an extensive burden of proof because their findings challenged the established theory. The assumption in science that the established theory should remain until significant evidence is generated against it gives one who wishes to overturn it a tremendous burden of proof. The presumption for the status quo is particularly strong in the sciences.

An argument warranted by the authority of scientific principle is considerably different from argument from authority in public argument. In public argument you might use authority to prove a claim ("Lower interest rates stimulate the economy, according to the chair of the Federal Reserve Board"). A scientist, however, is likely to use something more like a refutational argument. For instance:

1. The established theory has a lot of strength because of its longstanding success in predicting situations.
2. The countertheory has little evidence for its position.
3. Therefore, the established theory is still valid.

Whether as a constructive claim or a refutational one, such an argument does not look like the typical argument from authority as found in public argument (Albert Einstein is a credible scientist so we can trust his theory $E = mc^2$). For scientists as scientists making arguments in the scientific sphere, the only authority is the authority of established theory. It is probable in private that they are more likely to pay attention to, if not give adherence to, arguments advanced by highly reputable scholars over unknowns, or to place greater weight on theories advanced by persons with better credentials.

There is some suspicion that such credibility may be functioning in the case of the asteroid impact theory developed by Walter Alvarez and his team. Stephen Jay Gould, the evolutionary biologist is quoted as saying, "Paleontologists tend to be somewhat defensive. They suffer under the prejudice that theirs is a B science. And then some Nobel Prize-winning physicist [Luis Alvarez] tells them something" (Lessem 188).

Argumentation in the sphere of science concentrates on argument by generalization, cause, and sign. Its use of generalization is somewhat different from the usual understanding of that term because it is oriented to testing theory rather than just replicating it. Scientific arguments depend particularly on cause and, to a lesser extent, sign. Argument by analogy is used mostly as a method of explanation. In empirical argument it is rare, found in a form more like generalization. Argument by authority is considered inappropriate, though established principles have a kind of authority, and personal authority may play a role in private. Argumentation in science, as we have mentioned several times, is based on empirical evidence and we now turn to the subject of evidence.

SCIENTIFIC USE OF EVIDENCE

There are three forms of evidence, as we noted in chapter 7: specific instances, statistics, and testimony. All can be found in scientific argumentation. We noted earlier that science is not just a collection of observations or theories. It is a comprehensive system of empirical theory building. As we begin to examine the nature of scientific evidence we must look at that term *empirical* more carefully.

Empirically Grounded Claims

Traditionally, to be empirically grounded means that a claim must be based on sensory experience. Scientific explanations are empirical arguments when the evidence can be seen, heard, touched, smelled, or tasted. That understanding seemed reasonable in earlier centuries when our scientific theories were limited by our immediate senses, augmented by instruments such as microscopes and telescopes. Such limits are no longer applied to the term *empirical* because there is too much of what is known as reality that cannot be observed through even the augmented senses.

Quarks in physics, universes in astronomy, traits in biology, and the Jurassic period in paleontology are not available to the senses. "Nevertheless, science remains empirical in that its justification is in the interpretation of the material reality in which we function. In short, science makes sense of what we see, hear, and touch even though its explanation may incorporate much beyond that" (Anderson 12).

Specific Instances

Specific instances provide the empirical grounding for a scientific claim. That should be obvious. Colonies of bees, strata of rocks, actions of individuals all provide the empirical bases for forming generalizations about those events, actions of individuals, and phenomena that lead to hypotheses. Further examination of other instances serves to replicate, modify, or reject a theory.

From the time that the impact theory of dinosaur extinction was first proposed, there were two claims that were questioned: (1) was there such an impact as theorized, and (2) did it lead to extinction in a geological instant. By 1994 enough tests of the impact crater in the Yucatan were conducted that the theory seemed agreed on. But the question of instant extinction was still being questioned.

Research teams from universities such as The University of Washington, The University of Chicago, The University of California at Davis, Princeton, The Free University of Amsterdam, The University of Miami, and Florida State University looked for replication. They did so by examining the fossil records of microscopic marine protozoans called forams to determine when and how suddenly they died. In general, their findings supported the impact theory. There was, however, still some evidence that questioned it (Kerr). Such questioning is not unusual in science. No matter how many replications are achieved, the conditional nature of theories means that arguments are frequently based on statistical probability.

Statistics in Science

We noted in chapter 7 that statistics are essentially a numerical compacting of specific instances. They provide a means of talking about many specific instances without citing every one. That is a common approach to explanation for most public, even legal, argumentation. But science uses statistics in many more ways.

In scientific argumentation, statistics are not just a form of support. Ranging from relatively simple content analysis using some measure of an average to complex computerized programs of statistical analysis, statistics become a way of reasoning. Statistical reasoning provides the basis for generalizations about data and arguments about the cause for the evidence assembled.

The numbers that comprise statistics serve as a sign for conditions in the natural world. Their usefulness to science is determined by the extent to which they actually are representative (signs) of what they propose to measure. No one can ever "know" many natural phenomena, as we observed in the previous section on specific instances. To use statistics the scientist has to make assumptions about what makes a certain configuration of numbers a legitimate sign of the natural world.

The three tasks of statistics are:

1. To quantify a set of observations into a set of numbers. This is the descriptive use of statistics. Statistics reveal the central tendency of the numbers or the averages (mode, median, or mean), the distribution of certain characteristics, the dispersion of them, and the association among different characteristics in the set of numbers. Perhaps, there are 15,000 students in your university and 54 percent of them are women. The average age is 23.7. These are all numbers that describe.

2. To determine if the sample is representative (a sign) of the population from which it was drawn. A poll on your campus says that 58 percent of the students favor national health insurance. Were the students questioned representative of your student body?

3. To determine by a decision rule whether the characteristics found can be attributed to an error in sampling (the null hypothesis) or, if not, whether an alternate explanation, usually the hypothesis, is confirmed (Anderson 175–76).

Recall the study of children and the film sequence from *Swiss Family Robinson*? The researchers used a statistical test to determine how significant the results were.

The first task is to quantify observations into a set of numbers and relationships that will tell the researcher how to describe a population. It is concerned with measurement much like the general use of statistics discussed in chapter 7. The second and third tasks are concerned with meaning. These statistics are used to develop knowledge about a population. For these tasks, a decision rule is necessary to decide what is and what is not worth knowing. For the scientist, tasks two and three are at least as important as task one.

A look at these three tasks illustrates that there are assumptions that cannot be proven but must be taken as givens. For example, in measurement a primary assumption is that the numbers represent the phenomena. If not, then one's statistical descriptions have no real meaning. Another is that there is such a thing as a representative sample. If not, studies of public opinion, the behavior of chimpanzees, the effect of carcinogens on rats, or the physical properties of granite, would not be possible. If there is no such thing as a random sample that can be taken to be representative (a sign) of the population, the understanding of a natural phenomenon is impossible. But scientists do assume that a representative sample is possible. Another assumption is that the rate of error (the chance of being wrong) will identify the occasion of error (that the finding is false).

Statistics are important sources of evidence that link with argument by generalization, cause, sign, and analogy to form a composite system of argument.

Testimony

Testimony is a form of evidence that can stand alone as grounds for an argument from authority. For instance, you could argue as Jerry Jasinowski of the National Association of Manufacturers did (chapter 7) that "America is number one in the global competitiveness battle" because the World Economic Forum says so. However, that argument by authority is not strong in science. Is there a place for testimony? The answer in the human sciences is yes. Most of the evidence in some human sciences such as psychology and communication is testimony. In many others, such as sociology, anthropology, and political science, testimony is at least a significant basis of evidence. It is used, however, in a special way.

Testimony functions as evidence when in surveys or experiments, people express an opinion or indicate the facts that they know about a situation. For instance, Pamela and William Benoit were interested in discovering how people account for failure or success in an interpersonal argument and how they perceived the consequences for self and other relationships. They asked 27 students to write essays describing occasions of success and failure in interpersonal argument and answer questions about the consequences. Those written responses constituted the testimony that when analyzed provided the categories of explanations for success or failure.

Sometimes the evidence is taken from a set of categories that people judge. For instance, in chapter 9 we introduce a series of value terms by Milton Rokeach to represent the 18 major terminal and the 18 major instrumental values. People are given one or both lists and asked to rank order them, and the group's composite response is taken as a hierarchy of that group's values. Like Benoit and Benoit, Rokeach used open ended testimony to discover the values. But both studies rely on testimony in defining categories and in forming generalizations about their use by a group. The evidence is testimony (and hangs on the scientist's assumptions that the testimony is both true and real). It reflects the opinion and knowledge of the persons engaged in the experiment.

What you can see from this brief summary is that all three of the evidence forms are found in scientific argument. Statistics are clearly the most critical. Specific instances and testimony (in the human sciences) are the raw material from which statistical inferences are made. Statistical inferences are essentially linked to argument by generalization, cause, sign, and sometimes analogy.

CONCLUSION

The sciences examined here are the quantitative sciences, those disciplines and individuals who use the physical sciences as a model and mathematics as a foundation for explanatory theories. Scientists play a significant political role, but here we are interested in how they argue to one another as scientists. Scientific study begins with the value that there is order in nature that can be discovered. This order is explained through observation. These observations are characterized in claims of fact. They are combined with other already acknowledged claims of fact to develop a proposition that is a theory about fact. That theory can then be used to predict what will happen at another time or another place.

The tradition of argumentation in the scientific sphere can be preliminarily defined by four observations: scientific argument deals in claims of fact; it searches for truth over personal gain; it reveals results that are complete enough to test; and its theories change slowly.

Generalization, cause, and sign are the most important argument types in the scientific sphere. Generalization, in contemporary times, functions as abduction. That is, a generalization is established on the basis of its greatest probability rather than certainty.

Argument from cause is basic to scientific argumentation. When study reveals some previously unrecognized condition, the scientist wants to know its cause. To be established in theory it must be both necessary and sufficient to produce the effect. Argument from sign is important to establishing a scientific theory. Signs in biology indicate that an organism belongs to a particular species. All survey research is sign argument as is most social science argumentation.

Argument by analogy is used primarily to explain a phenomenon. To be the basis for an empirical argument it must have extensive similarities. In biology it must be homologous. Argument from authority is the least used type of argument in science. The review of literature section of research papers and articles and the authority of established theories function as a kind of argument from authority. Outward statements of authority as a basis for argument are not made, though they may be used in private.

Evidence in scientific argumentation is used to provide empirical grounding for claims. This is indicated in the specific instances that form the base of scientific reasoning. Statistics constitute the most elaborate kind of evidence and they have three tasks: (1) to quantify a set of observations into a set of numbers; (2) to determine whether the sample is representative; and (3) to determine if the characteristics found can be attributed to an error in sampling. Testimony has a function in the human sciences, in which people are called upon in surveys or experiments to express opinions.

PROJECTS

8.1 Interview a faculty member at your college or university who would be considered a scientist as we have defined a scientist in this chapter. Ask questions about the kinds of arguments and evidence he or she uses with peers (not those that might be used to convince others). Write a short paper (no more than five double-spaced pages) about what kinds of argument and evidence apply. Does the person you interviewed agree with what has been said in the chapter? How

, different is the interviewee's position from this chapter? Why do you suppose the difference exists?

8.2 Develop a speech about a controversy in science. There are many discussed in journals like *Science* and *Nature*. A librarian can help you locate an appropriate article or two. Explain the controversy by explaining what arguments and evidence are at issue.

REFERENCES

Anderson, James A. *Communication Research: Issues and Methods*. New York: McGraw-Hill, 1987.

Bakker, Robert T. *The Dinosaur Heresies*. New York: Morrow, 1986.

Benoit, Pamela J., and William L. Benoit. "Accounts of Failures and Claims of Successes in Arguments." *Spheres of Argument*. Ed. Bruce Gronbeck. Annandale, VA: Speech Communication Assoc., 1989: 551–57.

Broad, William J. "New Theory Would Reconcile Rival Views on Dinosaurs Demise." *New York Times* 27 Dec. 1994: C1+.

Campbell, John Angus. "Poetry, Science, and Argument: Erasmus Darwin as Baconian Subversive." *Argument and Critical Practices*. Ed. Joseph W. Wenzel. Annandale, VA: Speech Communication Assoc., 1987: 499–506.

Close, Frank. *Too Hot To Handle: The Race For Cold Fusion*. Princeton, NJ: Princeton UP, 1991.

"Cold Fusion Could Spark A Revolution in Science." *21st Century* May/June 1989: 12+.

Czubaroff, Jeanine. "The Deliberative Character of Strategic Scientific Debates." *Rhetoric in the Human Sciences*. Ed. Herbert Simons. Newbury Park, CA: Sage, 1989

Gouran, Dennis S. "The Failure of Argument in Decisions Leading to the 'Challenger Disaster': A Two Level Analysis." *Argument and Critical Practices*. Ed. Joseph W. Wenzel. Annandale, VA: Speech Communication Assoc., 1987: 439–47.

Gross, Alan G. "The Rhetorical Invention of Scientific Invention: The Emergence and Transformation of a Social Norm." *Rhetoric in the Human Sciences*. Ed. Herbert Simons. Newbury Park: Sage, 1989: 89–107.

Hoffner, Cynthia, and Joanne Cantor. "Factors Affecting Children's Enjoyment of a Frightening Film Sequence." *Communication Monographs* 58 (1991): 41–62.

Jones, Roger S. *Physics as Metaphor*. Minneapolis: U of Minnesota P, 1982.

Kerr, Richard A. "Testing an Ancient Impact's Punch." *Science* 11 Mar. 1994: 1371–72.

Leatherdale, W. H. *The Role of Analogy, Model, and Metaphor in Science*. Amsterdam: North-Holland, 1974.

Lessem, Don. *Kings of Creation*. New York: Simon and Schuster, 1992.

Lyne, John. "Argument in the Human Sciences." *Perspectives on Argumentation*. Eds. Robert Trapp and Janice Schuetz. Prospect Heights, IL: Waveland, 1990. 178–89.

Lyne, John, and Henry F. Howe. "The Rhetoric of Expertise: E. O. Wilson and Sociobiology." *Quarterly Journal of Speech* 76 (1990): 134–51.

Melosh, H.J. "Around and Around We Go." *Nature* 3 Aug. 1995: 386–87.

Rokeach, Milton. *The Nature of Human Values*. San Francisco: Free P, 1972.

Schultz, Beatrice C. "The Role of Argumentativeness in the Enhancement of the Status of Members of Decision-Making Groups." *Spheres of Argument*. Ed. Bruce E. Gronbeck. Annandale, VA: Speech Communication Assoc., 1989: 558–62.

Sharpton, Virgil L., Kevin Burke, Antonio Camargo-Zanoquera, Stuart Hall, D. Scott Lee, Luis E. Marin, Gerardo Suarez-Reynoso, Juan Manuel Quezada-Muneton, Paul D. Spudis, and Jaime Urrutia-Fucugauchi. "Chicxulub Multiring Impact Basin: Size and Other Characteristics Derived From Gravity Analysis." *Science* 17 Sept. 1993: 1564–66.

Suppe, Frederick. *The Structure of Scientific Theories*. Urbana: U of Illinois P, 1974.

Toulmin, Stephen, Richard Rieke, and Allan Janik. *An Introduction to Reasoning*. New York: Macmillan, 1984. 319.

9

Support: Values

Key Terms

stated values

implied values

positive values

negative values

terminal values

instrumental values

abstract values

concrete values

value systems

hierarchies of values

changing values

attacking values

values and decision makers

sphere dependence of values

Communication technology has made enormous strides in the past 50 years, especially in the last 20. Television satellites, cable, computers, fax-machines, cellular phones, cyberspace, and the internet all have increased by geometric ratios the availability of information to people and their ability to communicate with one another. Many feel this has been a mixed blessing, particularly when the influence on children is measured.

Children can find sex and violence on television and by surfing the internet. Most people believe this is a problem, but can it be solved? And how? Should media be censored? Should manufacturers be required to put V and S chips (so parents can blackout violence and sex) into the TV sets? How about similar blocks on computers? Should the government impose the restrictions on cable that are imposed on broadcast television? Would such restrictions infringe on freedom of speech? Does government censorship lead to restrictions on knowledge?

This problem is complex and made particularly difficult because it affects children. It is, as many have noted, a question of values. Think about the arguments that are generated on this question and note the values, stated and unstated, in this brief description: knowledge (information), communication, children (family, innocence), violence, sex, restriction, freedom (freedom of speech).

Not all argumentation is so obviously based on values. But all argumentation has values as a part of its development. Some would argue that values are the defining central factor of all argumentation (Sillars "Values"). One series of studies of unplanned reasoning by children and adults in various cultures indicates that value based reasoning is pervasive (Willbrand and Rieke 343). In this chapter we will examine values as they serve as support for claims at the same time that we remember that claims themselves may be values.

"A *value*," says anthropologist Clyde Kluckhohn, "is a conception . . . of the desirable that influences the selection from available modes, means and ends of action." A value may be "explicit or implicit, distinctive of an individual or characteristic of a group" ("Values" 395).

In chapter 3 we observed there are three kinds of claims: fact, value, and policy. Value claims are those that directly involve values, and policy claims require value claims to support them. Only a factual claim, which asserts that certain conditions exist in the material world and could be observed, would seem to be value free; but it is not. Even the scientist's careful statement about laboratory observations implies the values of rationality and knowledge. Thus, values are important even to choose one factual claim over another.

Values obviously relate directly to claims of value, and they are vital to policy and factual claims as well. Values, together with source credibility and evidence, are the grounds and warrants by which decision makers judge claims to be worthy of adherence.

Form of Values

Values, then, are concepts of what is desirable that arguers use and decision makers understand. Arguers use them with credibility and evidence to justify claims. But values come in a variety of forms and fit together in a variety of ways.

Stated and Implied Values

Some statements of value concepts are direct. People sometimes say that their *freedom*, *health*, or *wealth* is important. These words represent directly the value concepts they hold. Some value concepts are identified by several different words as is the case with *liberty*, *freedom*, or *independence*. Furthermore, there can be variations of a single word as in *freedom*, *free*, or *freely* depending upon the nature of the sentence in which they appear.

Value concepts are not always explicitly stated, however. Frequently, they are implied. Values are general concepts that define what arguers and decision makers believe are desirable, but, many values are implied in what we call *belief statements*. Milton Rokeach defines a belief as "any simple proposition, conscious or unconscious, inferred from what a person says or does and capable of being preceded by the phrase, 'I believe that. . . .'" (*Beliefs* 113).

Many statements of what a person believes do not directly state value concepts, but they imply them.

Equality
    STATED: *Equal* pay for *equal* work
    IMPLIED: Women deserve the same pay as men for the same work.

Science
    STATED: DNA research is a *scientific* triumph.
    IMPLIED: DNA research is virtually unquestionable.

Self-respect
    STATED: Every child's well-being is based on *self respect.*
    IMPLIED: Children need to learn to like themselves.

When you directly and frequently state value concepts you are more intensive in your use of values than if you imply values only through indirect statement. The closing argument of a trial frequently is more value intensive than is the examination of witnesses. In the legal sphere, the emphasis in the trial is on getting facts, which, along with other values that arise, is deliberately muted. The closing arguments of a trial provide more freedom for an attorney to openly attach values to the evidence.

Positive and Negative Values

Our definition of a value as "a conception of the desirable" puts a clearly positive cast on value concepts. However, for every positive concept there is at least one antithesis. So a statement of a value can be either positive or negative. Freedom opposes restraint, thrift opposes waste, knowledge opposes ignorance, pleasure opposes pain. Depending upon the strategy devised, if you argue against a specific proposal, you may do so by identifying positive values that oppose it or negative values that you associate with it. As a critic of argument you will want to note the extent to which an arguer focuses on either negative or positive values. You also need to ask yourself if a negative or positive emphasis tells you something about the nature of the argumentation.

Terminal and Instrumental Values

Values will reflect the ends a person admires (wealth, health, happiness, security) or the means to attain the ends (hard work, faith, helpfulness, responsibility). Milton Rokeach called these "terminal and instrumental values" (*Beliefs* 160). He also found the terminal values to be the most central to an individual's value system (*Nature* 215).

A caution is necessary on that point, however. People frequently make a terminal out of an instrumental value. For instance, they recognize that they must work hard (means) to achieve economic security (end), but for many people hard work becomes an end in itself. Retired people with secure financial situations frequently work hard at whatever they do because work has become a terminal value for them. For the scientist, a carefully worked out experiment brings pleasure. For the religious person, faith becomes more than a means to salvation; it is an end in itself.

Instrumental values such as hard work or faith sometimes become terminal values. Even so, it is worthwhile to remember the distinction when you are building and analyzing arguments.

Rokeach identified eighteen terminal and eighteen instrumental values, and while his lists are not exhaustive, they provide an understanding of possible terminal and instrumental value concepts (*Nature* 28).

Abstract and Concrete Values

A value is a conception, so it would seem that values are abstract. Words such as *freedom, justice,* and *truth* represent value concepts in society. However, there are also times when particular people, groups, institutions, or objects

---

TERMINAL VALUES

1. A comfortable life	10. Inner harmony
2. An exciting life	11. Mature love
3. A sense of accomplishment	12. National security
4. A world at peace	13. Pleasure
5. A world of beauty	14. Salvation
6. Equality	15. Self-respect
7. Family security	16. Social recognition
8. Freedom	17. True friendship
9. Happiness	18. Wisdom

INSTRUMENTAL VALUES

1. Ambition	10. Imagination
2. Broad-mindedness	11. Independence
3. Capability	12. Intellect
4. Cheerfulness	13. Logic
5. Cleanliness	14. Love
6. Courage	15. Obedience
7. Forgiveness	16. Politeness
8. Helpfulness	17. Responsibility
9. Honesty	18. Self-control

The instrumental values in this list have been adapted from Rokeach's original list to make them all nouns like his terminal values.

serve as values. These are called *concrete values* (Perelman and Olbrichts-Tyteca 77). The flag, the family, the Pope, the Star of David, and the Constitution are all concrete yet they are value concepts. The Constitution is a good illustration. It is an actual document, but in an argument it has all the power of an abstract value.

A statement that a law is unconstitutional is as value-laden for most people as it is to say that the law denies freedom. In a court of law, violation of the Constitution is a more forceful value argument than restriction of freedom. Civil justice frequently limits freedom. You have to leash your dog, drive at 20 miles per hour through a school zone, and restrict your speech when it maliciously damages another. However, no law can acceptably violate the Constitution. The Constitution is to American legal argument what God (another concrete value for believers) is to religious argument.

Abstract and concrete values work together. For instance, to use authority figures as support is to use concrete values. However, you don't say to a friend, "I believe we should study harder because my father says so." You are more likely to argue "we should study harder. My father says it will lead to greater success." The abstract value of "success" is linked to the concrete value of "father." The realization that abstract and concrete values work together leads us to another: that values, abstract and concrete, terminal and instrumental, positive and negative, stated and implied, work in systems.

VALUES APPEAR IN SYSTEMS

Values do not appear alone in argumentation. They appear in value systems, that is, as a set of linked claims. Clyde Kluckhohn calls these "value orientations . . . generalized and organized conceptions . . . of the desirable and non desirable" ("Values" 411). We hear people argue for better treatment of Native Americans, not on the basis of a single value of justice or mercy, but on the basis of a series of values that link together and reflect a unified system in which each value will be perceived as compatible with every other. Indeed, one of our major arguments over values is over the compatibility of values in a system. People are charged with inconsistency if they argue for their own freedom and discriminate against minorities. We know of people who wonder how someone can oppose legalizing marijuana and still drink alcohol. Some people consider it inconsistent to argue for morality and deny a belief in God. Others find it inconsistent to support capital punishment but oppose abortion.

These are examples of arguments about the consistency of values in a given system. They come about because values do not stand alone. They work in integrated systems. The theoretical and experimental literature supports the idea there is a limited and distinct group of value systems. There are many potential value patterns, Rokeach says, but the number will be limited because of the social factors involved (*Beliefs* 161).

In an extensive study of the value systems across cultures, Charles Morris found a dominant pattern of American value systems, although different from the value systems in other cultures (44).

Traditional Value Systems

There are several acknowledged American value systems that scholars from a wide variety of fields identify (Kluckhohn, *Mirror* 228–61; Morris 185; Ruesch 94–134; Steele and Redding 83–91; Weaver 211–32). To illustrate, we will examine one value system that is probably the dominant value system in American politics and government, the enlightenment value system.

America became a nation in the period of the Enlightenment. That was a new intellectual era based on the writings of scientists such as Sir Isaac Newton and philosophers such as John Locke. The Declaration of Independence is the epitome of an enlightenment document. In many ways America is an enlightenment nation, and if enlightenment is not the predominant value system, it surely is first among equals.

The enlightenment position stems from the belief that there is an ordered world where all activity is governed by laws similar to the laws of physics. These "natural laws" may or may not come from God, depending on the particular orientation of the person examining them, but enlightenment thinkers theorized that people could discover these laws by themselves. Thus, people may worship God for God's greatness, even acknowledge that God created the universe and natural laws, but they find out about the universe because they have the powers of observation and reason. The laws of nature are harmonious, and one can use reason to discover them all. They also can provide for a better life.

Restraints on humans must be limited because they are essentially moral and reasonable. Occasionally, people act foolishly and must be restrained by society. However, a person should never be restrained in matters of the mind. Reason must be free. Thus, government is an agreement among individuals to assist the society to protect rights. That government is a democracy. Certain rights are inalienable, and they may not be abridged: "among these are life, liberty, and the pursuit of happiness." Arguments for academic freedom, against wiretaps, and for scientific inquiry come from this value system.

Some of the words representing concepts from the enlightenment value system are:

POSITIVE: freedom, science, nature, rationality, democracy, fact, liberty, individualism, knowledge, intelligence, reason, natural rights, natural laws, progress, information

NEGATIVE: ignorance, superstition, inattention, thoughtlessness, error, indecision, irrationality, dictatorship, bookburning, falsehood, regression

People use the enlightenment value system in a wide variety of spheres and situations. They make judgments about the desirable in science, in politics, and in everyday life. All value systems, like the enlightenment system, are a set of linked claims about desirable ends and means. But the values in a system are more than linked to one another. Their relationship to one another is defined by a value hierarchy. In a particular argumentative situation, the values in a system are graded.

Values Are Graded in Systems

A particular set of decision makers is defined by the value system to which it adheres. Many Americans follow what we will call a personal success value system. For many Americans, family, career, health, self-respect, satisfaction, freedom of choice, accomplishment, material possessions, friendship, and similar values are most important (Gallup and Newport). The personal success value system represents Americans as success-oriented in an individual way that would not be found in other cultures (e.g., the Japanese culture).

However, as natural as such a value system is to Americans, it cannot be used in a particular argumentative situation until it has some kind of order to it. Any two values potentially contradict one another. A person may value both family and career as a part of personal success. Yet an argument can be made that career can interfere with family. The argument between Jeff and Joan, cited in Chapter 1, is this kind of value conflict. In such a case the two values are not just part of a value system; they have to be understood in relation to one another and the solution in this case involved using both (see p. 4).

"A particular audience," says Chaim Perelman and L. Olbrechts-Tyteca "is characterized less by what values it accepts than by the way it grades them." If you think of decision makers' values in isolation, independent of interrelationships, you "may neglect the question of their hierarchy, which solves the conflicts between them" (81–82; Walker and Sillars 141–45). Therefore, a claim that two parents should cut back on their work schedules to spend more time with their children is a matter of emphasizing family over career without denying the legitimacy of either value. Such an argument also may mean a lower rank in the hierarchy of other personal success values, such as material possessions.

Values, therefore, are concepts of the desirable ends and actions that are stated directly or implied. They are stated positively or negatively. They are terminal or instrumental, abstract or concrete. They are found in clusters that are value systems and, when applied to a particular situation, are graded to reveal their relative significance, one to another. With this understanding you are ready to see how you may use values in the argumentative situation.

GENERAL PRINCIPLES FOR THE USE OF VALUES

Because they are so basic to argumentation, values are essential both for criticizing the arguments of others and developing your own arguments. In this section we will examine seven principles for using values in argument. The first three apply most directly to criticizing the arguments of others. The last four are principles that will aid you in developing your own arguments.

Values May Be Found Anywhere in an Argument

We have already observed that there are no value-free arguments. Any part of an argument can state values. Some arguments may be made up completely of claims and subclaims that openly state values. In this example all the parts of the argument contain direct, positive values.

(Grounds) ————————————▶ *(Claim)*
You learn more when you study [Therefore] You should study
hard. hard..

(Warrant)

[Since] Learning is important.

Although such a value-intensive argument is possible, it is not a likely argument. In most arguments many values will be implied, not stated, and in some arguments, warrants or grounds will not be stated. Yet to function as a critic of arguments (your own or others) you will need to be aware that values may be found anywhere. You need to understand where an argument fits in a value system. You can do that only by actively looking for an argument's values.

As an arguer, you must be aware that you may be challenged at any time to state unstated values. That is a good reason for you to be aware of the values from which you argue. Two people are arguing. One says "The national economy is improving because unemployment is dropping." The other says "The national economy is worsening because the federal debt is increasing." Both claims can be supported. What is at issue is a conflict between work (employment) as a value and solvency (lack of debt) as a value. If you were one of these debaters, you would need to be aware of the unstated value you were defending because your opponent might call upon you to defend it.

Recognize Values in Warrants

Warrants are the most likely place to find values. Their role in an argument is to justify the reasoned movement from the grounds to the claim. Justification is clearly a value-using procedure.

The debate over the protection of wildlife has centered around the Endangered Species Act (ESA). Those who oppose the act claim that the ESA violates private property, hurts the economy, and wastes tax money. A strong argument is also made that it doesn't work. This claim is supported by a study by Charles Mann and Mark Plummer in their book *Noah's Choice: The Future of Endangered Species*. Their studies show that "by the end of 1994, only 21 species had been struck from the list, and of those 21, only 6 were delisted because they had gained enough ground to warrant removal." Others were removed from the list because they became extinct or were not endangered in

the first place. Even several of those whose status improved did not do so because of the ESA (Carpenter 43).

(Grounds) ──────────────────────▶ *(Claim)*
In 22 years until 1995 only 6   [Therefore] The Endangered
    species had been removed   Species Act is a failure.
    from the endangered cate-
    gory.

Some of those can be attributed to
    other reasons than ESA.

(Backing)
Charles Mann and Mark
Plummer study

(Warrant)
[Since] More than a questionable 6 in 22 years would be
needed to indicate success

(Backing)
The value of success

Those who argue for the Endangered Species Act claim that improvement has
to be measured not only by delisting but by other factors. Their argument is
really about how success is defined and the value of success remains central to
the controversy.

Find the Values in the Arguments of Others

Before you can decide whether to accept or refute arguments of others you
need to find the values they use. Here is a specific list of tools.

1. Look for specific language that directly states values.
   a. A statement ["I believe in *honesty.*"]
   b. A word [*freedom, truth, nature*].
2. Look for negative terms [*waste, immoral, filth*].
3. Look for concrete values.
4. Look for indirect values ["Vaccination is essential for all children" or "A
   cure must be found for AIDS" (health)].
5. Look for absent values that you might expect to find ["The purpose of
   government is to protect life and property."] (Why have liberty and the

pursuit of happiness been left out and property added to the traditional values of the Declaration of Independence?)]

6. Look for other factors that indicate values.
   a. Statistical evidence (science)
   b. Testimony of authorities who represent values [the Pope, Marx, Jefferson]
   c. Heroes and villians of stories
   d. Stylistic evidence [biblical, African American, or scientific style]

When you examine someone's argument with these tools you will have a good idea of the values in the arguer's value system.

Recognize the Limits of Value Change

Before you develop a case, you must think seriously about exactly what value changes you wish decision makers to make. Nicholas Rescher has pointed out that value changes usually take place by: (1) making a value more or less widely distributed within the society; (2) changing its relative importance to another value; (3) altering the range of a value's application; and (4) raising or lowering what one expects a particular value to mean when applied to a specific belief (14–16). These four options all have to do with shifts in the hierarchy, in application, and in the meaning of a value. None involve the almost impossible act of changing values by adding a new one or dropping an existing one.

The current public controversy over abortion is irresolvable so long as it is seen as a conflict between two prominent values in our society—life ("pro-life") and freedom ("pro-choice").

It is virtually impossible for the "pro-life" forces to accept the "pro-choice" position, and vice versa. Yet neither side denies the other's value. The pro-life position says a woman had a choice when she got pregnant, and the pro-choice group argues that quality of life must be considered, not just physical life. But, it can be argued, a woman did not have a choice in the case of rape, and the life of the mother is important. Also, there are arguments about when life actually begins.

Although the abortion debate is a rare case of two values in direct clash, there are modifications. Two proposed solutions have been to limit abortions to the first trimester or to cases of rape, incest, health of the mother, or severe fetal deformity. If either of these was generally accepted it would represent Rescher's third condition, altering the range of application. The first trimester proposal limits life to after the first trimester. The second proposal limits the freedom to choose abortion.

Some pro-choice advocates argue that life is important and abortion is wrong, but government should not interfere with the individual's right to choose. They are trying to change the relative importance of life and choice. Returning the issue to the states would be an attempt to change the distribution of the values of life and choice in the society. People are not likely to give up either value. Any resolution to satisfy both sides seems impossible. Perhaps it is. If there is to be general adherence to either position it will come, not with the extermination of one value or another, but by one of the four adaptations indicated above. If not, no matter what happens in courts and legislatures, the debate over abortion will continue to be unresolved.

Find the Best Point of Attack on Values

The method for analyzing claims of fact or value discussed in chapter 3 is used to determine the best point to attack value claims. First, you must determine what values support the claim. Second, you must determine what criteria to use in judging those values. Third, you must determine how to grade the values (Tuman).

Traditional journalistic standards, published in places like the Society of Professional Journalists' Code of Ethics, reveal a value system that has been labeled "accurate interpretation." That value system maintains that journalists should be truthful, communicate information, be objective, be fair, support freedom, and accept responsibility (Sillars, *Messages* 49–57).

FAIR (Fairness and Accuracy in Reporting) is a liberal journalistic organization like the conservative one Accuracy in Media (AIM). (You might note that both groups use terms out of this value system in their names.) FAIR published an analysis of conservative radio and television talk show host Rush Limbaugh subtitled "Rush Limbaugh Debates Reality." That he is objective, even Limbaugh would deny, but he does claim to be truthful and give people information ("I do not lie on this program"). He also believes that he supports freedom. He claims to accept responsibility (". . . if I find out that I have been mistaken . . . I proclaim it . . . at the beginning of a program—or as loudly as I can"). FAIR argues that Limbaugh is neither truthful nor fair. Those two values are the basis of their criticism of Limbaugh.

FAIR's criteria for truthfulness are quite strong. They claim that Limbaugh takes factual situations and draws untruthful conclusions. For instance, they claim that he says that human use of fluorocarbons does not destroy the ozone. It is a theory, says Limbaugh, developed by "environmental wackos," "dunderheaded alarmists," and "prophets of doom." To support his argument, he claims that volcanoes, like Mount Pinatubo, cause more ozone depletion by a thousand times "than all the fluorocarbons manufactured by wicked, diabolical, and insensitive corporations in history." FAIR cites the journal *Science*, to claim that chlorine from natural causes, such as volcanoes, is soluble and, therefore, rain prevents it from getting to the upper atmosphere to release the carbons. FAIR also quotes an atmospheric chemist at the University of California, Irvine, who says "Natural causes of ozone depletion are not significant." FAIR contrasts these experts with Limbaugh's expert who they claim is Rogelio Maduro who only has a bachelor's degree in geology (10–11). The criterion for judging truthfulness in FAIR's analysis is clearly the quality of the scientific supporters.

An example of their criticism on the value of fairness is Limbaugh's use of a joke reported by columnist Molly Ivins. On his TV show Limbaugh is said to have told this joke: "Everyone knows the Clinton's have a cat. Socks is the White House Cat. But did you know that there is a White House dog?" Then he showed a picture of Chelsea Clinton. The insult is seen as unfair, in part at least, because it is personal, not issue oriented, and is directed at a 13-year-old (17). In this case the traditional journalistic values apply and FAIR has chosen to emphasize and provide criteria for judging two of them.

Such a system, Joseph H. Tuman observes, leads to five alternative attack points on such an argument:

1. Dispute the values
   (Ex: "Fairness doesn't apply when attacking an evil").
2. Concede the values and hierarchy but dispute the criteria
   (Ex: "The comment about Chelsea was just a joke").
3. Concede the value and criteria but dispute the hierarchy
   (Ex: "The most important criterion is supporting freedom").
4. Concede the value but dispute the criteria and hierarchy
   (Ex: "There is a more important criterion for judging truth. These so-called experts are part of the "agenda-oriented scientific community").
5. Dispute all
   (Ex: "Fairness is an inappropriate value in this case and even were it appropriate, attacking a joke doesn't make sense and freedom is more important than either of these values") (93).

Obviously, the first and fifth alternatives are ones people would seldom use because, as we have already noted, values change very slowly. Still, this example illustrates how to challenge value claims. The three middle attacks (dispute the criteria, dispute the hierarchy, or both) are the most likely points at which Limbaugh supporters could attack the FAIR argument.

Relate Your Values to Decision Makers

The limited options of value dispute point to the role of the decision makers' values in making successful arguments. Adherence is most likely when the values in your arguments are ones that relate to decision makers. To achieve this you must pay close attention to the particular social group to which decision makers belong. Values are social, shared among the members of particular groups. Indeed, to a large extent, interaction among the members of a group defines the value system and its potential hierarchy. This is true of all kinds of groups: social, political, religious. It is true of families, and it is true of gangs. The values of your family (e.g., love, respect, cooperation, security) are positive to you because you are a member of that group. You probably think that gangs who hang out, get in fights over turf, bully people, and threaten authority are negative. To much of society, they are. The gang members, however, have defined their values much as your family has, and their values are positive to them. They see themselves, perhaps, as strong, proud, and standing up for their rights with members providing love, respect, cooperation, and security for one another. They reject the right of others to interfere with their freedom.

Although gangs probably will not be your audience, this example illustrates how groups define what values are positive, and link their beliefs and actions to these positive values. If you were to make an argument to change the behavior of gangs, you would need to start with the values they have (e.g.,

---

EXAMINING A VALUE SYSTEM

1. What *proportion* of a value system is represented by negative or positive values, abstract or concrete values, terminal or instrumental values, stated or implied values?
2. What *emphasis* does the value system have? How value intensive is it? What values are most salient?
3. How *consistent* are the values within the system?
4. How *significant* are the values in the system to the decision makers?

---

pride) and link that pride to socially acceptable behavior rather than anti-social behavior. You are not likely to change decision makers' values, but you can use the values they have to move toward a revised interpretation of them.

Use Evidence and Argument to Develop Values

We can talk about values by identifying specific words that reflect these values (e.g., *freedom, work, happiness, reason, salvation*). However, you need to keep in mind that you communicate values by the evidence and argument you use more than by direct statement. This is what we mean by *implied values*. Rather than telling someone that your argument is "reasonable" or "factual," demonstrate that it is. Remember the old writing dictum: "Show, don't tell." Direct statements make more value-intensive arguments. There are times when you will want to make your arguments value intensive. However, for most of your argumentation, values will usually be communicated by evidence and argument.

There are recent studies indicating that while people hold values such as those we have discussed in this chapter, they do not hold them in clearly defined systems. They live in a "fragmented intellectual culture" and a "fragmented popular culture" (Bellah, et al. 282–83). In the words of Conal Furay, Americans "dance around their values" (19). While individuals and groups can frequently identify values, they do not use them in a fully rational fashion. Consequently, care must be taken in stating values in too absolute a manner.

You need to make clear to decision makers that your values are their values, but if you overuse values you will make your case too obvious and open it to rejection.

Earlier we used the example of the controversy over the influence of the media on children. Newton N. Minow, Professor at Northwestern University and the former Chair of the Federal Communications Commission who labeled television a "vast wasteland" told his listeners what a child can find after school on TV programs in one week. Here are some of his examples:

A 13-year-old girl who has slept with 20 men
Transsexual prostitutes
Parents who hate their daughters' boyfriends

> Girlfriends who want too much sex
> White supremacists who hate Mexicans
> A woman who tried to kill herself nine times
> Sadomasochistic couples
> Dad by day, cross-dresser by night

In this partial excerpt there are a number of negative values used and most are unstated, but they are implied by these examples: sexual promiscuity, violation of childhood, hatred, racism, suicide, violation of family.

Making value-based arguments and examining the arguments of others involves finding values, understanding the limits of value change, learning to find a point of attack, and relating values to decision makers. However, these practices are tempered by a realization that value systems will differ from sphere to sphere.

SPHERE DEPENDENCE OF VALUES

Probably no other function of argumentation defines spheres so well as values. We have defined a sphere as a group of persons whose interstructured, repetitive, and therefore predictable patterns of communicative behaviors are used in the production and evaluation of argumentation. The criteria by which a group of people in a sphere appraise arguments form a value system. People are not admitted seriously to the sphere unless they have appropriate credentials (e.g., JD, MD, a successful election, ordination, a PhD in the right discipline). The permitted evidence, as we noted in chapter 7, is regulated by the criteria of the sphere. The preferred kinds of argument, how one argues, and appropriate language all depend on the criteria of that sphere. These criteria make up a system of values. So in one sense, a sphere is defined by its system of values.

Science and religion are two spheres that have frequently been at odds with one another. A comparison of the values in these two spheres helps to make their disagreements clearer. It is not just that their claims are sometimes at issue, but their defining values are much different.

Values in Scientific Argument

Scientific argument, as we use the term here (and in chapter 8), refers to those disciplines that use the physical sciences as a model to explain how physical, biological, human, and social entities function and interact. We mean to exclude humanistic study (literature, history, qualitative analysis) that aims at understanding individual phenomena. Scientific argument can be characterized by the values of order, usefulness, prediction, rationality, and knowledge.

Order in Science What we have called scientific argument assumes there is some *order* in phenomena. This means that a scientist builds "a world picture"

(Toulmin, Rieke, and Janik 328–30). Thus, scientific argumentation is judged by how well it can prove that the theory explains all related phenomena. Any sign that there is an inconsistency between one explanation and another must be accounted for or the explanation is deficient.

Scientists assume an order to data when they argue that one set of data will identify the natural state of related phenomena. For example, a social scientist will claim that an experimental examination of one group of children will provide a generalization about all similar children.

It is the rupture of order that interests scientists. A communication researcher discovers that TV takes up a good deal of a child's time until age 14. Then viewing time drops off sharply. Why? Because other factors interfere? Because parents monitor TV viewing more? Because TV programming is less interesting to teenagers? One does not decide to develop a theory about something that is explained by current theories. Theories are developed to explain a phenomenon that is different, and by developing or revising a theory to explain the change and accommodate the previous lack of change order is returned to the sphere.

Usefulness in Science   Closely related to order is the value of *usefulness*. If order is sustained by research then it is useful because it can be applied at other places and other times, the assumption goes. When a theory, no matter how much order it has, ceases to be useful, it is abandoned for another theory of greater usefulness.

Anthropologists in the nineteenth century considered it useful to know if people of different races and social status had different shapes and sizes to their heads. They used calipers to measure head sizes to explain their perceived differences in achievements. They believed that head size represented brain size and, thus, factors such as intelligence, social action, and language.

Today, serious social scientists consider such measurement humorous because the theory that used head size to determine intelligence has been rejected. There is a similar debate today over whether the Graduate Record Examination is a useful predictor of success in graduate school. Thirty years from now the GRE may be as useless as determining graduate school admission on the basis of hat size.

Prediction in Science   Implied in both order and usefulness is the value of *prediction*. It means that the theory represented in a claim will tell one not merely about the instance under consideration but it will predict how similar instances will occur. The theory of evolution is a good example of such a claim. It does not merely claim that a particular biological species changes. It predicts that all biological species evolve. It claims that they have evolved, are evolving, and will evolve according to certain principles. It asserts a high level of predictability. It is a forceful theory.

Rationality in Science   Although an ambiguous term, *rationality* is the clearest way to explain this value. It relates directly to the assumption that order exists.

Abraham Kaplan distinguishes between what he calls "logic-in-use," which describes the actual patterns of thinking used by scientists and "reconstructed logic," which describes the discourse through which scholars justify their conclusions (8–18). In the process of discovery, says Kaplan, imagination, inspiration, and intuition play an enormous role, but the discoveries must be justified to other scientists by reconstructing the imagination, inspiration, and intuition into a rational explanation that other scientists can follow and test as an intellectually coherent commentary. The rational explanation must provide a set of refined practices based on empirical evidence for the justification of claims.

Knowledge in Science   Nonprofessionals frequently describe science as the search for "scientific truth." Medical science has had a strong influence on this kind of thinking by suggesting there are certain diseases that it is learning to conquer one by one. Curiously, there is always plenty to work on, even after hundreds of years of conquest. A better term than *scientific truth* for this value is *verifiable knowledge*: an extended explanation based upon repeated attempts to justify related claims. Scientists seek knowledge that when lodged in theories links to the other values. It gives order to the subject under study and predicts what other useful knowledge may be known. Knowledge, then, is not some once-and-for-all final truth. Rather, science as Toulmin puts it, makes "the course of Nature not just predictable but intelligible—and this has meant looking for rational patterns of connections in terms of which we can make sense of the flux of events" (99).

The values of science identified here (order, usefulness, prediction, rationality, and knowledge) only begin to define the scientific value system. In addition, there are adaptations in the value system from one scientific discipline to another. Nonetheless, these five identify the system well enough to be used to contrast it with another major system: religion.

Values in Religion

Arguments about religion are surely as old as recorded history and as recent as today's newspaper. Because we write primarily for people in western society, this chapter discusses the religions in the Hebraic tradition: Judaism, Christianity, and Islam. These religions, George Kennedy has observed, are all highly verbal (120). As such, their values are clearly stated.

The existence of a wide variety of religious groups holding different theological interpretations makes it difficult to identify a specific set of values. Not all religious argumentation will cover all seven values we will discuss here, and other values are sometimes added. These seven, however, reasonably define the theological system: God; authority; human beings; moral behavior; faith; salvation; and the church.

God   The most forceful value in the Judeo-Christian-Islamic theological value system is the concrete value of God. God is understood as an entity of some kind with complete control over the world and all who inhabit it. For some, God controls every action. For others, such as deists, God is the source of natural law who sets the system into motion. In Christianity, God is frequently understood to consist of a trinity—Father, Son, and Holy Ghost—in which the son, Jesus Christ, is seen as a primary source for the understanding of the religion. So people speak of a "Christ centered religion" to define the value of God.

The three religions of the Hebraic tradition are monotheistic—they believe in one God—although some, such as Christian Trinitarians have one God in three persons. This one God, therefore, is all powerful and all knowing. God is usually perceived as an eternal father figure, judge, and provider.

Authority   At least in the religions of the Hebraic tradition, the starting point of most religious argumentation is an authoritative text, the Torah, the Bible, and the Koran being the most obvious examples. For the faithful, these books provide authoritative statements whose interpretations are the basis of argumentation. Robert Grant observes of Christian theology, "the interpretation of scripture is the principal bond between the life and thought of the Church and the documents which contain its earliest traditions" (9). This explains the desire among religious writers to find the earliest texts, those that are closest to the actual statements and actions of the originators of the religion.

Conflicts over the criteria for judging texts abound in theological argument. Conservative Protestants believe the Bible to be inherently and literally true. More liberal Protestants accept the Bible as metaphor in many cases. Roman Catholicism uses specialized analysis to explain the meaning of Biblical texts. For most Christians, the New Testament is more significant than the Old Testament. For Jews, of course, the Old Testament—the Torah—is the authoritative text. These differences among interpretive versions clearly illustrate the importance of authoritative texts to religious argumentation.

Although there are differences in emphasis and interpretation, all the religions of the Hebraic tradition are text based. For the conservative Protestant, for instance, almost as important to the understanding of religion as "Christ centered" (the value of God) is that it be "Bible based" (the value of authoritative text).

Humans   There is general agreement in the religions of the Hebraic tradition that humans are more important than other animals. But, do humans get this status from nature? From the ability to reason? From their possession of a soul? Thus, a persistent question in religious argumentation is about the basic nature of the human.

Despite all the disagreement about the nature of humans, the religions of this tradition clearly value humans over earth, sea, air, and all other creatures. God loves humans above all others, speaks to humans, designs laws by which humans are to live, and gives dominion to humans over everything else in the world:

> And God blessed them [Adam and Eve], and God said unto them, be fruitful, and multiply, and replenish the earth, and subdue it: and have dominion over the fish of the sea, and over the fowl of the air, and over every living thing that moveth on the earth (Genesis 2:28).

Moral Behavior   Knowing what is right and wrong is a value related to the value of humans. Some theologians argue that there are specific tests to discover what is morally right for a religious person. The *Catholic Catechism* says:

> The moral quality of our actions derives from three different sources, each so closely connected with the other that unless all three are simultaneously good the object performed is morally bad. . . . The object of the act must be good. . . . Circumstances . . . can make an otherwise good object evil. . . . Finally, the end or purpose . . . also affects the moral situation (Hardon 283–84).

Others would argue that determining religious morality is more complicated and more tentative than this statement implies.

There are also specific issues of interpretation. An important example is in the interpretation of the basic law, "You shall not kill." Is this law an absolute injunction against any form of killing? Animals? Fetuses? Criminals? Enemies in war? Such differences do not detract from the existence of the value of moral behavior in religious argumentation.

Faith   Faith is an instrumental value unique to religion. It extends human reason beyond rational observation. To it is linked the "power of prayer," the ability of the believer to communicate with God. Faith in God and faith in prayer are vital links between God and humans. Faith provides an important function of answering questions that fill in the gaps of traditional knowledge (e.g., Is there a God? Does God answer prayer? Is there life after death?).

Many acknowledge, try to learn about, and stand in awe of the deity. Others believe that God is very personal, and through prayer and other sacraments one can communicate with God. Some claim they actually talk directly with a divine being as if they were carrying on a conversation. Some believe that such communication marks a human as a special person, a prophet, for instance.

While in a Nazi prison in 1943, Dietrich Bonhoeffer, a German Protestant theologian, wrote to his parents of a more socially oriented idea of faith as the language of God:

> I have also been considering again the strange story of the gift of Tongues. That the confusion of tongues at the Tower of Babel, as a result of which people can no longer understand each other . . . should at last be brought to an end and overcome by the language of God, which everyone understands and through which alone people can understand each other again, . . . (Woelfel 197).

However one looks at it, faith that allows for this relationship of human to God is a very special and important value in any system of religious argumentation.

Salvation   For some people salvation is the most important issue in theology, because it is the most important benefit one receives from belief and its absence is the most horrible punishment. Others view it as less important or even personally nonexistent. They concentrate on the personal and social benefits of living a moral life on earth. Salvation can be seen as social, that is, the immortality of society. In such a view, individuals live on in what they contribute to others or through their children. Judaism has a concept of immortality, but it is a spiritual union with

God. There is no resurrection of the body, no physical torment for sinners, no pleasures. There is little detail one can discover about a Jewish heaven. It is not a place but a state of mind. Such a view is much less specific than the view held by most Christians or Moslems (Cohen 34–36).

Yet immortality is an important value in much of the Christian and Islamic world. For some it is a gift of faith and a very literal place. It is more than a spiritual condition for those people; it is an earned reward for a lifetime of following the other values in this system.

The Church   As immortality is a value that some put little stock in, so is the concrete value of the church. In Islam there is no church. Religious leaders come from the people, and they get their status from their ability to gain the adherence of others. Jews and evangelical Christians hold a similar view. Rabbis and ministers are chosen and dismissed by the congregation. The church is either an individual congregation or a loose confederation of individual congregations.

For Roman Catholics and some Protestant denominations, on the other hand, the church is an essential agency of the religion. Tradition is very important in Catholicism. To avoid error, the church interprets what God's word means. Members of the church become a part of something greater than what they are. There is a sense in which all members of religions in the Hebraic tradition are members of a spiritual church. *Islam, Judaism*, and *Christianity* are terms representing more than a series of values. They see themselves as a fellowship of believers.

This discussion of religious values has been brief, but it points out that any theology is a case that must be built using a value system from interpreting and grading these values. The decisions one makes on one value will affect what is possible for another. Thus, if humans are incapable of making proper decisions some agency, such as the church or direct fellowship with God, must be available to do so. The nature of God affects the nature of fellowship with God. How one interprets immortality relates to the nature of humans. These are only a few examples of how building a case for a particular theology involves the interrelationship of these values.

The Relation of Science and Religion

We have examined these two spheres of argumentation (science and religion) to illustrate how different two value systems can be. None of the value terms of one are found in the other. Religion, unlike science, has concrete values as four of its seven values (God, authority, humans, the church). In some ways science has the most abstract value system of all. Its five primary values (order, usefulness, rationality, prediction, and knowledge) are abstract. The only terminal value for science is knowledge and the usual terminal values for religion are God and salvation. How then do they coexist? An examination of the relationship between these two rival value systems provides a useful example of how values interact across spheres.

These two value systems have been the subject of controversy for many years. Early disciples of science, such as Copernicus and Galileo, found themselves in disputes with the Roman Catholic Church. In 1633 Galileo was forced to recant the publication of his belief in the Copernican theory, that the earth rotates on its axis and, with the other planets in the solar system, revolves around the sun. The basis for judging the Copernican theory a Christian heresy was the authority of the Church and the Bible that, taken literally, says that the sun revolves around the earth (Genesis 114–18; Joshua 10: 12–14). This controversy between religion and science can be extended far beyond the Copernican theory. However, the controversy illustrates at least a clash of values between the scientific values of rationality and knowledge and the religious values for authority in sacred text and Church.

For many people the sharp contrast in value systems between science and religion makes the two fundamentally antagonistic. For a natural system of order, there is the counterpart of God and the centrality of humans. Prediction is opposed by faith and salvation. Rationality is opposed by authority in sacred texts and the interpretation of the church. Accepting one value system can make the other its secondary value system. For instance, deists acknowledge God as a first cause. For them God created the universe with natural laws, wound it up like a clock, and set it to working. That working of the universe is rational because God's principles are rational. The scientific value system is, therefore, the dominant one because humans are to be scientists continually unraveling those laws. There are no miracles, answered prayers, or moral laws that are not rational and predictable. Faith is in the process, and the church is an institution that helps us to understand this gloriously ordered system.

The second way of using both value systems, and the one most interesting to us here, is to acknowledge the existence of two spheres of argument that can complement one another. For such persons, scientific order, rationality, and predictability is maintained and explained as science. God's role is with humans, morality, and salvation that cannot be explained by science because it is in a different argument sphere. An occasional miracle, for instance when prayer saves someone from a predicted death from disease, is just that—an occasional event. It is to be celebrated as an act of God but it does not refute the essential validity of scientific order. Neither does scientific rationality refute God, because God, operating in a sphere where science cannot argue, is the first cause of natural law.

Such a separation between spheres is not unusual. The separation of religion and science is one of the most dramatic, having received considerable attention, but the same is true with other spheres. Literary scholarship following a humanistic qualitative orientation can be seen as a different sphere and, therefore, not in conflict with behavioral psychology. Law and morality are frequently separated. Someone may not be seen to have broken the law but to have broken a moral code. Examples abound of people avoiding conflict by separating the values they live by into spheres of argumentation.

However, when spheres of argument are seen to overlap, serious value problems occur. In 1991, A. J. S. Rayl and K. T. McKinney asked scientists if science proves that God exists. Many argue that the question remains outside the sphere of scientific argumentation, but a few did not. One mathematical physicist said, "If science can't reach God, then God doesn't exist" (44). Such a point of view represents a total commitment to the scientific value system. This can be seen in his further statement: "Nature will tell us what sort of definition we have to use. . . . Matters of science are not open to opinion. . . . Physical evidence could greatly alter our view of God, but we need to redefine God in terms of physics, which won't be easy" (44–48).

Statements such as these clearly indicate that this mathematician believes that an argument about anything, even something as total as God, has to be argued by the values of science.

A similar situation occurs in the area of creation science. The Creation Science Association is a research and teaching organization that claims to provide scientific proof through research that the literal six day creation of the earth stated in Genesis is scientifically correct. However, one careful examination of their arguments shows that the proof is clearly based on textual authority, God, and faith. David Klope shows the relationship of science and religious values in one presentation of the Institute of Creation Research's "Worldview":

> In the transcendent portion of the ICR worldview "creation" and "revelation" have priority over "science," . . . The emphasis in this entire speech is that defense of "creation" comes first from the Bible, and the speech tries to show the ICR as acting in this manner through phrases such as "what we're saying at the Institute for Creation Research is this: look, we have a revelation from God who knows everything. . . . " Sequentially this priority is even enacted in the speech: Ham [the speaker] begins the speech by citing a Bible verse, and the entire first half of the speech involves primarily Biblical issues. Although the ICR maintains the value of "science," they are careful to prioritize theology. In this view a "creationist" must first be Biblical (123–24).

Some people, therefore, can bring these two spheres together but they do so mostly by acknowledging that each deals with different issues. When spheres come together and claim to deal with the same subject, however, it is clear that argument becomes the unusual case we noted earlier of a direct clash of values.

Religion and science are quite different spheres. They do not share values. There are many ways in which argumentation in these two spheres is quite different. They can work together if one is made secondary to the other. More likely, they will work together when they are clearly seen as being different spheres of argumentation. People must see that each has its place, subject matter, and method to answer different questions. In such a situation textual authority and faith, for instance, give answers to questions science cannot answer about moral life and salvation. Such values are compatible with order and rationality for they have their own order and rationality. Scientific values of order and rationality in such a situation have their own authority and faith.

When people do not accept such a separation the clash between the two value systems can become total. As you move into arguing issues in these spheres and other spheres where conflicting values exist, you need to keep this potential clash in mind. You need to consider where your decision makers stand and in which sphere they are likely to find their value warrants.

CONCLUSION

Values are an essential part of the analysis of every argumentative situation. They share with evidence and source credibility the grounds and warrant for a claim. No matter what kind of claim (fact, value, policy) is being argued, decision makers use values to judge whether it is worthy of adherence. A value is a general conception of a desirable mode, means (instrumental), or end (terminal) of action. It is differentiated from a belief, which is a simple statement about a specific situation. Many times values are openly stated (freedom) or implied in statements about specific beliefs ("people should vote").

Although values are usually treated as positive (freedom), they may be stated in the negative (restraint). They are usually thought of as abstract (freedom) but they can be concrete (the Constitution).

The values and beliefs used in an argumentative situation can be seen as a value system. That is, they work together and define each other's relation to the particular claim being argued. Because values are social as well as personal, decision makers can share them with the arguer. They can, therefore, be used in arguments to gain adherence. To gain adherence, however, decision makers must believe that the values in a particular system are consistent with one another.

There are a number of traditional value systems in America. Each of these not only has to be seen as having values that are consistent with one another, but also they must be graded. That is, the decision maker must be able to see the hierarchy of values. It has been said that more important than which values are in the system, is how each is graded in relation to every other value in the system.

There are some general principles for the use of values. Values may be found anywhere in an argument, although their use as warrants is probably most important. You can find the values in the arguments of others by using six specific tools discussed in this chapter. At the same time, you need to recognize the limits of value change. Changes in value systems rarely result from adding a new value or eliminating an old one. Most often changes will come through changing a value's distribution, rescaling it, redeploying it, or restandarizing it in the value system.

The best point of attack on a value system is found by using the procedure suggested in chapter 3 for analyzing the claims of fact or value: determine the values, the criteria for judging them, and the grading of them. This usually results in one of three attack points: dispute the criteria, dispute the hierarchy, or dispute both.

All arguments have values in them, but the most effective are those where the values are related to decision makers. However, even well-chosen values are not simply stated; they must be developed through evidence and argument.

Sphere dependence of values is illustrated by a comparison of science and religion. Scientific argumentation is characterized by the values of order, usefulness, prediction, rationality, and knowledge. Religious argumentation is characterized by the values of God, authority, humans, moral behavior, faith, salvation, and church. These two have frequently been in conflict with one another. There is no overlap in their value systems. Conflicts between them are resolved by making one a secondary value system to the other or by treating the two spheres as having completely different roles.

PROJECTS

9.1 Find a newspaper editorial and make a content analysis of its value terms. What value system does the writer follow?

9.2 Using a speech or essay provided by your instructor, diagram some of the key arguments to discover unstated values.

9.3 From contemporary magazines collect six or eight different full-page picture and written text ads for the same type of product (e.g., pain relievers, perfume, liquor, automobiles) and observe to what extent a single value system emerges.

9.4 Note the value differences between two magazines that aim at different audiences (e.g., *Playboy* and *Field and Stream*, *People* and *Ebony*, *Sunset* and *Better Homes and Gardens*).

9.5 Conduct a debate in class with some of your classmates on a value claim in which most of the support comes from other value statements. How effective is it? Under what circumstances can values stand alone?

REFERENCES

Bellah, Robert N., Richard Madsen, William M. Sullivan, Ann Swindler, and Steven M. Tipton. *Habits of the Heart: Individualism and Commitment in American Life*. Berkeley: U of California P, 1985.

Carpenter, Betsy. "Is He Worth Saving?" *U.S. News and World Report* 10 July 1995: 43–45.

Cohen, Simon. *Essence of Judaism*. New York: Behrman's, 1932.

FAIR. "The Way Things Aren't: Rush Limbaugh Debates Reality." *Extra!* July/Aug. 1994: 10–17.

Furay, Conal. *The Grass Roots Mind in America: The American Sense of Absolutes*. New York: New Viewpoints, 1977.

Gallup, George, Jr., and Frank Newport. "Americans Most Thankful For Peace This Thanksgiving." *Gallup Poll Monthly* Nov. 1990: 42.

Grant, Robert M. *A Short History of the Interpretation of the Bible*. New York: Macmillan, 1972.

Hardon, John A. *The Catholic Catechism*. Garden City, NY: Doubleday, 1975.

Kaplan, Abraham. *The Conduct of Inquiry*. San Francisco: Chandler, 1964.

Kennedy, George A. *Classical Rhetoric and Its Christian and Secular Tradition*. Chapel Hill: U of North Carolina P, 1980.

Klope, David. "The Rhetorical Constitution of the Creationist Movement." Diss. U of Utah, 1991.

Kluckhohn, Clyde. *Mirror for Man*. New York: McGraw-Hill, 1949.

———. "Values and Value-Orientations in the Theory of Action." *Towards a General Theory of Action*. Eds. Talcott Parsons and Edward A. Shils. New York: Harper and Row, 1951: 388–433.

Minow, Newton N. "Television's Values and the Values of Our Children." *Communication Policy Studies*, Northwestern University. The Annenberg Washington Program Children Now Conference Keynote. 2 Mar. 1995.

Morris, Charles. *Varieties of Human Values*. Chicago: U of Chicago P, 1956.

Perelman, Chaim, and L. Olbrechts-Tyteca. *The New Rhetoric*. Notre Dame, IN: U of Notre Dame P, 1969.

Rayl, A. J. S., and K. T. McKinney. "The Mind of God." *Omni* Aug. 1991: 43–48.

Rescher, Nicholas. "The Study of Value Change." *Journal of Value Inquiry* 1 (1967): 12–23.

Rokeach, Milton. *Beliefs, Attitudes and Values*. San Francisco: Jossey-Bass, 1968.

———. *Understanding Human Values*. New York: Free P, 1979.

———. *The Nature of Human Values*. San Francisco: Free P, 1973.

Ruesch, Jurgen. "Communication and American Values: A Psychological Approach." *Communication: The Social Matrix of Psychiatry*. Eds. Jurgen Ruesch and Gregory Bateson. New York: Norton, 1951: 94–134.

Sillars, Malcolm O. *Messages, Meanings, and Culture: Approaches to Communication Criticism*. New York: HarperCollins, 1991.

———. "Values: Providing Standards for Audience-Centered Argumentation." *Argumentation and Values*. Ed. Sally Jackson. Annandale, VA: Speech Communication Assoc., 1995: 1–6

Sillars, Malcolm O., and Patricia Ganer. "Values and Beliefs: A Systematic Basis for Argumentation." *Advances in Argumentation Theory and Research*. Eds. J. Robert Cox and Charles Arthur Willard. Carbondale, IL: Southern Illinois UP, 1982. 184–201.

Steele, Edward D., and W. Charles Redding. "The American Value System: Premises for Persuasion." *Western Speech* 26 (1962): 83–91.

Toulmin, Stephen. *Foresight and Understanding*. New York: Harper and Row, 1963.

Toulmin, Stephen, Richard Rieke, and Allen Janik. *An Introduction to Reasoning*. New York: Macmillan, 1984.

Tuman, Joseph H. "Getting To First Base: Prima Facie Arguments for Propositions of Value." *Journal of the American Forensic Association* 24 (1987): 84–94.

Walker, Gregg B., and Malcolm O. Sillars. "Where is Argument? Perelman's Theory of Values." *Perspectives on Argumentation: Essays in Honor of Wayne Brockriede*. Eds. Robert Trapp and Janice Schuetz. Prospect Heights, IL: Waveland, 1990: 134–50.

Weaver, Richard. "Ultimate Terms in Contemporary Rhetoric." *The Ethics of Rhetoric*. Chicago: Regnery, 1953: 211–32.

Willbrand, Mary Louise, and Richard D. Rieke. "Strategies of Reasoning in Spontaneous Discourse." *Communication Yearbook* 14. Ed. James A. Anderson. Newbury Park: Sage, 1991: 414–40.

Woelfel, James W. *Bonhoeffer's Theology*. Nashville, TN: Abingdon, 1970.

10

Support: Credibility

Key Terms

ethos	reputation
credibility	sincerity
competence	direct credibility
trustworthiness	secondary credibility
goodwill	indirect credibility
dynamism	sphere dependence

As President Clinton ran for office in 1992, and throughout his term in office, he was beset by arguments about his credibility. These ranged from matters like possible infidelity and sexual harassment to changing his mind on issues like Somalia, Bosnia, taxes, and a balanced budget. It is ironic that such should be the case for Clinton when his defeat of George Bush in 1992 was attributed to a credibility issue: Bush's 1988 campaign promise, "Read my lips! No new taxes!" that President Bush had to break. These prominent examples illustrate that sometimes credibility can be a central claim in argumentation. James M. Kouzes and Barry Z. Posner, researchers into business leadership, argue "Managers, we believe, get other people to do, but leaders get other people to want to do. Leaders do this first of all by being credible. That is the foundation of all leadership. They establish this credibility by their actions" (276). So, in at least two major spheres of argumentation, politics and business, credibility is a major factor. But *credibility*, as Kouzes and Posner argue, is not "some gift from the gods (as *charisma* is defined) but a set of identifiable (and hence learnable) practices, strategies, and behaviors" (275).

While credibility may serve as a claim in argumentation, its most important role is as a means to support a claim, just as evidence (chapter 7) and values (chapter 9) do. You will see as you read this chapter that credibility is closely related to evidence and values.

When Aristotle first defined credibility as one of the three forms of proof, he used the term *ethos*. For Aristotle, ethos is "proof" that is generated in the mind of the decision makers by "the speaker's personal character when the speech is so spoken as to make us think him credible" (1356a). The likelihood that adherence will be granted is increased, according to Aristotle, as the arguer is perceived as having good sense, good moral character, and goodwill toward the listener (1378a).

It is also worth noting that *ethos* is used to refer to the character of a whole people as well as individual character. The characteristics that Aristotle defined for the speaker are characteristics that will make the speaker compatible with the group.

CHARACTERISTICS OF CREDIBILITY

Modern social scientists have worked to find an empirical definition for credibility. Although there are differences among their studies, their judgments are not much different from Aristotle's. It is reasonable, therefore, to follow Aristotle's lead and define *credibility* as *the support for a claim that is developed by the decision makers' perception that the arguer is competent, trustworthy, and reveals goodwill and possesses dynamism.*

The first thing to observe about this definition is that it is the decision makers' perception that defines an arguer's credibility. When you say that someone has high *credibility* you mean you find that person credible. Your perception of a person's credibility may also be influenced by the context of the argument. Your friend, your mother, your religious leader, your professor, may all be credible to you but on different subjects at different times. Yet there are some characteristics about decision makers' perceptions that serve as a broad base for the judgments they make. Therefore, we will examine the most often perceived characteristics of credibility: competence, trustworthiness, and to a lesser extent, goodwill and dynamism.

Competence and Trustworthiness

A primary dimension that decision makers seek out is competence. A variety of value words have been used since ancient times as synonyms for *competence: sagacity, reliability, authoritativeness, expertise, qualification.* Common sense experience would confirm that decision makers find an argument more worthy of adherence when it is advanced by a person they believe competent on the subject.

Persons who are perceived as trustworthy also have high credibility. In literature since classical times, other value words have been used to define the meaning of being *trustworthy: probity, character, evaluative, honest, sincere,* and *safe.* Again, the commonsense is that ideas are more readily accepted from persons you trust.

Goodwill and Dynamism

The first two dimensions of credibility—competence and trustworthiness— are discussed by all writers. Two other factors—each of which is accepted by some and not by other writers—are *goodwill* and *dynamism.* Value terms such as *open-minded, objective, impartial, kind,* and *friendly* have been used to characterize the goodwill dimension. *Dynamism,* the only one of the four terms to be strictly modern, is characterized by words such as *showmanship*, *enthusiasm*, *inspiration*, and *forcefulness*.

It is easy to see how the research might have shown either goodwill or dynamism to be weak or nonexistent as separate dimensions. Goodwill could easily be classified as a subcategory of trustworthiness. People find trustworthy those persons whom they perceive to have goodwill toward them. Likewise, dynamism, when it functions in a positive manner, may well be a judgment about competence. Research shows that dynamism in a speaker increases audience retention of an idea (Schweitzer). A dynamic speaker would also appear more self-assured, and self-assurance conveys the impression that the persons who possess it "know what they are talking about." Even written argument that is direct in stating a claim with a sense of authority carries with it a dynamic quality.

Note this example of a direct, forceful argument about how much a person should invest in the stock market by stock market expert Peter Lynch: "I have one simple rule of thumb, and it's the same for Wall Street as it is for the racetrack: Only invest what you could afford to lose without that loss having any effect on your daily life in the foreseeable future" (Diehl 60).

However, dynamism has a feature not possessed by competence, trustworthiness, or even goodwill. Dynamism may be perceived negatively. The over enthusiastic salesperson exemplifies this problem.

While individuals' definitions of credibility are variable, there is enough agreement to identify decision makers' judgments of trustworthiness, competence, and goodwill as support for a claim. With some reservation about overdoing it, dynamism also serves as a factor in support of a claim.

FORMS OF CREDIBILITY

What decision makers know about an arguer's reputation will influence their perceptions of the claim. For instance, at the first meeting of your argumentation class, most of the members of the class probably know little about you. Your reputation is probably minimal. As time goes on in the class they know more and more about you. You develop a reputation. An arguer's reputation is important to credibility but cannot be changed instantly. Therefore, what you do to develop credibility in your argument is most important. The three forms of credibility that can be built into the actual arguments are direct, secondary, and indirect credibility.

Direct Credibility

The most obvious form of credibility is what we call *direct credibility*. This is the kind of credibility that you develop by making direct statements about yourself.

Every arguer brings a reputation to the decision making process. We quoted Peter Lynch above to illustrate a dynamic style. But Lynch has a reputation as a "Wall Street Wizard" for his management of the Fidelity Magellan Fund (Diehl 58). The President of the United States, the Speaker of the House, a company executive, an embezzler, a prominent athlete, all have a reputation: the opinion that decision makers have about a person's credibility before that person begins to argue. Advertisements for products frequently feature celebrities like Cybill Sheperd, Jerry Seinfeld, David Robinson, Steve Young, or Michael Jordan because of their reputations.

Chancellor Chang-Lin Tien of the University of California, Berkeley, uses direct credibility to open his article against blaming immigrants for America's problems. He observed that he is satisfied with his life. He is in charge of a "world class institution." His graduate students are successful. His research has contributed to America's engineering knowledge. Despite these accomplishments, when many people "see my face and hear my Chinese accent, they think of me as an immigrant . . . a drain on public services, a competitor for jobs and a threat to a cohesive society" (19).

Chancellor Chang-Lin lets the reader know directly about his success in education and research. His status as a successful immigrant, and as one who has experienced prejudice, makes him credible to speak on the subject. He implies he is competent and therefore his argument is worthy of adherence. Others will say, "I am a paramedic so I understand . . .," "I have studied the problem of trade imbalance . . .," "I play football at the University and I know how demanding it is." Direct credibility makes clear exactly why an arguer should be granted credibility by decision makers.

Secondary Credibility

We call another form of credibility *secondary credibility*. The arguer uses another person's credibility as the grounds for the argument, thus the term *secondary*. By associating the credibility of someone else with yourself you strengthen your own credibility.

Joseph P. Shapiro argues that there is a bias against disabled workers in our society and uses the secondary credibility of experts to reinforce his own credibility.

> More often the bias is subtle, as in the most serious problem—employment discrimination. According to a 1994 Louis Harris study commissioned by The National Organization on Disability, two-thirds of people with disabilities ages 16 through 64 are unemployed. A full 79 percent of them say they want to work. Arizona State University health economics professor William Johnson, Ph.D., and East Carolina University assistant professor of economics Marjorie Baldwin, Ph.D., found that even when people with disabilities do hold jobs, they make less than other workers and are less likely to be promoted (35).

Obviously, secondary credibility can work to diminish the credibility of the arguer and, therefore, of the arguer's claim. If the decision makers question the bias of a poll (even by the Harris Organization) that was paid for by a group that advocates for the disabled it may weaken, not strengthen, credibility.

A problem inexperienced arguers frequently miss is that credibility is not enhanced for decision makers simply because the arguer quotes a number of well-known people and agencies. Prominent people are not necessarily credible. The Chef's Choice company produces knife sharpeners and uses the photograph and testimony of Craig Claiborne who says, "My recipe for incredibly sharp knives. . . ." Most people who are not regular readers of the *New York Times* have no idea that Claiborne has written a cooking column for many years. But even those who do know him may doubt that a journalist who knows recipes really knows much about knife sharpeners.

Think of the reputation the quoted person has with decision makers. You may want to review the discussion about testimony evidence on pages 130–31. At this point you can see the close connection between evidence and credibility as forms of support for a claim. Secondary credibility is established from the testimony of sources the decision makers respect, not necessarily from the testimony of well-known sources.

Indirect Credibility

Unlike direct and secondary credibility, indirect credibility develops without direct statements from authority or personal statements about your personal character. Credibility is developed indirectly by the way you develop, support, and present your arguments. Your values influence decision makers' perceptions about you. The more effectively you argue the more credible you become.

Indirect credibility is probably the most forceful kind of credibility. While decision makers might rate you lower for speaking openly about your qualifications, they will not rate you lower for making an argument that gains adherence. In a sense, then, this entire book is about how to gain indirect credibility.

GENERAL PRINCIPLES FOR THE USE OF CREDIBILITY

The credibility you generate to support your claims—direct, secondary, or indirect—can play an important part in the response you get. However, there are no easy rules for how you should use it because this changes as decision makers and spheres change. Like beauty, it is in the eye of the beholder. Still, there are some general principles of credibility that apply to most situations.

Develop Credibility From Reputation

Reputation is the credibility you have with decision makers before you argue. It may be influenced by the success you are perceived to have (Andersen and Clevenger 73) and by the perception that you are from the same group as the decision makers (Andersen 220; Myers and Goldberg 174–79).

Madeleine K. Albright, the United States Representative to the United Nations, spoke to the Council on Foreign Relations at Washington, D.C., in January of 1995. In her introduction she associated herself with the Council and used that group's reputation to build her own.

> Good evening. It is great to be here among so many friends, and the timing couldn't be better. For decades, the Council of Foreign Relations has been at the heart of the bipartisan tradition of American foreign policy. Because we are a democracy, that tradition is never honored perfectly, nor in truth should we expect it to be. But the history of this century demonstrates that we are stronger and more successful when the two parties agree on core policies and principles than when we do not. On many past occasions the Council has helped bring us together. That capacity has continued relevance in this period of turbulence and transitions (354).

Difficulty occurs when arguers come to the argumentation situation with little credibility—not because they are unworthy of credibility, but because it is not recognized by decision makers. What we have said thus far about reputation would seem at least to reinforce half of the line from an old song, "The rich get richer and the poor get poorer." A person who comes to an argumentative situation with a favorable reputation in the area of the argument has an advantage over one who does not. Yet the person with a good reputation can make mistakes to damage his or her credibility. So it is important to reinforce your good reputation with decision makers.

Even if your reputation is limited, it can be improved. You must make special efforts, at least indirectly and with the use of secondary credible sources, to enhance your credibility. It is not uncommon for arguers to introduce statements of direct credibility about themselves that tend to increase credibility, if they are not too self congratulatory (Andersen 228; Ostermeier).

Sigrid Bathen, writing about child abuse, introduces her article with a series of examples of the problem that subtly reinforced her credibility:

> Of all the stories on children I have researched and written over the years, I especially remember the story of six-year-old Danny Balfour and the pictures police showed me of his bruised and near-lifeless body hooked up to futile hospital life-support machines. . . .
>
>   The story is seared more prominently in my memory even than the 1974 story about the mentally retarded child who was badly beaten in an understaffed and poorly supervised state hospital; more than countless interviews with juvenile criminals, including a 12 year-old who had murdered an eight-year-old. . . . More than the horrific stories of child abuse researched for speeches by state Attorney General John Van de Kamp. . . . More than the wrenching accounts of chronically hungry children and their parents in California's agriculturally rich Central Valley for a study I helped write for the California Rural Legal Assistance Foundation in 1991 (23–24).

Arguers' reputations can be enhanced in a formal situation by the way they are introduced (Andersen and Clevenger 64; Haiman). For instance, the editors of *California Journal* identify Sigrid Bathen as a former *Sacramento Bee* reporter, former press secretary to the Superintendent of Public Instruction and the Attorney General, a writer for publications including *Sacramento Magazine* and *California Lawyer*, and a teacher of journalism at California State University, Sacramento (22). When you introduce someone, emphasize the things about the person that will give them greater credibility with decision makers.

While it isn't likely to be a factor in your credibility right now, you should be aware of the influence of mass media on the credibility of less well-known people. The mere fact that a person is singled out of the millions of bits of information available for the six o'clock news will enhance credibility. Though persons may speak for organizations of no more than a dozen people, they gain credibility from their mere presence in the media. Never doubt that reputation is increased by an arguer being quoted in a book, reported in the daily newspaper, or seen on the *David Letterman Show*.

Take stock of your reputation. It is the starting point of your credibility. You can enhance it even if it is minimal. Your reputation is a benchmark that helps you to determine what you must do in your argument to enhance your credibility.

Be Sincere

Sincerity is probably the most commonly mentioned characteristic of credibility. It would seem a simple rule that to build credibility one should be sincere, but there is clear evidence, that sincerity cannot be determined by decision makers (Andersen and Clevenger; Eisinger and Mills). When someone says, "I believe her because she is sincere," that person really means, "I believe her because *I believe* she is sincere." It is the appearance of sincerity that decision makers judge, and this appearance may not constitute an accurate statement about the arguer.

This in no way implies that you should not be sincere. We have already noted that *sincerity* is frequently used as a synonym for *trustworthiness*. You need to be aware that sincerity alone does not mean that you will be perceived as sincere. However, your sincerity is a first step to convincing others that you are sincere.

Take care to avoid obvious signs that you mean to manipulate the decision makers. When you have a bias, and it is known, a clear and honest identification of it may actually advance your credibility. Decision makers usually put greater trust in the person who openly admits a bias. It is the decision makers' discovery of covert bias that is most damaging to sincerity (Mills and Aronson).

Identify with Decision Makers' Values

Perhaps the strongest indirect credibility is the arguer's identification with the values of the decision makers. A more complete discussion of social values and their role in argumentation is in chapter 9, but we make a few points here.

Unless you choose to speak or write on non-controversial points ("Motorists should slow down in school zones," "Cancer is a dangerous disease," "Everyone should have a friend") you will find controversy. Indeed, as we have observed before, you cannot have argumentation without issues. Those issues must be addressed as decision makers see them.

When you address issues you will be taking some positions with which some decision makers disagree. That is to be expected, and you will lose credibility if you try to agree with the audience on every point. Such a strategy will be transparent, and your sincerity will be questioned. A chameleon-like approach is in sharp contrast to what we mean by identification with decision maker's values.

Remember that audiences are collections of individuals. You can define a group of decision makers as an entity ("This is a Republican audience," "This is an audience of concerned parents," "This audience is pro-choice"), but this is *your* definition. The members are still individuals, and though they have some things in common, they are not identical. Furthermore, many audiences are segmented. Because it is "a Republican audience" does not mean they all agree on taxes, education, welfare, or foreign policy.

You must, of course, search for common ground with the majority of decision makers. Find as many points as you can on which to agree. Most important, show that your proposal is in keeping with their values (Reinard 44). Or construct a system of values showing clearly that while your proposal is contrary to some of their values, it is still consistent with others, and those other values are more important. In addition, show that those who would oppose your position have opted for a misleading system of values.

Consider how different members of your audience might respond to values, and address the various segments. In this hypothetical argument for building a new community medical clinic the values are linked to segments of the audience:

> A new medical clinic should be established in Porterville because it would bring new medical specialties into the town that are not now there (health—medical people). It will provide services for people who find it difficult to drive to other cities (safety, health—elderly). People from small surrounding communities will come to town and will shop here, instead of going to Fresno or Bakersfield (commerce—business people). The new center will open up 50 new jobs (employment—youth).

None of these values is likely to be questioned by any segment of the audience, yet each has a particular appeal to a particular segment. Identifying with decision makers' values can be complex at times but usually can be done without damage to your credibility.

The use of strong value-intensive arguments, in which heavy and repeated use of directly stated values dominates the argument, may have a negative effect on credibility. The research on fear appeals (e.g., appeals to fear of murder, rape, or mutilation) illuminates what probably happens with all value intensive appeals. Such appeals, it seems, are accepted only from an arguer with high credibility. Strong value intensive appeals may boomerang when used by an arguer with modest credibility (Hewgill and Miller). Credibility is weakened when invested in values that decision makers question and in too many value intensive arguments.

You may have this problem in your class. The others probably don't know you well. It would be best, therefore, for you to be careful of using strong value-intensive arguments. People who know you better, for whom you have credibility, would be more likely to respond positively to your intensity. They are more likely to see it as dynamic, particularly if they share those values with you.

Use Evidence to Build Credibility

Evidence appears to strengthen the credibility, especially of a low credibility arguer, and particularly if the evidence is not known to the decision makers (McCroskey 175). This is easy to understand. A highly credible arguer is much more likely than an arguer with lower credibility to be effective using assertion without evidence. People are less likely to wonder, "Where did you get that idea?" or "How do you know that is true?" Consequently, evidence becomes more important to a person with less credibility. One study shows that with apathetic decision makers, it takes twice as much evidence for an arguer with modest credibility to produce a movement toward adherence as it does for an arguer with high credibility (Lashbrook, et al. 262). Furthermore, evidence in the form of examples that are close to decision makers' experiences are more believable and, therefore, are more likely to enhance perceived credibility.

An authoritative source connected to an argument will make that argument more believable. One study shows that an authoritative group has higher credibility than an authoritative individual (Andersen and Clevenger 71; Ostermeier; Warren; Myers and Goldberg). An interesting phenomenon known as a *sleeper effect* seems to operate in the use of authoritative sources as secondary credibility. A source with high credibility tends to produce a strong initial change in people's views. In time that initial change weakens and a lower source gains (Andersen and Clevenger 67). This suggests that the credibility of the source has immediate impact, but for long-range adherence the quality of the argument and the evidence take on greater significance. The lesson you could learn from all this is that you need to build your competence with evidence that your decision makers respect.

Use Organization to Build Credibility

Well-organized cases may not increase credibility, but disorganized ones clearly weaken it, especially for low-credible arguers. Furthermore, showing disorganization by using phrases such as "I should have mentioned this earlier" creates the impression that speakers are disorganized and, therefore, less credible (McCroskey and Mehrley; Sharp and McClung; Baker).

In chapter 4 (Case Building) we discussed a number of different ways that a case can be organized. It is clear that the perception of disorganization can damage credibility. But what makes argumentation appear organized? One characteristic is that the decision makers know explicitly what claims are being made. When claims are vague, decision makers restructure information to correlate with their beliefs, even perhaps in the opposite direction of that intended by the speaker (Tubbs 18). First, therefore, explicit claims are preferred.

Second, a small group of well-developed arguments is preferable to a large number of unsupported arguments. Unsupported arguments invite decision makers to concentrate on their weaknesses. Well-developed arguments imply greater competence on your part. They also should be the arguments that are closest to decision makers' experience and knowledge. Thus, you are seen as having developed the most important issues.

Finally, show that you understand issues by acknowledging both sides of an argument. Even among decision makers who tend to disagree with your proposition, such two-sided argumentation creates the impression that you are fair and are not "dodging the issues." True, some decision makers who already support the arguers' proposition and who are less well-informed respond better to being shown only one side. However, showing both sides has better long term impact. The arguer is seen as being fair, and credibility is increased. This approach also provides the basis for what is called "inoculation." It strengthens the decision makers' resistance to later refutation. This has been demonstrated in a variety of situations, including public arguments and advertising (Pfau 27–28).

Argue Issues, Not People

It is easy, when argumentation leads to sharp differences of opinion, to believe that your opponent is not fair, is biased, or has ulterior motives. Resist this tendency. Center your argument on your claims; let *your* credibility show. Attempts to attack the credibility of an opponent have been shown to weaken, not strengthen, credibility. In one study, persons who initiated such attacks were seen by decision makers as less credible with less acceptable arguments while the credibility of the person attacked was given higher credibility (Infante et al. 188–89).

This phenomenon can be seen in political argumentation where people who raise claims about an opponent's credibility are found to be less credible, even with decision makers who agree with them on issues. Notice that most successful politicians carefully qualify attacks on opponents' credibility, emphasizing their records and positions on the issues. Direct attacks on a candidate's credibility are usually made by others, not the candidates themselves.

Your reputation is a benchmark of your credibility. No matter how limited it may be with the decision makers, it is the basis upon which credibility is built. To make your argument more credible to decision makers, be sincere, identify with their values, use your evidence and organization to build credibility, and argue issues, not people. In all of your plans to enhance your credibility use it to support your argumentation, keep in mind that credibility is a dynamic process, not a series of set rules.

UNDERSTAND CREDIBILITY AS A DYNAMIC PROCESS

You must realize that the process of argumentation is dynamic. Decision makers reject or accept your arguments on the interaction of credibility, values, evidence, and arguments that are both internal and external to the argumentation.

After studying two decades of credibility research, Jessie Delia concludes that the lack of consistent results can be explained in part by the failure to measure what takes place during the argumentative exchange itself. He says, "It is necessary to recognize that the communicator's image will, at least in part, consist of constructions made during the interaction itself." He goes on to claim that the decision to grant credibility to someone involves mental processes in which slight changes in the situation, for example the addition of another person to the discussion, may result in a decision to raise or lower that person's credibility.

A friend had just about convinced you to see a movie that she thought was great when another friend whom you consider an expert joins the conversation to point out the many flaws in the picture. Credibility granted on the basis of the first friend's opinion dissolves in the presence of an expert (375).

Decision makers are not given neat choices between highly competent and trustworthy arguers who show goodwill and are dynamic, versus their opposites. Thus, credibility is a composite of responses to the dimensions, and it may change even as the message is being received. Readers may know nothing of an author, but as they read a book they develop an appreciation for the author's competence based on what they have read. Similarly, experience with an arguer can change the trustworthiness dimension. To complicate matters further, there is reason to believe that for given decision makers, low credibility is not just the opposite of high credibility but a new configuration of dimensions (Schweitzer and Ginsburg).

The whole process of decision making from the highest level down through the single minor argument, constantly changes in the interaction among the elements that make it up. What we see when we talk about particular functions of credibility are arbitrarily frozen bits of information. Decision makers see a generalization or a movement in argumentation in which all the factors are seen together and simultaneously. They are always related to a particular argument, the arguers, the circumstance, and the decision makers. In politics this is called *image*.

SPHERE DEPENDENCE OF CREDIBILITY

Credibility is a dynamic process that must be seen in relation to particular circumstances, so different spheres of argument develop various standards for credibility. General principles such as those we have discussed will hold for most situations. They are modified, however, by the particular sphere in which the argumentation occurs.

Gary Cronkhite and Jo Liska have observed that credibility involves not just the inferred attributes that decision makers give to a particular source of an argument but also the specific subject matter and differing criteria of source acceptability. This point of view corresponds closely to our contention that credibility is influenced by the sphere of argumentation in which it operates.

You will recall that we defined a *sphere* of argumentation as a group of persons whose interstructured, repetitive, and therefore predictable patterns of communicative behaviors are used in the production and evaluation of argumentation. Credibility is subject to those criteria that people operating in a particular context or purpose agree upon.

Spheres are oriented around common needs, purposes, or what Stephen Toulmin calls, "doing what there is there to be done" (485). In a television hospital drama, "Chicago Hope," a young woman is told that she must have a mastectomy or die. It is unfair. "Why me?" is a reasonable response. But this is a question that medicine cannot answer. It has its own knowledge, evidence, values, and ways of arguing that define its sphere of knowledge. The physician has tests that show the breast tumor is malignant, and medical knowledge indicates that the only solution is to remove it surgically. The only alternative she has to death or surgery, he says, is a faith healer. It is clear that he is not serious about that alternative. The young woman eventually relies on the credibility of the physicians and has the operation.

In another part of the same drama, the hospital attorney questions a surgeon's decision to do a controversial brain operation. The physician tells the attorney he is not a doctor and is not qualified to make such a judgment. The attorney argues that he must defend the hospital from malpractice suits. Here, in one hour, three spheres are introduced: medicine, religion, and law, all with different ways of arguing and different standards of credibility. Cronkhite and Liska claim that arguers who show promise of helping spheres do "what there is there to be done" will be granted high credibility. As you may have guessed, if you didn't see the drama, in this television show the highest credibility goes to those who know and act in the medical sphere.

The old saying that "Politics makes strange bedfellows" suggests that if your sphere's purpose is electing candidates to public office, you make associations with others, no matter how offensive in other respects, who show promise of helping elect your candidates. Another cliché, "When does a gambler play in a crooked game? When it's the only game in town," suggests that even otherwise questionable activities may gain credibility when they offer the only hope of "doing what there is there to be done."

President Clinton looked the other way in 1995 when Iran, a nation of low credibility for most Americans, violated the arms embargo imposed on those fighting in the former Yugoslavia. He was willing to have Bosnian Muslims get weapons as long as the U.S. was not involved. So, he let Iran become his silent partner. Credibility, then, may be powerfully related to doing what you must do.

While competence, trustworthiness, goodwill, and dynamism may be general terms that cover all uses of credibility as support, they will look different from one sphere to another. What may be competence to a scientist will differ from competence in a law court, politics, or popular television. The three areas of credibility, and how spheres influence them, that we will examine here are the arguers' reputation, secondary credibility, and indirect credibility.

The Reputation of the Arguer

Some spheres, such as science, have firm definitions of who is competent. A beginning sign is the possession of advanced degrees (usually the doctorate) in the specific science being argued. Increased competence is assumed when a scientist's research is published in prestigious refereed journals, rewarded with research grants, and cited by other researchers.

In chapter 9 we discussed the debate between scientists and religionists over the Genesis story of creation. Scientists with all the necessary credentials argue that the biblical story of the earth's creation in seven days is inaccurate because it conflicts with the theory of evolution and the evidence of science. Some groups, such as the Institute for Creation Research, have organized to argue for the scientific validity of the biblical account. Their members, who call themselves creation scientists, argue that scientific evidence supports the biblical account of creation.

They have degrees in science, and they make arguments based on the analysis of scientific data. For some people, they have the reputation of scientists because of their professions and the fields in which they have their degrees. But for the established scientific community their reputations are suspect because of the nature of their research and their lack of credentials. Why? Some have only Masters' degrees, and those with doctorates have degrees in applied fields of engineering or mineral science, rather than basic research-oriented fields such as physics or genetics, and they have no record of refereed research (Klope 124). They are, therefore, seen by those in the sphere of traditional science as not having competence.

Creation Scientists also are seen as lacking trustworthiness in the scientific community because their religious orientation is perceived to lack scientific objectivity. Although we know they have assumptions of their own, scientists see themselves as objective and believe their research is not confounded by outside factors as is the research of creation science.

While religious affiliation does not enhance scientific argument when used counter to prevailing science, lawyers like to have a member of the clergy testify in court. Though the jury may not share many of the cleric's values and though they may not find the testimony very reasonable, they believe that a cleric is to be trusted and respected.

Sports figures and entertainment personalities are frequently used to argue for products on television: Shaquille O'Neill for All Sport, or Michael Jordan for Gatorade, may be perceived as particularly competent to argue the qualities for sports drinks. However, a soap opera star is no more competent than anyone else to say whether Tylenol is better than other pain relievers. In such cases, the qualification isn't competence, say Cronkhite and Liska, but something more like "likability, novelty, or entertainment" (104). Because the subject is about taste, a criterion that is almost impossible to define, no special sphere is involved even for arguments about sports drinks, and *competence* and *trustworthiness* take on different meanings.

Secondary Credibility in Spheres

Much of what we have noted about reputation holds as well for secondary credibility. When an arguer uses the credibility of others to support claims, those others need to be seen as credible by the standards of the sphere of the decision makers. Scientists acting as scientists need to be told about other scientists who support their views.

Lawyers frequently support their arguments with the testimony of people who are experts: psychiatrists, ballistic experts, professors of communication whose research is freedom of speech. There are areas, however, where credibility takes a serious shift and one of them is in the court of law.

Reluctant witnesses, in most situations, are not considered trustworthy. If you pressure a reluctant friend to tell you something against his or her will the potential for a distorted story is great. Such a person has a bias, so to speak; but, reluctant testimony is believable in a law court. The person giving it is forced by the potential of legal penalty to testify against personal biases and interests. Kato Kaelin reluctantly told a story that incriminated his friend O. J. Simpson.

Secondary credibility is not just a product of persons. Institutions also have credibility as a part of the evidence they provide. The *New York Times*, the *Christian Science Monitor*, and the *Los Angeles Times* are respected newspapers that lend their reputations to those who write for them and those who quote them. In business, the *Wall Street Journal* and *Forbes* magazine have great credibility. In the sphere of humanistic scholarship other institutional publications such as the *American Historical Review* or the *Publication of the Modern Language Association* (PMLA) are more powerful sources of secondary credibility.

An interesting source of credibility in the human and social sciences is the number of times a particular piece of research is cited by others. For instance, the *Citation Index* provides a record of how many times a particular research article is cited and in what sources. The understanding is that research is more valuable if it is used by others who publish in the most prestigious journals.

Indirect Credibility in Spheres

Arguers gain credibility from all they do in making the argument. All that we have said about the influence of spheres of argument on evidence and values applies here. For instance, we noted that hearsay evidence is usually not admissible in a court of law and its use will decrease the credibility of a lawyer who tries to enter it. If the lawyer attempts this too often, the competency of the lawyer will be questioned by the judge. But in interpersonal argument, where such rules are not established, arguers frequently increase their credibility because they have heard the report from a prestigious secondary source.

What we have said about credibility indicates that values are deeply embedded in credibility judgments. *Order*, *research*, *rationality*, and *prediction* are all values of the science sphere. *Faith*, *sacred texts*, and *salvation* are values associated with religious argumentation. *Aesthetic worth*, *form*, and *universality of theme* all stand as values of certain kinds of literary argument.

The use of values and evidence appropriate to a sphere support the claims of arguers and provide indirect credibility for the arguer. You will learn as you study and become expert in your chosen profession how decision makers assign credibility in that sphere.

CONCLUSION

People give adherence to arguments because they perceive them as reasonable, as employing values with which they agree, and as coming from a credible individual or group. Credibility has an important role in argumentation. It may serve as a claim in its own right, but most often it serves as support. It is generally considered to be developed by the decision makers' perception that the arguer is competent and trustworthy and reveals goodwill and dynamism.

There are three forms of credibility in arguments: direct credibility, used when arguers make direct statements about themselves designed to increase credibility; secondary credibility, from associating another's credibility with the argument; and indirect credibility, when the argument is developed in a way that makes the arguer more believable. Reputation adds to the likelihood of winning adherence, but only the first three forms of credibility can be directly controlled by the arguer at the time of any specific argumentation.

Credibility is very changeable because it is so related to the perceptions of the decision makers. However, there are some general principles for the use of credibility. You should use whatever reputation you have and build on it to develop credibility. Be sincere in expressing your own ideas. Identify yourself with the decision makers' values. Use evidence and organization to build credibility, and argue issues, not people.

Credibility, like argumentation, is a dynamic process. It is changed by what happens in the argumentative exchange itself. It is influenced by the situation. Furthermore, each of the factors such as trustworthiness, integrates with each of the other factors and are perceived together and simultaneously.

Credibility will be defined differently by decision makers in different spheres. Reputations are established by criteria that are different, in medicine, religion, and law, for instance. Credibility is given to the person believed capable of "doing what there is to be done" in a particular sphere. Reputation will be built by different credentials in different spheres. Secondary and indirect credibility will differ from sphere to sphere.

PROJECTS

10.1 Find two or more people who are not well acquainted engaging in argumentation such as a classroom discussion. Listen carefully to what they say and do that might affect their credibility to each other and to you. Write a summary of your observations.

10.2 Spend an evening watching television with a note pad in hand. Write down all the ways you can find that advertising agencies work to build credibility for their products. Engage in a discussion with others in class who have done the same. How well did what you see correspond to what is discussed in this chapter? Did you find additional principles about credibility not mentioned in this chapter?

10.3 Examine an event in a political campaign (e.g., a presidential debate, a student body officer candidate exchange in the newspaper, a club officer election). Take notes on the extent to which the candidates use direct, secondary, and indirect credibility. Explain in class which candidate had the most effective credibility for you and why.

10.4. Choose one of the following well-known persons and write a short paper discussing how that person's reputation might influence a specific audience you know well:

The president of the United States

The president of your university

The governor of your state

The mayor of your home town

Your religious leader

A student body leader

REFERENCES

Albright, Madeleine K. "The United States and the United Nations: Confrontation or Consensus?" *Vital Speeches of the Day* 1 April 1995: 354–58.

Andersen, Kenneth. *Persuasion: Theory and Practice*. Boston: Allyn and Bacon, 1971.

Andersen, Kenneth, and Theodore Clevenger, Jr. "A Summary of Experimental Research in Ethos." *Speech Monographs* 30 (1963): 59–78.

Aristotle. *Rhetoric*. Trans. W. Rhys Roberts. New York: Modern Library, 1954.

Baker, Eldon E. "The Immediate Effects of Perceived Speaker Disorganization on Speaker Credibility and Audience Attitude Change in Persuasive Speaking." *Western Speech Journal* 29 (1965): 148–61.

Bathen, Sigrid. "The Future for California Children." *California Journal* June 1995: 22–27.

Chang-Lin, Tien. "America's Scapegoats." *Newsweek* 31 Oct. 1995: 19.

Cronkhite, Gary, and Jo R. Liska. "The Judgment of Communicants Acceptability." *Persuasion: New Directions in Theory and Research*. Eds. Michael E. Roloff and Gerald R. Miller. Beverly Hills, CA: Sage, 1980: 101–39.

Delia, Jesse G. "A Constructivist Analysis of the Concept of Credibility." *Quarterly Journal of Speech* 62 (1976): 361–75.

Diehl, Digby. "Peter Lynch." *Modern Maturity* Jan./Feb. 1995: 58–68.

Eisinger, Richard, and Judson Mills. "Perceptions of the Sincerity and Competence of a Communicator as a Function of the Extremity of His Position." *Journal of Experimental Social Psychology* 4 (1968): 224–32.

Haiman, Franklin. "An Experimental Study of the Effect of Ethos on Public Speaking." *Speech Monographs* 16 (1949): 190–202.

Hewgill, Murray A., and Gerald R. Miller. "Source Credibility and Response to Fear-Arousing Communications." *Speech Monographs* 32 (1965): 95–101.

Infante, Dominic A., Karen A. Hartley, Matthew M. Martin, Mary Anne Higgins, Stephen D. Bruning, and Ghyeongho Hur. "Initiating and Reciprocating Verbal Aggression: Effects on Credibility and Credited Valid Argument." *Communication Studies* 43 (1992): 182–90.

Kouzes, James M., and Barry Z. Posner. *Credibility: How Leaders Gain and Lose It, Why People Demand It*. San Francisco: Jossey-Bass, 1993.

Klope, David C. "The Rhetorical Constitution of the Creationist Movement." Diss. U of Utah, 1991.

Lashbrook, William R., William B. Snavely, and Daniel L. Sullivan. "The Effects of Source Credibility and Message Information Quantity on the Attitude Change of Apathetics." *Communication Monographs* 44 (1977): 252–62.

McCroskey, James C. "A Summary of Experimental Research on the Effects of Evidence in Persuasive Communication." *Quarterly Journal of Speech* 55 (1969): 169–75.

McCroskey, James C., and R. Samuel Mehrley. "The Effects of Disorganization and Nonfluency on Attitude Change and Source Credibility." *Speech Monographs* 36 (1969): 13–21.

Mills, Judson, and Elliott Aronson, "Opinion Change as a Function of the Communicators' Attractiveness and Desire to Influence." *Journal of Personality and Social Behavior* 1(1965): 173–77.

Myers, Michele Tolela, and Alvin A. Goldberg. "Group Credibility and Opinion Change." *Journal of Communication* 20 (1970): 174–79.

Ostermeier, Terry H. "Effects of Type and Frequency of Self Reference Upon Perceived Source Credibility and Attitude Change." *Speech Monographs* 34 (1967): 137–44.

Pfau, Michael. "The Potential of Inoculation in Promoting Resistance to the Effectiveness of Corporate Advertising Messages." *Communication Quarterly* 40 (1992): 26–44.

Reinard, John C. "The Empirical Study of the Persuasive Effects of Evidence: The State After Fifty Years of Research." *Human Communication Research* 15 (1988): 3–59.

Schweitzer, Don A. "The Effect of Presentation on Source Evaluation." *Quarterly Journal of Speech* 56 (1970): 33–39.

Schweitzer, Don A., and Gerald P. Ginsburg. "Factors of Communication Credibility." *Problems in Social Science*. Eds. Carl W. Backman and Paul F. Secord. New York: McGraw-Hill, 1966: 94–102.

Shapiro, Joseph P. "The New Civil Rights." *Modern Maturity* Nov./Dec. 1994: 27–35.

Sharp, Harry, Jr., and Thomas McClung. "Effects of Organization on the Speaker's Ethos." *Speech Monographs* 33 (1966): 182–83.

Toulmin, Stephen. *Human Understanding*. Princeton: Princeton UP, 1972.

Tubbs, Stewart L. "Explicit Versus Implicit Conclusions and Audience Commitment." *Speech Monographs* 35 (1968): 14–19.

Warren, Irving D. "The Effect of Credibility in Sources of Testimony of Audience Attitudes Toward Speaker and Message," *Speech Monographs* 36 (1969): 456–58.

11

Values and Credibility in Business

Key Terms

retail
manufacturing
quality
bottom line
standard of living
government
freedom
manager
consultant

risk
product
success
competition
production
consumption
culture
context
sensemaking

It is only 3:00 p.m. on a typical Wednesday, and Henry Kenton, the owner of a retail business, is making his third major argument of the day. He started with a meeting at his bank where he was seeking a loan, then he went to a hotel where the representative of a sportswear firm talked about the need for a rush order of specially dyed material. Now Mr. Kenton is waiting his turn at the State Industrial Commission office to argue against a former employee's claim for unemployment compensation and money damages.

In another part of town, Rhonda McIntyre, President and Chief Executive Officer of a mid-size manufacturing firm, has spent the entire day in and out of meetings with Japanese executives trying to work out the details of a contract in which McIntyre's company is to supply a major component of the Japanese product. The arguments center around price, quantity, quality, and schedule.

Both of these people are engaging in business argumentation, and in each instance their arguments will rely heavily on support generated through credibility and values. In this chapter, we describe argumentation in business settings, with particular emphasis on the role played by credibility and values, and we will necessarily talk about other aspects of business argumentation as well. Although our comments are generally applicable to businesses, the wide diversity of argumentation practiced every day in business spheres makes it impossible for us to include observations on each variation.

We will look further into the argumentation of Henry Kenton and Rhonda McIntyre before talking about the nature of business in our society, credibility in business argumentation, and values in business argumentation.

THE NATURE OF BUSINESS ARGUMENTATION

Henry Kenton's first appointment of the day was at his bank to secure a loan, which will be guaranteed by the Small Business Administration. This took place at 9:00 a.m., by which time Henry had already visited three of his nine retail dry cleaning outlets spread throughout the metropolitan area, one of his two shirt laundries, the drapery and blind cleaning plant, and the new dyeing and chemical washing facility. During his 40-odd years at it, Henry has worked in all aspects of the business, and still fills in at shirt pressing or some other chore when an employee fails to show up and an order has to be sent out. His wife, Margaret, spends her days supervising the accounting and billing activities. Although they have plenty of money to support a comfortable retirement, both Henry and Margaret continue to work in the business that bears their name.

Argumentation in a Retail Setting

This morning, Henry sought to secure a loan of $250,000 to allow him to expand his dyeing plant to handle large orders. His major lines of argument in the application that must be submitted to the bank for a loan secured by the Small Business Administration include brief, simple, data-supported answers to these questions:

1. Who am I?
2. What is my company?
3. What am I going to do with the money?
4. How do I intend to pay it back?

"Actually," says Henry, "the first few applications I submitted were really difficult to write. But now, the bank's loan officers know me so well it's almost a rubber stamp. And I never missed a payment." In that brief statement, he identifies the power of credibility—"They know me so well"—and the key value of lending institutions—"I never missed a payment." His arguments will include claims such as these:

I. The bank can place their money in my hands with confidence.
   A. I have proved my character as a reliable debtor (credibility).
      1. Over the past 30 years, I have successfully repaid five loans from the SBA right on schedule.

    2. I have structured my debt service to allow complete repayment of all debts, including this one, by the time I reach 65 years of age.
    3. I have been honored by the SBA as a model for the responsible expansion of my business consistent with growth of income.
  B. My proposal for expanding the dyeing facility rests on sound business principles (values).
    1. The loan is secured by the equity available in the remainder of the business.
    2. The profit potential in dyeing is growing as domestic garment manufacturers seek facilities closer to home.
    3. Current dyeing capacity is too limited to allow us to take large orders, thus weakening our competitive position.

The bank will probably grant the loan request based on their past association with Henry Kenton and the reputation he has with them as a canny business operator. This is pure credibility. But if he did not also show ongoing awareness of the bank's value related to the security of their money (sound business principles, paying debts) his credibility alone might not suffice. Too many lending institutions have gone out of business by letting their money go into long-shot ventures.

The argumentation between Henry and the sportswear representative was quite different. He has no past reputation with them to provide a solid base of credibility, so Henry must generate credibility through the argumentation that occurs in the hotel room. During the "casual" conversation that starts off most business conferences, Henry will manage to work in the fact that he has been asked to address an international association of dry cleaners and that he is a member of Concepts 12, an exclusive national group of powerful dry cleaners who meet semimonthly from Boston to Hawaii to discuss effective business practices. This should lay a foundation of credibility.

Then Henry will provide data on his plant's access to temperature-sensitive dye that is tightly held and not available to most dye plants. This dye changes colors when the temperature changes, and a sportswear manufacturer who deals in, for example, ski clothing, can capture an exclusive market with garments that have one look in the lodge and then explode into different colors on the slopes. This will appeal to retailers' values relating to products that are both exciting to consumers and exclusive to the manufacturer.

Finally, Henry will demonstrate his plant's capacity to process the number of garments needed for the coming winter season. He will point to his plans for expansion and his method of financing it. This will aim arguments directly at the question of whether a national manufacturer can rely on this company to do what it says it will do, another aspect of credibility.

Now, it is 3:00 p.m., and Henry is about to act as his own advocate in a case before the State Industrial Commission. He has 125 people working for him, most of them are not highly educated, and the turnover rate is high.

When employees are fired or laid off, they may qualify for unemployment compensation. When they quit, they may not qualify. Often, the circumstances under which an employee leaves are not clear. If they come into dispute, they may result in an administrative hearing before the State Industrial Commission.

Today, the case involves Leda Calderon, a native of Costa Rica, who came to work for Henry at the counter of a dry cleaning outlet. Henry decided to keep his counters open on Saturday and announced that all counter personnel would have to take a turn on a Saturday shift. Leda objected on the grounds that she needed to be free on weekends because she made money selling items at a swap meet. Henry said if she refused the assignment, he would fire her. She did and he did.

Now, she has gone to the Industrial Commission asking for unemployment compensation and damages because of discrimination against her. She arrived with two lawyers.

Leda argues that since Henry forced her from her job, she should receive unemployment compensation, and since she was the victim of discrimination, Henry should pay her an additional amount of money as damages. Henry argues in return that she refused an assignment that was required of all his counter personnel. She was not singled out, and she disqualified herself by refusing the Saturday assignment.

The arguments seem deadlocked, and it is not clear what the arbitrators will decide. Henry needs an argument that will help them believe what he says: he needs to establish his credibility. So he announces that he is prepared to hire her back without prejudice if she will agree to take her turn on the Saturday shift. When Leda refuses, the arbitrators see that it is Henry's story that is more believable, and they decide to deny unemployment compensation as well as damages for discrimination.

Argumentation in a Manufacturing Setting

The argumentation of Rhonda McIntyre in the manufacturing corporation appears, on the surface, quite different from that of the small business. Yet they share the same fundamental regard for credibility and values. In the negotiations with the Japanese firm, Rhonda will need to establish her credibility in two ways. First, because they have not done business with each other before, she will need to establish a persona that will enhance her argumentation. Second, she knows that Japanese businesses tend to be even more suspicious of women than American firms, which still find it tough to deal with women chief executive officers. So she will need to establish a credibility that will transcend their sexist tendencies.

Doing business with Japanese firms presents an equally difficult problem in terms of values. American business values and Japanese business values are often at odds. Americans tend to concentrate on consummating the deal on the quickest most favorable terms. Japanese tend to work from established relationships in which an atmosphere of understanding has been developed.

They will take all the time necessary to build such relationships, while Americans become more and more impatient to get down to business.

To what extent will Rhonda be well advised to accept values that are unfamiliar to her just to win a contract? To what extent should she stick to her firm's values even though it may put the contract in jeopardy? Rhonda's argumentation proceeds along these lines.

First, she recognizes that building a strong interpersonal relationship is even more important in Japanese business transactions than it is in the United States. It will not do to push too hard for agreement. Because the Japanese representatives have chosen to come to her facilities for this first meeting, she will pay plenty of attention to scheduling time for informal interaction. Unlike many U.S. businesses, Rhonda has two members of her executive staff who are fluent in Japanese, and this is an asset she will use fully to build credibility. She will schedule tours directed by her executives and presented in Japanese, with accompanying printed materials, also in Japanese.

She will not spend too much time with the representatives herself. She will be aloof, playing the role of the most important person in the company. She will make appearances only at key times, and then she will behave clearly as the one in charge. She will allow most of the interpersonal networking and informal associating to be done by her male executives who speak Japanese. It would damage her credibility with the Japanese if she seems too friendly.

With regard to values, Rhonda will stress the quality of her product. She will give demonstrations that will dazzle the Japanese. She will show them her manufacturing plant that operates through teamwork and quality empowerment of teams, such as is common in many Japanese manufacturing facilities. She will provide data to prove that her product commands a 63 percent market share and has been known as the quality leader for 25 years. She will present the image of a sound and profitable business enterprise that would be pleased to do business with the Japanese but is certainly not dependent upon that business.

When the question of price comes up, Rhonda will present the catalog price of her product and make it clear that price is not negotiable. Her company has long had an informal company value that goes like this: "Make it good, and charge plenty." They have talked frequently over the years about this policy and whether they should try to position themselves as a discount company. They have consistently rejected the idea in favor of remaining a high-quality, high-price company. They will lose business rather than discount price. In this instance, Rhonda will hold to a company value even if it means the loss of this contract.

On the other hand, Rhonda happens to know that the Japanese firm accepted the prime contract a year ago with the intention of providing the component now under discussion themselves. They have spent a year trying and now realize they cannot make the component at the required specifications. They now are under the gun to come up with the component, do it fast, and at the specifications. Rhonda can bail them out of their difficulty by negotiating schedule, but it will cost them dearly. She knows that sometime in the future she will come to the Japanese firm with a similar urgent need, and they will exact a full price as well. It makes no sense to her to talk price now, she will wait until the shoe is on the other foot.

Rhonda will probably get the contract because the Japanese firm needs her product, she has a clear edge on quality, and she can ship according to their schedule. However, she will still not close the deal without several trips to Japan and several additional delegations from Japan to her plant. It will be a long process of building the credibility through interpersonal relationships necessary to satisfy the top executives of the Japanese firm that they can do business with this American woman. And it will take time to convince them that the price will not come down.

BUSINESS IN AMERICAN SOCIETY

In an era in which formerly socialist states are trying to develop market economies, there is much talk about what that means. Can the business practices developed in western countries be transplanted to those formerly socialist countries? Probably not. Each society will need to develop business practices consistent with their broad culture and special needs. Because of this, to be knowledgeable about business argumentation requires an understanding of how business relates to particular societies. We will briefly address the question of how business values are related to U.S. society.

The Concept of Business

Experts frequently debate the definition of *business*. Many hold to a traditional view that business "means an economic system coordinated by competitive markets, in which individuals and organizations, seeking profit and accepting risks, employ people and privately-owned resources to produce and distribute goods and services" (Ways xii). This definition points to the profit-seeking element of business enterprise. Traditionally, business has been seen as a single-minded effort to make money, and everything done in the name of business has been measured against the extent to which the effort produces returns in excess of the investment that went into the activity. The question, "What's the bottom line?" signals an interest in the net profit gained or expected from any endeavor. The "bottom line" is, of course, the last or bottom entry on any balance sheet that shows the funds remaining after all expenses have been accounted for.

Henry Kenton tells of an acquaintance who runs a dry cleaning operation in another state. The man represents bottom line values by his approach to competitors. He says, "Kill the bastards when they're young." Every time a competitor opens a dry cleaning business in the same town, Henry's friend immediately cuts his prices below a competitive level. Soon, the newcomer will be out of money and forced to close, and then the established dry cleaner raises his prices to recoup his losses and continue to dominate the market.

In recent years, people in business have been inclined to argue in favor of a broader concept of business values that places emphasis on the social values inherently associated with business. For example, another definition of *business* characterizes it as "the sum total of the organized efforts by which the people engaged in commerce and industry provide the goods and services needed to maintain and improve the standard of living and quality of life to which each of us may aspire" (Glos et al.). This concept adds consideration of the community's interests alongside the bottom line as a business value.

The president of Hanover Insurance was quoted in support of this view of business:

> The total development of our people is essential to achieving our goal of corporate excellence. Whereas once the morals of the marketplace seemed to require a level of morality in business that was lower than in other activities, we believe there is no fundamental tradeoff between the higher virtues in life and economic success. We believe we can have both. In fact, we believe that, over the long term, the more we practice the higher virtues of life, the more economic success we will have (Senge 140–43).

Government and Business

As government becomes increasingly active in business arguments, community values play a more important role. For example, the traditional U.S. idea of private enterprise was based on the value of freedom or free will. The workplace was deemed an "at-will" location. Workers were free to seek work, and they were hired subject to the will of the employer. The boss was free to fire an employee, and an employee was free to quit. No argument was needed to fire someone. No argument was needed to quit.

Today, however, government has taken an increasing interest in the hiring and firing process. Employers are not totally free to hire at will. They may not discriminate on such bases as race, age, gender, or disability. They may be subject to hiring standards to redress past discrimination. Employers may need to produce arguments to support hiring decisions.

Similarly, the employer is no longer as free to fire at will. Dismissing employees, once they have passed a probationary period, may require due process demanding the production of arguments to show the dismissal was based on employee performance and was not discriminatory. As in the case of Henry Kenton, business owners may be required to appear before government bureaus to justify their actions or face adverse decisions.

Henry Kenton claimed an employee who was planning to quit decided to take advantage of her job and do the dry cleaning for her entire family at Kenton's expense. When he discovered it, he fired her and deducted the time she had spent doing her private cleaning from her final paycheck. The Industrial Commission, however, said he had no right to take money properly owed her.

They ordered him to pay back the money regardless of his claim that she had misused her position.

Similar to the intervention of social values in the hiring and firing process is the community interest in working conditions. Employers have not been completely free to regulate the nature of work for some time. The number of hours worked, the minimum rate of pay, the age of employees, and other aspects of the workplace have been subject to government regulation for many years. Recent movement in providing for occupational safety and health demands that people in business be prepared to argue that their workers' well-being and the broader environment are properly being considered.

A dramatic change in business argumentation has come with the increased sensitivity to such employee rights as freedom from sexual harassment and age or disability discrimination. Job assignments, transfers, work demands, and on-the-job behaviors may lead to claims of harassment or discrimination that employers must be prepared to rebut with effective arguments.

Voluntary Social Action

In addition to these measures more or less forced upon business, there is a move toward voluntary considerations for employees that have never before been seen. Kirstin Downey Grimsley of the *Washington Post* reports that, "The nation's biggest and most prosperous companies are offering a large and growing array of generous offerings designed to help their workers cope with the stresses of managing their work and family lives."

Child care assistance, elder care programs, education allowances, and flex-time schedules are some of the benefits. The Calvert Group, a mutual fund company, invests $500 in the child's name when an employee gives birth. The Bureau of National Affairs allows male employees two weeks of paid paternity leave.

What is the motivation for these expensive programs? Evidence shows that such programs make employees more productive and loyal. And the company is more attractive to prospective employees.

CREDIBILITY IN BUSINESS ARGUMENTATION

As we have said in chapter 10, credibility is the perception that the arguer is competent and trustworthy, has good will toward the decision makers, and is dynamic. In business we have to expand that beyond a special arguer, such as Henry Kenton, to the larger context of the organization. Many business arguments are directed at generating credibility for an organization, its product, or its symbols. Consider, for example, an investment firm such as Salomon, Inc.

When people decide to purchase stocks or bonds or make other types of investments, they consider the reputation of the firm with which they intend to do business. Such terms as *solid, reliable, discrete, knowledgeable, trustworthy, profitable,* and *unblemished integrity,* come to mind. Recent years have revealed serious problems in financial institutions ranging from failures in savings and loans, to insider trading, to manipulation of junk bonds, to deep-seated weaknesses in a banking industry once thought to be impregnable to such problems.

Organizational Credibility

For these reasons, when it became apparent that some employees of the distinguished financial house of Salomon had "behaved egregiously" in dealing in the government securities market, the question of credibility became paramount. If the company could not restore its credibility quickly, it would soon be out of business.

Warren E. Buffett, the interim chairman of Salomon, placed a two-page ad in the *New York Times* to present an argument to restore the firm's credibility (Buffett). First, the argument admitted that some employees were guilty of wrongdoing and stated that the company would pay fines or penalties quickly and try to settle all valid legal claims promptly. This was aimed at settling fears that a protracted contest with the government and individuals would sap the firm's strength. Stating that "some" employees were guilty of wrongdoing implied that most people at Salomon did nothing wrong.

Second, the argument claimed that new rules and procedures had been instituted to prevent a recurrence of the problem. Further, the chairman appointed himself chief compliance officer and invited all 9,000 employees to help. This sought to relieve concerns about new troubles.

Third, the argument used a cost/benefit analysis to show that earnings continued high while a reserve fund had been set up to cover potential legal obligations. Those to whom the argument was addressed were assured of the continued financial viability of Salomon.

Finally, the argument discussed compensation. Salomon uses an incentive system through which employees can earn bonuses for excellent performance. However, the argument showed that some units of the company failed to produce earnings to match the bonuses, and this would be changed. Presumably, this addressed the need to reduce costs by bringing salaries in line with performance: in 1990, profits were flat in relation to 1989, but salaries increased more than $120 million (Buffett).

Ask yourself if this argument would satisfy you. Would you feel comfortable investing your money with Salomon, or would you find yourself inclined to try another company? In fact, the argument and the changes promised did the trick. By 1995, Salomon had restored its credibility and was once again a business with which people entrusted their money.

Managerial Credibility

In perhaps no other social organization is the judgment of one or a few people so important to argumentation as it is in business. Starting from the days in which a single entrepreneur or a few partners conceived, established, and managed businesses, there has been a strong authoritarian character to business arguments. In many businesses, both large and small, that continues today.

In their studies of leadership over the past 20 years, James M. Kouzes and Barry Z. Posner have surveyed a variety of respondent groups about what credibility means to them. "Honest, forward-looking, and competent. . . ." are the most consistently selected descriptors (26). You will notice how similar these terms are to the ones communication research has produced, which we report in chapter 10: *competence*, *trustworthiness*, *goodwill*, and *dynamism*. The most notable difference in the business setting is that credible leaders are expected to be "forward-looking." Business leaders ask people to join them in a plan for the future that will involve risk and may not produce a pay-off for many years. Under such circumstances, a leader must have high credibility, for that is essentially the basis on which people choose to accept or reject the arguments (27–28). Kouzes and Posner report that organizational members who believe their leaders to be highly credible tend to be more loyal to the organization, more committed to their team, see their values as consistent with those of the organization, and have a sense of ownership in the organization (26–27).

In some situations, it is sufficient to say, "The boss wants this." Subordinates frequently practice the strategy of insinuating an idea until the boss announces it. Then the claim comes with the credibility that it's, "the boss's idea." In fact, business leaders rise to prominence by being willing to make decisions and take risks, as long as they are associated with success.

On the other hand, when things go wrong, it is the managers who get fired. It was the interim chairman of Salomon who placed an ad in the *New York Times*, because his predecessor was removed when trouble emerged. Just as the manager or coach of an athletic team may be fired after too many losses, so can the CEO. Association with failure destroys credibility, making future arguments weaker. The coach or the CEO may need to go to another place for a fresh start with a new supply of credibility in order to perform effectively.

Managerial credibility operates at all levels of organizations. From supervisor to CEO, arguments are judged in large part on the basis of who is presenting them. If you have worked with a manager in the past and found that person to be forthcoming and reliable, you are likely to subscribe to future arguments. On the other hand, credibility is delicate and easily destroyed. One instance of a person misleading you, failing to follow through, or cutting you behind your back may make you suspicious of all future claims.

Consultant/Specialist Credibility

As business becomes more complex and highly technical, reliance on consultants and technical specialists has increased. A specialist may be someone outside the company brought in to work on a specific task, a person from within the company whose success or experiences in another unit promises insight, or one who has special training or expertise. Pamela Shockley-Zalabak lists these leadership responsibilities that may be sought from specialists: problem analysis, idea generation, idea evaluation, abstract ideas/vision identification, solution generation, solution implementation, goal setting, and agenda making (227–28). Arguments advanced in the name of the consultant or specialist are strengthened by the special credibility associated with a specific person.

Product Credibility

When Tylenol capsules containing arsenic were found, the company feared consumer confidence in the product would collapse. Discussions were focused on the question of whether all the time and expense that had been invested in building the name into the top selling, highly trusted acetaminophen pain reliever was lost.

The company chose to try to restore the product name's credibility rather than start all over with a new, untainted but unknown, name. They were successful, to the surprise of many. In a market where one acetaminophen product is pretty much the same as any other, most observers believed consumers would merely switch brands. But with the high credibility that Tylenol had possessed before the arsenic incidents, the manufacturer was able to win it back through a persuasive campaign focusing on the claim that hospitals, institutions with high credibility, continued to distribute Tylenol, even to new mothers.

By 1995, some competitors had conceded first-place in headache relief to Tylenol. They claimed in their ads only that their pain reliever was better for aches and pains, even though Tylenol was best for headaches. For its competitors to mention tylenol in an advertisement, and even acknowledge its strong position, is clear evidence that Tylenol had recovered its credibility.

The makers of Tylenol benefitted from having the first acetaminophen product ever marketed. "History shows," say Al Ries and Jack Trout, "that the first brand into the brain, on the average, gets twice the long-term market share of the number two brand. . . ." (43).

Tobacco companies have suffered much damage to their credibility in recent years. Their efforts to refute claims of health dangers from smoking have weakened while anti-smoking arguments have become increasingly successful. How could tobacco companies salvage their product's credibility under such adverse circumstances? Interestingly, they did it in part by claiming that cigarettes are not as bad as their critics claim. Here's the case.

We learn from a letter written by the American Broadcasting Companies and published in a Philip Morris ad in *The New Yorker* on September 11, 1995 that, on February 28, and March 7, 1994, the ABC television program *Day One* included segments reporting that, "through the introduction of significant amounts of nicotine from outside sources, Philip Morris 'artificially spikes' and 'fortifies' its cigarettes with nicotine and 'carefully controls' and 'manipulates' nicotine for the purpose of 'addicting' smokers." Philip Morris filed suit claiming ABC was incorrect in their claim. We do not know the details of how it came to pass, but we do know that in 1995, ABC published a letter in which they said, "We now agree that we should not have reported that

Philip Morris adds significant amounts of nicotine from outside sources."
Philip Morris took out ads in a wide variety of media with the implication that
ABC was conceding on a wide range of credibility-damaging arguments.
"APOLOGY ACCEPTED" was announced in big red letters. In the text at the
bottom, they said this:

> The tobacco industry is subject to relentless attacks. And our responses to accusa-
> tion . . . are often disregarded by the media and our critics. Here's all we ask:
> When charges are leveled against us, don't take them at face value. Instead, con-
> sider the information we provide, and then . . . subject the charges themselves to
> the scrutiny and skepticism they deserve. Fairness and a sincere interest in the
> truth demand no less ("Apology Accepted").

By forcing ABC to apologize, the tobacco companies regained some of the
"high ground" they had lost by proclaiming their dedication to the truth. They
also regained some of the presumption they had lost, and correspondingly
pushed the burden of proof back on the anti-tobacco arguments. Now reread
precisely what ABC actually apologized for.

VALUES IN BUSINESS ARGUMENTATION

Values in business argumentation can be generally grouped within the context
of five: the future, success, cost/benefit, competition, and production/con-
sumption. These concerns tend to constitute the criteria by which business arguments are critically assessed. Their relative importance in the evaluation of
a particular argument will depend upon the sub-sphere within which they are
produced and the issues under consideration. We will discuss each of them
briefly.

The Future

The essence of business is predicting the future. Businesses succeed or fail on
the strength of their ability to plan for what consumers will want in the time to
come, what research and development will be able to make practical next,
what the economic conditions of the state, nation, region, or world will be, and
what the condition of the labor market will become.

The future of the financial market alone, now that it is locked in ongoing
transactions worldwide, can spell success or failure. Businesses with curren-
cies from various countries must move their holdings from place to place in
anticipation of variations in relative value. Those seeking financing for business activities or looking for ways to put surplus cash to work must look all
over the world and gauge the future.

Businesses rarely rest on the claim that they have done well up to now;
typically, they claim they will do as well or better in the future. This point is illustrated in a rather ironic way in an advertisement by Federated Funds, an

investment company. Their ad in the *Wall Street Journal* shows a graph with the vertical axis indicating dollar amounts ranging from 9,250 to 10,750 (they do not say if these numbers represent thousands, millions, or billions of dollars) and the horizontal axis representing time ranging from 9/93 to 6/95. The lines on the graph show that over this period of time, their municipal fund outperformed a peer group consistently. The caption reads "Positively Boring Money Management," implying that their steady growth is so certain it is boring. Then, probably to satisfy the Securities and Exchange Commission, which strictly regulates the manner in which investments are presented to the public, they include this statement in small print at the bottom of the ad: "Past performance is not indicative of future results" ("Positively Boring"). This may be so, but the company knows that this is the kind of evidence people will use to judge business arguments about the future.

Success in Business

Perhaps no other institution in our society is as success oriented as business. This should not be surprising in light of the competitive character of business enterprise. Professional sports teams similarly point constantly to their wins. Claims are presented to financial institutions to convince them that the business is successful enough to warrant the granting of loans for continued growth, as in the case of Henry Kenton. Claims are presented to money managers to demonstrate success warranting high credit ratings for access to bonds, and investments in stock. Claims are made to customers and potential investors using success as an argument for winning their purchases.

American General, a company providing retirement annuities, consumer loans, and life insurance, made this argument to encourage purchase of its stock:

> Our record speaks for itself: *annualized total return to shareholders of 21 percent over the last 20 years* . . . increased dividends each year during the same period . . . and more recently, earnings have doubled over the last five years. Today, American General has assets of $58 billion. Financial strength has its rewards. . . . ("American General").

Does this argument effectively support the claim that this is a successful company?

Cost/Benefit

No matter how community minded a business may be, it must keep its eye on the bottom line to remain in business. Therefore, business argumentation is filled with claims relating to cost/benefit analysis.

The Coca-Cola company has for most of its history been perceived as a "plodding old giant." They were active and innovative in marketing their products, but when it came time to consider major changes in the business, they tended to give careful, fully considered scrutiny to the costs in relation to the benefits. For this reason, they did not make rapid decisions, and today that has proved costly. Robert Frank tells us Coca-Cola was

> . . . swamped by the wave of teas, juices, and flavored waters in the United States in the early 1990s. It was late entering India when that market began opening up in the late 1980s. It shrugged off attacks by private-label soft-drink makers in the United Kingdom until they had siphoned off sizable sales (A1).

So today, Coca-Cola has revised its thinking on cost/benefit to permit rapid decisions for change. They are still as interested in profit, but they have concluded that taking a long time to study proposals while competitors captured their potential customers was costing too much. An argument calling for an immediate decision to invest a great deal of money in a risky venture, in Russia for instance, survived critical scrutiny when there was evidence that speed would make the difference in market penetration.

Competition

Market share or penetration is the object of continuing claims in many businesses. Virtually no business can operate without regard to the actions of its competitors. Peter Senge uses the figurative analogy of the boiling frog to describe U.S. auto manufacturers. You can put a frog in boiling water, and it will easily jump out. But if you put the frog in cold water and gradually raise the temperature to boiling level, by the time the frog realizes it is in trouble, it will be too weak to jump out. Similarly, says Senge, U.S. auto manufacturers, holding command of the domestic auto market, remained calm while Japanese autos gradually took market share away. By the time they realized the problem, they were almost too weak to respond (22–23). Coca-Cola does not intend to make that mistake.

Competition and market share are brought into sharp relief in the emergence of the online information business. By the start of 1995, several ventures into online information were becoming established. America Online, CompuServe, and Europe Online SA are examples of companies that were claiming a share of the emerging market and using that position to argue that investors, subscribers, and media firms should join them. To succeed, such a company needs to offer information that is not easily available elsewhere so that subscribers will pay for it.

Then, in the summer of 1995, Microsoft Corporation introduced its Windows 95 program that included a new online service. That new source of competition spooked investors and subscribers in the other services. The arguments centered on the question of which of these competitors will become most powerful in the future. Microsoft had enormous credibility because of its past success in dominating its markets. Media/information firms were torn between two strong values: (1) the desire to see the online service with which they had already associated succeed; and (2) the need to remain competitive in a worldwide market. If they stayed where they were, they might find themselves left out in the cold. If they jumped to Microsoft, they might not negotiate as good a deal.

Production/Consumption

Production claims concern what can be produced, how it can be produced in relation to the firm's present or projected productive capacity, the labor and materials necessary, the speed of production, the timing of demand for the product, and the potential harmful side-effects of production.

A good example of the vagaries of production (and the challenge to argumentation) can be found in the oil industry. For many years, the Oil Producing and Exporting Countries (OPEC) have tried to control production of oil by their members to increase the price. This has been difficult as members have failed to fulfill their promises by producing more than their quota because they needed the income. Companies outside OPEC must base their production arguments not simply on the stated quotas, but on their expectation of actual production.

The viability of an oil company depends in large part on its ability to argue convincingly about the relationship of its future production to profitability. This is done either by buying reserves, which is expensive, or drilling for new oil deposits, which is also expensive as well as risky. For some time, major oil companies have avoided or abandoned oil fields when they did not promise the large production needed to maintain their high level needs.

Now, so-called junior oil companies have entered the picture. They employ the newest scientific methods to find oil, such as three-dimensional seismic exploration and horizontal drilling to hold down the cost and risk of exploration. They are small, have modest investment in the company, and can make a profit and increase the price of their shares by producing only 4,000 to 6,000 barrels of oil a day. This is a rate of production too small to be profitable to the huge oil companies (Carlisle). It's reminiscent of the time little computer companies produced a better product at a lower cost with a lower investment to sustain and managed to cause serious damage to the giant IBM.

CONTEXT OF BUSINESS ARGUMENTATION

We have already shown how values enter business argumentation at every level of organizational activity. Now we will discuss the characteristics of values within business organizations. As this discussion unfolds, you should begin to understand better how business units function as spheres.

Organizational Culture

In recent times, it has become common for organizational studies to examine businesses from the perspective of culture. Clyde Kluckhohn and William Kelly define *culture* as a "historically created system of explicit and implicit designs for living, which tends to be shared by all or specially designated members of a group at a specific point in time" (98).

Karl E. Weick, however, argues that these designs for living are not established in one time and then employed in a later time to direct action. On the contrary, says Weick, a company's past shared experiences provide the support for contemporary arguments about what should be done in the future work of the organization.

In an argument advanced today, claiming what should be done tomorrow, the arguer invokes shared past experiences making them salient and relevant. The decision makers may even attribute various meanings to the past experiences and still find that they provide acceptable support for today's argument. "Culture, in this revised view," says Weick, "is what we have done around here, not what we do around here" (189). Thus, much of business argumentation draws upon past experiences, and those who share them can, for that moment, act as a sphere by engaging in interpretations of their common experiences.

Charles Bantz develops the notion of culture as the generation of meaning:

> Culture . . . is an outcome and a process that arises in the meaningful activity of people. As action becomes meaningful, members of a culture develop expectations about the activities of members. . . . These patterns of expectations include norms, roles, agendas, motives, and styles. The development of cultural activity reflects the development of meanings and expectations (25).

Culture interacts with business arguments in the sense that it provides the value warrants on which arguments rest, while simultaneously and continuously arguments negotiate and revise the culture. Cultural meanings, with a system of values at their center (see chapter 9), are shared by members of the organization and emerge from the interactions of the group's members (Barnett 102–03).

Within a business organization, its value system is the intrinsic aspect of its culture. Values, says George Barnett,

> . . . provide the assumptions upon which organizational activities are based. They define its goals, and the criterion by which it is determined whether the goals have been successfully achieved. They are often thought of as the organizational or corporate ideology (108).

The value system provides focus for corporate consciousness and members' actions by "connecting social obligations with general ethical principles" that direct the day-to-day activities of workers on the basis of an overarching scheme, which cannot be violated without risk of punishment (Barnett 108).

In short, ongoing negotiation of culture (it is not a fixed context but one in continuous re-creation), relying as it does on past shared experience, is the process through which spheres form and change in business organizations.

Bantz's concept of organizations fits closely with our idea of spheres. He says organizing involves three or more people "who would define themselves as an organization, acting in concert to accomplish a common activity" (26).

Recall our definition of spheres in chapter 2. Spheres are three or more people in the process of interacting upon and making critical decisions. Their interaction is interstructured, repetitive, and thus predictable as they produce and evaluate arguments.

It is the members' symbolic representation of the sphere, says Bantz, that defines it. The limits of the sphere are identified through "members' symbolic representations of meaning and expectations" (26).

Contextualizing Values

Thinking of business argumentation in terms of organizational culture leads necessarily to the conclusion that specific arguments must be tied to specific cultures (spheres). The arguments will be assessed in terms of the particular context in which the decision is made. For this reason, it is dangerous to mention specific values as if they will support arguments with equal power no matter where they appear. Understanding business argumentation means *contextualizing,* putting in context, the values of the organization. Arguments occurring within the context of engineering specialists will be judged according to different values than the same arguments presented to the marketing department.

Each business organization negotiates its particular system of values as part of its culture, and that system drives the argumentation and decision making that occurs within the business (Shockley-Zalabak 241–73). Not every argument will be driven, for example, by the value of cost/benefit.

When Congress eliminated rules that prevented long-distance telephone companies from entering the local phone market, AT&T, MCI, and Sprint began spending billions of dollars on local switches, wireless services, cable connections, and other activities in order to penetrate the local market. The arguments focused on market share, not short-term profit. They could gain almost 30 percent of the market, and that share could well be the most profitable portion. "Their strategy is very rational," says an officer of Bell Atlantic Corporation, "AT&T could skim off the top 25 percent of our 11 million customers. . . ." These include businesses and affluent individuals who use everything from local services to call-waiting, voice-mail, and multiple phone extensions, which "account for 75 percent of our profit margin" (Keller).

At the same time, local phone companies were freed to enter the long-distance market. AT&T now holds about 60 percent of that market, but the so-called "Baby Bells" will spend billions to wedge in, again looking to market share rather than immediate profits.

Companies such as IBM and Digital Equipment valued a family feeling among employees with the implication of employment for life so highly that they allowed their profits to decline drastically rather than institute large-scale layoffs. When they finally gave in to the need to reduce their labor forces, the action changed their value systems so profoundly they had difficulty adjusting their approach to argumentation appraisal accordingly.

In engineering, both companies continued to work with the values of technical quality and permanence, while their competitors recognized that high tech today requires virtually continuous change. By failing to keep their products up to current standards and compatible with leading producers, Digital has virtually dropped out of competition.

Sensemaking in Organizations

Values come into play in business argumentation through the process of *sensemaking*. Karl Weick's concept of "sensemaking in organizations" is similar to what we mean by argumentation in organizations. Sensemaking, to him, means:

> . . . to talk about reality as an ongoing accomplishment that takes form when people make retrospective sense of the situations in which they find themselves and their creations (15).

Juries come to decisions by first agreeing on what the verdict should be and then looking back in the trial for material to justify their decision. People in organizations similarly employ justification: they start with a proposition in mind and then construct arguments to justify it. Using myths, metaphors, platitudes, fables, epics, and paradigms, says Weick, the argumentation develops in the form of a good story or a convincing vision as we discuss in chapter 4.

Through a story, values are enacted to build plausibility and coherence, embodying past experience and expectations, capturing both feeling and thought in making the arguments both reasonable and memorable. Weick observes: "sensemaking is about plausibility, coherence, and reasonableness. Sensemaking is about accounts that are socially acceptable and credible" (61).

CONCLUSION

Our look at the way values and credibility work in business argumentation has revealed the diversity of places in which argumentation occurs on a daily basis in a wide variety of organizations. From a small retail dry cleaner, to a midsize manufacturer, to giants such as Salomon, IBM, Digital, and AT&T, there is constant argumentation around such issues as price, quality, quantity, schedule, profit, market share, success, future conditions, growth, costs, competition, and production/consumption.

Credibility supports arguments on several levels. We have discussed organizational, managerial, consultant/specialist, and product credibility. The values that play a significant role in business argumentation include the future, success, cost/benefit, competition, and production/consumption.

The context in which business argumentation occurs is that of an organizational culture. Members of organizations engage in an ongoing creation and recreation of the set of past experiences they will use to support their arguments for future behavior. Each set of arguments, therefore, must be evaluated in terms of the context in which it occurs. Through stories based on past experiences, organizational members engage in sensemaking to build plausibility and coherence in their argumentation.

PROJECTS

11.1 Interview a person in the business world to discover how decision making occurs in their particular situation. Write a report on the interview.

11.2 Obtain a copy of an annual report sent out to stockholders by a corporation. Analyze the arguments contained in the report from the point of view of a stockholder interested in making money through growth in the value of the company's stock and through dividends.

11.3 Go to any stockbroker's office and ask to see analyses prepared to advise investors on the future of the economy, the future of an industry, and the future of a particular company. Analyze the arguments from the point of view of a prospective investor.

11.4 Read an article in the *Wall Street Journal* and write a paper on the particular argumentative practices evident in it. Use your paper to comment on business as a sphere.

REFERENCES

"American General." *Wall Street Journal* 14 Sept. 1995: A10.

"Apology Accepted." *The New Yorker* 11 Sept. 1995: 101.

Bantz, Charles R. *Understanding Organizations*. Columbia: U of South Carolina P, 1993.

Barnett, George A. "Communication and Organizational Culture." *Handbook of Organizational Communication*. Eds. Gerald M. Goldhaber and George A. Barnett. Norwood, NJ: Ablex, 1988: 101–30.

Buffett, Warren E. "Salomon, Inc." *New York Times* 29 Oct. 1991: D14–15.

Carlisle, Tomsin. "Canada's Junior Oil Companies Jump Into Exploration." *Wall Street Journal* 22 Aug. 1995: B4.

Frank, Robert. "Adding Some Fizz." *Wall Street Journal* 22 Aug. 1995: A1+.

Glos, Raymond, Richard D. Steade, and James R. Lowry. *Business: Its Nature and Environment*. Cincinnati: South-Western, 1976.

Grimsley, Kirstin Downey. "Nation's Biggest Firms Also Are Offering the Biggest, Best Perks." *Salt Lake Tribune* 24 Sept. 1995: F2.

Keller, John J. "AT&T Eagerly Plots a Strategy to Gobble Local Phone Business." *Wall Street Journal* 21 Aug. 1995: A1+.

Kluckhohn, Clyde, and William H. Kelly. "The Concept of Culture." *The Science of Man In The World Crisis*. Ed. Ralph Linton. New York: Columbia UP, 1945. 78–106.

Kouzes, James M., and Barry Z. Posner. *The Leadership Challenge*. San Francisco: Jossey-Bass, 1995.

"Positively Boring Money Management." *Wall Street Journal* 14 Sept. 1995: A4.

Ries, Al, and Jack K. Trout. *Positioning*. New York: McGraw-Hill, 1986.

Senge, Peter M. *The Fifth Discipline*. New York: Doubleday/Currency, 1990.

Shockley-Zalabak, Pamela. *Fundamentals of Organizational Communication*. White Plains, NY: Longman, 1988.

Ways, Max. *The Future of Business: Global Issues in The 80's and 90's*. New York: Pergamon P, 1978.

Weick, Karl E. *Sensemaking in Organizations*. Thousand Oaks, CA: Sage, 1995.

12

Refutation

Key Terms

process
cooperative
faction
framework
assessment
critical decision making
goals
decision makers

burden of proof
framebreaking
momentum
support
blocking
probing
questioning
flowsheet

Criticism is inherent in critical decision making, and refutation is the term we use to describe the process through which one person or faction (group of people) involved in a decision criticizes arguments advanced by another person or faction. The criticism may be addressed to other members of the same faction, to members of other factions, or to decision makers who are not a part of any faction.

THE PROCESS OF REFUTATION

While it is often useful to say that every issue has two sides, our concept of refutation embraces the idea of many factions subscribing to some point of view or advocating one decision over another. Refutation may need to move in several directions at once.

Some commentators have characterized refutation as a destructive process: one side tearing down the arguments of the other in a game of repartee. In our view refutation is a constructive process. Just as the sculptor must chip away stone and smooth over rough places to produce a work of art, critical decision makers must put their arguments to the most severe tests possible to make the best decisions.

It is in this vein that Douglas Ehninger and Wayne Brockriede characterize debate as a cooperative enterprise. They say a debater is "not a propagator who seeks to win unqualified acceptance for a predetermined point of view while defeating an opposing view" (vii). Instead, they say refutation serves an investigative purpose in the search for the best possible decision.

The concept of refutation as cooperative and constructive becomes clearer when we call attention to fundamental processes that have been so-cially constructed over centuries of practice. In critical decision making, refu-tation implies the following minimum essential principles:

1. All interested parties are given fair notice of an impending decision so that they can prepare their response.
2. Each faction has an equal opportunity to be heard.
3. Each faction grants the others the right to examine and criticize its argu-ments, including access to supporting persons and materials.
4. Decision makers hear arguments only in the presence of other interested parties.
5. People are not decision makers in their own causes.
6. Each faction accepts the delay of the final decision until the critical process has taken place.
7. All factions agree to accept the final decision no matter how far removed it is from their preference.

In chapter 13, we will discuss a view of fallacies that is based on rules such as these. The theory is that any action that impedes progress toward critical decision is a fallacy, and violating such rules does impede progress.

The constructive and ultimately cooperative character of refutation is evi-dent in some spheres, such as legislation, law, and scholarship. People often become impatient with legislative decision making as Democrats and Repub-licans debate each other, constantly finding weaknesses in the other's posi-tions, but they accept that such delay is a price well worth paying in the inter-est of making critical decisions. Totalitarian government operates much faster, but most people prefer the "agreement to disagree" that characterizes parti-san legislation.

In law, attorneys are instructed to disagree and criticize each others' claims in the overall cooperative search for justice. Failure to do their best to refute the opposition is a violation of legal ethics.

In scholarship, the presentation of research findings at conventions and in journals is just one phase in ongoing criticism. To be open to refutation, in-deed to seek it out, is the very essence of scholarship in the cooperative search for knowledge. *Refutation* as we use it in this book must be seen in contrast to many practices that reject opposing viewpoints uncritically. The history of po-litical decision making is filled with examples of governments silencing the op-position by putting leaders in jail, exile, or graves. *McCarthyism* denotes un-critical rejection of opposing ideas through accusation and intimidation. Talk show hosts show themselves to be uninterested in critical interaction. They use their position to talk over or cut off callers with whom they disagree, and then the audience hears the host's side of the issue when the caller has no fur-ther chance to speak. Professors who silence student opinions are equally dis-interested in critical behavior.

Refutation can be most unpleasant when it identifies weaknesses in ideas you believe in fervently, and many people lack the courage to listen to it. That is uncritical behavior.

In this chapter and the next, we set out basic processes of critical behavior. We cannot provide a "manual," and there are no litmus or phenolphthalein tests of argument available, but we do provide a sequence of considerations and potential strategies from which to draw and adapt to each decision.

APPROACHING REFUTATION

Refutation requires the open expression of disagreement with an argument made by someone else. Social rules in force in many cultures discourage such expressions. It is commonly considered impolite to question or challenge others, and linguists say people have a preference for agreement. Scott Jacobs and Sally Jackson say that in interpersonal argument this preference for agreement operates like a presumption in favor of the validity of what others have said. Because of this, "disagreement requires some compelling rationale, something definite enough and significant enough to overcome this presumption" (235–36). Jacobs and Jackson say that refutation is not a general attitude of skepticism, but the application of a specific argument to a specific decision.

A general attitude of skepticism may be a useful approach to refutation at times, but incessant challenging of others' statements can be obnoxious. Benjamin Franklin reports in his autobiography that challenging and refuting almost everything others say can be an ego-building practice for bright youngsters, but it should be set aside with maturity:

> I found this method safest for myself and very embarrassing to those against whom I used it . . . but gradually [I] left it. For, if you would inform, a positive and dogmatical manner in advancing your sentiments may provoke contradiction and prevent a candid attention (25–26).

Franklin concludes his discussion of this phase of his childhood with this quote from Alexander Pope: "Men should be taught as if you taught them not, And things unknown propos'd as things forgot."

Some former championship college debaters, in response to a survey conducted by the American Forensic Association in 1981 concerning the National Debate Tournament, said debate had merely reinforced what they now consider to be antisocial behaviors. They describe a tendency "to turn every conversation, whether social or academic, into a contest [in which they] always had to have the last word." "Truth, logic, tact, and just good manners were more often than not sacrificed for the sake of argument." They describe "mindless, knee-jerk" argumentation as an "insidious habit of pushing informal discussions to the argument stage," ego-gratification gained by winning, showing a superiority over others. One person says "Debate made me over argumentative, always finding problems with others' ideas. . . . It took a long time to get over it. . . . It [debate] may have increased my inability to work well with people on an interpersonal level." They found themselves seeking to conquer opponents rather than work out decisions through negotiation. One former debater concludes this way:

The road to agreement is not always won by argument; every encounter is not a debate. I undoubtedly applied techniques irrelevantly and inappropriately. Even in an argument, I subsequently learned, it is unnecessary, perhaps even counter-productive, to refute *all* of your opponent's case. The main points are enough, and humiliation is costly.[1]

Approaching refutation requires finding a working point somewhere between these extremes: a preference for agreement and silent acknowledgment of the validity of what others say; and the brash, hypercritical, competitive, and destructive practices described by Benjamin Franklin and some former college debaters. If you keep in mind that refutation is a cooperative part of the critical process, rather than a noncontact sport, you should fare well.

SETTING A FRAMEWORK FOR REFUTATION

Each decision and the arguments related to it require a new analysis from which to construct refutation. There must always be an inextricable link among the goals sought in decision making, the specific decisions proposed to meet the goals, and the arguments advanced in support of the proposed decisions. Before you can engage in refutation, then, you must lay a framework from which criticism will emerge. Just as the architect must adapt the structure of a building to meet the demands of the setting and its intended use, arguers must adjust their practices to the specifics of the situation at hand.

Assess the Argumentative Situation

Refutation is a response to the argumentative situation; unless you understand the situation at hand, you are not ready to participate in refutation. Even though people tell stories about talking the police out of tickets, for the most part interactions with police do not represent an argumentative situation. It is better to present your refutation of the charges to a judge. Dinner parties in which your politics or religion differ dramatically from everyone else are probably not the place to launch into an attack on their views. Conversely, when you are part of an impregnable majority, there is little point in refuting the minority arguments when those arguments stand no chance of influencing the decision.

Silence is often the most effective refutation. Remember that humiliation can be costly. But remember, too, that the decision to remain silent is always a gamble: you are resting your case on an assessment of the state of mind of the decision makers. If your judgment proves to be wrong, you will probably kick yourself for not speaking out. It's a tough choice, since speaking out can some-

---

[1]All quotations cited came from an anonymous data pool shared with the authors by Ronald J. Matlon, Lucy Keele, and others associated with the National Debate Tournament and the American Forensic Association. We stress that these critical comments reflected only a minority of those responding to the survey.

times do more harm than good. Only the most insightful have the courage to use silence as a refutation.

Think of the last essay exam you took. Did you find yourself trying to put down everything you could think of, turning the booklet in only when the time was up? This technique can either help you stumble on the correct answer or muddle it up. Next time, take a look at the students who finish before the time is up. They have chosen to write their best answer and stop. They have the same kind of courage needed to use silence as a refutation (or they just didn't have much to say).

The steps in critical decision making provide a guide in assessing the argumentative situation. As you check-off each step, you should become more sensitive to the potential paths for refutation.

Identify the Question or Claim   Keep your eyes on what the decision process is all about. When people lose sight of the key issues, bring them back. Constantly look at issues in relation to the proposition: if the issues are decided, will the proposition follow reasonably?

Ask about the status of the discussion. Where does the present argumentation stand in relation to deciding the proposition? During the preliminary interactions around any topic or decision, the focus of decision makers is likely aimed at gathering information and identifying and sorting relevant values. They are tuning in, paying attention, comprehending, generating relevant cognitions, and acquiring relevant skills (Trenholm 56). This is probably not the time to start refutation. It is possible that the search for a decision will move inexorably toward the decision you propose, and no refutation will be required. At this point, the best argumentative approach is to make a good impression on the decision makers: establish a rapport, obtain commitments, preview your point of view, and generally build high credibility (Rieke and Stutman 68–71, 109–16).

As alternative decisions begin to emerge and compete for the decision makers' attention, as the attractiveness of the alternatives approaches parity, forcing decision makers to struggle with discriminating among them, the time for refutation has arrived (Festinger 154–55). If you fire your refutational guns too soon, the effect may be lost because the decision makers are too early in their search to appreciate your points. If you wait too long, the opportunity to reduce adherence to other positions may have passed.

Survey Objectives and Values   Inherent in each sphere are overall objectives sought from argumentation and the values that will control the process. For example, find out about the rules of procedure. Different spheres prescribe different procedures of argumentation. In law, for example, refutation is restricted to specific stages in the trial and attempts to use refutation outside those limits may be denied. In business settings, criticism of a presentation is usually restricted to questioning rather than direct attack, and often this is limited to people in a high position. A lower-level person attacking a colleague may have what they call at IBM a "career-limiting experience." Before launching into your refutation, you are well advised to know the procedures.

A young negotiator going up against a seasoned veteran was determined to get the upper hand and decided to attack the other side's arguments immediately. The negotiators entered the room and had barely taken their seats when the younger man stood and delivered an impassioned, five-minute attack on the other side. There was a moment of silence, and then the seasoned veteran said, "Does anyone want a Coke before we get started?"

What are the operative cultural values? If you are familiar with film and television characterizations of lawyers at work, you may believe it is common to trash and brutalize the other side and then go out for drinks. If you have been a debater in high school or college, you may believe that tough, uncompromising attacks on others is appropriate behavior. Loud talking, rapid speech, ridicule, and other tactics make for good drama, but they are forbidden in many settings.

In our experience, these dramas do not reflect common practice. In most business settings, professional interactions, and even government sessions, restrained language, quiet voices, courtesy, and consideration for the "face" of opponents is demanded (Lim Tae-Seop 75–86). You may deliver a devastating refutation of another's position only to find you have alienated the decision makers. In countries other than the United States, this is often even more the case. Refutation, to be successful, must not unduly exceed the cultural boundaries of the decision making situation.

Canvass Alternative Decisions   Refutation can be powerful when it exposes the fact that little effort has been made toward testing a range of alternative decisions. Further discussion can be delayed pending research that may well uncover better approaches. Part of the defense in the O. J. Simpson trial was to force police to admit that O. J. was the prime suspect from the start, and they really hadn't looked for another suspect.

Weigh the Costs and Risks   Proposals may seem attractive on their face but lose support when the costs or risks are made clear. There are plenty of government services people would support if they did not require increased taxes. Many people who feel that more help should be provided to the homeless lose their enthusiasm when they learn that the shelter will be built in their neighborhood.

When Congress and the President debated ending welfare as it had been known up to that time, considerable attention was given to moving responsibility from the federal government to the states. This reflected widespread public opinion that the federal government had grown too large. But when the citizens of the various states realized that, even with federal block grants, states would either have to eliminate popular programs or raise taxes, many citizens lost their enthusiasm.

Search for New Information   Refutation does not mean shooting from the hip. If you have not done your homework, you're not ready for refutation.

Richard J. Herrnstein and Charles Murray, in their book, *The Bell Curve*, suggested that the intelligence of African Americans was inherently inferior to that of whites. Although there were many efforts at refutation, it became clear that additional information was needed.

In 1995, the American Psychological Association issued a report called, "Intelligence: Knowns and Unknowns," in which they reviewed relevant research. Among the new information they provided was the claim that standard tests do not measure all forms of intelligence, and while the lower scores on IQ tests by African Americans were reported accurately, there is no research support for a genetic explanation. In fact, evidence shows that both genes and environment contribute substantially to IQ and there is no research showing how those factors operate ("Footnotes"). Armed with this additional information, those who wished to refute the claims of *The Bell Curve* were more effective.

When skill in argumentation and communication are about equal, it is usually the faction with the newest and best information that will prevail. This is due in part to the fact that the better informed you are the less likely you are to advocate unwise positions.

Note Biases Underlying Positions   Identifying biases is an important part of refutation in critical decision making. Roadblocks can often be pushed aside by exposing preconceived notions and biases.

In the drive to end welfare programs as they were known at the time, Congress moved to put a dis-incentive on illegitimate births. They called it a "family cap." The plan was to deny benefits to women who had more than one illegitimate child. Behind this plan there were clear biases. Those favoring the cap said they did not want to "subsidize illegitimacy," presuming that illegitimate children were concentrated among welfare recipients. They further had a bias that suggested welfare mothers were consciously having children to increase their benefits, and behind that bias was an implicit racism suggesting that welfare mothers were mostly African American. There was virtually no evidence or research support for any of these assumptions.

Make Plans to Implement the Decision   Often, the best refutation is to take other proposals seriously and set out precisely what will be needed to implement them. The act of implementation often proves so complex, costly, or plagued with onerous side effects that enthusiasm for the decision vanishes.

Enthusiasm for national health programs frequently starts out high only to dissipate as problems associated with implementation become clear. Prior to 1993, the American people favored a program of national health insurance. The First Lady, Hillary Rodham Clinton, led a commission to plan such a program. But it was opposed and weakened when refutation focused on its implementation. The refutation was based not simply on costs, but access to medical care, choice, rapidity of response, quality of service, and other considerations. Such problems of implementation often cause proposals to die of their own weight.

Analyze the Decision Makers

How will the decision be made? The tone of refutation varies with the proximity to the decision and the likelihood of opposing points being stated after yours. If you are making the last statement, after which the decision makers will immediately make their choice, a more flamboyant, exhortative, and arousing style of refutation may be appropriate. If the decision will not be made for months or years after your refutation, as in congressional hearings, appellate courts, or businesses, the style and content of your refutation should be geared toward lasting impressions and specific recall that decision makers can use during their long deliberations.

If decision makers will not be exposed to counterargument, if they are not very well informed, if they are unlikely to raise objections to your position in their own minds, or if they clearly favor your position, you may concentrate on a one-sided, highly partisan refutation. If these conditions do not apply, however, you will probably be more effective if your refutation takes a multi-sided approach resembling an objective analysis of the alternatives (Trenholm 242).

Who are the Decision Makers?   We are constantly amazed to discover people debating each other without knowing who will ultimately make the decision. In academic debate, courts of law, and other highly formalized decision systems, this does not occur, but in the vast majority of decisions made each day, who finally decides may be obscure.

The police union was negotiating with the city government over their new contract. The city's negotiating team included a professional negotiator, the city attorney, a personnel officer, and a major of police. The union side included a professional negotiator, the president of the police union, and members of the executive committee of the union. After months of talks, the issues were narrowed to one: salary. It proved impossible to reach agreement on this issue, and at that point the question of who would really make the city's decision on pay raises became salient. The union asked for a conference with the mayor, and that produced no progress. It was only when the city's negotiator asked to leave the room every time a new proposal was presented that the police discovered it was the city director of personnel, a former aide to the governor, who was calling the shots. When she was asked to join the negotiations so she could hear the positions debated, she declined and talks broke off without agreement. It accomplished nothing to refute positions without her presence.

In many business settings, decisions are addressed and arguments exchanged with none of the participants knowing who will ultimately decide. People are asked to attend meetings without knowing their role or the purpose of the meeting. Curiously, our experience is that often the participants themselves are expected to decide, but *they do not know it*. Unless you know who will actually make the decision, you cannot generate useful refutation.

In legislation, the decision makers can be quite difficult to discover. On the surface, it is the elected representatives, senators or members of Congress, for example, who vote and thus decide. But a glance beneath the surface says the real clout may be in the hands of a few people who are recognized experts in the particular area of legislation, senior members holding party power, leaders of state delegations, or powerful lobbies (Matthews and Stimson 45). Unless your refutation gets to the real decision makers, it may have no impact at all.

What Are Decision Makers' Goals?   Refutation must not focus solely on the particular strengths and weaknesses of alternative decision proposals; it must relate ultimately to what is sought from the decision. It is possible that alternatives can be rejected *as a whole* rather than attacked point-by-point simply by showing that they fail to address the objective of the decision making. In law, the defense may reject the opponent's entire position by successfully arguing that no prima facie case has been advanced. What this means, simply, is that the judge could accept everything claimed by the prosecution and still not grant a decision in their behalf. In the midst of refutation, it is easy to lose sight of what the debate is about. Tit-for-tat argumentation may obscure what it is that constitutes the objective of all involved.

In legislation, for example, the overarching objective may be to manage the national economy, and opposing bills may call for deficit reduction, tax relief, reconciling the international balance of payments, controlling medical costs, or eliminating foreign aid. While each of these proposals has specific strengths and weaknesses that need attention, the ultimate goal, an effective national economy, must be the primary criterion by which they are assessed.

In partisan bickering, refutation often is focused on trivial issues to the point that everyone seems to have lost sight of what the debate is really about. Although you should criticize the arguments within the web of sub-issues on which the primary purpose rests, refutation should be based on criticism relevant to the decision objectives.

What Are the Presumptions of the Decision Makers?   In the chapters on argumentation and critical appraisal as well as case building, we discussed the concepts of presumption, probability, and burden of proof. These concepts are also crucial to refutation. There may be formal statements of presumption, such as that of innocence in U.S. criminal law, and there may be widely accepted presumptions, such as that in favor of the status quo, but each decision must be analyzed for the actual presumption in place.

In law, jurors who can truly accept the presumption of innocence of a particular accused may be so hard to find that the court will grant a change of venue. Time may be expended on behalf of proposed legislation that seems widely popular when the real decision makers have a strong negative presumption. After years of experience with television interviews of the leaders of a state legislature, we learned to ask off camera about specific bills under consideration, and almost invariably the leaders could accurately predict the outcome. Proponents would blithely continue their campaign, ignorant of a presumption against them that had to be refuted if they were to have any chance of success at all.

The character of your refutation must be responsive to the status of presumption. If your decision carries the weight of presumption, then your refutation should consist primarily of two components: (1) constantly demanding that all other positions accept the burden of proof and defining the nature of their burden; (2) constantly showing how they have failed to meet their burden of proof. The other side of that coin is this: if your position carries the burden of proof you may attempt a refutation that shifts the burden to the others.

This is successful only when the others are either ignorant of their presumption or are incompetent debaters, but it is surprising how frequently it works.

Coming into a meeting one day without having done his homework, an engineer started the discussion by asking the others how much work they had done. They became so focused on explaining their accomplishments and justifying their omissions that they failed to ask whether he had done his work. He successfully shifted the burden of proof.

Remember, both of these approaches rely on the fact that you *know the presumption of the real decision makers*. Also, at any point in decision making, presumption can change, and with it the burden of proof or rejoinder. Candidates for office have been known to shoot themselves in the foot by continuing a campaign based on early data showing a powerful lead even after research reveals that presumption has changed.

Senator Robert Packwood rather off-handedly rejected charges of widespread sexual harassment, and for the months after the charges surfaced continued to announced his intention to complete his term. He probably believed the traditional "old boys" network in the Senate would protect him by presuming his innocence. It was only when the Senate Ethics Committee recommended that Packwood be expelled from the Senate that he finally got the message and resigned.

Are Involved Factions Trying to Act as Decision Makers?   The problem about arguing with police is that they are actually involved in the issue: they aren't judges, they are givers of tickets. When you complain to a business or government agency about their products or services, chances are you will be talking to someone who has an interest in the outcome but who is also playing judge. You may be talking to the very person whose job it is that you are criticizing. If this is the situation, the solution is to find someone else with a smaller stake in defending the opposing point of view and more interest in resolving the dispute. Asking to talk with supervisors, managers, or a regulating agency often helps.

Similarly, such interactions may often involve question-begging tactics (see chapter 13), such as "Our policy is that. . . ." Instead of trying to refute the policy, ask to talk with a person who has the authority to circumvent the policy.

Finally, you need to get around what Tom Wolfe calls "the flak catchers." These are people in organizations whose job it is to listen to complaints (take the flak) and send people away. They are often programmed to mislead: "I wish I could help you, but there is nothing I can do." Instead of trying refutation on such people, you must get around them to real decision makers.

A woman allowed a teenage neighbor to repair her car in the high school shop class, and with the teacher's help he managed to cause $600 worth of damage. She went to the school district and spoke with the person in charge of all shop classes. He said, "I'm sorry, but the law does not allow us to carry insurance for this sort of problem. We are legally unable to help you." The woman asked a professional negotiator to go back to speak to him. He gave the same response, but this time the negotiator simply refused to accept the explanation. The administrator asked to be excused for a moment and returned with another person who introduced himself as the district insurance officer, who proceeded to give instructions about how to make a claim. The first administrator was merely acting as a flak catcher. If the woman had stopped with her first encounter, the district would have saved money. When the flak catcher failed to put off the negotiator, he brought in a real decision maker.

Analyze Opponents

Law provides "discovery" procedures that inform opponents in advance of a trial what witnesses or evidence will be presented. Opposing counsel have a chance to talk to each other's witnesses at length and to review documentary or physical evidence. The principle is that justice will be better served if opponents have time to prepare refutation carefully. The principle should be carried into all refutation: know as much as possible about opponents and their probable arguments.

SELECTING A POSTURE FOR REFUTATION

One of the most common mistakes of inexperienced debaters is the use of "the more you throw, the more will stick to the wall" theory of refutation. It's the same theory we spoke of earlier in relation to students writing essay exams: not enough courage to stop when you've said enough; not enough knowledge to know when enough is enough. This is a tactic used by the inexperienced or the desperate. We will suggest a variety of postures from which refutation can be conducted, in the hope of convincing you to think before you refute and to quit when you have done what you planned, even if you still have time, space, or arguments unused.

We posit a general theory of refutation: *aim refutation at the highest conceptual level possible*. When you can cut off the head, don't hack at the feet. A corollary of that theory is this: *when the decision is in your hands, shut up*. If the enemy is dead, hold your fire. We have seen times when defeat has been snatched from the jaws of victory simply because the obvious victor could not remain silent. Continued refutation actually moved decision makers to change their minds.

Refute from a Constructive Basis

Whether you are defending an established position with the protection of presumption or attacking it, refutation is most powerful when it comes from the perspective of a *viable constructive position*. It is one thing to hammer away at the prevailing policy, but its defenders are unlikely to abandon it without an alternative. In fact, defenders of the status quo will probably not even perceive your refutations for what they are because of selective perception.

Thomas Kuhn reports on what he calls scientific paradigms (sub-sets of spheres) such as ptolemaic astronomy, Newtonian physics, and quantum mechanics. Kuhn argues that "Once it has achieved the status of paradigm, a scientific theory is declared invalid only if an alternative candidate is available to take its place" (77).

In law, the defense can technically rely totally upon refutation of the plaintiff's case, but that is less powerful than generating at least a plausible alternative theory of the case. In the O. J. Simpson trial, the defense argued from the very start that racist police had set up O. J. by planting evidence. At first, this was seen as far-fetched, but when a key officer was revealed to be a racist by his own words, the story became at least plausible.

In public policy, naysayers are often turned aside with: "We know of all the weaknesses of our system, but it's the best there is." Challenges to public policy are strongest when they emanate from persuasive alternatives.

Defend Your Position

If you have constructed a viable alternative position or if you are defending the presumed position, stick with it. Too often, the heat of debate draws attention away from your home position as you sally forth to attack others. We suggest that every communication you produce in the debate begins with a restatement of your position and a discussion of how it remains intact despite the refutation of other factions. This may require some repairs. Your position may have been damaged by refutation, so your first priority is to put it back together. Remember, other factions will be trying to pull you away from your position and get you to debate on their ground. If they have the burden of proof, they will be trying to shift it to your shoulders.

Keep the Focus on the Goals of Decision Making

The highest conceptual level toward which refutation can be aimed is the goal of decision making. Constantly return the focus of the discussion to the goals sought from the decision to be made, and demonstrate any point at which other factions fail to generate those goals.

In a proposal designed to reduce spending to balance the state budget, a governor included a reduction in money given to welfare recipients offset by a new jobs program. Under refutation, the governor admitted that the costs of administering the jobs program would more than eat up money saved in welfare payments, but he said, "I feel everyone should make a sacrifice, and some work requirements seem reasonable." Focusing on the highest level of analysis, opponents argued that whether everyone should sacrifice or whether a jobs program was reasonable was beside the point. The issue was how to reduce state spending, and the governor's proposal simply did not fit that goal. In this way, opponents were able to reject the governor's bill as a whole without ever having to refute its individual elements.

Engage in Framebreaking

Chris Argyris reports research findings that suggest that people reason differently when they think about a program simply to understand it than when they intend to make a decision. They are able to detect and understand inconsistencies, errors, and other problems with decision proposals of others, *but not their own*, when under pressure to decide and act. Moreover, when they tried to refute other positions, "they created conditions that led to escalating error, self-fulfilling prophecies, and self-sealing processes" (39).

Argyris proposes *framebreaking* as the response to this problem. Helping others break their typical frame of reference in considering decision proposals allows them to see, for the first time, the problems with their positions.

Similarly, decision makers who are not otherwise involved in the argumentation need help breaking their frames of reference to see the problems you are pointing out in your refutation. Under pressure to decide, says Argyris, people disconnect from their reasoning process. These are the usual characteristics: people do not understand when their premises or inference processes are problematic; people perceive their analyses as concrete when they actually rely on abstractions and a complex series of inferences; people rarely see a need to test their own reasoning through interaction with others because they "know" their reasoning is clear and correct.

Argyris's plan involves what he calls *double-loop learning* in which "the basic assumptions behind ideas or policies are confronted, in which hypotheses are tested publicly, and in which the processes are disconfirmable, not self-sealing" (103–04). In argumentation, that process involves bringing into the open the assumptions that lie behind the arguments of others. It is used to discuss and challenge why grounds used may not be acceptable, why warrants employed may be irrelevant or without adequate backing, why reservations are overlooked or understated.

Refutation based on double-loop learning involves challenging the argumentation of others by bringing to light the fundamental assumptions, values, or frames of reference on which they necessarily rest. In this refutation, it is possible that entire lines of argument may be rejected simply by exposing their unstated foundation. If Argyris is correct, even those whose arguments you are refuting may be helped to see their own errors and move away from their original positions.

Many health insurance policies include a coinsurance payment by the insured. For example, it is common that a policy calls for the insurance to cover 80 percent of the costs with the insured paying 20 percent. When the patient receives a bill for, say, $200, it would be reasonable to assume that the total costs of the procedure were $1,000.

However, Robert Tomsho reports in the *Wall Street Journal*, that it is common for the insurance company to negotiate a discount of up to 50 percent with the health care provider without passing the savings along to the insured. So in this scenario, the insurance company paid a total of $500, and billed the customer for $200 which is actually 40 percent of the actual charge. It was only when a patient questioned the assumptions underlying the policy that this practice came to light (A1).

Framebreaking has been used widely to refute laws and practices that discriminate between men and women. The traditional frame of reference—that women are weaker and less intellectually and emotionally capable than men—supported laws that were proclaimed to be protective of women. When women sought to overturn the laws, they had to expose the assumption of inferiority and attack it directly. When the assumption fell, so did the concept of "protection," and that generated a new frame of reference that sex discrimination is hurtful, not protective. Many men who had opposed the women's movement shifted their position when they saw discrimination in this new light.

Test the Credibility of Other Factions

Review the discussion of credibility in chapter 10, and think about how challenges to others' credibility might form the basis of refutation. The credibility of key proponents may be used to damage a proposal. The credibility of evidence can be challenged by exposing bias, exclusion of important reservations, outdatedness, imprecision, or other criteria discussed in chapter 6. Credibility of sources of support can be the object of refutation.

In the long battle between the tobacco companies and their critics, credibility of evidence has played an important role. Critics claim research shows that smoking damages health but the tobacco interests continually reject this research by pointing out that the studies found only correlations, not causal connections. In return, when the tobacco companies produce research that suggests smoking is not the cause of health problems, critics note that researchers who are paid or otherwise supported by grants from tobacco interests are not reliable neutral scientists.

When a former lobbyist for the Tobacco Institute was diagnosed with cancer and decided to speak openly about his work, his testimony was granted high credibility. He was admitting he had participated in misleading the public by withholding information and providing inaccurate information. A former insider "coming clean" in a way that reflects badly on his own work has the highest credibility.

Stop the Momentum

When you perceive that a strong momentum is pushing a decision away from your position, delay may be a useful refutation. During World War II, General Douglas MacArthur, so the story goes, often kept controversial issues from his staff until just before 5:00 p.m. when all were anxious to get to "happy hour." At that point, they would approve almost anything without debate just to get out of the room. At such a juncture, requests for further information, a notice that some key person is not present, proposal of an amendment, indication of possible negative reaction from other distant interests, or other delaying tactics may prevent undue haste in decision making by halting the momentum.

Deny Support

The refutation aimed at the lowest conceptual level of analysis is a point-by-point attack on the support used by other factions. Review chapters 7, 9, and 10 on the various means of support, and consider how they can be the basis of refutation. Essentially, you proceed by denying other factions' support through challenges of authenticity, relevance, or sufficiency and by producing countersupport that neutralizes or overcomes their material.

The problem with this form of refutation should be obvious by now: you are hacking away at the lower extremities of opposition arguments, and often they can be repaired or replaced easily. Every time Hercules chopped off one of Hydra's heads she grew two more, and every time you chop off a piece of opposition support, they can grow two more. Like Hercules, you need to find a way to cauterize the wounds so they do not grow back: relate each challenge of support to the claim it backs. Demand that the *claim* be defended, and return the argumentation to the higher conceptual levels.

Sometimes debaters sandbag the opposition by presenting their weaker support first to draw an attack that they then replace with secondary support so powerful that decision makers discount any further challenges. Pilots talk of "sucker holes"—patches of apparently clear sky that lure in pilots who then find themselves in worse weather than what they were trying to escape. Apparently weak support can be a sucker hole. Your refutational energy is drawn toward what appears to be a weakness, and later you find to your horror that you have exhausted your opportunity for refutation on trivia, having overlooked more significant refutational targets. Then you are confronted with powerful secondary support the others had held in reserve. If you read military history, you will find this strategy behind many victorious generals.

COMMUNICATING REFUTATION

It is exciting to read about daring feats written in ways that make them sound easy; it is quite another to try them yourself. In military history heroism may sound attractive, but it takes on another aspect in the midst of battle. It's not as easy as it sounds. Neither is refutation.

What we often forget when reading about battles or debate is that others will be trying to do to you what you are trying to do to them. In a Walter Mitty fantasy, you may picture yourself delivering a brilliant and powerful refutation to an opponent who cringes under your eloquence and bows to your superior analysis. When you really try it, the opponent will probably give you just as much in return.

The first time you are forced to hear or read what others think of your ideas, and their comments are not complimentary, you may find yourself gravitating toward escape from the process or giving an angry, flailing response. It will take considerable cool to stay on course. Because our society does not typically condone refutation, preferring agreement or silence instead, you may lack the emotional preparation for it. As a result, there are important steps to take in communicating your refutation. The more prepared you are the more you will be steeled against the emotions that necessarily are involved. Simulations, practice sessions, are an absolute necessity. Even the president of the United States conducts practice sessions before major press conferences.

Here is a basic format for communicating refutation that works in most situations:

1. State the point to be refuted.
2. State your claim relevant to the point.
3. Support your claim.
4. State explicitly how your criticism undermines the overall position of those you are refuting.

These four steps make clear what is being refuted and why, and it links your individual refutation to a higher conceptual level. It makes clear how this refutation weakens not just this one point, but the whole case. In the remainder of the chapter, we will discuss refutation processes that fall within this general pattern of communicating your refutation.

Block Arguments

Refutation can be prepared in advance by briefing opponent's arguments in a form that can readily be accessed in an actual argument. This allows you to plan your response systematically through argumentative blocks—outlines that set out the opponents' arguments one by one with your response opposite. When, in the heat of debate, an argument comes up, you can glance at your prepared block on that argument and review what you planned to say in response. Most professional advocates use the blocking system to assure a basic refutation that is consistent with their overall position and help avoid unwise arguments made in haste.

In the summer of 1995, the Microsoft company announced, with great fanfare, its Windows 95 software update. Competitors knew that the dominance of Microsoft in its markets would make the new product instantly attractive to buyers. When talking to customers, IBM and the Apple Computer company knew the presumption would favor Windows 95, and it would be their burden to refute the claims of Microsoft if they intended to sell their own products successfully.

They had obviously prepared their refutation in advance because immediately following the announcement of Windows 95, both IBM and Apple published full-page ads refuting the claims of Microsoft. As we said at the start of this chapter, there are often more than two sides to a proposition, and so we will provide sample blocks to illustrate how two companies sought to refute Microsoft. If you are deciding on what software to buy, you will need to consider all three arguments, and maybe more.

Notice the difference in refutation strategies between IBM and Apple. The IBM refutation focuses heavily on a constructive position—their product is better in specific ways. They do not directly engage the Microsoft arguments very often. On the other hand, Apple takes a more direct refutation approach, specifically countering claims of Microsoft with their own.

Sample Refutation Blocks

Block #1

Microsoft Windows 95	*IBM OS/2*
Unlock the Potential of the Computer	0S/2 Does Everything Windows 95 Does and More
I. Make it work easier	I. A full family of products all easy
A. Easy to use tools	A. Serve different size needs
1. Start button taskbar	
2. Windows Explorer	
B. Plug and Play frees from manual setting CD-ROM, etc.	
C. Long file names 250 characters	

Block #2

Microsoft Windows 95	*IBM OS/2*
Make it work faster: faster file and disk access 32-bit architecture; faster printing 32-bit architecture	OS/2 has one smooth, seamless operating system that works on PC's large computers, to your notebook
II. Compatible with current software	II. OS/2 is part of the world's business fabric
A. 16-bit programs and drives for Windows to MS-DOS and workgroups	A. Runs bank ATM's
	B. Controls cash registers in fast-food chains and department stores
	C. Airline reservations
	D. Used where down time cannot be tolerated

Block #3

Microsoft Windows 95	*IBM OS/2*
III. A world of possibilities; several tasks at once, 32-bit programs; preemptive multitasking	III. OS/2 offers true multitasking and crash protection
A. Microsoft Network online, e-mail, news, internet access	A. Dependable connections in house and out to internet
	B. Powers more PC

application servers than any
system on the planet
C. OS/2 is polished and
perfected, battle tested
1. In use seven years
2. In third release

Block #4

Microsoft Windows 95
IV. Unlock the Potential
Computer; make it work
easier

A. Easy to use tools
1. Start button
taskbar
2. Windows explorer
B. Plug and Play frees
from manual setting,
CD-ROM, etc.
C. Long file names
250 characters
D. Compatible with your
current software
1. 16-bit programs
and drives for
Windows to MS-DOS

Apple Power Macintosh
IV. Windows 95 Unproven;
Windows works poorly; "bailing
wire, chewing gum and Prayer."
Stephen Manos, the *New York
Times* 1 Aug. 1995
A. Most people will need to
upgrade hardware and
software to get Windows 95
close to Macintosh

Block #5

Microsoft Windows 95
V. Make it work faster

A. Faster file and disk
access 32-bit
architecture
B. Faster printing

Apple Power Macintosh
V. Macintosh runs twice as fast as
a 120 MHz Pentium running
Windows
A. Uses advanced RISC-based
processor

B. Independent research
proves Power Macintosh
9500 is 63 percent faster
on average

Block #6

Microsoft Windows 95
VI. A world of
possibilities
A. Multitask work

Apple Power Macintosh
VI. Macintosh offers
possibilities, too
A. Multitask work

1. Several tasks at
   once with 32-bit
   architecture
2. Preemptive multi-
   tasking

B. The Microsoft Network
   1. E-mail
   2. News
   3. Internet access

C. One-Step In Box
   1. Easy to view and
      work with e-mail
      from multiple
      sources, bases, comments,
      bulletin boards

D. Network Ready
   1. 32-bit access to
      network resources

E. Mobile
   1. Dial-up networking
   2. Battery monitor
   3. Plug and play support
      for PCMCIA

1. 3-D graphics
2. Videoconference
3. Speech recognition
4. Telephone
5. Virtual reality

B. Windows is weak
   1. Runs on aging chip
      architecture
   2. Only runs on other
      people's hardware

C. Macintosh offer a seamless
   integration of both
   hardware and software using
   RISC-based processor

Probe Opponents

In the military, it is standard practice to send out patrols to discover the location, strength, and response patterns of the enemy. In debate, early refutation should send out tentative questions and challenges to discover where other factions are weak, where they are sandbagging, and where they are loaded for bear. Listen carefully for questionable support or repetition of original support rather than secondary support. At the same time, use a continued analysis of the decision makers to learn where they perceive weaknesses in other positions as well as your own.

Based on this probing, you can match your strength against others' weaknesses. Choose your challenges to bring together your greatest strengths opposite others' greatest weaknesses *as defined by your reading of the decision makers*. If you have already won decision makers' support on a major point, don't keep going over it; just review it from time to time to keep it on their minds. Concentrate refutation on those points in other positions that remain open in decision makers' minds and on which you have some reasonable expectation of success. Don't waste time flogging an issue you cannot win.

Use Questioning to Probe   In most decision making situations, there is some opportunity for interrogation, and if used properly it can be powerful. The most frequent mistake is to confuse probing questions with refutation itself. Rarely do you seriously damage another's position during actual questioning. Instead, you discover weaknesses, expose contradictions, challenge credibility, and extract admissions that can then be used as part of your refutation. This will strengthen your refutation because you can remind decision makers that your point is based on what the opponents themselves have said.

Follow basic rules of questioning:

1. Prepare and practice questions in advance.
2. Ask questions to which you know the probable answers from prior research.
3. Phrase questions to allow a reasonably brief, preferably yes or no answer.
4. Be courteous in tone of voice and content of question, unless you want a dog fight.
5. Don't ask a question that demands that the other side capitulate—Perry Mason is pure fiction.
6. Ask the question and shut up; if you don't get the expected answer, move on rather than try to give your preferred answer yourself.
7. If the response is evasive, rephrase and try again, courteously.

The paradigm of ideal confrontation, according to Scott Jacobs, is for the questioner to elicit a declarative statement and then request a series of brief informative replies, followed by a rhetorical question that is, at once, a reply to the original declaration and a demonstration of its contradiction. Here is an example:

> Mother: I have a perfectly good will.
> Daughter (a law professor): Will it have to go to probate?
> Mother: I don't know.
> Daughter: Is it subject to estate taxes?
> Mother: I don't think so.
> Daughter: Will it adjust to your changing circumstances?
> Mother: I'm not sure.
> Daughter: Mother, don't you think it would be a good idea to have your will checked out for these things?

Prepare to Respond to Questioning Answering questions well is a part of refutation, though few prepare for it. Lawyers spend plenty of time preparing witnesses and politicians prepare to answer the press, but few others do so. Follow these principles:

1. Never answer until you understand the question.
2. Take your time.
3. Recognize that some questions don't deserve answers.
4. If the questioner interrupts, allow it.
5. Don't elaborate if it won't help you.
6. Ask permission to elaborate if it will help you (if permission is denied, remain silent).
7. Answer only those parts of the question that you believe deserve an answer.
8. Answer a question that was not asked, if that makes more sense to you.

9. If given an opportunity to repeat your argument, accept it in full.
10. Remember that during your refutation you will have a chance to explain or discount the effect of your answers; don't try to do this during questioning as it will only make you appear to be whining.

Follow Good Communication Practices

The most fundamental rules of good communication should be used in refutation, even though excitement often works against such clear practices. One way to keep yourself together even under pressure is to take notes that keep you informed at a glance on what arguments have emerged around each issue.

A flowsheet is a form of note taking or outlining that shows the progress of arguments and their various refutations. The flowsheet on pages 246–247 follows the arguments of four people debating the proposition that *A Virtual University Should Be Established.* The left column shows the arguments of the first affirmative constructive and the next column the first negative. The arrows show how the negative arguments relate to the affirmative and the flow of arguments through the second affirmative and negative speeches.

CONCLUSION

Refutation must come from a balanced posture that is neither too silent nor too brash. It should be approached as a cooperative, critical process important to good decision making. Before you can begin refutation, you need to assess the argumentative situation to learn the way the argumentation is functioning in the particular sphere, including who the appropriate decision makers are and what are their presumptions.

Before refutation begins you should prepare yourself for it by assessing the situation in light of the steps in critical decision making. You should also analyze the decision makers and your opponents to gain the necessary information to select a posture for refutation.

Once refutation begins, it should be aimed at the highest conceptual level possible. Often it will include a constructive basis for your criticism that you can defend. Sometimes refutation rests on framebreaking, or helping decision makers adopt a different way of thinking about the issues. You may also test opponents' credibility, stop momentum, and deny support.

In communicating refutation it is well to follow a format of stating the point to be refuted, then your refutation and support, and finally show how it undermines the opponent's position. To prepare for refutation it is a good idea to build refutational blocks that summarize each argument to be refuted and your refutation of it. A flowsheet will help you keep track of an argument and visually identify what you must refute.

PROPOSITION: A VIRTUAL UNIVERSITY SHOULD BE ESTABLISHED

Affirmative	*Negative*	*Affirmative*	*Negative*
I. Expanding current universities to meet future needs is too costly.	I. You are assuming high costs needs without providing necessary data.	I. The demands on higher ed. in the future are well documented.	II. In a technical era, truly educated citizens will become even more important than in Plato's time.
A. Construction costs will be high.	A. You have not specified what will be needed. You provide no figures on the cost of establishing a virtual university.	A. John Mosley, VP for Academic Affairs, U. of Oregon writes in <u>Managing and leading the University of the 21st Century: Megatrends and Strategies</u> provides data.	A. Technology changes quickly, and if students are only filled with current information, they will soon be obsolete.
1. Current physical facilities are deteriorating.			B. The most practical education is one that prepares students to think, learn, communicate, decide, and act effectively.
2. The number of students is increasing.			
3. Construction is expensive.			
B. Costs to students will be high.	B. You have provided no comparative data showing the differential between traditional higher ed. and a virtual university.	B. Quantitative data is provided in <u>Postsecondary OPPORTUNITY</u> No. 36, June, 1995.	
1. Living away from home is costly.			
2. Commuting long distances is costly.			
3. Tuition will be raised to pay for construction, etc.			
C. Costs to students will be high.	C. What will be the amount of increase in personnel costs? Again, you give no data.		
1. Faculty salaries will increase.			
2. Additional faculty must be hired.			
II.	II. Cost must be measured against the criteria of what is needed in higher education.	II. The criteria for higher education must be adjusted for the 21st century.	
	A. Higher education aims at preparing people to think critically, learn effectively, interact socially, and be good citizens.	A. The criteria you list come from Plato's time, and the world has changed.	
	B. A virtual university is not able to meet these criteria,	B. The future will demand citizens with knowledge and skills in technical fields.	
	1. Technology is best in giving information.		
	2. Technology is worst at developing critical thinking.		
	C. Damaging our children's education is a cost that cannot be measured in dollars.		

III. A virtual university will be practicable and desirable. →

A. New technology is practical,
1. Computers,
2. Videoconferencing
3. Internet tutorials
4. Off shelf CD-ROMS

B. New technology is preferable to spending money on conventional higher education.
1. It will remove the need to construct new buildings.
2. It will cost students less.
3. There will be no need to hire new faculty.

IV. There are no serious disadvantages to a virtual university,

A. Interaction is possible in a virtual university: students can talk with each other and the teacher.

B. The best teachers can be used no matter where they are geographically.

C. Quality control in instruction will be easier, more certain.

III. A virtual U. is impracticable and undesirable, →

A. There is no substitute for shared human spaces of a campus.

B. Face-to-face meetings with instructors is essential.

C. Physically going to the library and conducting research is essential.

IV. There are serious disadvantages to a virtual university, →

A. This is not real interaction.

B. No teacher can be effective in a disembodied format.

C. In fact, studying by themselves, students need not do their own work.

III. Virtual universities are now working successfully, →

A. National Technical U. represents a consortium of fifty American universities.

B. Canada has an on-line MBA.

C. Britain has an Open University.

IV. The disadvantages have not been supported by evidence.

III. Experience with technology-based education has not been good.

A. We learn that hundreds of students watching TV sets don't learn much.

B. National Technical U. is mostly talking heads and graphs.

C. Britain and Canada are not replacing their excellent universities with these experiments.

PROJECTS

12.1 Select a newspaper editorial with which you disagree. Prepare a refutation of it with the aim of convincing the other members of the class to sign a letter to the editor rejecting the editorial.

12.2 Present your refutation to a group of other students and ask them to give you critical responses. Ask them to help you improve your refutation.

12.3 Write a letter to the editor expressing your refutation of the editorial. Then write a commentary on your work that identifies how your original refutation changed after talking to other students and then changed again to be effective with all potential newspaper readers.

12.4 Engage in a class debate in which you do refutation. Then talk to the other students to determine how well received your refutation was.

REFERENCES

Argyris, Chris. *Reasoning, Learning, and Action*. San Francisco: Jossey-Bass, 1982.

Ehninger, Douglas, and Wayne Brockriede. *Decision By Debate*. New York: Dodd, 1967.

Festinger, Leon. *Conflict, Decision, and Dissonance*. Stanford: Stanford UP, 1964.

"Footnotes." *Chronicle of Higher Education* 29 Sept. 1995: A10.

Franklin, Benjamin. *The Autobiography of Benjamin Franklin*. Ed. Gordon S. Haight. New York: Black, 1941.

Jacobs, Scott. "How to Make an Argument from Example in Discourse Analysis." *Contemporary Issues In Language and Discourse Processes*. Eds. Donald G. Ellis and William A. Donohue. Hillsdale, NJ: Earlbaum, 1986. 149–67.

Jacobs, Scott, and Sally Jackson. "Conversational Argument: A Discourse Analytic Approach." *Advances in Argumentation Theory and Research*. Eds. J. Robert Cox and Charles A. Willard. Carbondale: Southern Illinois UP, 1982. 205–37.

Kuhn, Thomas S. *The Structure of Scientific Revolutions*. Chicago: U of Chicago P, 1970.

Lim, Tae-Seop. "Politeness Behavior in Social Influence Situations." *Seeking Compliance*. Ed. James P. Dillard. Scottsdale: Gorsuch Scarisbrik, 1990. 75–86.

Matthews, Donald R., and James A. Stimson. *Yeas and Nays: Normal Decision Making in the U.S. House of Representatives*. New York: Appleton, 1975.

Rieke, Richard D., and Randall K. Stutman. *Communication in Legal Advocacy*. Columbia: U of South Carolina P, 1991.

Tomsho, Robert. "Some Health Insurers Leave Patients to Foot Excessive Copayments." *Wall Street Journal* 21 Aug. 1995: A1.

Trenholm, Sara. *Persuasion and Social Influence*. Englewood Cliffs, NJ: Prentice, 1989.

13

Refutation by Fallacy Claims

Key Terms

fallacy claim

incorrect logic

sophistry

informal logic

tu quoque

begging the question

authority

popularity

post hoc

ad hominem

discussion rules

burden of proof

deception

refusal to reason

cooperation

irrelevant

obfuscation

quantity maxim

conflict of interest

reckless disregard

One of the critic's tasks in refutation is to examine arguments to see whether they contain fallacies. If the critic can successfully claim that an argument is fallacious, the person making the argument has the burden to correct or abandon the position. However, looking for fallacies is not like checking the oil in your car to see if you're a quart low. It's rather complicated.

We will start with a definition. A *fallacy claim asserts that an argument must be rejected because it violates a significant rule of argumentation relevant to the appropriate decision makers*. Central to this concept of fallacy are four characteristics:

1. Charging that an argument commits a fallacy requires that you undertake the burden of proving it to the satisfaction of the decision makers. This is in contrast to pointing out, for example, that a computational error has been made in solving a mathematical problem or that a word has been misspelled. In math or spelling, the error may well be self-evident once attention is focused on it. In argumentation, a fallacy claim is rarely self-evident (Lyne 3).

For example, we often hear in conversation the claim, "You're being inconsistent." And the other person merely replies, "No, I'm not." If you intend to make the fallacy claim of inconsistency, you need to say something like this: "When you oppose abortion on the grounds that life is sacred but at the same time support capital punishment, you argue against yourself. That is inconsistent." When you state the fallacy claim that directly, the other person must do more than deny the charge.

2. A fallacy claim charges significant deviance from appropriate argumentation practices; it does not make nit-picking criticisms that score debate points rather than advance critical decision making. Sometimes people trounce on a slip of the tongue, a minor error, or an overstatement as though it were a triumph. A bit of hyperbole, such as

> WILLIE: "In his entire career, Sean Connery never appeared in a truly bad movie,"

may produce a response like,

> JOE: "Oh yeah. What about *First Knight?*"
> WILLIE: "Oh. I guess I forgot about that one."

This may weaken Willie's credibility but it is not what we mean by fallacy, because he can hold the claim by qualifying it with, "I meant most of his movies."

3. A fallacy claim charges a violation in argumentation rules that may not be appreciated by appropriate decision makers until it is made an issue. It opens to discussion a violation at once so significant and so subtle that appraisal itself becomes an issue. One function of a fallacy claim is to pinpoint the issue that in principle needs resolution (Lyne 3).

Elder Paul H. Dunn was widely respected among members of the Church of Jesus Christ of Latter Day Saints (Mormon) for his inspirational talks and books. He used his exploits in World War II and as a professional baseball player to make religious claims. Then it was discovered that these "experiences" never happened. He fabricated them. He was accused of the fallacies of misuse of authority and deception.

This forced public debate on a moral principle that was significant but had not been explicitly discussed: must the parables used by religious teachers be true? Some claimed that if the examples were merely intended to inspire people to live a better life, then it did not matter that they were false. Others said Dunn's work must be rejected because of the violations of trust.

More recently, reports the *New Yorker*, Father Michael Kennedy who is a curate in Dungarvan, Ireland, delivered a shocking sermon. He announced that a woman with AIDS had come to town and slept with 80 men, of whom five are now HIV positive. Dungarvan is a town of only seven thousand people, and this announcement caused quite an uproar.

Extensive searching by townspeople and journalists has totally failed to find any evidence of such a woman or the alleged exploits. It would seem that Father Kennedy made up the story for whatever reason he had in mind. Yet, because it came from the local priest in the midst of a sermon, people could not lightly dismiss it. Father Kennedy is also susceptible to the claim of the fallacies of misuse of authority and deception as was Elder Dunn (Toibin).

4. While a fallacy claim rests upon a significant rule of the sphere, the appropriate decision makers must reaffirm the rule for the claim to succeed. For example, while courts have a rule to follow past precedents, individual courts sometimes choose to ignore it. To claim that an argument is fallacious because it violates precedent requires the court to reaffirm its commitment to the precedent.

In the remainder of the chapter, we discuss competing views of fallacy and examine selected social guides to the development of fallacy claims.

VIEWS OF FALLACY

Aristotle is credited with formalizing logic, and his work in the *Sophistical Refutations*, *Prior Analytics*, and *Rhetoric* is cited as the origin of the concept of fallacy (Hamblin 50–88). As logicians sought to make sense of Aristotle's ideas, they did so from a world view powerfully shaped by a sense of order and certainty. They were sure that the universe is orderly and that humans possess the rational capacity to understand and deal with it. Logic was perceived to be the tool of that rationality.

Logicians believed that just as numbers and abstract symbols, such as P and Q, could be manipulated within mathematical or logical analyses with certain and consistent meaning, so could ordinary language. For most of our intellectual history, people have believed that words have precise meaning and the primary task of the arguer is one of interpretation: discovering meaning and using the correct word to say what is meant. For a discussion of this, examine chapter 15.

Fallacy as Incorrect Logic

The view of logic that has emerged over the past 500 years in Europe and ultimately the United States, is one that seeks order and certainty by removing the disorderly and unpredictable aspects of human behavior. In this view, dialogue, conversation, and human feeling are "mere nuisances" (Ong 251). Logic is a system existing outside of human discourse (Howell 350–61). It has little patience for the pragmatics of language as practiced by ordinary people where the meaning of words is negotiated through usage and may vary within a single argument.

From this world view, it is no wonder that some philosophers understand Aristotle's idea of fallacy as identifying *incorrectness* in logic. They are like old-fashioned grammarians in that respect. In traditional grammar, the task is to locate grammatical errors such as this: "The books is on the table." The error is in agreement between noun and verb, because the first is plural and the second is singular. In logic, the task is to locate logical errors, for example, the fallacy of the undistributed middle term in a categorical syllogism (described in chapter 2):

Japanese eat raw fish.
Sharks eat raw fish.
Therefore, Japanese are sharks.

The error is failing to have a premise that logically links Japanese with sharks.

In the discussion of informal logic in chapter 2, we introduced you to the hypothetical syllogism that takes the "If A, then B" form. For example, "If it rains, then the streets will get wet." You can logically use this in two ways: (1) affirm the antecedent, a *modus ponens* (it did rain, so the streets are wet); (2) deny the consequent, a *modus tollens* (the streets are not wet, so it did not rain).

On the other hand, drawing a claim from affirming the consequent or denying the antecedent can be called fallacious because they do not yield valid conclusions. That is, if you see that the streets are wet and conclude it must have rained, you could be making an error. There is more than one way the streets can become wet. Similarly, if you know it has not rained and presume, therefore, that the streets are dry, you could be committing a fallacy.

A fundamental fallacy in the eyes of some is to mistake validity for truth (Fearnside and Holther 126). This may occur when ordinary language and real issues are presented in logical form (what we call quasi-logic in chapter 2). For example, this argument follows a valid form: Any structure built on my property belongs to me, and your fence is on my property, so it belongs to me.

While the claim seems clear-cut and valid as stated, the real problem is with the substance of the argument, not its form. Any lawyer will tell you that fences and property lines are not simply a matter of a surveyor's report. To make good on this claim, you must successfully argue not only that the property line is where you claim it is, but that you have consistently and publicly continued to claim the property. If you have allowed the fence to stay there without asserting your claim, you may have no case. A critic who stopped with the observed validity of the argument would miss the key issues.

In one view, it is not worthwhile to study fallacies based on violations of the rules of formal logic because strengths and weaknesses in argumentation are too variable (Ehninger and Brockriede 99–100). In another view, although argumentation is admittedly inexact and ambiguous, taking note of such fallacies serves as a point of reference by which arguments "might be critically analyzed" (Lyne 4).

The more knowledgeable you are on the rules of logic and the ways they can be violated, the more likely you are to sniff out some of the problems in people's arguments and come up with effective refutation. But you must keep in mind that argumentation does not conform to strict rules of logic, and logical incorrectness may not be an effective fallacy claim.

Fallacy as Sophistry

A fallacy, to some, is more than an error. It is an error that leads, or could lead, rational people toward mistaken or dangerous conclusions. Those holding to this view are dedicated to more than correctness. They seek to rid the world of sophistry, the use of plausible but fallacious reasoning. The study of fallacies is a way to protect people from being led astray by persuaders who care nothing for truth in their fervor to get their way (Walton 2–15).

A typical introduction to textbooks on fallacies predicates the study on the rising intensity in the "constant battle for our minds and allegiances that is such a distinctive feature of life . . . through the mass media particularly" (Engel 4). "The triumph of rhetoric is like the spread of a virus infection," say Fearnside and Holther, "it would be a good idea if the community could somehow develop a serum against some forms of persuasion" (1). Howard Kahane believes the study of fallacies is the serum that attempts to "raise the level of political argument and reasoning by acquainting students with the devices and ploys which drag that level down" (xi). He says persuasion is often successful when it ought not to be, and so he defines a fallacy as an "argument which *should not* persuade a rational person to accept its conclusion" (1).

> For example, people may be taken in by this argumentation: When the attorney general of the state announced an investigation of the university president for possible misuse of funds because it had been discovered the president had lavishly remodeled his office, the president responded by revealing that the attorney general had recently spent $10,000 just for a new door into her office.

This *tu quoque* argument (responding to a charge by making a counter-charge) is a fallacy in the eyes of some because, first, it is logically erroneous in not addressing the issue of the university president's actions and, second, it may seem plausible to the public. For example, some people seemed quick to forgive President Richard Nixon for Watergate and President Ronald Reagan for Iran/Contra partly in the belief that other presidents have done the same or worse.

While pointing to another wrong rather than dealing with the immediate issue may be objectionable in some contexts, it may not always be so. Dennis Rohatyn notes that "He that is without sin among you, let him first cast a stone at her" (John 8:7), the New Testament quotation attributed, with widespread approbation, to Jesus Christ, is a *tu quoque* argument. Jesus used it to spare a woman accused of adultery while avoiding damage to himself by seeming to violate religious rules. We know of no one who has charged Christ with committing a fallacy. Rohatyn is not approving of *tu quoque* in general, he is merely saying it is not always a fallacy to use that argumentative form (1).

We will briefly introduce you to some commonly mentioned fallacies arising from the concern over sophistry. This is not a complete list, nor are these forms of argument always sophistic.

Begging the Question   When an answer or definition seems plausible but, upon closer examination, assumes as fact that which is not proved, it may be *begging the* *question*. To beg the question is to assume as true that which you are trying to prove. It is also called circular reasoning. Circular definitions fall within this classification. Douglas N. Walton says that an argument " . . . that commits the fallacy of begging the question uses coercive and deceptive tactics to try to get a respondent to accept something as a legitimate premise that is really not, and to slur over the omission, to disguise the failure of any genuine proof" ("Begging" 285). Walton says this is like pulling yourself out of the quicksand by your own hair (290).

In law, the defense may successfully object if the prosecutor says, "At what time did the murder occur?" The object of the trial is to determine *if* a murder occurred, and the prosecutor assumed it into fact. We may know someone is dead, but whether it is *murder* is still at issue.

Similarly, to condemn abortion as murder because it is taking the life of an unborn human being is to beg the question. The statement uses the point at issue (at what point does life begin) to support the claim, and thereby fails to carry the discussion any further along.

Appeal to Authority   To assume a claim is a fact simply because someone with high credibility says it is may constitute a fallacious appeal to authority. Argumentation by its nature relies heavily on support from authority, so the fact that someone uses that kind of support does not necessarily call for criticism. A fallacy claim on authority occurs when the appeal is thought to be improper because the so-called authority is not an authority on the question at issue. Our discussion of testimonial evidence in chapter 7 develops these ideas.

Appeal to Popularity   Similar to the objection over uses of authority is that over appeals to popularity. Claiming that something is good because it is popular runs the risk of criticism. Modern advertising employs both authority and popularity, often with questionable justification.

Is it reasonable to say that a product is good because it is a best seller? Even those who compile the best seller lists of books caution people against assuming they will enjoy any book that has been at the top of the list for many weeks. Are the television shows with the highest ratings the best? Again, popularity may be the result of criteria that are not relevant to you or your decision makers.

Post Hoc *Fallacies*   Many arguments rest on a claim of causality, as we explained in chapter 6. A fallacy may be claimed when it is believed that a faulty causal relationship is at hand. The Latin phrase *post hoc, ergo propter hoc*, from which the fallacy gets its name, calls attention to the tendency to assume a causal relation among events because they are related in time or space.

This kind of reasoning is common in politics. When a new governor or president comes into office and shortly thereafter interest rates fall, employment is up, and the economy is booming, politicians claim that they caused these effects. As often as not, the particular leader had nothing to do with it, in which case the claim could be susceptible to a *post hoc* charge.

People are quick to ascribe causes, often with little or no justification. You come down with a cold, and your mother says, "I told you not to go outside without your coat." You get in trouble, and your father says, "I told you not to run around with that bad crowd." Your grades go up at the same time that you are frequently absent from class, and you announce, "Attending class doesn't have anything to do with getting high grades." Such pat causal arguments invite close scrutiny and may deserve the label of *post hoc* fallacy.

Fallacies in Language   Following Aristotle's lead, a great many fallacy claims are based on problems with the language in which an argument is expressed. Since argumentation uses ordinary language to deal with questions within the realm of uncertainty, ambiguity is always a possibility. Still, a critic can sometimes find instances in which language problems are of such significance as to warrant a fallacy claim.

When the U.S. Supreme Court interpreted the Thirteenth, Fourteenth, and Fifteenth Amendments to the U.S. Constitution, which were passed during the post-Civil War period, to rule that only Congress, not state and local governments, could pass affirmative action laws, Justice Thurgood Marshall accused the majority of turning the language on its head. The language was designed, he said, to keep state and local government from harming minorities, not from helping them (Richmond v. Crosen).

Ad Hominem Fallacies   When people turn their criticism against a person rather than the person's ideas, they may commit an *ad hominem* fallacy. There is plenty of evidence that we do this regularly in our own minds by giving more credence to the arguments of attractive people and less to the unattractive (Rieke and Stutman 128–29). It would be as if you said "Your argument is weak because you're ugly." While you may not be as blatant as that in using *ad hominem* arguments, you may have heard people say something like this:

> Senator Ted Kennedy had no business criticizing Justice Clarence Thomas's behavior. When the argument is about sexual misconduct, Kennedy should keep his mouth shut.

To the extent that Kennedy's argument is rejected only on the grounds that the senator's personal behavior is not above reproach, it could count as an *ad hominem* fallacy claim. In chapter 15 we talk about verbal aggressiveness as opposed to argumentativeness. Verbal aggressiveness is largely defined as resorting to *ad hominem* attacks.

These are only a few illustrative forms of fallacies commonly mentioned in the efforts against sophistry. Other potential fallacies are appeals to pity, fear, ignorance, force, prejudice, and the pressure of the mob.

We have discussed two theoretical foundations on which fallacies can be identified: logic and sophistry. Both of these premises have come under attack in recent times.

The relevance of logic to practical argumentation is in serious doubt. Although its patterns are still recognized and used, as we discuss in chapter 2, as a way to structure argumentation, its rules of validity are generally seen as inapplicable. Since, in this theory, a fallacy is a violation of a logic rule, fallacies become suspect when the rules of logic are deemed irrelevant.

Sophistry has always been a difficult posture from which to identify fallacies because of the extreme ambiguity of the concept. What is sophistic to one is acceptable to another. Who is to say an argument "ought not to be persuasive?" Who has the authority to say an authority ought not to be believed in this instance? Who decides when a *tu quoque* is okay and when it is fallacious? By what rule do we say that this *ad hominem* argument is inappropriate as used and is, thus, fallacious?

Fallacies as Violations of Discussion Rules

Because of these concerns, contemporary scholars have sought a new and acceptable theoretical basis on which to rest the concept of fallacies. Frans H. van Eemeren and Rob Grootendorst of the University of Amsterdam have developed what they call a *pragma-dialectical* approach to argumentation. By this phrase, they mean a combination of normative rules (a philosophical ideal of reasonableness) with a pragmatic study of speech acts (what people actually say and mean in argumentation).

From the pragma-dialectical perspective, van Eemeren and Grootendorst develop a theory of fallacies that first sets out ten rules for critical discussion (see chapter 2). They include such prescriptions as allowing everyone to speak; requiring that claims be supported; demanding relevance of arguments; calling for honesty in representing arguments presented; expecting that arguments be logically valid or capable of being validated; and avoiding confusing arguments (209).

The concept of fallacy follows directly from these ten rules: any move in argumentation that blocks critical discussion by violating one of these rules is a fallacy. They conclude their discussion by arguing that all the traditional fallacies, such as those we discuss under sophistry, can be reasonably organized under one of the ten rules of critical discussion.

Douglas Walton basically agrees with this characterization of fallacies. His pragmatic view of fallacy differs in only two respects. First, he notes that van Eemeren and Grootendorst do not make a distinction between fallacies and simple blunders in argumentation. Second, he says the idea of fallacy should be extended beyond critical discussion to include such contexts as inquiry, negotiation, deliberation, quarrels, and information-seeking dialogue (*A Pragmatic* xii).

Walton says the concept of fallacy presumes that the concern is with moves within argumentation. Merely incorrect statements do not meet his definition of fallacy. He also claims that fallacies involve a " . . . serious kind of infraction that involves a systematic technique of deceptive argumentation" (*A Pragmatic* 233–34). People may commit a blunder that does, in fact, violate a rule of dialogue, but it is not serious because it is not systematic or deceptive. He says an argument is a fallacy if it twists some aspect of argument to one's advantage (*A Pragmatic* 235). A fallacy, says Walton, is an argumentation technique used wrongly, as defined by these three criteria:

1. A failure, lapse, or error, subject to criticism, correction, or rebuttal

2. A failure that occurs in what is supposed to be an argument

3. A failure associated with deception or illusion (*A Pragmatic* 237)

Further, a fallacy involves the violation of some maxim of reasonable dialogue, is a systematic kind of wrongly applied technique of reasonable argumentation, and is serious, not a blunder (*A Pragmatic* 238).

Drawing upon all of these views of fallacy as well as our own thoughts, in the remainder of the chapter we will discuss how fallacy claims are a part of refutation. You should remember that the contemporary image of fallacy is tied to the actual rules governing argumentation and the willingness of decision makers to see an argument as a violation of one of those rules.

USING FALLACY CLAIMS IN REFUTATION

Claims of logical incorrectness, sophistry, and violations of discussion rules must be considered in your plan of refutation. Recall from chapter 12 that you should always aim at the highest conceptual level and that pointing out specific mistakes or embarrassing slips may not do much to damage other positions.

The highest conceptual level can usually be found by looking for the ultimate purpose sought from the argumentation. In the debate over welfare, it was sometimes difficult to identify the highest conceptual level. In the Congressional debate on ending "welfare as we know it" during the summer of 1995, many justified eliminating federally funded welfare because of the need to balance the federal budget. Some justified ending all welfare for able bodied adults in order to force people to seek work rather than let society support them.

Opponents, however, argued that the reasoning in both cases contained a fallacy of faulty causal generalization. If Congress merely shifted from direct funding to block grants to the states, opponents claimed, there would not be significant savings to use to balance the budget. If the states picked up the responsibility for welfare, opponents argued further, there would still be situations in which able bodied adults were being supported. Aiming refutation at the highest conceptual level, these claims asserted that if the legislation would not accomplish its purpose due to a lack of causal relationships, it should not be adopted.

Before using refutation by fallacy claim, be sure it is consistent with your overall critical pattern. If you decide to argue a fallacy claim, remember to communicate it clearly by following the steps listed below, which were detailed at the start of the chapter.

1. Accept the burden of proving that what you claim as a fallacy is fallacious in this circumstance.

2. Identify the significant argumentation practice that you claim has been violated.

3. Show why it is an issue worthy of consideration.

4. Charge the decision makers to reaffirm their commitment to this practice in this instance.
5. State explicitly how your fallacy claim undermines the overall position you are refuting.

SOCIAL GUIDES TO FALLACY CLAIMS

While it is impossible to identify inherently fallacious ways of arguing, we can list some relatively enduring patterns on which fallacy claims can be based. Like the common patterns of criteria for argument appraisal (logical, good reasons, scientific, good story) listed in chapter 2, these guidelines are not universal but are widely seen as potentially problematic procedures in argumentation. You can use these guidelines in the development of fallacy claims.

Intent to Deceive

Earlier we said that simple errors or misunderstandings do not form the basis of fallacy claims because they can be brought up, discussed, negotiated, and corrected. But errors or misunderstandings that can be shown to be intentionally deceptive are commonly seen as fallacious. People may forgive the former but not the latter. Rohatyn makes an analogy between reason-deception and eroticism-pornography:

> One is loving, the other possessive. One respects both persons and flesh, the other objectifies and dehumanizes. One is dialogic: sensual, but never exploitative. . . . The other is monologic: vengeful and authoritarian. One is frank, vulnerable and open, whereas the other lusts for power (10).

When a scholar in the work of Dr. Martin Luther King, Jr., announced that parts of King's doctoral dissertation apparently were taken from other sources without credit, a debate ensued. On the one hand, plagiarism constitutes intentional use of another's work without credit with the intent that readers believe it is your own work. If so, King's behavior would seem to be fallacious. On the other hand, King's defenders have argued that King's purpose was benign: he was always a political activist, not a scholar, and when he used others' work he did so to make a point, not to deceive. Most agreed that if King did it simply to get his doctorate without doing his own work, it was unacceptable. The debate was over intent to deceive.

Chris Raymond reports that studies of patient histories suggest that Sigmund Freud suppressed or distorted facts that contradicted his theories. He rested his case heavily on the case histories of six people, of whom one left therapy dissatisfied after three months, two were never treated by Freud or any psychoanalyst, and another never really had therapy. Of the two remaining cases, Freud's claims of effecting a cure were refuted by a confession of Freud himself and a denial by one of the patients. A research professor of psychiatry at the University of Pittsburgh said, "It is clear that Freud did what euphemistically might be called editing of his case material . . . [but that] isn't tantamount to dishonesty" (4–5). Again, there was deception leading to a debate over intent. To establish a fallacy claim, the critics must show that Freud doctored his cases with the intent to deceive.

Advertisers come in for considerable criticism because of their apparent willingness to deceive people to win them over. Communication scholars who specialize in the study of advertising, however, do not identify deception as central to advertising. They do say it relies upon the force of *our own* self-deceptions, fantasies, values, personal realities, or world views. Loose analysis may lead you to charge deception when an advertiser is merely using intense language, hyperbole, and dynamism alongside appeals to our own realities.

On the other hand, there are examples of those who have knowingly sought to deceive us in order to gain our adherence, and these become the object of fallacy claims. During the Vietnam War, the Defense Department daily issued body counts of enemy soldiers to maintain popular support for the war, when they knew the high counts were fabricated. This has been the basis for fallacy claims. Fundraisers have argued for donations to worthy causes knowing that more than 90 percent of the money will go to pay for the campaign itself and that little help will actually go to those in need. This has been claimed as a fallacy.

Merchants try to get us to buy products we would not otherwise purchase by telling us they are gifts when, in fact, we will pay for them. Encyclopedia companies used to tell people they wanted to give them a set worth hundreds of dollars, if only they would agree to purchase some other items. The total amount paid more than covered the cost of the books. We get cards in the mail almost weekly announcing that we have been chosen to receive something free. All we need to do is pay a handling charge. One person won a boat and an outboard motor, and only had to pay a few hundred dollars for shipping and handling. When the boat arrived, it was a toy worth far less than our friend had paid. That can form the basis of a fallacy claim based on the intent to deceive.

Refusal to Reason

In a pure sense of the term, critical decision making means having a basis for a decision that can be examined critically. It does not demand any particular kind of rationale, it merely demands a rationale. To make a claim but refuse to give reasons in its support may give rise to a fallacy claim. Even to rely on altruism or one's own authority—"Believe it because I ask you to"—is a reason that can be critically examined. To say, "Believe it just because," or "Believe it for no particular reason," is to deny others (including yourself) the opportunity for critical appraisal.

Children around the age of three use the word *because* as a reason, when older children and adults almost never do so. This is not so much a refusal to reason as it is a childish understanding of the process of reasoning (Willbrand and Rieke 435).

By the same token, when someone over the age of four asserts a claim without any support, or with "because, just because," as a basis, we conclude it is a refusal to reason and may form the basis of a fallacy claim. Parents do their children no good by answering the multitude of "why" questions with "just because" answers. Government does citizens no good by answering challenges to public policy with a refusal to reason hidden behind national security. Critical decision making rests upon the ability to consider reasons, so refusal to reason denies the critical process and constitutes a potential fallacy.

We know a high-tech firm that does business with the government, and both sides play a refusal to reason game. The government auditors demand access to complete financial data to determine whether the firm is overpricing its products, and the firm refuses to provide the data, claiming its catalog prices are set competitively.

On the government side, a strict percentage markup, including research and development costs, is allowed, and no reasons are given. The government just enforces its rules, it does not justify them. The firm, on the other hand, claims (privately) that research and development costs are so great in their industry that if they told the government auditors how much they must mark up prices to cover the research and development costs, it would be denied. Both sides are susceptible to fallacy claims. We suspect the better approach would be to open the case up to negotiation on a product-by-product basis to allow reasonable markup and still hold government costs to a minimum, but so far neither side is budging.

Breach of Conversational Cooperation

H. P. Grice says that when people engage in argumentation they do so within a presumption that anything said is intended to be "cooperative," that it contributes toward the goal of the interaction. He posits four conversational maxims of such cooperation that govern each utterance: the utterance is topically relevant; it is expressed perspicuously (clear, easy to understand); it is sufficient for the meaning needed at that juncture, says neither too much nor too little; and it is believed to be true ("Logic"; "Further Notes"). Robert Sanders says that breaches of this process of conversational implicature may constitute the bases of fallacy claims (65). We will discuss each briefly, again focusing on intent. Innocent breaches of conversational implicature can, presumably, be repaired through further dialogue.

Irrelevant Utterance   Since the cooperative principle guides people to presume comments are relevant, it is possible to damage the critical process by making irrelevant statements with the intent that they be taken as relevant. We stopped at a small-town gas station recently, only then noticing that the price was ten cents a gallon more than the place across the street. The attendant, in response to our request for a justification for his high prices, said, "Well, you can go across the street if you are willing to put cut-rate gas in your car." We were supposed to presume that the quality of the cheaper gas was lower and even dangerous to use. An acquaintance who runs a station in the city says the difference in price was probably a function of one station being a "name" outlet and the other a cut-rate place. He says the gas at both places was probably about the same since cut-rate stations often buy their gas from major name producers. That the other place was cut-rate was relevant, but not to gas quality.

Obfuscation   The cooperative principle leads us to presume that our interlocutors are doing their best to be clear and as easy to understand as possible. *Obfuscation* as we use it here, is an intent to make communication unclear in order to secure adherence from those who trust in the commitment to clarity. The common paradigm case of unclarity—the IRS tax instructions and other publications of the federal government—probably would not count as obfuscation as defined. "Bureaucrat-ese" may be a disease, but it is usually not *intended* to confuse.

Some years ago, our colleagues at the university wanted a color television monitor for a research project, and they asked for one in a grant proposal. The request came back with the notation that funding for color monitors was not allowed. Instead of accepting this rejection, our friends resubmitted their request, but this time they asked for a "nonmonochromatic" television monitor, and it was granted. That is winning adherence through obfuscation, and may form the basis of a fallacy claim.

Today, many food products include some variation of the word *light* in their name or description. *Diet* is used similarly, as are *low-fat* and *no-cholesterol*. In these instances, there is the possibility of obfuscation by oversimplification. A diet or light product may contain a few calories or a hundred or more. A no-fat product may still be fattening, and a diet product may contain dangerous cholesterol while a no-cholesterol product may contain dangerous fat. The Food and Drug Administration tries, with limited success, to keep such practices under control, but each time it must advance a fallacy claim and sustain the burden of proof.

Violations of the Quantity Maxim   The cooperative principle says we presume that our communications say enough to make sense and no more. Violations of this *quantity maxim* seek adherence by taking advantage of that presumption while saying more or less than would otherwise be appropriate. Closely related to this potential fallacy claim is the concept of conflict of interest, in which some information that would be significant to a critical decision is withheld to mask multiple motives.

Tax advisers say that people get themselves in more trouble than necessary during audits with the Internal Revenue Service by saying too much. They advise people to answer questions with the minimum necessary to respond, and no more. The problem comes, say the advisers, when the audit seems over, people are standing up to leave, and the urge toward normal conversation returns: "Well," says the taxpayer, "I'm glad that's over, because I'm leaving tomorrow for my place in the Bahamas." "What place in the Bahamas?" asks the tax auditor, "Maybe we'd better sit back down."

There is a fine line between an honest withholding of information that is not legally required, such as is recommended by tax advisers, and saying more or less than is reasonably needed for understanding just to secure adherence. In court, this took place:

PROSECUTOR: Did you sleep with this woman?
DEFENDANT: No.

The answer is true in one sense (they did not sleep), but untrue in the meaning communicated. If exposed, the defendant may be the subject of a fallacy claim of violating the quantity maxim. The waste disposal company that publishes data showing that a shipment contains "no hazardous waste" without saying that the shipment was originally hazardous by government standards but has barely fallen out of that definition through chemical changes, is a potential object of a fallacy claim.

This maxim can be violated by overstatement as well. The same waste disposal company may try to mask the danger of its shipment by publishing page upon page of details documenting what hazardous substances are *not* contained, just so the elements that *are* hazardous can be buried in excessive detail and thus be overlooked. This, too, may be the basis of a fallacy claim.

Conflict of Interest   Withholding of relevant information is usually the basis for charging a conflict of interest. When the ophthalmologist recommends an optical shop nearby, it is relevant to know it is owned by the ophthalmologist.

An acquaintance went to a lawyer to discuss a suit against a local company she believed had cheated her. The attorney advised her to forget about the incident and sent her away. Only later did she discover that the attorney had for many years been on retainer to represent the company in question. That discovery could count as the basis of a fallacy claim through conflict of interest.

A prominent law firm was retained by the state of Utah to defend an anti-abortion law that was under challenge by such entities as the Utah Women's Clinic. After billing the state for $170,000 in fees, the firm was discovered to represent the Utah Women's Clinic in tax and employee benefit matters. Was it a conflict of interest to serve as attorneys for the clinic in some legal matters while at the same time opposing them in the suit over the anti-abortion law? The firm claimed there was no conflict of interest and refused to withdraw, but the state attorney general fired them.

More to the point is the question of why the firm had not notified the state at the outset about its representation of the clinic. Their failure to be "up-front" about the matter was probably more damaging than the fact of the representation itself. Knowing that the same firm had been ordered to withdraw from another case by the state supreme court because of conflict of interest simply added to their low credibility (House).

Reckless Disregard for the Truth   We have already discussed the intent to deceive; however, here we interpret the cooperative principle from a concept developed in law (see *New York Times* v. *Sullivan*). When someone participates in communication by providing information, we presume through the cooperative principle that they not only believe what they say but have some basis for that belief. In law, it may be considered malicious to communicate facts with reckless disregard for the truth, and that is the basis of this fallacy claim.

Newspapers usually make a practice of verifying stories before printing them, particularly when reporting sensitive facts such as that a banker is a heavy gambler. Independent sources are sought along with parallel confirmation. To make little or no effort to confirm a story may constitute reckless disregard for the truth, a fallacy claim. The CBS program *60 Minutes* interviewed people who claimed to have been paid as sources for news stories for which they had no information. What CBS was doing was making a fallacy claim of reckless disregard for the truth against some supermarket tabloids.

CONCLUSION

Fallacies are violations of significant rules of argumentation relevant to the appropriate decision makers. The notion of fallacy as incorrect logic is identified with the tradition of formal logic. While this perspective is generally not appropriate for the realm of argumentation, knowledge of specific fallacies within the system may serve as a critical guideline. Three formal fallacies are: affirmation of the consequent or denial of the antecedent; undistributed middle term; and mistaking validity for truth.

Identifying fallacies with sophistry has been a key element of informal logic. Here fallacies are seen as arguments that are persuasive when they should not be. Some specific fallacies are: *tu quoque*; begging the question; appeal to authority; appeal to popularity; *post hoc, ergo propter hoc*; fallacies in language; *ad hominem*; appeal to pity; appeal to fear; appeal to ignorance; appeal to force; appeal to prejudice; and pressure of the mob. While you cannot be sure a fallacy is present simply by noticing these argumentative forms, they can direct your attention toward such questions as whether or not an intent to deceive can be argued successfully.

Contemporary theories tend to see fallacies as violations of discussion rules. In critical interactions, there are some basic rules of rationality that can be suggested through a dialectical perspective. Fallacies occur when one of these discussion rules is violated. Mere blunders or misstatements of fact are not classified as fallacies. A fallacy must occur within argumentation and serve as a deliberate violation of accepted rules in order to gain an improper advantage.

We suggest that in making a refutation by fallacy claim, you integrate it with your overall refutation strategy. First, arguing a fallacy should make a substantial contribution to critical analysis at the highest conceptual level. Second, the fallacy claim must be effectively argued. You must accept and satisfy your burden of proving not only that a fallacy is present, but that its presence constitutes a significant and relevant consideration to the appropriate decision makers at the time.

Finally, there are enduring, socially negotiated guidelines for the development of fallacy claims that, while they do not point to certain fallacies, can be used to discern what may prove to be convincing fallacy claims: intent to deceive; refusal to reason; breach of conversational cooperation; irrelevant utterance; obfuscation; violations of the quantity maxim; conflict of interest; and reckless disregard for truth.

PROJECTS

13.1 Select a letter to the editors published in a newspaper that commits what you believe to be a fallacy. Identify the fallacy and develop your argument proving why.

13.2 Exchange your paper written in the first exercise with another student. Each of you write a response to the other's paper that argues one or both of these claims: (1) The alleged fallacy really is not fallacious; (2) The alleged fallacy would not be a fallacy used in another sphere.

13.3 Read the Federal Trade Commission rules on product labels, the National Institutes of Health Office of Scientific Integrity rules governing research reports, or the Codes of Ethics published by the American Medical Association, the American Bar Association, or any other professional association relating to improper argument practices. Write a report on the specific rules of fallacy in the sphere represented by the rules or code you have read.

REFERENCES

City of Richmond v. J. A. Crosen Company: 1989, 109 S. Ct. 706.

Ehninger, Douglas, and Wayne Brockriede. *Decision by Debate*. New York: Harper, 1978.

Engel, S. Morris. *With Good Reason*. New York: St. Martin's, 1986.

Fearnside, W. Ward, and William B. Holther. *Fallacy: the Counterfeit of Argument*. Englewood Cliffs, NJ: Prentice Hall, 1959.

Grice, H. P. "Logic and Conversation." *Syntax and Semantics, 3: Speech Acts*. Eds. Peter Cole and Jerry L. Morgan. New York: Academic, 1975. 41–58.

———. "Further Notes on Logic and Conversation." *Syntax and Semantics, 9: Pragmatics*. Ed. Peter Cole. New York: Academic, 1978. 113–28.

Hamblin, C. L. *Fallacies*. London: Methuen, 1970.

House, Dawn. "Law Firm Fired, But Utahns Will Still Pay Abortion-Defense Bill." *Salt Lake Tribune* 10 Oct. 1991: A1–2.

Howell, William S. *Logic and Rhetoric in England, 1500–1700*. Princeton: Princeton UP, 1956.

Kahane, Howard. *Logic and Contemporary Rhetoric*. Belmont, CA: Wadsworth, 1971.

Lyne, John R. "The Pedagogical Use of Fallacies." *Iowa Journal of Speech Communication* 13 (1981): 1–9.

New York Times v. Sullivan. 376 US 254 (1954).

Ong, Walter J. "Ramist Rhetoric." *The Province of Rhetoric*. Eds. Joseph Schwartz and John Rycenga. New York: Ronald, 1965. 226–54.

Raymond, Chris. "Study of Patient Histories Suggests Freud Suppressed or Distorted Facts that Contradicted His Theories." *Chronicle of Higher Education* 29 May 1991: A4–6.

Rieke, Richard D. "The Judicial Dialogue." *Argumentation* 5 (1991): 39–55.

Rieke, Richard D., and Randall K. Stutman. *Communication in Legal Advocacy*. Columbia: U of South Carolina P, 1990.

Rohatyn, Dennis. "When Is a Fallacy a Fallacy?" International Conference on Logic and Argumentation. Amsterdam, 4 June 1986.

Sanders, Robert E. *Cognitive Foundations of Calculated Speech*. Albany: State U of New York P, 1987.

Toibin, Colm. "A Kennedy and His Flock." *New Yorker* 2 Oct. 1995: 36.

van Eemeren, Frans H., and Rob Grootendorst. *Argumentation, Communication, and Fallacies*. Hillsdale, New Jersey: Erlbaum, 1992.

Walton, Douglas N. *Informal Fallacies*. Philadelphia: John Benjamins, 1987.

———. *Begging the Question: Circular Reasoning as a Tactic of Argumentation*. New York: Greenwood, 1991.

———. *A Pragmatic Theory of Fallacy*. Tuscaloosa: U of Alabama P, 1995.

Willbrand, Mary Louise, and Richard D. Rieke. "Strategies of Reasoning in Spontaneous Discourse." *Communication Yearbook* 14. Ed. James Anderson. Newbury Park, CA: Sage, 1991. 414–40.

14

Refutation in Government and Politics

Key Terms

public sphere
political claims
political issues
the public
committee hearings
applying legal practice
using the record
good stories
majoritarianism

amendment process
credibility function
issues and images
the people
media
political debates
values and evidence
leave no shot unanswered
inoculation

Political argumentation is the oldest recorded argumentation sphere. It can be found in the ancient myths of the Babylonian King Gilgamesh, the Homeric debates of the *Iliad* and the *Odyssey*, ancient Chinese records, and the Old Testament record of the ancient Jews. One modern form of political argumentation has taken its name from an Old Testament prophet: the Jeremiad. If you could penetrate fully to the earliest actions of our species you would probably find that political discussion emerged virtually with language itself.

Wherever groups exist in the form of families, communities, organizations, states, or nations, political decisions are necessary. It is impossible to be apolitical, for inaction is also a decision. If the people who live across the street beat their children mercilessly and you do not report the fact to the authorities because you do not want to get involved, you have taken a political action based on a political reason. However, the political action we are interested in here is *political argumentation: the process of using verbal and visual arguments among citizens, leaders, and government agencies to influence the policy decisions of a political community*. This argumentation produces "consequences that are widespread and enduring; and affect persons other than oneself for good or evil" (Bitzer 230–31).

THE NATURE OF POLITICAL ARGUMENTATION

In its broadest sense political argumentation is synonymous with argumentation per se. However, we will be talking about argumentation that directly involves what has been called the "public's business." It is the argumentation that G. Thomas Goodnight says is characteristic of the public sphere:

> A public forum is . . . a sphere of argument to handle disagreements transcending private and technical disputes. . . . [It] inevitably limits participation to representative spokespersons [and provides] a tradition of argument such that its speakers would employ common language, values, and reasoning so that the disagreement could be settled . . . (219–20).

We define political argumentation further by examining its claims, its content, its development, and its refutation.

The Claims of Political Argumentation

In chapter 3 we identified three kinds of claims—factual, value, and policy. One of the defining characteristics of political argument is that it always aims at policy. A lawyer may argue the factual claim that a chemical spill was harmful to a client and, subsequently argue for a legally appropriate remedy. Both claims are treated in law as factual claims. When the same lawyer appears before a state legislative committee on the same subject, the aim is to bring about regulations that will constitute a new policy. Policy claims are argued by building a case on subclaims of fact and value, but the aim is to gain adherence to the policy claim.

The Content of Political Claims

When Aristotle referred to the relatively simple society of ancient Greece, he defined five general categories of political argumentation that are still important today: (1) ways and means; (2) war and peace; (3) national defense; (4) exports and imports; and (5) legislation (21–24). In modern terms, ways and means refers to issues emerging from consideration of fiscal and monetary policies. War and peace includes all of our foreign policy and national defense programs. Imports and exports suggest the full range of issues arising from interstate and foreign commerce—whether free trade agreements like the North American Free Trade Agreement (NAFTA) or the General Agreement on Tariff and Trade (GATT) are beneficial to the American economy. Legislation ranges from modification of the Constitution to statutory revisions. Legislatures must set policies as general as legal rights for women and as specific as the use of "low fat," "fat free," or "diet" labels on food.

Equal rights for women and food labels are good examples of the way in which Aristotle's five classifications have expanded. Decisions like these and many others that would have been personal then, are political today. We have reached the place in our complex society where every policy question is potentially political.

Political argumentation is, as J. Robert Cox says, "a normative sphere." That is, it is not defined by a specific set of claims with which it deals. Rather, the participants in political argumentation generate reasons "for a course of action and in interpreting the consequences of their decision . . . invoke a notion of 'the public'" (131). There is always implied in argumentation the idea that its policy claims are designed for the common good of some social collective that we call the public. The usefulness of such public policy is determined by the immediate needs of the community. Should local communities censor cable television? Should the federal government regulate airline prices? Should English be the official language of a state? These are all claims about what the public is and wants.

The Development of Political Claims

Initially political claims are vague. They become more specific as argumentation develops. No court of law would tolerate a claim as unclearly stated as most political claims initially are, and no scientists could proceed without a firm statement of a hypothesis. Yet most political claims begin the argumentative process in a very general form (Cobb and Elder 400):

> Air quality in American cities should be improved.
> Taxes should be reduced.
> The chuckholes in Atlanta's streets should be repaired.
> The reading level of children in Denver should be improved.

These are examples of claims with which government agencies usually begin. They represent (as we noted in chapter 3) the recognition of a problem, a "feeling of doubt." Frequently, they are almost issueless because they are claims with which everyone will agree. However, as public bodies examine these claims and interest groups argue them, they become more specific. To become a working policy the claim must become more specific. Take the reading example. Virtually no one in Denver would object to improving the reading level of children. But how? At what cost? What will the new policy replace? and, What will children read? The answers proposed to these questions make the policy more specific and more controversial. Compare these two claims:

1. The reading level of children in Denver should be improved.
2. With funds now used for the education of children with disabilities, the Denver school board should hire 50 reading specialists to provide individualized reading programs in the fourth grade.

Issues Emerge As Claims Become More Clearly Phrased   Some people, even those who want the reading ability improved, will object to taking funds away from children with disabilities. They may argue that the money should come from other sources or new taxes, and a whole host of issues will emerge. Others will argue that direct attention to reading is not the best way to improve reading, rather reading instruction should be integrated into other instruction. Issues that did not seem very important when the original general claim was advanced will arise. Some parents at a public hearing may be frustrated, saying, "I'm interested in better reading instruction for my children. Why are we talking about cutting programs for children with disabilities?" Their frustration comes from the need for claims of political argument to become specific.

Claims and Issues Will Change as Argumentation Emerges   Policies need the widest possible consensus of the members of the affected group. Therefore, claims are often amended to protect them from possible refutation. So, a school board may propose that social studies time be cut and more time allotted to reading instruction. Then they may propose greater emphasis on reading in all instruction. As a matter of fact, they may come out with a curriculum revision that seems completely at odds with the original intent to improve reading instruction. The new revision may actually cut the amount of time specifically devoted to reading!

Most Claims Do Not Become Policy, and Most That Do Are Noncontroversial   Many interest groups expend great amounts of money and time researching and arguing policy claims, yet most policy claims never become policy. Even those policy claims that become legislative bills have a high rejection rate. More than 20,000 bills are proposed each session to the U.S. Congress, yet less than six percent of them ever become law. Of those bills that pass, two-thirds are supported by both major parties (Matthews and Stimson 6–7).

Many bills, both simple and complex, are passed without argument. While it is difficult to characterize those claims that pass easily, they most probably represent efforts to reduce conflict, reconcile varying interests, and compromise opposing goals. Political decisions that go through the modification process we have described are the product of a broad compromise-based consensus. The dramatic case of a hard-fought partisan argument on a well-defined policy claim is unusual.

In the first two years of the Clinton administration, the President and a Democratic Congress pushed through a number of controversial pieces of legislation such as the Brady Bill, restricting handgun purchases, a ban on the sale of certain assault weapons, and a budget that passed by a single vote in the Senate. Even so, all of these bills had changes from their original versions (like the exclusion of some assault weapons) in order to get the votes necessary to pass them.

Perhaps, in part because of these controversial bills, the House and Senate got a Republican majority in 1994. In the election of 1994 the Republican candidates for the House argued for a series of 34 measures that they called their "Contract With America." However, in the first year of their control of Congress they were able to pass only those items that were agreed to by a consensus in both House and Senate (Popkin and Borger). The legislative process has more than a dozen points in committee and floor action where legislation may be delayed or defeated (Wise 22). The political party system, the Presidential veto, and outside pressure all serve to make most political claims develop through continual cooperative modification until a consensus is reached.

To say that cooperative modification to consensus is the nature of political argumentation is not to maintain that there are no issues, no debates. The modifications necessary to consensus are discovered when issues are revealed in debate. The issues are likely to be over modifications of policy, but issues are there nonetheless.

Refutation in Government and Politics

Even in political campaigns, where conflict would seem most likely, disagreements are more likely to be over the degree or nature of a proposition rather than over a direct yes or no. On health care, taxes, foreign policy, or environmental protection, for instance, disagreements are over the degree of governmental action. In political campaigns a diverse electorate usually makes it impossible for a politician with an absolutist position to win.

When debate is present, refutation of opposing arguments is essential to the decision making process. Much of the legislative process is taken up with identifying potential rebuttals to a policy proposal. If the rebuttals come with political clout, the legislative policy is usually revised to accommodate them. The final draft of a bill will sometimes seem to lack clarity and coherence because it includes so many changes inserted in order to win votes by countering refutation.

Argumentation in government and politics includes a variety of situations from a televised presidential campaign commercial to a newspaper advertisement for a local city council candidate, from a congressional hearing to a mayors' debate. Although there are similarities, there are also differences. We will try to deal with these differences by looking at how refutation functions in the argumentation of three sub-spheres: committee hearings, legislative action, and political campaigns.

REFUTATION IN COMMITTEE HEARINGS

In recent years Americans have been able to see firsthand how committee hearings function. Segments have been shown on television. The most dramatic, like the 1995 Congressional investigations of the Ruby Ridge, Idaho, eleven-day standoff between federal agents and white separatist Randy Weaver, and the federal raid on the Branch Davidian's compound in Waco, Texas, have been shown on C-SPAN. The 1991 Senate Judiciary Committee hearings over the appointment of Judge Clarence Thomas and the charges of sexual harassment against him by Professor Anita Hill were covered live on the three major television networks, CNN, and C-SPAN and seen in over fourteen million homes. ("Viewers").

Involving as they did highly controversial charges about the actions of governmental personnel, they provided extensive examples of how refutation can function in committee hearings. The same principles apply to thousands of other hearings in congress, state legislatures, and city and county government. Committee hearings are vital decision making scenes where the claims of argumentation are modified through refutation.

During the 96th Congress, the House Appropriation Committee and its sub-committees "held 720 days of hearings, took testimony from 10,125 witnesses, published 225 volumes of hearings that comprised 202,767 printed pages" (Davidson and Oleszek 220). Committee hearings are the place where "state and society meet to discuss what the laws should be. Committees invite interested parties—individuals, groups, businesses, and others—to make recommendations and discuss with the committee what the law ought to be" (Boynton, "When Senators" 132).

When you add to congressional policy and personnel hearings, the many administrative hearings that administrative agencies hold to involve the public in the actual application of laws once written, you realize how important hearings are to defining and applying policy. We will look now at the characteristics of such hearings and the form that refutation takes in them.

Characteristics of Hearings

Hearings are characterized by the need to convert solutions into law to develop, and focus on, a record that will justify the action taken. Refutation in this setting involves the legal questioning format and telling good stories.

Hearings involve controversy over policy. Controversy leads to refutation but refutation is blunted because claims are made through a questioning process. It resembles the type of fact finding questions used in a court of law (Asbell 108). That is, those who hold the hearings ask questions rather than make claims. The format implies that they are gathering evidence. Frequently, it is evidence they already have. The testimony of witnesses is used to "build a record" from which specific provisions of laws or administrative decisions are justified.

Using the Record in Hearings

Although the questioning format limits how one may argue, there is still considerable potential for refutation. This refutation comes mostly from the committee members as they "set the record straight." For instance, when the Senate Environmental Protection Sub-Committee, held hearings on the reauthorization of the 1977 Clean Air Act, Senator Max Baucus of Montana asked questions designed to prepare arguments for refutation. He asked the four presidents of health organizations what the best arguments were against their conclusions and how they would respond to them (Boynton, "When Senators" 11).

Later, Chairman George Mitchell used this record when "an executive of a research and development organization for electric utilities . . . claimed there was no environmental precipice over which the nation was hurtling." George Mitchell asked him to read the testimony (that Senator Baucus had solicited) of the four presidents of the health organizations. Mitchell told him he would change his mind about the seriousness of the problem if he read that testimony (Boynton, "When Senators" 143).

Focus for the Record in Hearings

In most hearings (the Ruby Ridge, Waco, and Thomas hearings are exceptions) there is little disagreement among the members of the committee. Those who serve on committees generally agree on the basic direction of legislation. Everyone on the Senate Agriculture Committee wants to help the farmer and generally they know how they want to do this and what the pitfalls are. They are there to find the best way to do it (Boynton, "When Senators" 10). This focus restricts the arguments that can be made.

Dennis Jaehne illustrates this restriction on arguments of wilderness groups in the administrative appeals of Forest Service implementation decisions. The conflict he observed between the Utah Wilderness Association and the Forest Service involved a basic value disagreement "between the idealistic concept of *preserving* land in its 'natural' state and the pragmatic concept of *protecting* land in . . . administrative rules and regulations" (496). However, in the cases he studied, the Utah Wilderness Association became pragmatic and technical in arguing modification of administrative practice in order to influence changes. He found that "rational collaboration" has problems for [participants with] "environmental ideals, particularly in the degree of cooptation of environmental ideals by administrative discourse. Speaking like the natives [bureaucrats] makes you rather more like the natives than not speaking like the natives" (501).

Even though witnesses might have idealistic views of the situation they must adapt to the pragmatic questions of policy building or administration. Witnesses must follow the focus of the questioners or be without influence.

The Forms of Refutation in Committee Hearings

The questioning format that produces a focused record of testimony works from specific forms of refutation. G. R. Boynton has identified four main ones in the hearings on the 1987 Clean Air Act ("When Senators" 145–47). Notice that each is based on the record and relies on questions, yet serves to refute the testimony of the witness.

1. "Here is what you say; someone else says; how can you sustain what you say?" The example given earlier when presidents of health organizations were asked what opponents might say and how they would respond to these opponents is an example of such an argument. Here is a case where refutation is used on a friendly witness. The witnesses are refuted, even asked to refute their own positions, to bring out the positive answer the questioner wants.

2. "Here is what you say, and another witness has said something quite different. How can you account for this counter testimony?" This form looks very much like the first but it is not friendly. Boynton gives this example:

A witness from the Department of Energy said that installing scrubbers on old power generating plants would cost more than the original capital investment in the plants. Senator Mitchell questions this claim by noting that another witness had said scrubbers were being installed in all German power plants for $100 per kilowatt hour. What, more precisely, will they cost in the U.S., he asks. And why would they cost more in the U.S. than in Germany? Senator Mitchell knows that cost is an important part of the argument against scrubbers, and the discrepancy between the cost estimates of the two witnesses is the trigger for raising the question ("When Senators" 146).

3. "Here is what you said, and here is what I know. How can you justify what you said?" This is a simple variation from the second form except that the questioner uses his or her credibility to support the refutation. This poses a difficult problem for the witness because, for the moment, at least, the person asking the question is the decision maker. Thus, it is difficult for the witness to answer that the questioner is wrong. Furthermore, the traditions of the Senate ("the world's most exclusive club") are such that open attacks on a senator will usually bring even political opponents to the senator's defense. This makes the answer to such refutation doubly difficult.

4. "Here is what you said today and what you said [or did] at another time. How do you justify the discrepancy?" Inconsistency, as we have discussed in chapter 4, is a powerful basis for any refutation. Some believe it is the most powerful because it uses your own arguments (or actions) against your position. One should not be surprised then to see it used as a basis of refutation in hearings. In the Clean Air Act hearings, Senator George Mitchell argued to the auto industry representatives:

> Today you have said that the improvements we are proposing are impossible for you to meet and even if you could meet them the improved health would not be worth the cost. But, that is exactly what your industry has said every time the law has been changed from 1965 to [the] present, and despite these claims you have met the standards of each new law. Why should we take seriously what you are saying today? (Boynton, "When Senators" 146).

Telling Good Stories

G. R. Boynton's examination of the Senate Agricultural Committee hearings illustrates that all this building of a record, focus, and refutation can be put in a narrative argument:

> The "good story" told in the hearings of the Senate Agriculture Committee is "a" story. The individual narrative accounts are bits and pieces of this larger story. They do not stand alone. You cannot understand any one of these stories without understanding the larger story of which each is a part. An important role for the narratives is carrying the cognitive complexity which is the "good story" ("Telling" 437).

Many bills are omnibus measures that cover a number of subjects. A farm bill has to have narratives about potatoes, cotton, corn, and wheat; about regions; about size of farms; about methods of harvesting. These narratives have to fit together into a good story. These stories have real characters in them: farmers, workers, market specialists. They proceed through a series of events that lead to a satisfactory conclusion for all under the proposed policy. If they do not, the policy is modified to make the story right.

In a situation such as the Clarence Thomas hearings the story is primarily about the credibility of a person. So the day after Hill and Thomas testified, their supporters came forward to confirm their statements. The *New York Times* headlined: "PARADE OF WITNESSES SUPPORT HILL'S STORY, THOMAS'S INTEGRITY." Friends of Anita Hill affirmed that as long as ten years earlier she had mentioned the sexual harassment to them. These bits of testimony supported and became a part of her story. In the same way those who testified that Clarence Thomas was completely businesslike and could never be guilty of sexual harassment, supported his story.

Committee hearings, the first of the three sub-spheres of political argumentation discussed here, serve as a means to clarify policy legislation, confirm participants in the process, and define administrative action. They are characterized by applied legal practice and building and using a record. These same characteristics are carried forward into the second sub-sphere: legislative action.

REFUTATION IN LEGISLATIVE ACTION

Committee hearings are a vital and time consuming part of congressional action. They serve to define a proposition from a more general proposal and to make that proposition (a bill) more immune to refutation. After a bill is drafted, it must pass both houses of Congress and be approved by the President (or the President's veto overridden). In addition, public opinion, spurred on by specific events, special interest groups, and sometimes legal action can influence what will happen.

As we noted earlier, most of the problems on about two-thirds of all legislation are worked out in the committee hearings. Therefore, controversy or rebuttal in their passage through the legislative process is limited. For the one third of the bills that are the subject of controversy, refutation is an important part of their movement through the system.

Refutation Is Usually Not Confrontational

You will recall from chapter 12 that refutation should not be seen as an attack on an opponent to win a decisive victory. Nowhere is this principle more true than in the legislative process. It is a reflection of what has been called the first cardinal rule of politics: "Don't make enemies you don't need to make" (Dowd). More than that, however, an important value of the legislative process is majoritarianism. Sponsors of legislation try to get the greatest support that they can. They want a significant majority. The larger the better. Noncontroversial legislation is the ideal.

Refutation in this system is frequently about resolving small problems in the legislation to make it acceptable to a larger majority. For instance, a clean air act that emphasizes acid rain may be criticized for not doing enough about ambient air quality, a point of interest to more states than acid rain. The following is a paraphrase of an actual refutation. It refutes the proposed law by agreeing with it but supporting an amendment.

> We need to pass this bill to deal with the problem of acid rain. The chief sponsors of the bill have understandably, considering the problems in their New England states, emphasized acid rain. However, in the Middle West and West, ambient air quality is of greater concern. Because of the seriousness of that problem, I support the amendment to the Clean Air Act that would require modifications for ambient sulfur dioxides, sulfate, and particulate standards.

The argument is not against what is in the bill (acid rain control), it argues for an addition to the bill to regulate ambient air quality.

Refutation Is Usually Not Personal

We have noted that much legislation depends on as large a majority as possible. Such majoritarianism is important because larger majorities provide political protection. If a legislator can say that the law was supported by most Republicans and Democrats, its supporters are less vulnerable to the charge that they are "too liberal" or "too conservative." In addition, the tradition of treating one another without personal rancor is a part of the American legislative tradition.

In the floor debate over the confirmation of Clarence Thomas and in response to Republican Arlen Spector of Pennsylvania who had led the questioning of Professor Hill, Senator Edward Kennedy said, "There's no proof that Anita Hill has perjured herself and shame on anyone who suggests that she has." Senator Specter replied, "We do not need characterizations like shame in this chamber from the Senator from Massachusetts." To this, Senator Kennedy responded, "I reiterate to the Senator from Pennsylvania and to others that the way that Professor Hill was treated was shameful" (Apple A13). That exchange is about as personal as you will find in congressional debate.

Eric M. Uslander has argued that there is a declining emphasis in the U.S. Congress on comity. He says that there is less attention, particularly since the 1980s, to reciprocity and courtesy than was previously true (23–33). While there may be a decline, there is still far less personal attack, particularly in the Senate, than might be expected of a partisan assembly.

The Amendment Process as Refutation

The amending process has always been an active one in committees. When a bill came to the floor of the House or Senate, amendments were usually extensions of committee hearings. However, in recent years the amendment process has been used more as a basis of refutation. Former Arizona Congressman Morris Udall noted a few years ago that the House of Representatives has become a "fast breeder reactor. . . . Every morning when I come to my office, I find that there are twenty more amendments. We dispose of twenty or twenty-five amendments and it breeds twenty more amendments" (Keefe and Ogul 208).

Many amendments are friendly. They are designed to strengthen, without changing in any significant way, the bill's essential purpose. Other amendments may look innocent enough but will actually weaken a bill and make it less likely to pass. Political scientists William Keefe and Morris Ogul explain how this can work:

> A favorite gambit in attacking a bill is to "perfect" or amend it to death. Under this plan, amendment after amendment is submitted to the bill, ostensibly to make it a "better" bill. With each amendment a new group can be antagonized and brought into opposition to the bill. Nor is it very difficult to make a bill unworkable, even ridiculous. Thus the president of the Illinois Retail Merchants Association succeeded in getting a committee in the Illinois House to adopt an amendment to a minimum-wage bill, a measure he vigorously opposed, setting up a $500,000 fund to be used in enforcement of the law. This move was calculated to stimulate new opposition to the bill. . . . Many a bill has been threatened or emasculated by a carefully drawn and skillfully maneuvered amendment (209).

By such procedures, amendments become the basis on which a bill is refuted. If an arguer is not careful, a bill can be amended to refute its original intention.

Refutation Has an Important Credibility Function

Although debate is important to a democratic society and refutation is central to it, floor debate has limited influence on legislation. A well-developed argument, a new way of looking at an issue, or a well thought out refutation that strikes at the center of a policy can influence undecided members. Mostly, however, floor debates, like committee hearings, are oriented to establishing a record. Speakers say what they say in supporting or refuting arguments to demonstrate their positions for their constituents. The C-SPAN coverage of debates in the House of Representatives, though few people watch them, have aided some, like Georgia Republican Congressman Newt Gingrich who used his appearances in C-SPAN covered speeches attacking Democratic leaders to build a record that increased his credibility among some voters, eventually leading to his election as Speaker of the House.

Perhaps more important than building a record or influencing a few fence sitters to move one way or another is a frequently overlooked credibility function of floor debate:

> It is a good way for members to persuade their colleagues of their competence in a public policy field; it enables them to affirm a personal position or to support or back off from a past position; it presents an opportunity to gain publicity, to consolidate old support, and perhaps to attract new followers (Keefe and Ogul 218).

Relations Between Legislature and the Executive

In recent years the federal government has been characterized by what has been called "divided government" where the Congress is controlled by one party while the President is from another. In the 40 years between 1952 and 1992, a Democrat was president for only 14 years. The Democrats have controlled both houses of Congress for all but four of those 40 years. In 1994 the situation was reversed and a Democrat was president while both houses of Congress were controlled by the Republicans. Although not as dramatic, similar divided government has occurred in some state governments. Even where the same party controls both legislative and executive branches, differences between the branches can occur.

In such situations debate can be quite vigorous and even acrimonious. The president or governor has a veto that is difficult to override. So even when the opposition has a majority in the legislative branch, its power is curbed. Some presidents (Harry S. Truman holds the record with 250) earned a reputation for their frequent vetoes (Keefe and Ogul 329). The debate between a hostile majority in Congress and the president increases as an election nears.

In the autumn of 1991 there was a debate over whether or not the United States was in a recession. Much of this argumentation was definitional. This was not a depression such as the great depression of the 1930's. But, was it a recession? Certain economic indicators were weak but President George Bush assured the nation that the economy was growing out of this minor sluggishness. He proposed to accelerate that growth by repealing the tax on capital gains to stimulate investment and thus to create more jobs. The Democrats said that was "trickle down economics" to benefit the rich.

The Democrats wanted to extend unemployment benefits for people whose benefits had run out. President Bush vetoed that move as "budget busting." It would increase the deficit, he said. The Democrats proposed a tax cut for lower and middle income people, paid for from cuts in defense, to stimulate the economy. Bush opposed that because he favored his cut in capital gains.

The issues were over definition: is this a recession? They were about process: are economic conditions getting worse or better? They dealt with credibility: is the President uninterested in the poor and middle class? Do the Democrats actually want to solve the problem or just make political points? Value issues were actively involved: is the suffering serious? Will tax cuts increase economic insecurity? And, of course, there were policy issues: should unemployment insurance coverage be extended? Should the capital gains tax be repealed? The debate frequently emphasized the support and refutation of the fact and value claims behind the policy claims along with a host of other issues (e.g., limits on the military budget and restrictions on imports) linked to these policy decisions.

Eventually, some compromises were worked out between Congress and the administration. The president approved the extension of unemployment benefits, for instance, although it was not for as long as the Democrats had proposed. The lesson to be learned from this is that refutation is frequently a complex problem because single issues can have implications on a wide variety of claims. Debate involves party politics, public opinion, the media, the responsibilities of government branches, the state of the economy, and the state of the world.

ARGUMENTATION IN POLITICAL CAMPAIGNS

A political campaign is a complex mixture of activities. It includes speeches, debates, mailings, television and radio ads, sound bites for the media, person to person campaigning by candidates and supporters, telephone contacts, getting people to the polls, and many more activities. They all are argumentative in their nature and involve refutation. A closer examination of campaign argumentation is in order.

Campaigns Involve Issues and Images

All argumentation in the political sphere has, hidden in its attention to policy questions, an element of the personal: is this person (or party) a fit representative of his or her constituents? This dual emphasis on issue and image, present throughout the legislative process, becomes increasingly important as campaign and election time nears. The process described earlier of "building a record" becomes more focused on how that record will influence voters.

Candidates look to the opponent's record to find a basis for attack. In the 1992 presidential election Democrats attacked President Bush because he did not keep his famous 1988 pledge "Read my lips—no new taxes." Republicans and Independent Ross Perot pointed to the Arkansas record on economic development and the environment to attack candidate Bill Clinton, then Governor of Arkansas.

In a campaign, then, questions of a candidate's image and issue positions become confused. Some argue that image takes over and the issues are pushed aside by the image constructed through short commercials and media sound bites. Even debates, they argue, emphasize the candidate's image and play down the public policy issues. Says Lloyd Bitzer, "the stuff of ordinary campaigns consists of arguments, position statements, testimonials, commercials, and other materials relating to the prudence, good character, and right intentions of the candidates—to the image. . . . Thus, discussion of issues . . . tends to be subsumed under the discussion of images" (242–43).

It is natural that political campaigns should be seen as image centered. After all, the central issue of every campaign is personal: should the candidate be elected? But the debate over image is not as clearly personal as many believe.

Mary E. Stuckey and Frederick J. Antczak characterize the image that George Bush assigned to Bill Clinton, and Clinton assigned to Bush, in the 1992 election.

> To understand Bill Clinton in terms of George Bush, for instance, is to see Clinton as a youthful, unpatriotic, inexperienced, rash, and fundamentally untrustworthy

character. Throughout the campaign, Bush tried to undermine the status of his opponent, making comments like, "My feisty little friend from Texas, Ross Perot, had one thing right. He said the grocery store is no preparation for Walmart. Well, I think the man's on to something" (120).

In Clinton's rhetoric, George Bush and the Republicans were responsible for the ills that afflicted America. "Families are coming apart, kids are dropping out of school, drugs and crime dominate our streets. And our leaders here in Washington are doing nothing to turn America around." That pain and that fear were occasioned by the economic policies of the Reagan/Bush administrations, which were established as the defining issue of the 1992 general election (121).

The contrast in these two images is a product of the position each holds. Clinton is a young man with no federal experience and a record as a Vietnam war protester with accusations against him for sexual infidelity. Bush's image of him is quite personal and more clearly fits the usual idea of image as not being related to the issues. But Bush is the incumbent President; he has a record. So Clinton's image of George Bush is about the issues that he claims Bush has not attacked. Each will refute his negative image by calling attention to the issues he has delt with. Clinton will talk of successes in the Arkansas economy and education while he was Governor, and Bush will point to his record in domestic and foreign policy.

Candidates are usually reluctant to attack an opponent directly with charges about character. That function is usually carried out by others, as when Gennifer Flowers claimed that she had a long affair with Bill Clinton. Depending on how much credibility voters are inclined to give to such persons, a candidate may need to respond. That is what Clinton and his wife did when they went on television to refute the image of Clinton as a philanderer.

Candidate Clinton further changed the image question by emphasizing the difference between private character and public character. He reinforced that claim throughout his 13 month campaign with statements like:

> The truth is that I have demonstrated the public character that this country needs as president. I have consistently fought for the same things for more than ten years. I fought for economic modernization, . . . education advancement, . . . to clean up the political system (Miller 349).

The reason most candidates avoid direct negative attacks on their opponents is that the potential is too great for such attacks to backlash against the person who made them. Backlash is less likely when negative advertisements are based on issues than on the personal characteristics of an opponent (Roberts 181). Even the now famous 1988 negative ads the George Bush campaign used against Michael Dukakis (the Willie Horton and Boston Harbor ads) were linked to issues as they attached Dukakis' record on crime and the environment.

For instance, the most notorious of these ads (about Willie Horton, an African American from Dukakis's state of Massachusetts, who, when released on a prison furlough program, brutalized and raped members of a Maryland family) was used as a personal, and many argued racist, attack on Dukakis.

However, it was also linked to the furlough program and the issue of toughness toward crime. Republicans argued that the ad was not personal, but issue oriented.

Another image problem that has to be contended with, in this era of heavily mediated campaigns, is the tendency of journalists to change "the story of the election from 'who should govern' to 'who can win'" (Smith 295). The image that a candidate is a loser decreases the attention paid to the candidate and thus decreases the chance that the candidate can refute this or any other charge. Refutation obviously functions only if it is communicated, and it can only be communicated when the journalists pay attention or when the candidate has a lot of money to purchase rebuttal advertisements.

The decision of the electorate on the proposition: should the candidate be elected? looks like a simple question of image. It is not. It is influenced significantly by a candidate's record and position on issues. Credibility may be more important in political campaigns than in some other situations, but credibility is influenced by the arguments and values an audience comes to associate with a candidate. Even negative ads have more influence if the credibility of a candidate is linked to issues.

Campaign Arguments Are Linked to "The People"

A political campaign is based on an argumentative strategy. The strategy has to cast the candidate as a leader who will achieve the public policy that the people want. Terms like *the people* and *the public* are myths constructed by candidates to define the whole population as embodying the candidate's point of view (McGee). One study of the 1984 presidential debates found that both Ronald Reagan and Walter Mondale claimed to speak for *the people* although with quite different interpretations of what that meant (Werling, et al. 234). Such a strategy can be seen in every campaign strategy. Candidates defend their claims as designed to support "the people," and refute opponents' claims as attacks on "the people." Even though "the people" is a campaign myth, it is an important base for the story that a candidate must tell and maintain at the center of the campaign.

Telling the Right Story

Each campaign should add up to a convincing story of a candidate whose record shows, and statements reinforce, that he or she is in tune with the people to provide a wise public policy. Developing such a story has been transformed in many cases into "the speech" where the same arguments, values, credibility, and even examples are used by a candidate throughout a campaign. Emphasis is shifted, introductions or conclusions are changed to orient a speech to a particular audience. However, the campaign speeches turn out to be essentially one speech. The term *the speech* was first used in Ronald

Reagan's pre-campaign for governor in 1966 (Ritter). It is a standard campaign procedure now. It defines the story of the campaign.

In 1992 Ross Perot was the most successful independent or third party candidate since Theodore Roosevelt in 1912. He was a successful billionaire businessman who had never run for office but had gained some fame by Ken Follett's book, commissioned by Perot. *On Wings of Eagles* was the story of Perot's rescue of his company's hostages held in Iran at the same time that the government could not free the American Embassy hostages. Perot's campaign was built around the use of half-hour infomercials where Perot used charts and interviews to tell his story.

Ross Perot's story was of a man from a poor family who rose to be a leader in business. He did this by applying the things he learned in his close-knit family. There he learned that self-sacrifice and working for others, for community, was the way to make things better, not only for others but for the individual. In this way he got things done, as he did in Teheran and in business. He is no politician because he does not complicate and confuse things as traditional candidates do. He analyzes the situation and sees what has to be done and he does it. He will take these principles of analysis, family, self-sacrifice, and community and use them to solve the deficit, increase employment, free MIAs, and restore people's trust in the American government and confidence in themselves (Kern).

Maintaining the Story

The story does come under attack and when that happens a campaign must use refutation to answer the charges and restore the story.

George Bush and Bill Clinton, realizing that they had more to lose than gain, did not attempt to refute Ross Perot's story.

However, after the election Perot was hurt badly and his story began to come apart when he debated Vice President Albert Gore on the NAFTA agreement in 1993. Gore attacked Perot's story that he would use the principles of self-sacrifice and community. He pointed out, for instance, that the Perot family had a tariff free airport in Texas that they used to benefit themselves while denying the free trade advantages of NAFTA to others. Perot was unable to refute such charges. His inability to maintain his story undoubtedly contributed to his drop in popularity after the debate.

The most disastrous example of an inability to maintain a story was of Michael Dukakis, the Democratic Presidential candidate in 1988. Michael Dukakis had no well-developed story. His story was "mushy" and "incoherent" (Lewis 160). His emphasis on the "Massachusetts Miracle" (economic development under his leadership as Governor) and a campaign based on "competence," fit into George Bush's story of Michael Dukakis as a "technocrat" not a "man of the people." The Bush campaign was able to tell a story of a Dukakis presidency that would weaken America, encourage crime, increase taxes, and destroy the environment and the family.

Dukakis was somehow unable to refute the Republican version of the Dukakis story, in part because the Dukakis campaign treated each campaign event as a separate unit and delayed rebuttal so long that the only real story was Bush's story of Dukakis (Madsen 109).

Politicians from presidents to city council members build a record through legislation and public argumentation. It is combined, in the political campaign, with the candidate's credibility, policy claims, and values to sustain a reasonable story. Defending that story is the central focus of political refutation.

Media and Refutation

Because of the multi-media used in contemporary campaigns, the need to defend the story may come from many different sources. For instance, the Bush campaign itself did not use Willie Horton's picture. The picture came from political action committees and local Republican party groups. A Republican fund-raising letter in Maryland, for instance, featured photographs of Michael Dukakis and Horton, and asked, "Is this your pro-family team for 1988?" (Lewis 159).

Furthermore, the press can become an adversary. In the 1988 vice presidential debate, Judy Woodruff listed prominent Republicans who had expressed reservations about Republican vice presidential candidate Dan Quayle and asked why he had "not made a more substantial impression" on them (Weiler 215). These members of the questioning team frequently used what J. Michael Hogan calls "preemptive refutation" in debates. They attacked a candidate's position with a question. Andrea Mitchell asked Governor Dukakis this question in the third debate of the 1988 campaign:

> Governor, you've said tonight that you set as a goal the steady reduction of the deficit, . . . No credible economist in either party accepts as realistic your plan to handle the deficit by tightening tax collection, investing in economic growth, bringing down interest rates and cutting weapons systems. . . . So let's assume, now, for argument's purpose, that it is the spring of 1989, and you are President Dukakis, and you discover that all of those economists were right and you were wrong. You are now facing that dreaded last resort—increased taxes. Which tax do you decide is the least onerous? (222).

No candidate wants to debate the reporter, particularly when she or he can say, "I was just asking a question," but that is what the candidate has to do.

The media also pose a problem for a campaigner who wants to refute an argument from whatever source because of controlled access. Media managers can control the extent to which a refutation gets covered. This is true in less visible or less highly financed campaigns. It is also part of the reason campaigns are increasingly more expensive.

Kathleen Hall Jamieson points out that media reporters such as Dan Rather, Tom Brokaw, Peter Jennings, Lesley Stahl, Lisa Meyers, and newspaper reporters as well, told voters the principles by which they should interpret the campaign. She found fifteen principles, such as "Candidates believe that symbols win more votes than substance" and "At the end of a campaign those ahead in the polls adopt the motto: "No news is good news" (163–64). All of these principles, in one way or another, tend to portray the candidate as an actor with no concern for issues, only the strategy for winning.

THE SPECIAL ROLE OF DEBATES

Increasingly, politics involves debates. There was a time not too many years ago when political debates were rare. Incumbents would not debate their lesser known opponents because they had nothing to gain. The first presidential debate was between two non-incumbents, Richard Nixon and John Kennedy, in 1960. The next presidential debate was in 1976, when Gerald Ford, although an incumbent, agreed to debate Jimmy Carter because Ford was vulnerable in the polls and because he was not an elected president. Since that time, it has been an expected routine. Also since that time, debates have become an expected part of campaigning in most state and local races.

Debate experts and others have examined these debates and found them less than ideal. The general agreement is that they are not debates in the sense that candidates directly confront, question, and refute one another. Rather, they are seen as "joint appearances" with minimum exchange between candidates. The Lincoln-Douglas Illinois Senatorial debates of 1858 are held up as models against which contemporary political debates are judged negatively. However, as David Zarefsky has noted, those debates had some of the characteristics we decry in contemporary political debates.

The Lincoln-Douglas debates "were often repetitive; they are characterized by the trading of charges, often without evidence; the arguments were incompletely developed . . . the moral question received scant attention in the debates, . . . With rare exceptions, moreover, the candidates set out their own beliefs but did not grapple with the opponent's conception" (224).

Political debates are what they are because they are like the campaign, and the campaign is a reflection of the mixed American political condition in the late twentieth century. A wealth of research findings points to debates as the place where people believe they can find out about the candidates and their stands on issues (Rowland and Voss 239). Campaign debates have greater attendance or viewership than any other campaign messages (Jamieson and Birdsell 121).

The status of argumentation in these debates is a response, not to partisan, issue-oriented voters, but to the diverse nature of the electorate. Political parties and candidates represent voters who hold a variety of positions on issues. Some Democrats may favor better unemployment benefits, less taxes on the middle class, federal health insurance, and a strong national defense, be undecided on civil rights, oppose abortion, and support or oppose many other ideas. Other Democrats will be stronger, weaker, or ambivalent on any of these issues. The same will be true of Republicans. In addition, there is a growing tendency for voters to consider themselves independent or to associate themselves with narrower special interests such as abortion, gun control, federal-state powers, or school prayer. Therefore, no candidate can take a strong stand on a controversial issue without risking a loss of support. Such a reality influences the nature of refutation in a political campaign.

REFUTATION IN THE POLITICAL CAMPAIGN

We have already discussed several implications for refutation in the political campaign, but we now look at refutation more specifically. Refutation in the political campaign is concerned with values, evidence, and credibility. It must preserve the story of the campaign and it must leave no shot unanswered.

Refutation Is Usually About Values

Favoring a controversial policy can damage a political candidate. When Walter Mondale argued in 1984 that he would raise taxes and, if elected, so would Ronald Reagan, he committed political suicide. In 1988 when George Bush said "Read my lips, no new taxes" he took a position with which most Americans agreed. In the 1990s the debate is not over taxes—yes or no. Virtually no politician favors tax increases and those who do, favor them on someone other than their constituents. The central argument is about how we do what we do without raising taxes. This is only one example of how specific policy choices are limited in a campaign because people agree on values but reject policies. There are others: How do we oppose abortion but provide for choice? How do we cut the military and provide for national defense? How do we protect the environment and produce more jobs?

Candidates faced with the need to argue for what people want without the specifics that people reject find the basis of their arguments in values. The values are usually shared by the candidates and the public (Werling, et al. 231). Bill Clinton was able to make a strong value argument that every American should be guaranteed health protection. But as the Clinton health plan emerged and was subjected to refutation on the specifics of how it would work, it fell in popularity and was abandoned. Polls still indicated that health was an important value for most Americans but finding a plan and paying for it is no easy task.

Evidence Is Important to Refutation

While refutation is usually about values, that does not mean that campaigns do not use evidence. A successful campaign will provide evidence, statistics, and testimony to support the value orientation of the campaign. There is considerable use of evidence in speeches and debates. Adrian W. Frana observed it in the 1988 presidential debates:

> Many examples could be provided because so much was employed. One was the use of *statistics* (Dukakis claiming the U.S. having 5% of the world's population but 50% of its cocaine use, Bush noting that taxes had been cut and that revenues

were up 25% in three years). Another was the use of *examples* to personalize or illustrate a larger point (Dukakis, in talking of the 37 million Americans who have no health insurance, citing a Houston father who had been laid off and lost his coverage and now he can't let his son compete in Little League because he's afraid he will get hurt and he can't provide the health insurance; Bush using the St. Louis experience as the wrong approach to low-cost housing) (200–01).

Credibility Is Significant in Refutation

In any political campaign, credibility is important because, as we have noted, the overarching proposition is about the candidates: should this candidate be elected? Therefore, all that we have said about issue and image is appropriate here. Credibility becomes important as a candidate works to sustain an image. Sometimes credibility is attacked directly as in some examples we have noted about the 1988 Bush campaign. We might add to George Bush's characterization of Michael Dukakis, Democratic vice presidential candidate Lloyd Bentsen's remark to his Republican counter-part Dan Quayle, "You're no Jack Kennedy, [after Quayle compared his age to Kennedy's at the time of Kennedy's election as President]" or Michael Dukakis' label for George Bush as the "Joe Isuzu [a character in an automobile commercial who tells lies] of American politics."

It is indirect credibility, however, that most often causes problems for candidates. When candidates are seen as being on the wrong side of, confused about, or ignorant of issues, credibility problems are serious. A candidate in danger of such credibility problems must take immediate action to refute the charges so as to restore the story crafted for the campaign.

The Story Is Significant in Refutation

When we say the candidate must "restore the story crafted for the campaign," we acknowledge refutation as more than just saying "that's wrong." Each argument has a place in the campaign. You will recall from chapter 12 that one needs a posture for refutation, a constructive base from which to refute the position of others. We also observed that the framework of refutation that works in most situations follows these steps: state the point to be refuted, state your claim relevant to the point, support your claim, and state explicitly how your criticism undermines the overall position (the story) of those whom you are refuting. We might add to this last point that the undermining of an opponent's position (story) should reaffirm yours.

In chapter 3 we analyzed the 1994 California Ballot Proposition 187 that proposed to deny public services to illegal immigrants. You will recall that when opponents argued that Proposition 187 conflicted with state and federal laws and U.S. Constitutional protections, the supporters' reply was "Nonsense." The only refutation to this claim, supported by legal authority, was to say it was not true. Such a response, and it's not uncommon, is a weak refutation because it fails to advance the debate. It provides no new argument or support to strengthen the story or to undermine the opponent's story.

Leave No Shot Unanswered

If the story of the campaign is to be sustained, then the dictum of Christopher Matthews, a political aide with considerable inside experience in the political campaign process, is worth remembering: "Leave no shot unanswered" (117). Perhaps no recent election represents this maxim so well as the election of 1988. In that election the George Bush campaign chose a strategy of devoting 50 percent of its efforts to "negative campaigning" or attacks on Michael Dukakis. It was late in the campaign when the Dukakis campaign adopted a similar strategy. Republican strategist Roger Ailes had said, "There are three things that get covered: visuals, attacks, and mistakes" (Bennett 129). The Bush campaign attacked Dukakis on conservation (the pollution in Boston Harbor), his membership in the American Civil Liberties Union (a "liberal" organization for a person who said he was not a "liberal"), on crime (the Willie Horton case), his softness on defense, and others. These attacks came in commercials (picture of Willie Horton, turnstiles of released and returning prisoners, Bush boating on Boston Harbor, pictures of medical waste in the water) speeches, and debates. And, as we noted earlier, Bush maintained the story of his opponent. In one debate, for instance, he said that one of Dukakis' answers was "as clear as Boston Harbor" (Frana 202).

Dukakis, virtually every political observer agrees, waited too long to respond. He somehow believed these were superficial charges that voters would see through and concentrated on his own "positive" campaign. He was wrong. Some negative campaigning backfires, but it always has to be refuted.

Refutation by Inoculation

Refutation is usually thought of as something that takes place after a candidate has had a story and the image it projects attacked. However, there is considerable evidence to show that answering the argument before it is made can have a significant effect and even prevent it from being used. Such a refutational strategy is called *inoculation*. It is a metaphor for inoculating humans against disease in which a weakened form of a virus is introduced into the body to stimulate resistance to the disease. There are two factors in political inoculation: first there is a warning of an impending attack that causes a voter to be motivated to strengthen support, and then to establish resistance to any future attack arguments (Pfau and Kenski 85).

Studies of a South Dakota senatorial race and the 1988 Bush-Dukakis presidential election by Michael Pfau and Henry C. Kenski show that inoculation "deflects the specific content of the attacks, and it reduces the likelihood that the political attacks will influence receiver voting intention. In addition, because inoculation precedes attack, it even provides defenses against attacks that are launched late in the campaign" and therefore, are particularly difficult to refute (100).

The major difficulty of such a strategy is that it brings out charges that might not have been made and is, therefore, subject to the credibility claim that the refuter is putting up a "strawman," of manufacturing an argument that no one would use, in order to refute it. Still, where a candidate knows that a challenge is likely, inoculation against it is a useful refutational strategy.

CONCLUSION

Political argumentation is the oldest recorded argumentation sphere. It is the process of using verbal and visual arguments to influence the policy decisions of a political community. Political argumentation is characterized by the use of policy claims. The content of those claims emphasizes ways and means, war and peace, national defense, exports and imports, and legislation according to Aristotle, though those categories have expanded meanings in modern times. In addition, many things that would have been considered personal in other times are public now. Political claims begin in a vague form, but they become more specific as argumentation about them develops. Claims and issues also change as argumentation emerges. Most claims that are advanced do not become policy, and most that do are noncontroversial.

The first of three major sub-spheres of political argumentation is committee hearings. There, argumentation is characterized by applying legal practice. Arguments are developed as questions as if the questioner was only searching for facts, however, the questions are designed to build a record that can be used in subsequent hearings and legislative debates. The actual forms these questions take reveal the argumentative intent of their use. The overall objective of the questioning, record building, and refutation is to tell a good story that will stand up to criticism.

In the second sub-sphere, legislative action, refutation is usually non-confrontational. Under the influence of the value of majoritarianism the objective is to get the largest possible majority. Refutation is usually not personal. The amendment process serves as a kind of refutation. Refutation has an important credibility function in building a reputation for the legislator. This process of resolving differences through the amendment process is extended to the relationship between the legislature and the executive.

In the third sub-sphere, political campaigns, there is a complex mixture of activities. Campaigns involve both policy issues and the images of the candidates. Campaign arguments are made in the light of an understanding of the "people" or the "public." These concepts are used as a basis for telling the right stories about the candidate and about the opponent. These stories together form the story of the campaign and its relationship to the people. That story must be maintained, not only against the refutation of opponents but that of the media as well.

Debates have a special role in political campaigns. They are probably the single most important campaign activity, despite frequent complaints that they do not involve extensive attention to the issues. Debates reflect the mixed political condition in the country.

Refutation in a political campaign tends to be about values more than specific policies. Evidence and credibility are important to refutation because they help to sustain the story propagated by the campaign. To maintain that story a candidate and campaign must answer attacks on the story. Sometimes that refutation comes in the form of inoculation before the attack is actually made.

PROJECTS

14.1 Attend a committee hearing of a campus or local government group. Write a short analysis of the argumentation used there. To what extent does it reflect the principles of committee hearings discussed in this chapter? What is your opinion of the quality of the hearings?

14.2 Attend a meeting of a special interest group in your town or on your campus, a meeting centered on an issue such as nuclear arms reduction, disposal of nuclear waste, protection of the environment, improvement of the food in the student union, or the role of student government. You can locate such groups by looking for announcements of meetings in the newspaper. Prepare a critique on the argumentation used.

14.3 Interview a person who is or has been a member of a public decision making body. Ask him or her to discuss how arguments are stated and refuted in that body. Prepare a report on the interview.

14.4 Choose a current public controversy and, with a partner, debate against two other members of the class on that controversy. Your instructor will explain how to organize the debate.

REFERENCES

Apple, R. W. Jr. "Senate Confirms Thomas 52–48, Ending Week of Bitter Battle; 'Time For Healing,' Judge Says." *New York Times* 16 Oct 1991: A1, A3.

Aristotle. *The Rhetoric*. Trans. Lane Cooper. New York: Appleton-Century-Crofts, 1932.

Asbell, Sally L. "Understanding the Rehabilitation Act of 1973: A Rhetorical Analysis of Legislative Hearings." Diss. U of Utah, 1989.

Bennett, W. Lance. "Where Have All the Issues Gone? Explaining the Rhetorical Limits in American Elections." *Spheres of Argument*. Ed. Bruce Gronbeck. Annandale, VA: Speech Communication Assoc., 1989: 128–35.

Bitzer, Lloyd F. "Political Rhetoric." *Handbook of Political Communication*. Eds. Dan D. Nimmo and Keith R. Sanders. Beverly Hills: Sage, 1981: 225–48.

Boynton, George R. "When Senators and Publics Meet at the Environmental Protection Sub-Committee." *Discourse and Society* 2 (1991): 131–55.

———. "Telling a Good Story: Models of Argument; Models of Understanding in the Senate Agriculture Committee." *Argument and Critical Practices*. Ed. Joseph W. Wenzel. Annandale, VA: Speech Communication Assoc., 1987: 429–38.

Cobb, Roger W., and Charles D. Elder. "Communication and Public Policy." *Handbook of Political Communication*. Eds. Dan D. Nimmo and Keith R. Sanders. Beverly Hills: Sage, 1981: 391–416.

Cox, J. Robert. "Investigating Policy Argument as a Field." *Dimensions of Argument*. Eds. George Ziegelmueller and Jack Rhodes. Annandale, VA: Speech Communication Assoc. 1981: 126–42.

Davidson, Roger, and Walter J. Oleszek. *Congress and Its Members*. Washington, DC: Congressional Quarterly, 1981.

Dowd, Maureen. "Sununu Sayonara: He Broke 7 Cardinal Rules." *New York Times* 5 Dec. 1991: A14.

"Excerpt From a Statement By Senator Kennedy." *New York Times* 16 Oct. 1991: Al, A3.

Frana, Adrian W. "Characteristics of Effective Argumentation." *Argumentation and Advocacy* 25 (1989): 200–02.

Goodnight, G. Thomas. "The Personal, Technical, and Public Spheres of Argument: A Speculative Inquiry into the Art of Public Deliberation." *Journal of the American Forensic Association* 18 (1982): 214–27.

Hogan, J. Michael. "Media Nihilism and the Presidential Debates." *Argumentation and Advocacy* 25 (1989): 220–25.

Jaehne, Dennis. "Administrative Appeals: The Bureaucratization of Environmental Discourse." Diss. U of Utah, 1989.

Jamieson, Kathleen Hall. *Dirty Politics: Deception, Distraction, and Democracy*. New York: Oxford, 1992.

Jamieson, Kathleen Hall, and David S. Birdsell. *Presidential Debates: The Challenge of Creating an Informed Electorate*. New York: Oxford, 1988.

Keefe, William J., and Morris S. Ogul. *The American Legislative Process: Congress and The States*. Englewood Cliffs, NJ: Prentice-Hall, 1985.

Kern, Montague. "The Question of a Return to Basic American Values: 'My Mother and Winston Churchill' in the Heroic Narrations of Ross Perot's Infomercials." *Presidential Campaign Discourse*. Ed. Kathleen E. Kendall. Albany: State U of New York P, 1995. 157–78.

Lewis, William F. "'Getting Away With Murder': George Bush, Lee Atwater, Willie Horton and the Political Logic of Common Sense." *Spheres of Argument*. Ed. Bruce Gronbeck. Annandale, VA: Speech Communication Assoc., 1989: 158–66.

Madsen, Arnie. "Partisan Commentary and the First 1988 Presidential Debate." *Argumentation and Advocacy* 27 (1991): 100–13.

Matthews, Christopher. *Hardball*. New York: Summit, 1988.

Matthews, Donald R., and James A. Stimson. *Yeas and Nays: Normal Decision-Making in the U.S. House of Representatives*. New York: Wiley, 1975: 6.

McGee, Michael C. "In Search of 'The People': A Rhetorical Alternative." *Quarterly Journal of Speech* 61 (Oct. 1975): 235–49.

Miller, Greg R. "Incongruities in the Public/Private Spheres: Implications of the Clinton Presidential Campaign." *Argument and the Postmodern Challenge*. Ed. Raymie E. McKerrow. Annandale, VA: Speech Communication Assoc., 1993: 345–51.

"Parade of Witnesses Support Hill's Story, Thomas's Integrity." *New York Times* 14 Oct. 1991: A1.

Pfau, Michael, and Henry C. Kenski. *Attack Politics: Strategy and Defense*. New York: Praeger, 1990.

Popkin, James, and Gloria Borger. "They Think They Can." *US News and World Report* 10 April 1995: 26–32.

Ritter, Kurt W. "Ronald Reagan and The Speech: The Rhetoric of Public Relations Politics." *Western Speech* 32 (1968): 50–58.

Roberts, Marilyn S. "Political Advertising: Strategies for Influence." *Presidential Campaign Discourse: Strategic Communication Problems*. Ed. Kathleen E. Kendall. Albany: State U of New York P, 1995. 179–200.

Rowland, Robert C., and Cary R. W. Voss. "A Structural Functional Analysis of the Assumptions Behind Presidential Debates." *Argument and Critical Practices*. Ed. Joseph W. Wenzel. Annandale, VA: Speech Communication Assoc., 1987: 239–48.

Smith, Craig Allen. "The Struggle for Interpretive Dominance." *Presidential Campaign Discourse: Strategic Communication Problems*. Ed. Kathleen E. Kendall. Albany: State U of New York P, 1995. 293–304.

Stuckey, Mary E. and Frederick J. Antczak. "The Battle of Issues and Images." *Presidential Campaign Discourse: Strategic Communication Problems*. Ed. Kathleen E Kendall. Albany: State U of New York P, 1995. 117–34.

"Viewers Tune In." *New York Times*. 14 Oct 1991: A17.

Uslander, Eric M. *The Decline of Comity in Congress*. Ann Arbor: U of Michigan P, 1993.

Weiler, Michael. "The 1988 Electoral Debates and Debate Theory." *Argumentation and Advocacy* 25 (1989): 214–19.

Werling, David S., Michael Salvador, Malcolm O. Sillars, and Mina A. Vaughn. "Presidential Debates: Epideictic Merger of Issues and Images in Values." *Argument and Critical Practices*. Ed. Joseph W. Wenzel. Annandale, VA: Speech Communication Assoc., 1987: 229–38.

Wise, Charles R. *The Dynamics of Legislation*. San Francisco: Jossey-Bass, 1996.

Zarefsky, David. *Lincoln Douglas and Slavery*. Chicago: U of Chicago P, 1990.

15

The Language of Argumentation

Key Terms

social process	definition
context	intensity
meaning	qualifiers
interpretation	vivid details
style	power
figures of speech	aggression

Language is the subject of the last chapter in this book, yet in many ways it is the foundational element of argumentation. All argumentation is dependent upon the symbol system by which it functions. Shared language interpretative strategies have been identified as starting points of argumentation, and evidence, argument, values, credibility, and all the others topics we have discussed are built on language.

In this chapter we will first talk about the role of language in communicating arguments, noting particularly its social basis and thus its inherent ambiguity. Then we will discuss some of the most important ways that you can use language to strengthen your arguments. We will see how language influences your definitions, credibility, power relationships, qualifiers, and interpersonal aggression.

LANGUAGE AND THE COMMUNICATION OF ARGUMENT

Fundamentally, *language* is a collection of noises, movements, and marks people speak or set down on paper or some other substance. Language is not connected to things "in the world," it is simply a tool people use to interact with each other. Over many years, people have come to assign general meanings to noises, movements, and marks, and these meaning assignments have achieved enough regularity to allow the assignment of labels and the codification of the meanings in such repositories as dictionaries and textbooks. But it would be a good idea, as we launch into a discussion of language in argumentation, to keep in mind that language is an ever-changing process that we use to gain and maintain human relationships. In fact, "Language becomes language only when it is used, and this use of language . . . defines its nature" (Kent 11).

Our discussion of language in this first section, will identify its social nature, its dependence on interpretation, and the meaning of style. Then we will turn to definitions, the way language influences credibility, and language choices as power relationships.

Language Is Social

Language is commonly referred to as human symbolic activity. The symbols that make up language are arbitrarily assigned meaning, when people interpret them as part of interaction. Words don't have meanings, people have meanings. You have meanings in mind when you speak or write, but they are based on your prior experience and education. In the immediate context in which you are speaking, writing, or reading, the meanings of the words will depend upon the context in which you find yourself at the time, and the people with whom you are interacting. That is why we say language is social.

While people often talk about "conveying" meaning, this is misleading. Meaning is not delivered like the mail or a fax. It is, instead, constructed within social processes. Every time you set out to communicate, at least three meaning processes are involved. First, there is the meaning you intend to communicate. Second, there are the conventional, established meanings (what is found in textbooks and dictionaries). Third, there is the interpretation made by those with whom you are communicating (Anderson and Meyer 48).

In 1980, when George Bush was Vice President of the United States, he was standing in a receiving line at a reception when a reporter came through and, noting Bush's suede blazer, said, "That's a handsome coat. What poor animal was sacrificed to make it?" Bush is reported to have replied, "We don't bother with animals. We use humans" (Maestas 3). What did Bush mean? Was it a smart-aleck quip? Was it a quick facetious retort intended to put off an animal rights challenge? Did Bush mean to say his coat was made with human hides? We cannot know the answers to these questions without knowing more about the social context.

The Bush statement was quoted in a newspaper article published in 1995 dealing with charges that the U.S. Government, without fully warning the public, conducted nuclear tests in Nevada so that the effects of radiation could be studied. The reporter's use of the Bush statement, "We use humans," in this context suggests quite a different potential meaning. Is the reporter claiming that Bush knew in 1980 that the government had used humans as guinea pigs? Is it unfair for the reporter to take a statement made fifteen years earlier, and in quite another context, to introduce a criticism of government action?

Obviously, the reporter can do whatever she pleases with the language, as can everybody else. But when you interpret the language, if you take the social conditions into account, you may come up with different meanings. Then, some people will say the Bush statement had nothing to do with nuclear testing and therefore cannot be used in evidence for that argument. Others may conclude that Bush, like most other federal bureaucrats, is in on the nuclear conspiracy along with lots of other conspiracies. So there are many possible interpretations of the one simple statement, "We use humans," and no one can say with finality which is correct, because meanings are socially established.

The social basis of language becomes apparent when you consider it in relation to argument spheres. One of the characteristics of arguments within a particular sphere is language usage and meanings. When you present an argument, it is important to take into account the sphere in which the argument is to be evaluated and the language characteristic of the sphere. Can you guess the sphere in which this sentence appeared: "In this paper we will expand and revise the structurational conceptual scheme by closely analyzing an example of climate emergence as a meaning-making undercurrent in a changing organization" (Bastien, et al. 87). If you guessed an academic sphere, you are correct. The chances are that you do not know what some of the words mean, and you probably suspect that some of the familiar words do not mean what you think they mean. Scholars often create new words to communicate a precise meaning: *structuration*. They also use ordinary words in ways peculiar to the academic sphere: *climate*. When students are assigned to read research reports or other scholarship, they often become frustrated by having to adjust to such a peculiar language usage. To another academic, the language seems perfectly clear.

Sometimes, words that seem to be simple and straightforward can take profoundly different meanings as they move from sphere to sphere. Take these words, for example, "A well regulated militia being necessary to the security of a free State, the right of the people to keep and bear arms, shall not be infringed." When this statement, the Second Amendment to the Constitution of the United States, is said within a constitutional law sphere its interpretation is quite different from that used by the National Rifle Association (NRA) or a citizens' volunteer militia. The Supreme Court puts emphasis on the word *militia* and concludes that it applies to such state government sponsored organizations as the National Guard in opposition to a federal standing army (*U.S. v Miller*). The NRA and some constitutional historians look mostly at the words *the right of the people to keep and bear arms*, and conclude it means government cannot restrict individuals' possession of firearms (Levy 341). Now, possibly in order to come within the court's interpretation, people are forming what they call militias, which may be well regulated but are not state sponsored.

In each case, the users claim to know what the words meant when they were written more than 200 years ago even though, as one historian says, "The Second Amendment is as vague as it is ambiguous" (Levy 341). Another commentator calls attention to the use of the word *militia*, which is no longer in common usage, as the source of the problem (Young xv). He thinks, as does the NRA today, a well regulated militia really meant an armed populace (Young li-lii). These people behave as if the words mean the same today as they did long ago, and that they mean the same thing in all contexts. In fact, the social basis of language tells us that words mean what the people using them at any given time choose to interpret them to mean.

Language Depends on Interpretation

Even when language has been codified as to meaning, and when you are aware of the language practices peculiar to the sphere within which you are presenting your arguments, you can still be unsure what meaning your words will generate. When you argue, you make a guess as to what meaning others will attach to your words. You have an interpretation of meaning for the language you use, but when you communicate with others, you will discover that they have an interpretation for your words that is often different from your own. Communication relies upon people making good guesses about the interpretation others will make. In direct interaction, it is possible to advance your arguments, listen to others' response, and adjust your arguments according to the apparent interpretation that has been given to your words. Gradually, you and others can develop a common set of interpretations that allow you to conduct argumentation. Words are like pieces of a jigsaw puzzle: what any single piece is or does can be understood only in relation to all the other pieces (Odell 36). But it is the toughest of all puzzles in that it is three-dimensional and in constant movement.

In your families, neighborhoods, religious institutions, among close friends and coworkers, you can make quite good guesses as to the meaning your words will be given because all are using a similar interpretation strategy. However, the inherent ambiguity of language, its unique meaning for each person, means that your guesses will never be perfect (Kent 31). The further removed you are from the decision makers, the more hazardous will be your guesses. In writing, for example, we must make extremely tenuous guesses as to the interpretations that will be given to our language by people who come from a wide geographic area, different ages and backgrounds, and over many years.

It is not enough to ask someone, "What do you mean by that argument?" Their answer will require more interpretation on your part, and the fit will never be perfect. Anatol Rapoport feels that before a real dialogue can take place, the participants should satisfy these essential features of what he calls an "ethical debate":

1. The ability and willingness of each participant to state the position of the other people to their satisfaction.
2. The ability and willingness of each participant to state the conditions under which the position of the others has merit or is reasonable.
3. The ability and willingness of everyone to assume that all participants are very much like themselves and that they have a lot in common (80).

What he emphasizes by these criteria is the interpretative character of language. What passes for disagreement or misunderstanding in argumentation may simply reflect a failure of the parties to work out a common strategy for interpretation. If you are thinking only about your own arguments and feeling that those who disagree with you are unreasonable, bullheaded, or just mean, you probably have not been doing the interpretative work needed to resolve your disagreement. Before expressing your disagreement, you must work on interpreting what others are saying, and that requires hard work.

Style Is Saying the Same Thing in Different Ways

Style is one of the key things that distinguish one argument from another when both are supporting essentially the same claim (Hickey 2). When you are planning your argumentation, keep in mind that at every step you have linguistic choices to make. The more you understand this, and the more choices you perceive for every thought, the more effective you will be in terms of language style. "The contribution of language to reasoning cannot be doubted . . ." (Odell 22).

What are some of the criteria to consider in making your stylistic choices? The *degree of formality* is important. Writing tends to call for more formal style than speech. The tenor of the situation, for instance a party discussion or Congressional testimony, will suggest the style of language to be used. The *social relationships/hierarchies* between the people involved will suggest style. With friends we tend to use a different style of language than we do with strangers. We are probably less formal with peers than with people we perceive as more powerful or important. The characteristics of the *sphere* will dictate style. Internal auditors at Merrill Lynch are not allowed to use a word stronger than *adequate* to rate a department's practices. The *physical setting* will influence stylistic choices. Speaking to a thousand people in an auditorium tends to demand a certain word choice that would not be appropriate in a conversational setting. The *argumentative status* of the interaction, ranging from cooperative to antagonistic, will dictate certain language choices. In fact, argumentation can be changed abruptly from cooperative to antagonistic by word choice alone. *Timing*, whether it is the time of day or the stage in the argumentation, can influence style. Highly oratorical or poetic language choices can fall flat at one time and move people at another.

SOME FIGURES OF SPEECH

METAPHORS\SIMILES

A direct or implied comparison between two concepts: compliment a cop by saying, "Your shield is made of gold." "ALS (Lou Gehrig's disease) is like having a live brain in a dead body."

HYPERBOLE

Use of exaggeration for emphasis: "The Contract with America could change the lives of every child in every family in America."

ANTITHESIS

Juxtaposition of contrasting ideas: "Let us never negotiate out of fear. But let us never fear to negotiate."

RHETORICAL QUESTION

Asking a question not for an answer but to make a claim: "Do you want to learn a billion-dollar secret?"

IRONY

Using a word to communicate the opposite of its usual meaning: "They cut the budget by only increasing it by a few billion dollars."

Effective style is associated with breaking away from predictability (Hickey 5). Good style choices surprise and delight people because, when they are expecting just more of the same, they get something different, original, creative, exciting. Language choices can be used to amuse, clarify, annoy, insult, exhort, manipulate, convince, tempt, exonerate, excuse, warn, promise, avow, threaten, punish, and ridicule. You can use puns, word play, poetic devices, rhetorical devices, and figures of speech to give added strength to your arguments. "What makes one natural language user more interesting and captivating than another is [the] ability to use language in innovative and unique ways—ways no other has traversed" (Odell 22; 34–37).

DEFINITIONS ARE ARGUMENTS

One of the basic characteristics of good language use is the practice of definition. What is often overlooked, however, is the fact that definitions are claims that must be supported by effective argumentation, because meanings are based on consensus. Value-laden words such as *love, knowledge, government, god,* clearly have no single precise definition. Neither do such apparently straightforward words as *agnostic, geranium, planet,* or *reconsider.* When you use words, you cannot appeal to a single, correct definition. You must present a convincing argument in support of your interpretation. Definitions can be used as support for your arguments only if you have, through argument, generated a common interpretation with the decision makers. There are several common ways to build an argument in support of your definition, and we will discuss some of them.

Formal Definition

A formal definition involves the development of a logic-based argument (see chapter 2) founded on identifying a general class for which there is a high probability of a common audience interpretation, and then locating the term you are defining within that class and differentiating it from other aspects of the class. Essentially, you can use the syllogism format to argue for a definition:

A *democracy*, as Americans use the term, is a government [general class] in which the people either directly or through elected representatives exercise power [differentiation].

Psychology is the science [general class] of mental processes and behavior [differentiation].

Fundamentalism is a movement in American Protestantism [general class] based on a belief that the Bible is a literal historical record and incontrovertible prophecy [differentiation].

Definition by Example

Just as examples can serve as support for any argument (see chapter 7), they can be used to support your argument for a definition. The process is the same: you locate a specific concept for which there is high likelihood of a common interpretation in your audience, and then relate your concept to it.

> *Graphic arts* are, for example, such works as engravings, etchings, woodcuts, or lithographs.
>
> The *New Deal* is characterized by, for example, Social Security, the Federal Deposit Insurance Corporation, and the Securities and Exchange Commission.
>
> To *proselytize* is, for example, what the Mormons do when they send two young people around knocking on doors to talk about their religion.

Functional Definition

Sometimes a good way to make a convincing definition is to illustrate how a concept functions.

> *Spark plugs* ignite the fuel mixture in an internal combustion engine.
>
> *Dental floss* cleans the areas between your teeth.
>
> A *heuristic device* gives students a guide to use for learning on their own.

Definition by Analogy

You can establish a clear meaning for a concept by using argument by analogy (see chapter 6) to show how a term is like or unlike other familiar concepts. Remember, arguments by analogy work by placing a concept under study alongside one on which there is agreement. If they can be shown to have significant similarities, the unknown concept can take on meaning from that which is already agreed upon.

Definitions by analogy resemble formal definitions, but they are subtly different. In formal definitions, concepts are identified logically as part of a class. In definition by analogy, concepts are explained by their similarity to a more familiar concept.

> *Chewing coca leaves* is like taking cocaine, because that is where cocaine comes from, but it is different because it gets into the bloodstream more slowly through the mouth than by inhalation or injection, which deliver cocaine quickly and directly into the bloodstream.
>
> A *historical novel* is like a history book in that it is based on the study and interpretation of the past, but it differs in the fact that the author is free to include imagined characters, conversations, and events.
>
> An *oboe* is like a clarinet in that it is a slender woodwind musical instrument, but it differs in that it has a double-reed mouthpiece.

Definition by Authority

Arguments based on authority (see chapter 6) are common in definition. The most obvious authority is a dictionary, which for many situations is all the authority you need. Resist being entrapped, however, by a veneration of authority leading you to believe that the dictionary is the final or only authority on word meanings. Often, it is the worst because dictionaries cannot possibly be published fast enough to keep up with the dynamics of language. However, they will give you a general guide to three factors that will strengthen your argument in many situations.

Usage identifies how a word commonly appears in our communication; what people usually mean. Widespread use of a word for a certain meaning provides some authority for that meaning or definition.

Etymology reports the history of a word from the earliest languages. In the past, an argument for a definition that was based on what the root of a word meant, for instance in Greek or Latin, was more powerful than it is today. Today, such an argument is mostly effective with people who still believe that words possess inherent meaning.

Wordsmiths, or the people who create or modify words, can be used authoritatively to support a definition. When physicists theorized the existence of subatomic particles as the fundamental units of matter, they needed a new word for them. They turned to literature in James Joyce's *Finnegan's Wake*: "three quarks for Mr. Marks," and named their particles *quarks*. Academics, adolescents, gangs, ethnic groups, musical groups, and others commonly create new words and can serve as the authorities on definitions. Dictionaries frequently identify these wordsmiths.

With this general discussion of language behind us, we can now turn to some specific aspects of how language and argumentation work together. None of the specific observations we will make can be presumed to function the same way in every context. Remember, you are always making guesses about how others will interpret your language, and your guesses will never be certain.

LANGUAGE CHOICES AFFECT CREDIBILITY

In addition to the information provided in chapter 10, we can point to some aspects of language choice that can enhance your credibility. Using language that is seen as logical, factual, emotional, assertive, and unambiguous tends to increase credibility, as does a personal, conversational style (Rieke and Stutman 118).

In their book on credibility, James M. Kouzes and Barry Z. Posner tell us to speak with confidence in order to build credibility (211). Your language behavior affects the confidence you communicate, and therefore, it plays a part in the credibility you develop. Here are a few of the language choices you can make to communicate confidence.

Use Intense Language

Think of neutral language as colorless, fact-oriented, informative. "Lauren Jones tries to get along in a world that has not been friendly to her." That is neutral language. Now, here is the same idea expressed in intense language, that is, language that moves away from neutral: "Lauren Jones tries to be faithful to her own cause—a cause of survival in a world that has tried to rip out her soul." Language is more intense when adjectives that make evaluations or reflect potency (*beautiful*, *strong*, *dumb*) are used. Intensity is increased with the addition of adverbs that reflect strong probability (*certainly*, *surely*), frequency (*always*, *never*), or intensity (*very*) (Bradac, et al. 416).

Winston Churchill, then Prime Minister of England, reported, in 1940, that British and French armies successfully escaped from German attack by crossing the English Channel from Dunkirk, Belgium. But he did not say it in such neutral language: "A miracle of deliverance, achieved by valor, by perseverance, by perfect discipline, by faultless service, by resource, by skill, by unconquerable fidelity. . . ." Intense language tends to be associated with confidence and thus credibility. However, remember our warning in chapter 10 that when language becomes too intense, credibility suffers. Intense language is more powerful so long as it does not exceed what decision makers think is appropriate.

Use Strong Qualifiers

In the Churchill statement above, you can see examples of strong qualifiers: "perfect," "faultless," "unconquerable." Think of weaker qualifiers he might have used: "very good," "capable," "great." In his review of Ralph Fiennes' performance of Hamlet, John Lahr says, " . . . Ralph Fiennes has pitched his drop-dead matinee-idol profile and the modesty of his sensitive soul into a post modern 'Hamlet'" (97). Does "drop-dead matinee-idol" do a better job of qualifying Fiennes' appearance than, say, "handsome"? What about "sensitive" and "post modern" as qualifiers? Do they communicate greater confidence than less strong words might?

Use Vivid Details

In description, you can provide general information, or you can use vivid details. For example, in describing a new office occupied when a company fell on hard times, you could say the office was small and furnished with inexpensive furniture. Or you could, as did Stephen Schiff, make the details more vivid: "[The offices] have low ceilings and cheap carpeting and the kind of black-painted desks that you can buy by the dozen from an office-supply firm" (52). Notice the vivid detail in the following statement intended to get us to subscribe to an investment publication. The point is to frighten older people about the security of their savings.

Generation "X" is peopled with real barbarians, tattooed and be-ringed, carrying clubs and chains and wearing leather and metal body armor. . . . Like the invaders of Rome, they seek to conquer and destroy. Nihilism is their religion—which means they worship the idea of destruction (*TaiPan* 3).

LANGUAGE CHOICES AFFECT POWER RELATIONSHIPS

For some people, power is a dirty word. Many react negatively to what they see as someone's efforts to manipulate or gain power over them through the use of language. Yet every interaction has the potential for establishing and changing the power relationships among interactants. This is especially so in argumentative interactions, so it is important for the student of argumentation to understand how language affects power relationships.

Linguistic and interactive skill give some people power over others (Tannen 10). Everyone has been in a discussion with someone who is clearly skilled and practiced in argumentation, and have felt as if they were unable to give their ideas a fair expression because of the powerful use of language by the other. The remedy for this is for everyone to develop the language skills of argumentation (Odell 39).

Control of the topic leads to control of the interaction, and control of the topic is achieved, in part, by language choices (Tannen 8). To assert directly, "I want to talk about. . . ." or when someone shifts to another topic, to assert, "Let's get back to the topic," or "That's not the issue," can give one the power to set the topic. To interrupt others, to talk over them, and take the floor away from them, tends to establish power. Use of leading questions, those that call for a yes or no answer, allow one to control the interaction (Rieke and Stutman 154–57; Thomas 138). Of course, the impact of language choices depends on the interpretation of the decision makers. Such strategies as these could alienate them by appearing overbearing and rude. To be effective, power must be established as tactfully as possible.

All of these language behaviors and others, which establish and maintain interpersonal power, can be seen in the legal environment. The legal system has evolved over the years to give the officers of the court maximum power. The power of lawyers and judges comes in part from the ability to compel responsive answers, maintain role integrity ("I'll ask the questions, you give the answers"), control the agenda ("We'll talk about that now"), and choose the type of question to narrow the choices for the respondent and allow the examiner to state the evidence (Walker 1–2).

A speaker can gain dominance over the interaction by introducing a "master speech act," which serves to define the topic and limit the discussion. "Let me tell you how I hurt my shoulder," creates " . . . an expectancy on the part of the listener as to what is in store. . . . It creates discoursal space for the dominant . . . speaker" (Thomas 138). To say, "I have three points to make . . ." has the same effect. We have said that meaning is influenced by context. The same is true of what is relevant in an interaction, but typically, one person in the conversation becomes the dominant participant by setting the topic and thereby assuming the power to say what is and is not relevant throughout the interaction. This is often the first speaker, but not always.

The dominant speaker uses a variety of linguistic devices in maintaining the right to set the topic and determine relevance, including the ones we have listed above (Thomas 144). Speaking first and using powerful language increases the chances of one becoming the dominant participant.

In a debate, you want your understanding of the situation (your case) to be the center of the argumentation, even for your opponents. You want your story or version of the events to grind the lenses through which the decision makers interpret all the arguments. By the same token, the opponents will be maneuvering to have their interpretation take center stage. As you recall from the discussion of case building in chapter 4, if the negative or defending position can provoke the others to respond rather than stick with their initial position, the power relationship will have shifted.

Another way of thinking about power relationships and language is to focus on the use of powerless language, which can reduce your chances of being a dominant participant. Powerless language has been identified in the research as consisting of certain language forms such as those below. Generally speaking, you should avoid them if you intend to gain or maintain power in the interaction.

Unnecessary Verbal Intensifiers

Curiously, by increasing the intensity of some statements you can actually weaken your language. Unnecessary adverbs can weaken language: "It was a *very*, *very* good movie." "I *really and truly* believe it." If, instead of saying simply and forcefully, "I am angry with you," you say, "I am so angry . . . " you can reduce the power of the statement.

Inappropriate Verbal Qualifiers

Listen to yourself and see how often you use such expressions as "I guess," "In my opinion," "You know?" "Okay?" "I think." These qualifications are sometimes appropriate; we will talk about communicating qualifiers later. However, if you listen to yourself and others you will notice people using qualifiers for no clear reason. Inappropriate qualification tends to reduce the power of your language.

Tag questions or hedges are a form of unnecessary qualifiers. In class, when you are asked a question by the professor and you know the answer, do you protect yourself on the off chance you are wrong by adding a tag question or a hedge at the end: "Isn't it?" "Didn't they?" "I think," "Sort of," or simply ending your answer on a rising inflection (as in a question)? This communicates powerlessness. So does the use of hesitation forms such as "um," "ahhh," "well," "you know," "uh," "okay?" "like" (Rieke and Stutman 154–55; Infante et al. 226).

Indirect/Lengthened Requests

When requesting someone to do something, language can range from a direct command to an indirect speech act that does not even look like a request at first glance. For instance, you have not been invited to go along with some people to the movies, but you want to. However, you are hesitant lest you get a turn-down and lose face. The answer to that is an indirect request or a lengthened request.

An indirect request might look like this, "I've finished my work earlier than I thought, so I have some time for fun." If the group wants you to come along, they will recognize the statement as a request and say, "Why don't you come with us?" If they don't want you along, they can treat the statement as informative, "You probably need some peace and quiet."

A lengthened request might look like this, "I haven't seen that movie, and I have some time free, so, I would like to come along with you, but if you don't have room in the car I'll do something else." Again, you have communicated your request while allowing for a face saving out.

You may think of these language forms as the expression of politeness, and they do serve that function. But their use may make you appear to be tentative, hesitant, and weak (Infante, et al. 226).

On the other hand, " . . . only the truly powerful can make direct requests" (Tannen 6). If you had complete confidence in your power or status among your friends, you could say, "I'm coming along with you to the movie." Think of the times when people virtually command you. The boss says, "Take this report down to accounting." Your mother says, "Clean up your room." The police officer says, "Step out of your car." Think of instances where a direct request without politeness is effective: "Will you take off your clothes and put on this robe?" says the physician. "Can you prepare a report on that and get it in my hands by tomorrow morning?" says the president.

In any argumentative interaction, then, decision makers will form impressions of the power relationship among participants, and frequently their perception of one arguer as more powerful will increase the chances of subscribing to that person's arguments. This is not always the case, and there are important roles to be played in argumentation other than being powerful. But you should be aware of how language use affects power relationships.

LANGUAGE COMMUNICATES QUALIFIERS

Look back to chapter 6 for the discussion of qualifiers. When you advance an argument, you must be aware of the strength of your reasoning and evidence and remember that your choice of language to qualify your claims is tied to that strength. The stronger you believe your reasoning and evidence to be, the stronger is the qualifier. Ultimately, the statement of qualifier is a report of the extent to which you authorize the decision makers to put more or less faith in what you claim and to what extent you suggest they should trust and act on your claims. The choice of language used in qualifiers defines the extent to which you present tentative, guarded, qualified, or enthusiastic claims (Toulmin 93).

The identical claim, expressed in two social contexts, may have different qualifiers. When talking among friends, you might say, "Lutece is the world's finest restaurant." When speaking to a group of French chefs, you might find yourself saying, "Lutece is an excellent restaurant, comparable to some of the best in France." Why did you say it differently? Perhaps because you expected a different critical scrutiny in the two groups. Maybe because your confidence in the claim was strong enough for friends but not as strong among the most knowledgeable. Upon hearing that Lutece has been sold to a restaurant chain, you might say, "Lutece may or may not still be a superb restaurant. Time will tell." In each instance, you communicated the extent to which you wanted to qualify your claim, to guard yourself by restricting the extent to which you are willing to be held accountable for the claim.

In some instances, you graduate the strength you wish to communicate along a continuum: *certainly, probably, maybe, perhaps, might/may*. To qualify your claims by identifying them with your credibility (your opinion), you can use such language as, *I think, I guess, I suppose, It is my opinion*. (Remember that only those with high credibility can use this without other forms of support.) To indicate that your claim is based on statistical or sensory evidence, you can use such language as, *It seems, Observations suggest, It looks like, Research supports, 95 percent reliability, P < .05*. To use authoritative evidence, you can say, *X says, They report, It has been said by, Apparently*. Evidence by example might be qualified by, *must, obvious, seems, evidently*. Arguments of a quasi-logical style might use, *should, could, can, would, conclusively, presumably*. To reduce the extent to which you want to authorize others to believe or act on your claims, you might say, *sort of, kind of, about, of course, oddly enough, actually, at least, even, only, but* (Barton, "Evidentials" 745–46; Barton, "Discourse" 10–12).

The qualifier you use has significant influence on your argumentation. It determines the extent of commitment you have to a claim, the amount and nature of the proof you must provide, and the extent to which you want decision makers to believe or act on your claim. Careful use of qualifiers is a key element in the language of argumentation.

LANGUAGE COMMUNICATES AGGRESSION

In chapter 1, we define an argument as the intersection of a claim and its support. Speakers of English also know that the word *argument* can suggest an angry exchange of attacks. Most cultures find the latter kind of argument unpleasant and try to avoid it. In conversational argument, there is a (preference) presumption for agreement (Jackson and Jacobs 253). One of the things that makes argumentation degenerate into destructive interaction is language choice.

Language choices associated with the destructive use of argument fall within the concept of *verbal aggression,* which " . . . denotes attacking the self-concept of another person instead of, or in addition to, the person's position on a topic of communication" (Infante and Wigley 60). It has the effect of inflicting, and may be intended to inflict, psychological pain (Infante 51). These attacks can take many forms: questioning others' intelligence; insults; making people feel bad; saying others are unreasonable; calling someone stupid; attacking character; telling people off; making fun of people; using offensive language; yelling and screaming (Infante and Wigley 64). People can attack one's competence, physical appearance, background; they can tease, ridicule, make threats, use profanity, and nonverbal emblems (Infante, Chandler, and Rudd 167).

Sometimes, people resort to verbal aggressiveness because of their psychological makeup and their lack of argumentative skills (Infante, Chandler, and Rudd 164–65). All of us have at one time or another resorted to these forms of attack. However, even when decision makers think your charges are accurate, verbal aggressiveness reduces your credibility (see chapter 10). In some cultures, even the direct expression of disagreement is perceived as in bad taste.

In western culture, what is important to emphasize is the difference between the language of assertiveness and argumentativeness on the one hand, and hostility and verbal aggressiveness on the other. Assertiveness involves being interpersonally forceful in expressing your ideas. Argumentativeness is characterized by presenting and defending positions on issues while attacking others' positions (Infante 52). Hostility is manifest by the use of the language of negativity, resentment, suspicion, and irritability. Verbal aggressiveness involves using language to inflict pain and weaken or destroy another's self-concept (Infante 52).

It is unnecessary to give more examples of the language of hostility and verbal aggressiveness because you are familiar with it through MTV, movies, records, contemporary politics, and your own experiences. We must emphasize, however, that at any time, you have a choice whether or not to use such language. If you are conscious of your language choices and avoid hostility and aggressiveness, others with whom you are interacting will be less likely to use it. If, when others are verbally aggressive, you refuse to respond in kind, it is more likely to disappear from the discussion. If others persist in being hostile and aggressive, you can always walk away. The more comfortable you are with yourself and your skills in argumentation, the easier it will be to concentrate on the positive aspects of argumentation.

CONCLUSION

Human symbolic behavior is a social process. While meanings may be generalized enough to be given apparently firm definitions in dictionaries, meaning is a function of the varying interpretations people make as they seek to interact. The influence of spheres on argument practices includes the determination of appropriate language usage and meaning. Because people in different spheres or from different social situations use different interpretation strategies, arguers must make guesses about how their arguments will be understood. Effective argumentation rests upon the willingness of the participants to do the work necessary to develop common interpretative strategies. Style in language identifies that there are many different ways to say the same thing. Effective style comes from having a wide range of choices in the language employed, and using delightfully unexpected language forms.

It is frequently necessary to develop an effective argument in support of a definitional claim before using that language as a part of a larger argument. Definitional arguments can use formal structures, examples, functions, analogies, and authority. Use of language affects credibility. Intense language, strong qualifiers, and vivid details, when used carefully and in moderation, can increase credibility.

The way people use language in the process of argumentation can shape the power relations that develop. Control of topic, leading questions, introducing a "master speech act," speaking first, and using powerful language tend to give power to an arguer. Powerless language, such as unnecessary verbal intensifiers, unnecessary verbal qualifiers, and indirect or lengthened requests, frequently are associated with loss of power.

The qualification step in argumentation is accomplished through the careful use of language. The arguer must take account of the strength of arguments and support as well as the extent to which decision makers are to be authorized to take seriously, act upon, or hold the arguer accountable in selecting the language used in qualification.

Language can communicate aggression. There is a difference between being forceful in supporting your own arguments and criticizing those of others (assertiveness and argumentativeness), and in attacking the self-concept of someone with the intention of inflicting psychological pain (aggressiveness). In most argumentative situations, aggressiveness reflects one's lack of self-esteem and argumentative effectiveness, and in most cultures it is considered an objectionable behavior.

PROJECTS

15.1 Select a newspaper editorial and read it in groups of about six or eight people. Without talking to each other, write what you think the editorial writer means, being specific about the meanings of words, phrases, colloquial expressions, allusions, and so on. Then, in group discussion, talk about each person's interpretation. Notice where there are significant differences in the interpretation strategies you and others have used. Try to work out a common interpretation strategy for the entire group.

15.2 Now, still working in the group, rewrite the editorial with the intention of making it clear to other members of the class. Exchange your rewrite with that of another group, and read it individually. Are there still differences in interpretation? Note them.

15.3 Select a topic and prepare an argument supporting your position. Now, rewrite it adding significantly more figures of speech, intense language, and vivid detail. Review the two versions and compare and contrast them. Exchange your work with someone else, and then critique their argument. Did they go too far in adding figures and special forms of language? Suggest editorial changes.

15.4 Look at a segment of a debate such as one from the *Congressional Record* or *Burden of Proof* on TV. Discuss the language and identify ways in which power was asserted and assertiveness and argumentativeness are employed. Identify any places where the debate reveals instances of verbal aggressiveness. What impact did it have on the debate?

REFERENCES

Anderson, James A., and Timothy P. Meyer. *Mediated Communication: A Social Action Perspective*. Newbury Park, CA: Sage, 1988.

Barton, Ellen L. "Evidentials, Argumentation, and Epistemological Stance." *College English* 55 (1993): 745–69.

————. "Discourse Epistemics and the Structure of Argument in Written Language." Unpub. Manuscript, 1995.

Bastien, David T., Robert D. McPhee and Karen A. Bolton. "A Study and Extended Theory of the Structuration of Climate." *Communication Monographs* 62 (1995): 87–109.

Bradac, James J., John Waite Bowers, and John A. Courtright. "Three Language Variables in Communication Research: Intensity, Immediacy, and Diversity." *Human Communication Research* 5 (1979): 257–69.

Hickey, Leo. *The Pragmatics of Style*. London and New York: Routledge, 1989.

Infante, Dominic A. "Teaching Students to Understand and Control Verbal Aggression." *Communication Education* 44 (1995): 51–63.

Infante, Dominic D., Teresa A. Chandler, and Jill E. Rudd. "Test of an Argumentative Skill Deficiency Model of Interpersonal Violence." *Communication Monographs* 56 (1989): 163–77.

Infante, Dominic A., and Charles J. Wigley, III. "Verbal Aggressiveness: An Interpersonal Model and Measure." *Communication Monographs* 53 (1986): 61–69.

Jackson, Sally, and Scott Jacobs. "Structure of Conversational Argument: Pragmatic Bases for the Enthymeme." *Quarterly Journal of Speech* 66 (1980): 251–65.

Kent, Thomas. *Paralogic Rhetoric: A Theory of Communicative Interaction*. London: Associated UP, 1993.

Kouzes, James M., and Barry Z. Posner. *Credibility: How Leaders Gain and Lose It, Why People Demand It*. San Francisco: Jossey-Bass, 1993.

Lahr, John. "Matinee Idolatry." *The New Yorker* 15 May 1995: 97–100.

Levy, Leonard W. *Original Intent and the Framers of the Constitution*. New York: Macmillan, 1988.

Maestas, Amy. "Carole Gallagher: One Woman vs. The Bomb." *The Event* 25 May 1995: 3.

Odell, S. Jack. "The Powers of Language." *Power Through Discourse*. Ed. Leah Kedar. Norwood, NJ: Ablex, 1987: 19–39.

Rapoport, Anatol. "Strategy and Conscience." *The Human Dialogue*. Eds. Floyd W. Matson and Ashley Montagu. New York: The Free P, 1967: 79–96.

Rieke, Richard D. and Randall Stutman. *Communication in Legal Advocacy*. Columbia: U of South Carolina P, 1990.

Schiff, Stephen. "Master of Illusion." *The New Yorker* 15 May 1995: 52-69.

TaiPan. Special Millennium Fever Edition, 1995.

Tannen, Deborah. "Remarks on Discourse and Power." *Power Through Discourse*. Ed. Leah Kedar. Norwood, NJ: Ablex, 1987: 3–10.

Thomas, Jenny A. "Discourse Control in Confrontational Interaction." *The Pragmatics of Style*. Ed. Leo Hickey. New York: Routledge, 133–56.

Toulmin, Stephen E. *The Uses of Argument*. London: Cambridge UP, 1964.

U.S. v *Miller* 307: 174 1939.

Walker, Ann Grafton. "Linguistic Manipulation, Power, and the Legal Setting." *Power Through Discourse*. Ed. Leah Kedar. Norwood, NJ: Ablex, 1987. 57–80.

Young, David E., Ed. *The Origin of the Second Amendment*. Ontonagon, MI: Golden Oaks, 1991.

Index

309